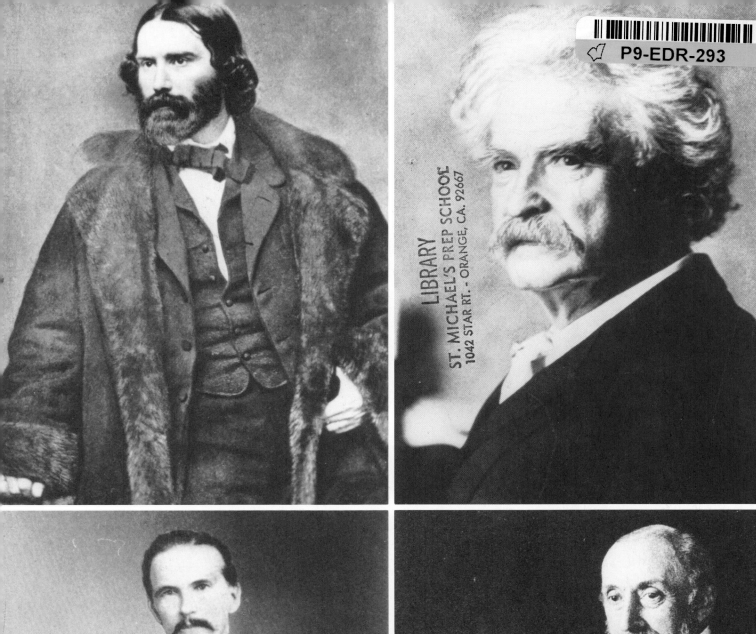

Endsheets: (left to right, top) Edmund Clarence Stedman, James Burrill Angell, James Russell Lowell, Samuel Clemens; (left to right, bottom) Bret Harte, William Dean Howells, Paul Hamilton Hayne, Charles Eliot Norton

Dictionary of Literary Biography • Volume Sixty-four

American Literary Critics and Scholars, 1850-1880

Dictionary of Literary Biography

1: *The American Renaissance in New England*, edited by Joel Myerson (1978)

2: *American Novelists Since World War II*, edited by Jeffrey Helterman and Richard Layman (1978)

3: *Antebellum Writers in New York and the South*, edited by Joel Myerson (1979)

4: *American Writers in Paris, 1920-1939*, edited by Karen Lane Rood (1980)

5: *American Poets Since World War II*, 2 parts, edited by Donald J. Greiner (1980)

6: *American Novelists Since World War II*, Second Series, edited by James E. Kibler, Jr. (1980)

7: *Twentieth-Century American Dramatists*, 2 parts, edited by John MacNicholas (1981)

8: *Twentieth-Century American Science-Fiction Writers*, 2 parts, edited by David Cowart and Thomas L. Wymer (1981)

9: *American Novelists, 1910-1945*, 3 parts, edited by James J. Martine (1981)

10: *Modern British Dramatists, 1900-1945*, 2 parts, edited by Stanley Weintraub (1982)

11: *American Humorists, 1800-1950*, 2 parts, edited by Stanley Trachtenberg (1982)

12: *American Realists and Naturalists*, edited by Donald Pizer and Earl N. Harbert (1982)

13: *British Dramatists Since World War II*, 2 parts, edited by Stanley Weintraub (1982)

14: *British Novelists Since 1960*, 2 parts, edited by Jay L. Halio (1983)

15: *British Novelists, 1930-1959*, 2 parts, edited by Bernard Oldsey (1983)

16: *The Beats: Literary Bohemians in Postwar America*, 2 parts, edited by Ann Charters (1983)

17: *Twentieth-Century American Historians*, edited by Clyde N. Wilson (1983)

18: *Victorian Novelists After 1885*, edited by Ira B. Nadel and William E. Fredeman (1983)

19: *British Poets, 1880-1914*, edited by Donald E. Stanford (1983)

20: *British Poets, 1914-1945*, edited by Donald E. Stanford (1983)

21: *Victorian Novelists Before 1885*, edited by Ira B. Nadel and William E. Fredeman (1983)

22: *American Writers for Children, 1900-1960*, edited by John Cech (1983)

23: *American Newspaper Journalists, 1873-1900*, edited by Perry J. Ashley (1983)

24: *American Colonial Writers, 1606-1734*, edited by Emory Elliott (1984)

25: *American Newspaper Journalists, 1901-1925*, edited by Perry J. Ashley (1984)

26: *American Screenwriters*, edited by Robert E. Morsberger, Stephen O. Lesser, and Randall Clark (1984)

27: *Poets of Great Britain and Ireland, 1945-1960*, edited by Vincent B. Sherry, Jr. (1984)

28: *Twentieth-Century American-Jewish Fiction Writers*, edited by Daniel Walden (1984)

29: *American Newspaper Journalists, 1926-1950*, edited by Perry J. Ashley (1984)

30: *American Historians, 1607-1865*, edited by Clyde N. Wilson (1984)

31: *American Colonial Writers, 1735-1781*, edited by Emory Elliott (1984)

32: *Victorian Poets Before 1850*, edited by William E. Fredeman and Ira B. Nadel (1984)

33: *Afro-American Fiction Writers After 1955*, edited by Thadious M. Davis and Trudier Harris (1984)

34: *British Novelists, 1890-1929: Traditionalists*, edited by Thomas F. Staley (1985)

35: *Victorian Poets After 1850*, edited by William E. Fredeman and Ira B. Nadel (1985)

36: *British Novelists, 1890-1929: Modernists*, edited by Thomas F. Staley (1985)

37: *American Writers of the Early Republic*, edited by Emory Elliott (1985)

38: *Afro-American Writers After 1955: Dramatists and Prose Writers*, edited by Thadious M. Davis and Trudier Harris (1985)

39: *British Novelists, 1660-1800*, 2 parts, edited by Martin C. Battestin (1985)

40: *Poets of Great Britain and Ireland Since 1960*, 2 parts, edited by Vincent B. Sherry, Jr. (1985)

41: *Afro-American Poets Since 1955*, edited by Trudier Harris and Thadious M. Davis (1985)

42: *American Writers for Children Before 1900*, edited by Glenn E. Estes (1985)

43: *American Newspaper Journalists, 1690-1872*, edited by Perry J. Ashley (1986)

44: *American Screenwriters*, Second Series, edited by Randall Clark, Robert E. Morsberger, and Stephen O. Lesser (1986)

45: *American Poets, 1880-1945*, First Series, edited by Peter Quartermain (1986)

46: *American Literary Publishing Houses, 1900-1980: Trade and Paperback*, edited by Peter Dzwonkoski (1986)

47: *American Historians, 1866-1912*, edited by Clyde N. Wilson (1986)

48: *American Poets, 1880-1945*, Second Series, edited by Peter Quartermain (1986)

49: *American Literary Publishing Houses, 1638-1899*, 2 parts, edited by Peter Dzwonkoski (1986)

50: *Afro-American Writers Before the Harlem Renaissance*, edited by Trudier Harris (1986)

51: *Afro-American Writers from the Harlem Renaissance to 1940*, edited by Trudier Harris (1987)

52: *American Writers for Children Since 1960: Fiction*, edited by Glenn E. Estes (1986)

53: *Canadian Writers Since 1960*, First Series, edited by W. H. New (1986)

54: *American Poets, 1880-1945*, Third Series, 2 parts, edited by Peter Quartermain (1987)

55: *Victorian Prose Writers Before 1867*, edited by William B. Thesing (1987)

56: *German Fiction Writers, 1914-1945*, edited by James Hardin (1987)

57: *Victorian Prose Writers After 1867*, edited by William B. Thesing (1987)

58: *Jacobean and Caroline Dramatists*, edited by Fredson Bowers (1987)

59: *American Literary Critics and Scholars, 1800-1850*, edited by John W. Rathbun and Monica M. Grecu (1987)

60: *Canadian Writers Since 1960*, Second Series, edited by W. H. New (1987)

61: *American Writers for Children Since 1960: Poets, Illustrators, and Nonfiction Authors*, edited by Glenn E. Estes (1987)

62: *Elizabethan Dramatists*, edited by Fredson Bowers (1987)

63: *Modern American Critics, 1920-1955*, edited by Gregory S. Jay (1988)

64: *American Literary Critics and Scholars, 1850-1880*, edited by John W. Rathbun and Monica M. Grecu (1988)

Documentary Series

1: *Sherwood Anderson, Willa Cather, John Dos Passos, Theodore Dreiser, F. Scott Fitzgerald, Ernest Hemingway, Sinclair Lewis*, edited by Margaret A. Van Antwerp (1982)

2: *James Gould Cozzens, James T. Farrell, William Faulkner, John O'Hara, John Steinbeck, Thomas Wolfe, Richard Wright*, edited by Margaret A. Van Antwerp (1982)

3: *Saul Bellow, Jack Kerouac, Norman Mailer, Vladimir Nabokov, John Updike, Kurt Vonnegut*, edited by Mary Bruccoli (1983)

4: *Tennessee Williams*, edited by Margaret A. Van Antwerp and Sally Johns (1984)

Yearbooks

1980, edited by Karen L. Rood, Jean W. Ross, and Richard Ziegfeld (1981)

1981, edited by Karen L. Rood, Jean W. Ross, and Richard Ziegfeld (1982)

1982, edited by Richard Ziegfeld; associate editors: Jean W. Ross and Lynne C. Zeigler (1983)

1983, edited by Mary Bruccoli and Jean W. Ross; associate editor: Richard Ziegfeld (1984)

1984, edited by Jean W. Ross (1985)

1985, edited by Jean W. Ross (1986)

1986, edited by J. M. Brook (1987)

Concise Series

The New Consciousness, 1941-1968 (1987)

Dictionary of Literary Biography • Volume Sixty-four

American Literary Critics and Scholars, 1850-1880

Edited by
John W. Rathbun
California State University, Los Angeles
and
Monica M. Grecu
University of Nevada at Reno

A Bruccoli Clark Layman Book
Gale Research Company • Book Tower • Detroit, Michigan 48226

Manufactured by Edwards Brothers, Inc.
Ann Arbor, Michigan
Printed in the United States of America

Library of Congress Cataloging-in-Publication Data

American literary critics and scholars, 1850-1880.

(Dictionary of literary biography; v. 64)
"A Bruccoli Clark Layman book."
Includes index.
1. Criticism—United States—History—19th century. 2.
Criticism—United States—Bio-bibliography. 3. Critics—
United States—Biography—Dictionaries. 4. Literary histo-
rians—United States—Biography—Dictionaries. 5. Amer-
ican literature—19th century—History and criticism. I.
Rathbun, John Wilbert, 1924-   . II. Grecu, Monica M. III.
Series.
PS74.A45   1988   801'.95'0973   87-25802
ISBN 0-8103-1742-7

For Pauline A. Rathbun and Cornelia Grecu-Arghir, mothers

Contents

Plan of the Series

The advisory board, the editors, and the publisher of the *Dictionary of Literary Biography* are joined in endorsing Mark Twain's declaration. The literature of a nation provides an inexhaustible resource of permanent worth. We intend to make literature and its creators better understood and more accessible to students and the reading public, while satisfying the standards of teachers and scholars.

To meet these requirements, *literary biography* has been construed in terms of the author's achievement. The most important thing about a writer is his writing. Accordingly, the entries in *DLB* are career biographies, tracing the development of the author's canon and the evolution of his reputation.

The purpose of *DLB* is not only to provide reliable information in a convenient format but also to place the figures in the larger perspective of literary history and to offer appraisals of their accomplishments by qualified scholars.

The publication plan for *DLB* resulted from two years of preparation. The project was proposed to Bruccoli Clark by Frederick G. Ruffner, president of the Gale Research Company, in November 1975. After specimen entries were prepared and typeset, an advisory board was formed to refine the entry format and develop the series rationale. In meetings held during 1976, the publisher, series editors, and advisory board approved the scheme for a comprehensive biographical dictionary of persons who contributed to North American literature. Editorial work on the first volume began in January 1977, and it was published in 1978. In order to make *DLB* more than a reference tool and to compile volumes that individually have claim to status as literary history, it was decided to organize volumes by topic, period, or genre. Each of these freestanding volumes provides a biographical-bibliographical guide and overview for a particular area of literature. We are convinced that this organization—as opposed to a single alphabet method—constitutes a valuable innovation in the presentation of reference material. The volume plan necessarily requires many decisions for the placement and treatment of authors who might properly be included in two or three volumes. In some instances a major figure will be included in separate volumes, but with different entries emphasizing the aspect of his career appropriate to each volume. Ernest Hemingway, for example, is represented in *American Writers in Paris, 1920-1939* by an entry focusing on his expatriate apprenticeship; he is also in *American Novelists, 1910-1945* with an entry surveying his entire career. Each volume includes a cumulative index of subject authors and articles. Comprehensive indexes to the entire series are planned.

With volume ten in 1982 it was decided to enlarge the scope of *DLB*. By the end of 1986 twenty-one volumes treating British literature had been published, and volumes for Commonwealth and Modern European literature were in progress. The series has been further augmented by the *DLB Yearbooks* (since 1981) which update published entries and add new entries to keep the *DLB* current with contemporary activity. There have also been *DLB Documentary Series* volumes which provide biographical and critical source materials for figures whose work is judged to have particular interest for students. One of these companion volumes is entirely devoted to Tennessee Williams.

We define literature as the *intellectual commerce of a nation:* not merely as belles lettres but as that ample and complex process by which ideas are generated, shaped, and transmitted. *DLB* entries are not limited to "creative writers" but extend to other figures who in their time and in their way influenced the mind of a people. Thus the series encompasses historians, journalists, publishers, and screenwriters. By this means readers of *DLB* may be aided to perceive litera-

---

ture not as cult scripture in the keeping of intellectual high priests but firmly positioned at the center of a nation's life.

DLB includes the major writers appropriate to each volume and those standing in the ranks immediately behind them. Scholarly and critical counsel has been sought in deciding which minor figures to include and how full their entries should be. Wherever possible, useful references are made to figures who do not warrant separate entries.

Each *DLB* volume has a volume editor responsible for planning the volume, selecting the figures for inclusion, and assigning the entries. Volume editors are also responsible for preparing, where appropriate, appendices surveying the major periodicals and literary and intellectual movements for their volumes, as well as lists of further readings. Work on the series as a whole is coordinated at the Bruccoli Clark Layman editorial center in Columbia, South Carolina, where the editorial staff is responsible for accuracy of the published volumes.

One feature that distinguishes *DLB* is the illustration policy—its concern with the iconography of literature. Just as an author is influenced by his surroundings, so is the reader's understanding of the author enhanced by a knowledge of his environment. Therefore *DLB* volumes include not only drawings, paintings, and photographs of authors, often depicting them at various stages in their careers, but also illustrations of their families and places where they lived. Title pages are regularly reproduced in facsimile along with dust jackets for modern authors. The dust jackets are a special feature of *DLB* because they often document better than anything else the way in which an author's work was perceived in its own time. Specimens of the writers' manuscripts are included when feasible.

Samuel Johnson rightly decreed that "The chief glory of every people arises from its authors." The purpose of the *Dictionary of Literary Biography* is to compile literary history in the surest way available to us—by accurate and comprehensive treatment of the lives and work of those who contributed to it.

The *DLB* Advisory Board

Foreword

This volume of the *Dictionary of Literary Biography* is the second of three designed to survey comprehensively contributions of nineteenth-century literary critics and scholars to letters in the United States, and covers the period 1850-1880.

These years were witness to a time of intense social and political strain, internecine warfare, and profound cultural transformations in the history of the United States. With the Gadsden Purchase in 1853 the present continental boundaries of the country were established, but not much else was stable. The population boomed during these years from twenty-five million in 1850 to double that number in 1880. Over ten million of this increase were immigrants, mainly of Irish and German origin, who encountered sporadic outbreaks of nativist prejudice. The 1850 census, the first to provide reliable figures, indicates that manufacturing had displaced agriculture as the dominant factor in the economy; by 1880 this dominance was readily apparent, for one of every three persons in the population lived in an urban setting. As a consequence, national purpose came increasingly to be phrased in urban terms as the emotional and behavioral characteristics of city individuals and groups prevailed over others in the culture.

With economic authority vested in such urban centers as Boston and New York, it was inevitable that these centers would also wield cultural authority. In letters, the majority of literary theorists and practicing critics lived in New England and New York, with the publishing industry being the only concrete nexus between them. Of the thirty-five critics covered in this volume, only three—William J. Grayson, Paul Hamilton Hayne, and Sidney Lanier—represent the South. The small number may be attributed to the havoc of the Civil War followed by the disorders of Reconstruction. Western literature was embraced as a new force in the culture, but only after eastern critics called attention to it. Bret Harte and Samuel Langhorne Clemens are the only western critics included in this volume, and both left the West shortly after they came to popularity.

Despite the concentration of critics in the East, surprisingly few called for literature to register urban experience, Cornelius Mathews being virtually alone in this respect. Their sights seem to have been raised higher to train on some common ground that would explain what Americans had participated in or lived through: national character, for example. To such a critic as Grayson or Charles Eliot Norton literature should correspond to all that he saw as perdurable in the American mind: a solid moral code, respect for precedent, traditional values, deference to the most skilled or best members of the culture. To another critic, say Evert Augustus Duyckinck, the national character was seen as emergent rather than existent, so that literature should embody principles of democratic equality and social reform in order to advance the people's growth into democratic consciousness. Still another critic, in anticipation of Frederick Jackson Turner's thesis that the frontier formed an American temperament, might extol western literature as most clearly capturing and dramatizing the archetypal confrontations with circumstance which helped to forge the national character. Whatever the critics' points of departure, an aim obviously common to most of them was to examine literature in terms of complexes of expectations that had little to do with whether literature was aesthetically good or bad.

Another megaprinciple that critics used for examining literature was the moral sense. Frequently tied to the argument that the ultimate value of literature is truth, even while the immediate aim is pleasure, the moral testing of literature is a much more complicated and persistent problem than the examination of literature within the context of national temperament. On its most reductive level, a literary work can be dismissed because it does not conform to the rules for conduct held by the critic. An extension of this level is the idea that literature should instruct people in what is good and bad behavior. Fortunately neither of these views is much in evidence in the critics under review, though even Walt Whitman could explode on occasion at the "filth" he had encountered. Moral concerns as they verge on the ethical pose greater problems for critics, since here one becomes involved with conflicting views of human nature and therefore needs to adopt a more philosophical stance. A measure of William Dean Howells's stature as a critic, for example, was his ability to recognize the strengths of such younger and more radical writers as Hamlin Garland, Stephen Crane, Frank Norris, and Robert Herrick even though they ran counter to his own literary interest in acquired virtue as the value his characters gain in having to make hard choices.

While critics of this period all tended to agree that literature should be judged at least partly on how it served the greater national purpose and on its truthfulness in representing the moral natures of human beings, there were sharp differences otherwise as they presented, defended, and applied the principles of the critical schools to which they loosely adhered. Unlike the literature published at this time, which is widely disparate and ranges from the soft sentimentalism of the 1850s through local color to the darker notes of an incipient naturalism, the critical positions were few in number and easy to spot. Generally speaking, they include impressionism, aestheticism, critical idealism, critical realism, and scholarly historicism.

Impressionism and aestheticism enlisted few advocates. Many of the New York critics—somewhat bohemian, often superficial—used details and mental associations to evoke subjective impressions rather than subject literary works to social or aesthetic analysis. It is no accident that some, Henry Theodore Tuckerman and Edwin Percy Whipple for example, also tried their hands at the type of travel literature which emphasizes suggestions of mood, place, and natural phenomena. On a deeper note, the impressionism of John Burroughs combined personal response with a transcendentalist appreciation of nature to focus on the character of the writer as a means of determining what animated him and made his experience of life unique. Sidney Lanier and Edmund Clarence Stedman best represent the aesthetic position. Both men affirmed beauty as the basic principle from which all other principles were derived, but neither went so far as to say that art is free of any obligation or responsibility other than that of striving for beauty. Chiefly they concentrated on the expressive nature of poetry—Lanier in *The Science of English Verse* (1880) and Stedman in *The Nature and Elements of Poetry* (1892)—in which balance, rhythmic flow,

and general inflection serve to stir the readers' aesthetic responses and thereby enhance appreciation of the invention and insights of the authors themselves.

While Stedman paid a great deal of attention to the aesthetic side of literature, he is more properly ranked with those who subscribed to critical idealism during these years. Critical idealism descends from the interests and work of antebellum romantics like Ralph Waldo Emerson and James Russell Lowell (both of whom actually continued to publish in the years following the Civil War). Because literary romanticism gave way to realism in the postwar period, literary historians have assumed a like diminution in the vitality and relevance of romantic critical theory. That is a difficult position to maintain. Lowell's criticism and range of appreciation establish him as the leading critic of the postwar period, and the later work of such critics as Brander Matthews reveals that critical idealists could fully appreciate the emergence of talents like Samuel Clemens.

Furthermore, the romantic emphasis on imagination as a revelatory power of the mind to form images of things not present to the senses or within the actual experience of the person involved—a concept central to the romantic vision—continued to be a viable tool employed even by critics whose allegiances were to other critical theories. Whipple, for example, while his practical criticism falls short of solid insight, had a defensible critical theory that owed much to the New England romantics. Much the same can be said for Walt Whitman. Nor are the critical idealists as reactionary as sometimes charged. Both Stedman and Richard Watson Gilder opened the pages of *Century Monthly Magazine* to new talent and recognized the strengths of writers like Whitman, Howells, and Henry James, and Charles Eliot Norton performed a like editorial service in the pages of *Atlantic Monthly*, *North American Review*, and the *Nation*.

In opposition to critical idealism, critical realism denied the primacy of subjective experience and proposed two principles in its place: that objects of perception exist independently of the perceiver, and that their artistic representation should be factually accurate. These principles obviously are more relevant to fiction than to lyrical poetry, and the triumph of critical realism as a set of expectations owes much to the fact that the short story and novel displaced poetry as the most popular literary forms for critics and the reading public alike. The insistence on factual representation had several natural consequences. As David E. E. Sloane points out in his entry on Bret Harte, realism opened the way for writers to expand the scope of their work by dramatizing lower-class and even disreputable characters who as human beings warrant sympathetic consideration, and by going beyond forms of literary expression to include the nonstandard or substandard everyday speech of a country or locality.

As sensitive as realists like Howells and Clemens were to the circumstantial influence of experience on human behavior, few were willing to limit literature to no more than a factual, dispassionate description of events as lived. Anthony Trollope, for example, was regularly criticized for being no more than a photographic realist (to use Henry James's term) who piled up detail upon detail without reference to what it all meant. Obviously, then, realism involved some selection (as romantic theory also held), and it also involved some sense of the moral consequences of human behavior. In the over 1,700 book reviews that Howells wrote, he returns repeatedly to the idea that critics should describe, interpret, and classify the works under review: the critic's job, he argues, is "to identify the literary species and then to explain how and where the specimen is imperfect or irregular" in the light of what the author tried to do.

Side by side with these currents of critical theory and practice, scholarly historicism went its way quietly, scarcely noticed. Yet it produced some of the best critical work written during 1850-1880 and accounts for a quarter of the critics under consideration in this volume: James Burrill Angell, Francis James Child, John Fiske, Horace Howard Furness, Henry Norman Hudson, William G. T. Shedd, Moses Coit Tyler, Richard Grant White, and Lowell in his later career. Of these scholars, Fiske was mainly a popularizer of others' views, while the work of Child, Furness, and Tyler continues to make its contribution to our knowledge of the subjects they addressed. In its origins scholarly historicism was heavily indebted to German theories relative to secular history and biblical criticism, and examples of this indebtedness can be found in the work of Angell, Shedd, and Tyler. Speaking more generally, however, scholarly practice in the years 1850-1880 is less given to theorizing on the nature of history than to an immersion in a historical age and place, building on previous scholarship. Its intention is not to be determinative in the sense of passing judgment on literary works, but when skillfully done its discernment and appraisals can be so discriminating as to constitute authoritative opinion.

—John W. Rathbun and Monica M. Grecu

Acknowledgments

This book was produced by Bruccoli Clark Layman, Inc. Karen L. Rood is senior editor for the *Dictionary of Literary Biography* series. J. M. Brook was the in-house editor.

Art supervisor is Gabrielle Elliott. Copyediting supervisor is Patricia Coate. Production coordinator is Kimberly Casey. Typesetting supervisor is Kathleen M. Flanagan. Laura Ingram and Michael D. Senecal are editorial associates. The production staff includes Rowena Betts, David R. Bowdler, Charles Brower, Cheryl Crombie, Mary S. Dye, Charles Egleston, Sarah A. Estes, Judith K. Ingle, Maria Ling, Warren McInnis, Kathy S. Merlette, Sheri Neal, Joycelyn R. Smith, and Elizabeth York. Jean W. Ross is permissions editor. Joseph Caldwell, photography editor, and Joseph Matthew Bruccoli did photographic copy work for the volume.

Walter W. Ross and Rhonda Marshall did the library research with the assistance of the staff at the Thomas Cooper Library of the University of South Carolina: Lynn Barron, Daniel Boice, Kathy Eckman, Gary Geer, Cathie Gottlieb, David L. Haggard, Jens Holley, Dennis Isbell, Marcia Martin, Jean Rhyne, Beverley Steele, Ellen Tillett, and Virginia Weathers.

The photographs on page 45 and 284 are reproduced by permission of the Yale Collection of American Literature, Beinecke Rare Book and Manuscript Library, Yale University.

American Literary Critics
and Scholars,
1850-1880

Dictionary of Literary Biography

James Burrill Angell

(7 January 1829-1 April 1916)

Dennis R. Perry
University of Missouri-Rolla

BOOKS: *The Reminiscences of James Burrill Angell* (New York: Longmans, Green, 1912);
Selected Addresses, by James Burrill Angell (New York & London: Longmans, Green, 1912).

OTHER: Margaret E. Foster, *Hand-Book of French Literature: Historical, Biographical, and Critical,* revised and edited by Angell (Philadelphia: Cowperthwait, 1857).

PERIODICAL PUBLICATIONS: "Emanuel Geibel," *Bibliotecha Sacra,* 12 (1855): 770-789;
"Lewes' Life of Goethe," *Christian Review,* 21 (July 1856): 412-424;
"Influence of English on German Literature," *North American Review,* 84 (1857): 311-333;
"The Life and Works of Jean Racine," *Bibliotecha Sacra,* 14 (July 1857): 597-622;
"Royal House of St. Cyr," *North American Review,* 85 (October 1857): 369-392;
"Royal Literature," *Christian Review,* 22 (October 1857): 571-580;
"Influence of English Literature upon the French," *North American Review,* 86 (April 1858): 412-434.

James Burrill Angell's literary scholarship has become a minor footnote in an active life that included political journalism, international diplomacy, and university administration. His out-

put as a literary critic and scholar consists of a handful of periodical publications and a revised edition of the *Hand-Book of French Literature: Historical, Biographical, and Critical* (1857; originally published in London by Chambers in 1855). He based his literary criticism on the Scottish Common Sense philosophy he learned at Brown University during the 1840s. This perspective led him to dislike literature in which immoderate passion, trivial subject matter, dark or mystical romanticism, philosophical pessimism, and antireligious sentiment were to be found. As an intellectual conservative Angell viewed literature from a religious perspective; but as a scholar of French and German literature he tried to balance religion and aesthetics in his criticism. In addition, like the Cambridge Brahmins, Angell was a literary internationalist who believed that a nation's literature must be judged according to universally applicable criteria.

A descendant of Thomas Angell, a prominent founder and citizen of Rhode Island, James Burrill Angell was born on 7 January 1829 to Andrew Aldrich Angell and Amy Aldrich Angell on the family farm that was settled in 1710 near Scituate. Following a grammar school education, Angell entered Brown University at the age of sixteen and graduated valedictorian in 1849. While on a European tour in 1852 he was offered the choice between the chair of civil engineering or

James Burrill Angell

modern languages at Brown University. He chose the latter and spent additional time abroad studying French and German. He returned to teach at Brown in 1853 as the youngest member of the faculty, recording in *The Reminiscences of James Burrill Angell* (1912) that he "strove and not without fair success, I hope, to imbue them [his students] with some enthusiasm for the study of the great authors to whom I introduced them."

During these early years as a professor at Brown Angell began to stake out the principles he thought most fruitful in the study of literature. His first article, "Emanuel Geibel," published in the Congregationalist quarterly *Bibliotecha Sacra* in 1855, declared his intent to "notice the life and the works of a single living poet, and his relation to his age." For Angell psychological and social context is an essential element in the analysis of an author: "We must see the conflicting elements by which he is surrounded in order to know his temptations and to appreciate

his virtues." After describing several schools of German poetry, Angell locates a context by which to sketch Geibel's life and evaluate his work. He approves of Geibel's early political poems because he "appeared as an advocate of reform and a friend of liberty" yet positioned himself "as a Christian opponent to the Quixotic schemes of the [revolutionary] red republicans." A moderate conservative, Angell only approved gradual reform. The provincial and immediate nature of these poems give them only historical interest for Angell, however, and he much prefers Geibel's nature poems: "But if we would know the man, we must see him in communion with nature."

Angell praises Geibel's sensitivity to the landscape and his ability to interpret nature's spiritual meaning. Throughout the analysis Angell finds Geibel's greatest strength to be his adherence to a religious aesthetic. Like other critics educated in the Scottish doctrine, Angell considered nature a moral force to be understood in moral terms: "Again, the spring is a proclaimer of the love of God. The world is a temple; and fragrant exhalations from every flower tremble their way towards heaven as the holiest incense...." He also applauds Geibel's love poetry for moral reasons. Unlike the work of some poets, which "is ever hovering on the verge of indecency," Geibel's "impulses are exalted, his aspirations noble, his whole nature sound and healthful." He also finds the poet's ability to avoid self-aggrandizement in his poems one of the "characteristics of a great poet," aesthetically fulfilling Christ's proverb about the exaltation of the humble. Angell finally commends Geibel's poetry, regardless of its lack of boldness and sublimity, for modeling the correct pattern for future German poetry. While other German poets "are loading the air with misanthropic lamentations or impious complaints," Geibel, Angell writes, exudes "a cheerful Christian hopefulness." To Angell's credit, he had enough critical objectivity to see Geibel's pietism in perspective: "It is rather as a pure and a Christian poet, than as a great and a brilliant poet, that he deserves our respect and esteem."

Angell's review of George Henry Lewes's *The Life and Works of Goethe* (1855) appeared in the *Christian Review* in 1856. Angell evaluates Lewes's critical and biographical approach to Goethe and then uses the resultant context to discuss the nature of the critic's and the poet's moral obligations in society. In assessing Lewes's approach,

Angell as a young man

Angell commends him for his sympathetic identification with the author. However, Lewes identifies with Goethe to such an extent that Angell finds him unable to recognize moral errors in the poet's life: "We disagree with Mr. Lewes in his views of many questions of propriety and morality, [although] we thank him for his facts."

Angell's own reaction to Goethe, as well as to Lewes, is mixed. While he recognizes his poetic greatness and can excuse Goethe of such petty charges as haughtiness, he cannot ignore Goethe's moral lapses. Angell notes that because criticism and teaching both introduce literature to young scholars, the critic must not, like the "genius lovers," forgive a poet's immorality because of his great talent or knowledge. Angell's Scottish Common Sense training taught him that genius and morality went hand in hand. Goethe was a gifted poet; his romantic egocentrism disqualified him as a genius. Angell decries the self-centered, antisocial impulses of contemporary poets: "Genius has no element of selfishness; and selfishness always underlies excessive introspection." In effect, Angell proclaims that poets engaged in an aesthetic of self-scrutiny are morally lazy and avoid the greater social responsibility of presenting universal rather than personal truth.

His ideal examples of poets who fulfill this responsibility are Shakespeare and Dante.

Angell uses this opportunity of writing about Goethe to discourse on the theme of the "sacred office of Poetic Teacher" in Miltonic terms. In Angell's view, the most basic assumption about art is that "the highest Beauty must always co-exist with the highest Goodness." That poet "who continually disregards the truths which his mind reveals," Angell contends, "soon lose[s] the power of clearly perceiving those truths." Then, as genius ignores moral truth, it loses its ability to perceive pure beauty. Angell encourages poetry that does not "picture scenes which offend natural delicacy and elevated taste." He does not, however, "desire to fill the world with stories of good boys and girls, who lived and died without an impulse or passion." Neither is he interested in an art that merely points to a moral. "If it ever teaches, it is because it pleases." This idea had emerged among the more liberal critics of the Scottish school for whom morality in literature did not mean religious didacticism, and Angell followed in their wake.

Angell's first article for the *North American Review*, "Influence of English on German Literature" (1857), came at the request of its editor, Andrew T. Peabody. Patterned after the *Edinburgh Review*, the *North American Review* had been a haven of Scottish ideas since 1815, a tradition that Peabody partially continued. Angell's article is a comparative study in which he demonstrates the influence English literature has had on German literature. This basic principle is that all the nations in Europe are culturally interdependent and that to determine the growth and progress of a nation's literature one must view it in relation to other nations. That interdependence is not an unmixed good, for Angell concludes that German imitators of English models have generally retarded Germany's literary progress. He specifically mentions the morbid and unnatural pietism and aestheticism of Edward Young's imitators. On the other hand, Angell rates Shakespeare as the greatest English genius and the supreme interpreter of nature and applauds his important and healthy influence on Goethe and on other German writers.

In 1857 Angell also revised the Chambers *Hand-Book of French Literature*, to which he added a brief history of the French language and a number of explanatory notes to the text. In addition he briefly mentions lyric poet Jean Baptiste Rousseau and introduces a theme developed later as a

Angell in his office at the University of Michigan

major criticism of French literature: its slavish adherence to classical models. "The man who will travel to Rome or to Greece to describe what he feels, may have some enthusiasm himself, but it will rarely affect his readers." For Angell lyric poetry "ought to be the expression of the author's own thoughts and feelings."

Angell further examines French literature in two articles. In "The Life and Works of Jean Racine," which appeared in *Bibliotecha Sacra* in July 1857, he recounts aspects of Racine's biography and reviews his major works. Angell is highly critical of Racine's first tragedy, *La Théobäide*, because the characters have nothing pleasing in their natures. "By what grouping of such repulsive figures could the artist hope to form a work of beauty or of interest? It is a law of aesthetics . . . that the merely horrible should never be presented alone." He also criticizes the lack of variety in the action of the play and the lack of feeling in its single love relationship. However,

these early problems were overcome, and Angell is able to trace in Racine's work a growing poetic power which finds a way to dramatize the "purity" of love and to balance the beautiful with the horrible. In Racine's selfless search for truth Angell perceives the qualities of genius lacking in Goethe. For Angell great art can only be created by great men. "There are a chosen few, like Racine, whom we cannot but love and admire."

Angell published his last literary article, "Influence of English Literature upon the French," in the *North American Review* in 1858. Similar in structure to his essay on English influences on German literature, the article examines the differences between the English and French literary minds. He had noted at the end of the Racine essay a tolerant relativism that seems to run counter to his theory of cultural interdependence: "Shall the builder of the Strasburg Cathedral deny all genius to the architect of St. Peter's? Or is not, rather, each work good in its

Angell family portrait taken on the steps of the president's house at the University of Michigan: (front row) Constance McLaughlin Green; Robert Angell; Esther L. McLaughlin Donahue; David B. McLaughlin; Rowland H. McLaughlin; James B. Angell II; James A. McLaughlin; (middle row) James W. Angell; Marion Angell McAlpin; James Burrill Angell holding Isabel McLaughlin Stevens; Lois A. McLaughlin; (back row) Mrs. James R. Angell; James R. Angell; Andrew McLaughlin; Mrs. Alexis C. Angell; Alexis C. Angell; Sarah C. Angell

kind? Is not each suited to its place?" While each literary impulse may have its place, Angell invokes a higher principle: the increased literary possibilities that freedom from strict rules allows a writer. Had he written the book on the comparative study of French, German, and English literatures as he had once hoped, his theme might have been that English literature is the most balanced of the three. For Angell the English literary mind represents a healthy middle ground between the extremes of French conservatism and German individualism. Such comparative methods seem to have been the direction Angell's criticism might have developed had he continued to pursue his literary career.

In 1858, when Henry B. Anthony, editor and proprietor of the *Providence Journal*, was elected to the senate, he asked Angell to assume

his editorial duties and Angell accepted. Offered the editorship of the journal in 1860, Angell resigned his chair at Brown in part because curriculum changes limited his opportunities to teach beyond the elementary stages of the French and German languages. "This elementary teaching soon became rather uninspiring to me. I used to say it did not seem to stretch the flexor muscles of the mind." In 1866, after six years of writing and editing for the Republican journal during the intense political climate of the Civil War, Angell accepted the presidency of the University of Vermont. He proved an able administrator who garnered needed support from the state. Never an intellectual, withdrawn elitist, he won many friends for the university through his readiness to lecture throughout the state.

His success as an administrator soon

brought him in 1871 to Ann Arbor as president of the University of Michigan, where he advocated coeducation, graduate research, and broader selections of electives. He applied Scottish ideas of intellectual democracy to academics and became a champion of popular education. His reputation as an innovative administrator and an intellectual of the people also brought him a number of diplomatic missions. In 1880 he was sent to China as part of a three-man commission appointed by Rutherford B. Hayes to negotiate a new immigration treaty. Angell's guidance and the ability of the commission to make a treaty quickly with the reportedly difficult Chinese led to his appointment by Grover Cleveland to the Anglo-American Northeastern Fisheries Commission and to the Canadian-American Deep Waterways Commission. His last diplomatic position came in 1897, when William McKinley appointed him minister to Turkey. He retired from the University of Michigan in 1909 and died on 1 April 1916.

Angell spent only four years of his fifty-four-year professional career writing literary scholarship and criticism. While he wore many of the critical blinders of his contemporaries in overemphasizing the need for optimism and perhaps placing art on too high a pedestal, he avoided the harsh prescriptive negativism (though superior theorizing) of critics like Edgar Allan Poe. He also avoided, in his international perspective, many of the literary provincialisms of the Young America group clustered around the Duyckinck brothers. Ultimately, however, Angell contributed little that was new to the critical theory of his day, even though his adoption of German historicism might have developed into an important approach to the comparative study of European literature. Above all, Angell believed that truth was not to be found in extremes, and he always sought a balance between aesthetic and moral concerns in his literary criticism. As scholar and critic his intellectual creed can perhaps be best summed up in his hope for the future of German literature which he notes in "Emanuel Geibel": "May we hope that a school will arise, who shall join all that is vital in the conservatism of the past, and all that is good in the progressiveness of the present, to a fulness and depth of Christian faith which the future alone can reveal."

Letters:

From Vermont to Michigan; Correspondence of James B. Angell: 1869-1871, edited by Wilfred B. Shaw (Ann Arbor: University of Michigan Press, 1936).

Biography:

Shirley W. Smith, *James Burrill Angell: An American Influence* (Ann Arbor: University of Michigan Press, 1954).

Papers:

The papers of James Burrill Angell dating from 1845 to 1916 are located in the Historical Collections of the University of Michigan.

John Burroughs

(3 April 1837-29 March 1921)

Peter Crawford
Statement Magazine

BOOKS: *Notes on Walt Whitman, as Poet and Person* (New York: American News Company, 1867);

Wake-Robin (New York: Hurd & Houghton, 1871; London: Low, 1871; revised and enlarged edition, New York: Hurd & Houghton, 1877);

Winter Sunshine (New York: Hurd & Houghton, 1876; London: Low, 1876; revised and enlarged edition, New York: Hurd & Houghton, 1877);

Birds and Poets with other Papers (New York: Hurd & Houghton, 1877; Edinburgh: Douglas, 1884);

Locusts and Wild Honey (Boston: Houghton, Osgood, 1879; Edinburgh: Douglas, 1884);

Pepacton (Boston: Houghton, Mifflin, 1881; London: Low, 1881);

Essays from "The Critic" by John Burroughs and Others (Boston: Osgood, 1882);

Fresh Fields (Boston: Houghton, Mifflin, 1885; Edinburgh: Douglas / London: Adams, 1885);

Signs and Seasons (Boston & New York: Houghton, Mifflin, 1886; Edinburgh: Douglas / London: Adams, 1886);

Indoor Studies (Boston & New York: Houghton, Mifflin, 1889);

Riverby: Essays on Birds, Trees, and Prairies (Boston, New York & London: Houghton, Mifflin, 1894);

Whitman: A Study (Boston & New York: Houghton, Mifflin, 1896; London: Watt, 1896);

The Light of Day: Religious Discussions and Criticisms from the Naturalist's Point of View (Boston, New York & London: Houghton, Mifflin, 1900);

Squirrels and Other Furbearers (Boston, New York & London: Houghton, Mifflin, 1900);

John James Audubon (Boston: Small, Maynard, 1902);

Literary Values and Other Papers (Boston & New York: Houghton, Mifflin, 1902; London: Gay & Bird, 1903);

Burroughs in 1857

Far and Near (Boston & New York: Houghton, Mifflin, 1904; London: Constable, 1905);

Ways of Nature (Boston & New York: Houghton, Mifflin, 1905; London: Constable, 1905);

Bird and Bough (Boston & New York: Houghton, Mifflin, 1906; London: Constable, 1906);

Camping with President Roosevelt (Boston & New York: Houghton, Mifflin, 1906); enlarged and republished as *Camping and Tramping with Roosevelt* (Boston & New York: Houghton, Mifflin/London: Constable, 1907);

Leaf and Tendril (Boston & New York: Houghton, Mifflin, 1908; London: Constable, 1908);

Time and Change (Boston & New York: Houghton Mifflin, 1912; London: Constable, 1912);

The Summit of the Years (Boston & New York: Houghton Mifflin, 1913);

The Breath of Life (Boston & New York: Houghton Mifflin, 1915; London: Constable, 1916);

Under the Apple-Trees (Boston & New York: Houghton Mifflin, 1916);

Field and Study (Boston & New York: Houghton Mifflin, 1919);

Accepting the Universe: Essays in Naturalism (Boston & New York: Houghton Mifflin, 1920; London: Constable, 1921);

Under the Maples (Boston & New York: Houghton Mifflin, 1921);

My Boyhood, with a Conclusion by Julian Burroughs (Garden City & Toronto: Doubleday, 1922);

The Last Harvest (Boston & New York: Houghton Mifflin, 1922; London: Cape, 1923);

John Burroughs at Troutbeck; Being Extracts from his Writings, Published and Unpublished (Amenia, N.Y.: Troutbeck Press, 1926);

The Heart of Burroughs's Journals Edited by Clara Barrus (Boston & New York: Houghton Mifflin, 1928).

OTHER: "Walt Whitman and his Recent Critics," in *In Re Walt Whitman*, edited by Horace Traubel and others (Philadelphia: McKay, 1894), pp. 93-108;

"Walt Whitman and the Common People," in *In Re Walt Whitman*, edited by Traubel and others (Philadelphia: McKay, 1894), pp. 363-365;

"Henry D. Thoreau," in *A Library of the World's Best Literature, Ancient and Modern*, volume 37, edited by Charles Dudley Warner and others (New York: International Society, 1897), pp. 14,871-14,876;

"Walt Whitman," in *A Library of the World's Best Literature, Ancient and Modern*, volume 39, edited by Warner and others (New York: International Society, 1897), pp. 15,855-15,891;

"Walt Whitman," *Encyclopaedia Britannica*, 10th edition, volume 23 (Cambridge: University Press, 1902).

PERIODICAL PUBLICATIONS: "Expression," *Atlantic Monthly*, 6 (November 1860): 572-577;

"Analogy," *Knickerbocker*, 60 (December 1862): 477-484;

"Walt Whitman and His 'Drum Taps,'" *Galaxy*, 2 (1 December 1866): 606-615;

"Carlyle," *Century Magazine*, 26 (August 1883): 530-543;

"The Poet of Democracy," *North American Review*, 154 (May 1892): 532-540;

"The Poet and the Modern," *Atlantic Monthly*, 78 (October 1896): 565-566;

"Science and Literature," *North American Review*, 416 (March 1914): 415-424;

"A Critical Glance into Thoreau," *Atlantic Monthly*, 123 (June 1919): 777-786.

John Burroughs is still revered by some conservationists and bird watchers as the Homer of the nature essay. As a literary critic, however, he has been met since his death in 1921 with a silence that belies the influence he exercised during a half century writing for the nonacademic yet thoughtful reader. Indeed, many fancied him a sage, a distinction which he perhaps did too little to discourage. His literary talents are influenced mainly by the American transcendentalists and their English precursors. As a young man he befriended Walt Whitman; combined with his own growing popularity, his warm evaluations of Whitman's work helped convince the public to recognize a writer they would have as soon condemned.

Burroughs was born on 3 April 1837 to Chauncey A. and Amy Kelly Burroughs on a small farm at Roxbury, New York, the seventh of ten children. He received what schooling he could from country schoolhouses. At age seventeen, he began teaching and was able to save enough money to place himself in better schools. In his spare time, he sought to improve his writing by imitating Samuel Johnson. In 1856 he studied briefly at the Cooperstown Seminary where he became enthralled with the writings of Ralph Waldo Emerson. So profound was the influence that, four years later, James Russell Lowell, then editor of the *Atlantic Monthly*, checked through all of Emerson's work to rule out the possibility of plagiarism before publishing an essay by Burroughs called "Expression." Perhaps conscious of how unEmersonian it was to imitate Emerson, Burroughs began writing the distinctive nature essays for which he is best known. In 1863 he moved to Washington, D.C., where he met Whitman. The two became instant and lifelong friends.

It is impossible to say how much of Burroughs's first book, *Notes on Walt Whitman, as Poet and Person* (1867), was actually written by

Ursula North, whom Burroughs married in 1857

Whitman. Much of the prose is at the very least Whitmanesque; Burroughs admitted in a 1920 letter, "I have no doubt that half of the book is his." Beginning with an account of the friendship and of the early publishing history of *Leaves of Grass* (1855), the book soon turns to a discussion of Whitman's concerns–"Life, Love, and the Immortal Identity of the Soul"–and his method, which is to condense a number of thoughts into one word or image. In spite of this compression, Burroughs finds that Whitman's poetry is "death to epigrams" because the ideas and their expression are so vast as to "approximate to a direct utterance of Nature herself." As in Nature, beauty is not removed from "the wide background of rudeness, darkness, and strength." "Where others bring a flower from the woods or a shell from the shore, [Whitman] brings the woods and the shore also" and manages at the same time to repeat "the act of creation itself."

Agreeing with Whitman that nature gives the human spirit its best access to "the highest Philosophy and Religion," Burroughs goes on to say that nature plays a dominant role in Whitman's concept of a New Man who derives his morality from Nature's "material forms and shows" and celebrates "the purity of the Body in its juices . . . and all its organs." Burroughs praises Whitman's

refusal to criticize human failings as do other writers, stating that the poet's aim is not to teach "a good lesson" but to "take down the bars to a good lesson": thus might a person acquire and maintain the moral fiber necessary to take advantage of the wealth and progress of modern civilization.

Notes on Walt Whitman, as Poet and Person gained hardly any notice at all in the United States but received a warm review by William Rosetti in London where perhaps the threat to propriety that Whitman posed was moderated by his being a novelty from abroad.

Burroughs stayed in the capital until 1885, working as a clerk in the Department of the Treasury and later as a special bank examiner. Every two or three years he gathered a group of essays, some previously published, into a book. *Birds and Poets with other Papers*, which appeared in 1877, contains the essay "Before Beauty," which develops the idea set forth in *Notes on Walt Whitman, as Poet and Person* that beauty must be accompanied by "a rank, material basis." For Burroughs the problem with poets of the day was that they wanted to "spare us the annoyance of the beast." But in so doing, he thought they enfeebled both their poetry and the reader. In a companion essay, "Before Genius," Burroughs proposes that while the common perception may be that literature is read for ideas or for pleasure, in fact it is read to acquaint oneself with the personality of the artist. From this simple observation, very likely borrowed from Charles-Augustin Sainte-Beuve, Burroughs derives the major part of his critical methodology, which is to examine the character of the artist as revealed in his work.

This he does in the essay "Emerson." He finds Emerson too refined, lacking "broad, massive effect"; he is too much the "close-browed miser of the scholar's gains," interested in the spirit to the exclusion of the flesh. Consequently, he is shut out from "emotional poetry, the poetry of fluid humanity" and his "field of vision and enjoyment" is curtailed. According to Burroughs this explains the loosening of his powers in his later years; "he is a husbandman who practices no rotation of crops." Nevertheless, for Burroughs Emerson is eternally "the prophet and philosopher of young men," taking "almost an unfair advantage" of the youth "fed upon the penny precepts and staple Johnsonianism of English literature." Indeed, those who have never been swept away by him are to be pitied.

Pages from the manuscript for Burroughs's essay "The Flight of the Eagle," with emendations by Walt Whitman (The Life and Letters of John Burroughs, *1925)*

Burroughs on Yale University campus, 1910, receiving an honorary Doctor of Letters degree (photo © Paul Thompson)

By the time *Indoor Studies* (1889) was published, Burroughs had quit Washington, had built a house at West Park on the Hudson, and, to keep from idling, had planted a vineyard and a berry farm. *Indoor Studies* begins with a look at Thoreau. Burroughs found that like Emerson, Thoreau lacked sympathy, comparing him to a crusty loaf of bread, "forbidding to tender gums, but sweet to those who had good teeth and unction enough to soften him." If Thoreau had been flexible, more prone to self-surrender, he might have become a great poet. In the same man, Burroughs discovered the trifler who refused to pay "a paltry tax" and the visionary who defended John Brown. This knotty character makes *Walden* (1854) "the most delicious piece of brag in literature." Thoreau's strategy is to make the most common things look strange: "he squeezes his subject as in a vice" to force "something out of nothing." Burroughs claims that Thoreau was not a good

natural historian because he would not surrender to Nature; it "must surrender to him" and hand over the Ideal. Nevertheless, he concludes, "his happy literary talent makes up for the poverty of his observation."

In "Science and Literature" and "Science and the Poets" Burroughs suggests that, although the scientific treatment of Nature can never replace its literary treatment, artists nevertheless should be aware of scientific developments, such as Darwin's theory of evolution, and should not refrain from incorporating scientific facts into their work. "Matthew Arnold's Criticism" is a solid assessment of Arnold's work and character. Arnold brings "a classic mind to modern themes"; his Hellenism is a love of institutions and a distrust of the individual. But Burroughs finds his social criticism weak due to a soft temperamentalism, as is his promotion of the truths of Christianity minus the rituals; to Burroughs this is "no more Christianity than the extract of lilies or roses is a flower-garden." Burroughs maintains that Arnold is best as a critic of literature, the vocabulary he created being particularly valuable to the scholar. Contrasting Sainte-Beuve and Arnold, Burroughs finds the former more able to judge sympathetically a work based on its own merit and the latter to indicate where the work "transgresses the law" of perfect taste. Arnold's books function together as a whole, each one "entirely subordinated to plan, to structure, to total results." Rarely novel or forceful, usually consistent and clear, "he is as free from the diseases of subtlety of thought or expression . . . as any of the antique authors." Still, Burroughs finds faults with Arnold's forever "unclouded intellect" and purported disinterestedness, suggesting that they block Arnold from appreciating the revolutionary genius who, by nature, has "a certain bias, a certain heat and onesidedness."

In 1896, four years after Whitman's death, Burroughs finished *Whitman: A Study*. Each chapter of the book deals with a different aspect of the poet's life and art while revolving around the theme of Whitman as the poet of democracy and the New Man. Being such he "shows us all things in and through himself " with a kind of "altruegotism." It is a mistake, says Burroughs, to assume that the ever-present personal pronoun stands for the private individual, Walt Whitman. It stands for all people. Against Whitman is his monotony and lack of humor which sometimes places him, according to Burroughs, "on the verge of the grotesque without knowing it." This

Burroughs with inventor Thomas A. Edison and tire manufacturer Harvey S. Firestone, 1916

does not, however, prevent him from being "a poet plus something else"–a poet with a gospel that contains "the word of faith and power."

Literary Values and Other Papers (1902) is a collection mostly of theoretical essays. The title essay shows a development of the ideas set forth in "Before Genius." The source of literary value is always "the man behind the record," not the record itself. "The personal element is the salt of literature. Without it, the page is savorless." This element is lost in the classroom where the students are trained to fall upon the text "like hens upon a bone in winter . . . every line is literally picked to pieces." Instead of emphasizing analysis, the teacher should equip students to recognize the genuine from the counterfeit in literature; this can only happen through "direct sympathetic intercourse with the best literature."

"Style and the Man" draws a distinction between style and stylistics, the former arising from a "vital, intimate, personal relation of the man to his language," the latter from an effort "to find meaning for words." In effect, the stylist's "thoughts are word-begotten." Furthermore, the stylist's efforts are often marred by obscurity, both in thought and syntax, and seem to the reader "obviously studied." Burroughs contrasts Walter Pater, the stylist, with Arnold, the writer with style who succeeds by allowing his personality to dictate his words, not words to dictate the personality of his writing.

"Criticism and the Man" and "Recent Phases of Literary Criticism" examine the task of the critic. To Burroughs all criticism is impressionistic and subjective. Faith that one can judge a poem according to objective standards and fixed classifications while avoiding sympathy and intuition amounts to a "poetical creed, [the same as] a political or religious creed." "Love must come first," the emotions before the intellect. The highest task of the critic is to inspire and to awaken ideas in the reader, not to hand down judgments. Great artists are self-expressive, whereas great critics find "complete self-expression in and through the works of other men." Finally, as sensitive registers, critics can rise above the babel of schools and movements, even contain opposites, for they respond less to what is said than to who says it.

"Democracy and Literature" proposes that a writer might address the people without descending to the "loud and vulgar." The "great, modern democrats in literature," such as Tolstoy and Whitman, lift popular taste from its current vulgarity through their "deeply religious way of looking at mankind." Furthermore, they have discovered in the modern industrial and scientific age "new artistic motives and values." If Dante could make poetry out of Hell, Burroughs asks, could not genius do the same among factories and machines? The essays on Emerson and Thoreau in *The Last Harvest*, published posthumously in 1922, are more anecdotal in their approach but do not represent any significant change in attitude toward the two men.

Throughout his career as a literary critic, Burroughs maintained a core of ideas and attitudes from which he rarely strayed. The writers he preferred refrained from abstractions, strove for a democratic tone, and followed Nature in building beauty within a framework of elemental and brute forces. His advice to readers was to read impressionistically, not judgmentally, and to realize that they approach the literary work not to gather great ideas but to meet a great personality.

During the last fifteen years of his life, Burroughs became a minor legend. He was awarded honorary degrees by Yale, Colgate, and the University of Georgia and received several cars as gifts from Henry Ford. A friend of Edison and Roosevelt, the subject of a number of articles by Dreiser, he was the focus of many a pilgrimage to his rustic farm by the Hudson. Regardless of the change in critical tastes that followed soon after his death and which almost entirely dismissed his work, Burroughs still provides an excellent introduction to Whitman, Emerson, Thoreau, and Arnold. He should especially not be overlooked by the more serious students of Whitman.

Letters:

Clara Barrus, *The Life and Letters of John Burroughs*, 2 volumes (Boston & New York: Houghton Mifflin, 1925).

Interview:

Theodore Dreiser, "Fame Found in Quiet Nooks," *Success*, 1 (September 1898): 5-6.

Bibliographies:

Jacob Blanck, comp. "John Burroughs," *Bibliography of American Literature*, volume 1 (New Haven & London: Yale University Press, 1955), pp. 433-448;

Joseph M. Garrison, Jr., "John Burroughs," *Bulletin of Bibliography*, 24 (May-August 1964): 95-96, 94.

Biographies:

Theodore Dreiser, "John Burroughs in His Mountain Hut," *New Voice*, 16 (19 August 1899): 7, 13;

Clara Barrus, *Whitman and Burroughs: Comrades* (Boston: Houghton Mifflin, 1931);

Elizabeth Burroughs Kelly, *John Burroughs: Naturalist, the Story of His Work and Family* (New York: Exposition Press, 1959).

References:

Joel Benton, "John Burroughs," *Scribner's Monthly*, 13 (January 1877): 336-341;

Norman Foerster, *Nature in American Literature* (New York: Russell & Russell, 1923);

Henry James, *Views and Reviews* (New York: Books for Libraries Press, 1968);

Perry Westbrook, *John Burroughs* (New York: Twayne, 1974);

Westbrook, "John Burroughs and the Transcendentalists," *Emerson Society Quarterly*, 55, part 2 (Second Quarter 1969): 47-55.

Papers:

The major collections of Burroughs materials are in the John Burroughs collection in the Clifton Waller Barrett Library at the University of Virginia, the Henry W. and Albert A. Berg Collection in the New York Public Library, and at the Henry E. Huntington Library and Art Gallery in San Marino, California.

George Henry Calvert

(2 June 1803-24 May 1889)

Christina Zwarg
Harvard University

See also the Calvert entry in *DLB 1, The American Renaissance in New England.*

BOOKS: *A Volume from the Life of Herbert Barclay,* anonymous (Baltimore: Neal, 1833);

Count Julian; A Tragedy (Baltimore: Hickman, 1840);

Miscellany of Verse and Prose (Baltimore: Hickman, 1840);

Cabiro: A Poem. Cantos I and II (Baltimore: Hickman, 1840);

Scenes and Thoughts in Europe. By an American (New York: Wiley & Putnam, 1846; revised edition, Boston: Little, Brown, 1863); republished with *Scenes and Thoughts in Europe. By an American. Second Series* as *Travels in Europe: Its People and Scenery, Embracing Graphic Descriptions of the Principal Cities, Buildings, Scenery, and Most Notable People in England and the Continent* (Boston: Cottrell, 1860);

Poems (Boston: Ticknor, 1847);

Scenes and Thoughts in Europe. By an American. Second Series (New York: Putnam's, 1852; revised edition, Boston: Little, Brown, 1863); republished with *Scenes and Thoughts in Europe,* first series, as *Travels in Europe* (Boston: Cottrell, 1860);

Introduction to Social Science: A Discourse in Three Parts (New York: Redfield, 1856);

Comedies (Boston: Phillips, Sampson, 1856);

Joan of Arc: A Poem. In Four Books, anonymous (Cambridge: Privately printed, 1860); republished under Calvert's name (Boston: Lee & Shepard/New York: Dillingham, 1883);

The Gentleman (Boston: Ticknor & Fields, 1863);

Arnold and André. An Historical Drama (Boston: Little, Brown, 1864; revised edition, Boston: Lee & Shepard, 1876);

Cabiro. A Poem. Cantos III and IV (Boston: Little, Brown, 1864);

Anyta and Other Poems (Boston: Dutton/New York: Hurd & Houghton, 1866);

Portrait by William Edward West, 1839 (courtesy of the Hon. John Ridgely Carter)

First Years in Europe (Boston: Spencer, 1866; London: Trubner, 1866);

Ellen: A Poem for the Times, anonymous (New York: Carleton, 1867); enlarged and repub-

16

lished under Calvert's name (New York: Sheldon, 1869);

Goethe: His Life and Works. An Essay (Boston: Lee & Shepard/New York: Lee, Shepard & Dillingham, 1872; London: Trubner, 1872);

Mirabeau: An Historical Drama (Cambridge: Printed at the Riverside Press, 1873; revised edition, Boston: Lee & Shepard/New York: Dillingham, 1883);

The Maid of Orleans: An Historical Tragedy (Cambridge: Privately printed, 1873; revised edition, New York: Putnam's, 1874);

Brief Essays and Brevities (Boston: Lee & Shepard/ New York: Lee, Shepard & Dillingham, 1874);

Essays Aesthetical (Boston: Lee & Shepard/New York: Lee, Shepard & Dillingham, 1875);

A Nation's Birth and Other National Poems (Boston: Lee & Shepard, 1876);

The Life of Rubens (Boston: Lee & Shepard/New York: Dillingham, 1876);

Charlotte von Stein: A Memoir (Boston: Lee & Shepard/New York: Dillingham, 1877);

Wordsworth. A Biographic Aesthetic Study (Boston: Lee & Shepard/New York: Dillingham, 1878);

Shakespeare. A Biographic Aesthetic Study (Boston: Lee & Shepard/New York: Dillingham, 1879);

Coleridge, Shelley, Goethe. Biographic Aesthetic Studies (Boston: Lee & Shepard/New York: Dillingham, 1880);

Life, Death, and Other Poems (Boston: Lee & Shepard/New York: Dillingham, 1882);

Angeline. A Poem (Boston: Lee & Shepard/New York: Dillingham, 1883);

Threescore, and Other Poems (Boston: Lee & Shepard/New York: Dillingham, 1883);

Sibyl. A Poem (Boston: Lee & Shepard, 1883);

The Nazarene. A Poem (Boston: Lee & Shepard/ New York: Dillingham, 1883);

Brangonar. A Tragedy (Boston: Lee & Shepard/ New York: Dillingham, 1883).

OTHER: *Illustrations of Phrenology,* edited by Calvert (Baltimore: Neal, 1832).

TRANSLATIONS: *Don Carlos: A Dramatic Poem, by Frederick Schiller* (Baltimore: Neal, 1834);

Correspondence between Schiller and Goethe, from 1794 to 1805 (New York & London: Wiley & Putnam, 1845);

Joubert. Some of the "Thoughts" of Joseph Joubert (Boston: Spencer, 1867).

PERIODICAL PUBLICATIONS: "Prologue in Heaven," *Chronicle of the Times* (13 November 1830): 243-270;

Review of *The Life of Friedrich Schiller, North American Review,* 39 (July 1834): 1-30;

"A Lecture on German Literature," *Southern Literary Messenger,* 2 (May 1836): 373-438;

"Ralph Waldo Emerson. Essays.–Lectures and Orations,–Nature.–Poems.–Representative Men," *New York Quarterly,* 1 (January 1853): 439-447;

"Weimar in 1825," *Putnam's Monthly Magazine,* 8 (September 1856): 257-267;

"Göttingen in 1824," *Putnam's Monthly Magazine,* 8 (December 1856): 595-607;

"Dante and his Latest Translators," *Putnam's Magazine,* new series 1 (February 1868): 155-167;

"Sainte-Beuve, the Critic," *Putnam's Magazine,* new series 2 (October 1868): 401-411;

"Matthew Arnold's Wordsworth," *Literary World* (Boston), 10 (25 October 1879): 339.

Discussing how to strengthen the *Dial,* Ralph Waldo Emerson suggested to Margaret Fuller that George Henry Calvert be asked to contribute and Fuller understood by this that the journal needed to enlarge its coverage of European literature. A true cosmopolitan, Calvert was a prolific writer of poetry and prose and one of the early translators of German literature in America. Readers prized him less for his artistic and critical skills than for his work in promoting neglected or controversial European masters. One of the group of Americans who pursued postgraduate study at the University of Göttingen (in 1824 he met and became friendly with Emerson's brother William), Calvert was an early translator of Goethe, Schiller, and Joseph Joubert. He also wrote the first American biographies of Goethe, Charlotte von Stein, Rubens, and Wordsworth. He never did write for the *Dial.*

Calvert ran a curious if ironic parallel to the lives of both Fuller and Emerson. Like Emerson and unlike Fuller, he attended Harvard University; like Fuller and unlike Emerson, he adored travel and spent a good part of his career crossing through Europe. He greatly admired Goethe and wrote the biography Fuller never managed to write. More prolific than Emerson and Fuller combined, Calvert produced over thirty published volumes (including epic poems, dramas, biographies, critical essays, and several interesting works of travel literature). Yet his work has received little critical attention.

Calvert was born eight days after Emerson on 2 June 1803, the son of Rosalie Stier and George Calvert. Calvert's early experiences were quite different from those of his contemporaries, for his European descent on his mother's side of the family encouraged an oddly cosmopolitan provincialism. Calvert's mother had fled to America from Belgium after Napoleon seized the country, and Calvert grew up on tales of the exodus. These fostered an appreciation of European culture (he recalled how his mother's family crated and shipped a number of famous paintings to America in their flight) but did not always help him to appreciate the artistic treasures at home. Indeed, he was often highly critical of American writers. For example, according to his biographer, Ida Gertrude Everson, he considered the work of Walt Whitman an "enormous joke." Yet sometimes his ambivalence about America could yield sharp critical insights. Not surprisingly, it was a new writer for the *Nation*, Henry James, who recognized that ambivalence when he received Calvert's late work, *Essays Æsthetical* (1875).

Prolific as he was, Calvert only wrote one work of fiction. Published anonymously in 1833, *A Volume from the Life of Herbert Barclay* gave play to several themes that would reappear in the life of its author, notably the virtues of education and the "education" of travel. Calvert's interest in travel developed naturally during his childhood on his father's estate near Baldensburg, Maryland, where his mother charmed him with tales of her early days in Antwerp. Calvert's bond with his mother proved vital. She not only told elegant and exotic narratives of Europe for him to dream about (and identify as his own–his mother, after all, was a descendant of Peter Paul Rubens) but carefully monitored his education, making sure that he received training suitable for a "gentleman" traveling in European circles. Calvert's early aristocratic yearnings were not the product of his mother's grooming alone, however. On his father's side, Calvert was related to the founder of Maryland, George Calvert; and his great-grandfather was the fifth Lord Baltimore. The trappings of this distinguished family gave Calvert a sense of entitlement.

Calvert attended Harvard from 1819 to 1823, but along with thirty others, he was denied his degree due to his participation in the "Great Rebellion," the protest dividing the class of 1823. Even this event seemed oddly tailored to

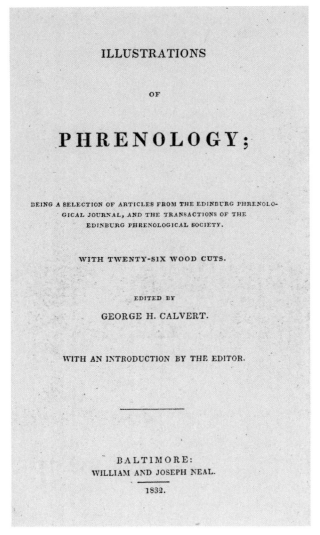

ILLUSTRATIONS

OF

PHRENOLOGY;

BEING A SELECTION OF ARTICLES FROM THE EDINBURG PHRENOLO-
GICAL JOURNAL, AND THE TRANSACTIONS OF THE
EDINBURG PHRENOLOGICAL SOCIETY.

WITH TWENTY-SIX WOOD CUTS.

EDITED BY

GEORGE H. CALVERT.

WITH AN INTRODUCTION BY THE EDITOR.

———

BALTIMORE:
WILLIAM AND JOSEPH NEAL.
1832.

Title page for the essays Calvert gathered to illustrate his belief "in the vast importance of the Phrenological discoveries . . ."

Calvert's divided loyalties, since, as his biographer notes, the protest emerged out of the "influence of Bancroft, Cogswell, Everett and Ticknor, all of whom had studied in Germany." The primary goal of the rebellion was to restrict the rule of the "Immediate Government" over student activities, but the protest inevitably encouraged students to express their dissatisfaction with the type of instruction that they were receiving at Harvard. In the summer of 1823, soon after his dismissal from the university, Calvert journeyed to Europe, first visiting an uncle who lived near Antwerp and then settling in Göttingen, where he studied philosophy and history for fifteen months. After meeting Goethe in Weimar and entering society there, Calvert traveled next to

Edinburgh, Paris, and Antwerp before returning to America.

These experiences proved formative for Calvert. Though deprived of an official degree from Harvard, his travel and education in Europe "certified" him as a cosmopolitan. When he returned to America, he married Elizabeth Steuart and first settled in Baltimore. There he coedited a journal entitled the *Chronicle of the Times* (which changed its title to the *Baltimore Times* before it closed in 1832). The journal attempted to expand beyond the horizon of the average American periodical by making occasional reference to European literature. In it, Calvert made an early translation from the prologue of Goethe's *Faust*.

During this period, Calvert developed an interest in phrenology and in 1832 edited a collection of essays from the *Edinburg Phrenological Journal*. Calvert's passion for the science of phrenology was as casual yet positive as his later interest in the water cure and the "scientific" socialism of Charles Fourier and Jean Baptiste Godin. In many ways, these interests developed out of his desire to connect with the "promise" of American culture. Calvert had something of Benjamin Franklin's appetite for newfangled theories, though less of his talent for applying them. Oddly this bent did not impede a contrary desire to sow European culture onto American soil. The reform theories he admired, after all, were invariably generated in Europe.

In 1834 Calvert wrote the first American translation of Friedrich Schiller's dramatic poem, *Don Carlos* (1787), and almost simultaneously published a review of Thomas Carlyle's *Life of Schiller* (1824) in the *North American Review*. These efforts gave him a small readership which perhaps encouraged him to write and publish his own dramatic tragedy, *Count Julian*, in 1840. Calvert continued throughout his life to write and publish poems and plays, but his talents were better displayed in his translations and, more crucially, his critical appreciation of Europe and its literary scene. Upon his return from a second European tour, Calvert began to gain even more recognition for these skills. In 1845 he translated the first section of the *Correspondence between Schiller and Goethe, from 1794 to 1805* and in 1846 published his first travel essay, entitled *Scenes and Thoughts in Europe. By an American*. Both works benefit by Calvert's growing sense of his role as mediator between the Old World and the New.

In his introduction to the *Correspondence Between Schiller and Goethe*, Calvert criticized the Phi Beta Kappa oration delivered by George Putnam one year earlier in Cambridge for its narrow attack on Goethe. Calvert not only dismissed the harsh moral judgments made against Goethe's character as irrelevant but added the scandalous suggestion that his work was probably enlarged by the "errors" into which his "ardent temperament" drew him. Art was "mental procreation," according to Calvert, "and the mind of a people can no more grow without Art than its body can without generation."

Calvert's desire to mediate between the Old World and the New takes on a peripatetic quality in *Scenes and Thoughts in Europe. By an American*. Moving from England to France and then to Italy, Calvert attempts to distinguish each country for Americans by upsetting some of their most tenacious clichés. Though England "looks everywhere aristocratical" Calvert insists that one cannot "ascribe the short-comings of England to the aristocratic principle" any more than one can "claim for it her many glories." If Europe has more "idlers" than America, it is because "capital being wanting in the United States, almost the universal energy is busied in supplying it."

Calvert's work is most interesting when he finds himself confronted with American attitudes that resist their response to a broader European sensibility. A case in point is his impatience while in Italy when he heard about the controversy brewing back home over the "nudity" of Greenough's statue of George Washington. As always, Calvert is nettled by the curious censoriousness of Americans. The charm of Calvert's irritation, however, lies in the oddly prudish rhetoric that he uses to educate his reader. According to Calvert, "Washington . . . ought to be beheld, not as he came from the hand of a tailor, but as he came from the hand of God." There are times, however, when Calvert's American sentiments obtrude upon European matters, particularly when he discusses France and things relating to Napoleon. Goethe created great works, but Napoleon merely created great havoc, according to Calvert, and could not be forgiven for his immoderacies. "His name will hereafter be a gorgeous emptiness: his memory is not vitalized by a principle."

Like Emerson, Calvert elected throughout his career to describe and analyze the men who were shaping the intellectual climate of the nineteenth century. Goethe and Shakespeare were crucial to both critics, though Goethe was considerably more problematic for Emerson than Calvert. And like Emerson, Calvert also found himself inexplicably drawn to Napoleon. Both critics tend to mention the French utopian socialist Charles Fourier whenever they discuss Napoleon, as if the two somehow represent opposing possibilities for American culture, though Calvert tends to be more extreme both in his distrust of Napoleon and in his confidence in Fourier.

F. O. Matthiessen thought that the "American Renaissance" could also be named the "Age of Fourier." Certainly Fourier's social theories had saturated the American intellectual community by the time Calvert began lecturing to American audiences on their behalf. This suggests that Calvert's interest in Fourier represented a new acceptance of and desire to develop his American birthright. Indeed, in 1844, Calvert chose Newport, Rhode Island, as the site of his permanent residence. He soon became chairman of the school board and in 1852 ran for political office. Calvert delivered a series of general lectures inspired by Fourier while he served as Democratic mayor from 1853 to 1854. His book *Introduction to Social Science: A Discourse in Three Parts* (1856) collects and prints those lectures. Once again, Calvert finds himself at war with Napoleon, casting off one prototype of leadership in search of another. Within the overall argument of the lectures, Napoleon emerges as the bad model, a man "who knew how to lead soldiers but not how to lead men." He stands as proof for the argument that "civil rule and mere municipal organization" were no longer suitable principles of social organization.

Calvert's interest in the development of the "natural law" of work reveals his desire to situate himself firmly on American soil even as it suggests the limitations of his ability to do so. His brand of socialism, it is true, was well suited to the tenets of American capitalism (he believed for example that the idea of a "community of goods" was a "social solecism") and therefore posed little real threat. Yet it also revealed a sad blindness to the gathering racial crisis in the culture. To be sure, Calvert picks up on the growing concern over slavery in America, but his manipulation of the term "slave" in his *Introduction to Social Science* ("however democratic may be his political relations, however white his skin, he is not free: he is a slave") subverts his distaste for that institution. If anything, it reveals Calvert's belief in the superiority of the Anglo-Saxon race. Calvert turns Fourier's "progressive" view of history to this notion rather easily, arguing that some people ("the natives of Central & Western Africa, the Malays in Asia, the Indians in America") "never reach the adult state."

In 1863 Calvert wrote his most curious treatise: *The Gentleman*. Published at the height of the Civil War, it was reprinted four times. The work was his most popular effort, perhaps because its concentration on the decorous behavior of a "gentleman" provided an escape for the horrors of fratricide, or, more deeply, because the internal ambiguities of Calvert's thought gave allegorical play to the tension felt by the American public during this traumatic time. Calvert's argument spins on several crucial notions: that the history of the world is progressive and that America finds itself admirably situated within that historical thrust; that the gentleman is a rather passive, unobtrusive character; and that above all the "moral element" is central to the gentleman's character.

Sometimes, of course, these ideas collide, and it is the friction of their collision that generates interest. The Civil War exposed the confusion that could occur when the gentleman's careful demeanor (he "takes no liberties; is chary of questions") is challenged by a moral issue. This was as true for the Southern "Gentleman" as for his Northern counterpart. The pathos of Calvert's choice of topic at this time lies in the way it exploits the conflicting sense of manhood (which is to say, white manhood) in both sections of the country, for according to Calvert, "the gentleman is above all things, free."

Calvert's gentlemen are not drawn from literary history, though he concedes that certain artists did attempt to develop the concept of the gentleman. He finds in Homer only one specimen, Hector, though Calvert argues that Homer's portrait is limited by the time in which he writes. Even Plato is shown to fail; Christianity was necessary for the development of the true Gentleman. Thus Calvert's models, the Chevalier Bayard and Sir Philip Sidney, are drawn from history; both lived, according to Calvert, in a time of "corruptions and affectations of decay." The men around them were given over to perfidious behavior, and the two stand out more starkly for their lack of egotism.

Bayard is drawn as a gallant soldier, generous in victory and skilled in military decorum. He formed the model in Calvert's mind for the Northern soldier who, like Bayard, should be victorious but giving in his victory, remain stern, and refuse as did Bayard the seductions of a base, impoverished class who would sell flesh and blood. Sidney was another kind of ideal, closer to

GOETHE:

HIS LIFE AND WORKS.

AN ESSAY.

BY

GEORGE H. CALVERT.

BOSTON:
LEE AND SHEPARD, PUBLISHERS.
NEW YORK:
LEE, SHEPARD AND DILLINGHAM.
1872.

Title page for the first American biography of Goethe

Calvert's heart because he was forced to travel abroad and become learned and accomplished in the culture of the countries he toured. His dying gesture on the battlefield (giving up his armor for a lord only to be mortally wounded in the process) in many ways provides the counternarrative to the victorious Northern soldier embodied in Bayard. If the North were to lose, it seems to suggest, dignity in defeat is more important than the issue of battle. One cannot help but see a tinge of autobiography in this portrait, as if Calvert felt himself sacrificed by the culture he so obediently served.

The relative popularity of his work seems to have released him from this gloomy self-image, for he was soon able to write about himself in a lively and engaging way. In his *First Years in Europe* (1866), Calvert tells about his early experiences as a young man abroad. By describing the early divisions emerging from this experience, Calvert in effect shows how he was compelled to culti-

vate a critical point of view. The description of his visit to Antwerp does this well; there he tells how he ascended the steeple of the church where his mother first viewed the battle which prompted her flight to America. Calvert then turns to analyze Rubens's *Descent from the Cross* hanging on the walls of the same church. Calvert's complex appreciation of Rubens involved a powerful sympathy for the artist that resulted from the close personal bond Calvert's mother made him feel for his ancestor.

It can be said that this extremely subjective view informs all of his critical essays. Whenever possible, Calvert attempts to understand a work of art by entering into a sympathetic reading of the author's life. Calvert was affirmed in this approach through his October 1868 critique of the French critic Sainte-Beuve. His *The Life of Rubens* (1876), the first American biography of the artist, strengthened this tendency further. Thus *First Years in Europe* marks a kind of critical turning point for Calvert in which the distance that he felt from his environment, European or American, is increasingly turned to advantage.

Once he "situated" himself as he did in *First Years in Europe*, Calvert was released to do his most engaging work. In 1872 he published the first American biography of Goethe, the beginning of a series of critical biographies (Calvert called them "Biographic Aesthetic" studies). Calvert's biography of Goethe represents the culmination of his lifelong admiration for the artist.

In the book he attempts to use his reading of Goethe to break down and shake up prudish reading habits of the American public. This sometimes led him into readings that have about them a faint if inverted feminist quality. (He defends *Elective Affinities*, for example, as "a thrilling protest against conjugal infidelity.") Yet the biography is perhaps most important for the distance Calvert draws between himself and Goethe. It enables him to use his impatience with Goethe's political orientation to define his own. Goethe is criticized for his failure to acknowledge the necessity of "revolt and revolution" because Calvert had come to accept these as "the only means of clearing the atmosphere when the moral and social equilibrium" is "chronically disturbed."

Here is revealed a curious patriotism on Calvert's part, a winning over of his American side which simultaneously marks an accommodation of his European background. Starting in 1872 he published a new book every year, and each gives clearer indication of this critical accommodation. His confidence is reflected in two volumes of his collected essays, *Brief Essays and Brevities* (1874) and *Essays Aesthetical* (1875).

Because Calvert wrote on so many topics, his selection for these two volumes is revealing. In addition to essays such as "Genius and Talent," "Ladyhood," and "Art," it is not surprising that he summons his old interest in travel, though it *is* interesting that he does so in order to make a distinction between Napoleon and Fourier. In an essay, "Travel," Napoleon is characterized as a "terrible traveller." The alternative model for travel emerges from the essays "Organization," "Work," and "The Social Palace at Guise," which emphasize travel of another kind, the great socialist "movement" from "wages and the isolated household" to a social harmony where "men, women and children" are "united in cheerful rivalry."

This underlying tension between Fourier and Napoleon neatly allegorizes Calvert's divided allegiance between the promise of America and the legacy of Europe and becomes even clearer in "Brevities," a collection of epigrams included toward the end of the volume. Here Calvert's thoughts are collected in fragments, something like journal entries, and their cumulative effect suggests a faith in history both informed by the past and stirred by the imaginary possibilities of the future. On one level "history" is on the side of Napoleon, yet this is a negative attribute which generates the need for an imaginative thinker like Fourier who can reorganize history as he would a text. At the same time Calvert acknowledges the imperious control of language, since "the vice of written histories is, that they are not HISTORY." In the best of worlds Napoleon's history is a bad text, a poor play, one to be rewritten and improved upon in a climate where the curious imbrication of history and imagination can flourish. In effect Calvert reconciles his divided allegiance to Europe and America by describing America as the new "stage" of history; hence his essay "A National Drama" in *Essays Aesthetical*. This is the volume that Henry James reviewed favorably in the *Nation* in 1875 and not without cause. It contains some of Calvert's most controlled writing. James responds to the way that Calvert attaches ethical and cultural value to style: "the weakest as well as the strongest must have a manner; but few can have a style."

Calvert attempts to master a style of his own in his critical biographies: *Wordsworth* (1878), *Shakespeare* (1879), *Coleridge, Shelley, Goethe* (1880), and

Charlotte von Stein: A Memoir (1877), the subject of which was an intimate friend of Goethe. His work on both Wordsworth and Shakespeare is the least satisfying as an attempt on the one hand to reinforce Matthew Arnold's good opinion of Wordsworth and on the other to regroup some of his earlier comments on the inevitable authority of Shakespeare. This is also true of his essay on Goethe. Yet his two sections on Coleridge and Shelley achieve a balance of critical and biographical insight, and his decision to have the two essays published together was a happy one. His work on von Stein forms a final defense of Goethe's controversial love life; but it also reflects Calvert's continued effort (however flawed) to include women in the text of history.

This impulse no doubt lay behind his fascination with Joan of Arc, who received his unembarrassed praise in a long poem written in 1860 and then dramatic treatment in his play *The Maid of Orleans: An Historical Tragedy* in 1873. It no doubt also generated and encouraged the publication of his long poem about a woman's rescue from prostitution (*Ellen: A Poem for the Times*) in 1867, just after the close of the Civil War. Yet Calvert was no more successful in these efforts than he was in his final attempt to write a tragic drama about Napoleon (*Brangonar. A Tragedy*, 1883). If the "style" of American history was to change and improve upon the drama of the past, Calvert was fated to predict rather than produce it.

References:
Ida Gertrude Everson, *George Henry Calvert: American Literary Pioneer* (New York: Columbia University Press, 1944);
Orie W. Long, *Literary Pioneers; Early American Explorers of European Culture* (Cambridge: Harvard University Press, 1935);
Bayard Quincy Morgan, *A Critical Bibliography of German Literature in English Translation, 1481-1927* (Stanford: Stanford University Press/London: Oxford University Press, 1938);
H. W. Pfund, "George Henry Calvert, Admirer of Goethe," in *Studies in Honor of John Albrecht Walz* (Lancaster, Pa.: Lancaster Press, 1941).

Papers:
The largest collection of Calvert's letters (106) is at the John Hay Library, Brown University. Other letters are in the Butler Library at Columbia University (32 letters and memorabilia), the

Houghton Library at Harvard (16 letters), the Milton Eisenhower Library at Johns Hopkins University (9 letters), the Beinecke Library at Yale (6 letters), the Enoch Pratt Free Library in Baltimore (5 letters), and the William Perkins Library at Duke (5 letters). A photostatic copy of his "Autobiographic Study," is at Columbia University.

Francis James Child

(1 February 1825-11 September 1896)

Steven Swann Jones
California State University, Los Angeles

See also the Child entry in *DLB 1, The American Renaissance in New England.*

BOOKS (Editions and Compilations): *Four Old Plays. Three Interludes: Thersytes, Jack Jugler, and Heywood's Pardoner and Frere: and Jocaste, a Tragedy by Gascoigne and Kinwelmarsh,* edited, with an introduction and notes, by Child (Cambridge, Mass.: Nichols, 1848);

The Poetical Works of Edmund Spenser, 5 volumes, edited, with biographical and philological notations, by Child (Boston: Little, Brown, 1855);

English and Scottish Ballads, 8 volumes, selected and edited by Child (Boston: Little, Brown, 1857-1858); enlarged and republished as *English and Scottish Popular Ballads,* 10 volumes (Boston: Houghton, Mifflin, 1882-1898; London: Henry Stevens, Son & Stiles, 1882-1898);

Il pesceballo, opera in un atto; musica del maestro Rossibelli-Donimozarti, Italian words by Child, English version by James Russell Lowell (Cambridge, Mass.: Riverside Press, 1862);

Observations on the Language of Chaucer (Based on Wright's edition of the Canterbury Tales) (Cambridge, Mass.: Welsh Bigelow, 1862);

Poems of Religious Sorrow, Comfort, Counsel and Aspiration, selected and edited by Child (New York: Sheldon, 1863; revised edition, New York: Hurd & Houghton, 1866);

War-songs for Freemen, compiled by Child (Boston: Ticknor & Fields, 1862);

Observations on the Language of Gower's Confessio

Amantis (Boston: F. B. Dakin, 1868);

The Childe of Bristowe, a Legend of the Fourteenth Century (Cambridge, Mass.: Wilson & Son, 1886).

OTHER: "Ballad Poetry," in *Johnson's New Universal Cyclopaedia: A Scientific and Popular Treasury of Useful Knowledge* (New York: Johnson, 1884), pp. 365-368.

Francis James Child was a persevering scholar and punctilious editor who contributed significantly to both literary and folkloric research. His significant contributions to literary study include his 1855 edition of Spenser, which was called by George Lyman Kittredge, shortly after Child's death, the best edition in existence, and his 1862 *Observations on the Language of Chaucer (Based on Wright's edition of the Canterbury Tales)*, which was praised by W. W. Skeat as providing the only full solution to the question of the proper scansion of *The Canterbury Tales*. Child's major folkloric accomplishment is his comprehensive compilation of English and Scottish popular ballads, in which he attempted to include authentic versions of the best-known ballads from those countries. His work so definitively established the canon of folk ballads that they have become known to folklorists as the Child ballads, according to the number that Child gave them, which is perhaps the most fitting and flattering tribute that could be paid to Child's achievement. Each of these accomplishments marks Child as a scholar of exceptional talent, meticulousness, and industry, and all together they assure him an enduring place in the fields of medieval literature, linguistics, and folklore.

The promise of Child's accomplishments was evident fairly early in his life. While growing up as the third child of eight in a Boston sail maker's family, he was enrolled in the normal English High School, but the headmaster soon recommended that the boy be transferred to the Boston Latin School in preparation for admission to Harvard College. In 1846 he graduated from Harvard first in his class and was chosen by his classmates as their orator at commencement. He immediately entered the service of Harvard as a tutor, first in mathematics, then in history and political economy, and eventually in English.

In 1849 he obtained leave from the college to travel and study in Europe, particularly in Berlin and Göttingen, where he concentrated on Germanic philology. He had the advantage of two influential and inspiring models, Jacob and Wilhelm Grimm, whose work had led the way in combining linguistic and folkloric research (according to Kittredge, throughout his life, Child kept a picture of them on the mantel over his study fire-

place). When he returned to America in 1851 Child was offered the Boylston Professorship of Rhetoric and Oratory at Harvard, and in 1854 the University of Göttingen, in recognition of his performance while studying there, awarded him the degree of Doctor of Philosophy *honoris causa*.

Child balanced his academic accomplishments with a well-rounded personal life. He married Elizabeth Ellery Sedgwick on 23 August 1860, fathered four children, tended his rose garden, and developed close relationships with a number of friends, including James Russell Lowell and William and Henry James. Child continued to live in Boston and to fulfill diligently the duties of teaching English composition for over twenty years, until in 1876, as part of Harvard's reorganization into a university, a Harvard chair of English was instituted, affording Child the opportunity to teach classes more closely related to his fields of specialization. He continued in this capacity for another twenty years until June of 1896, when he completed his fiftieth year of teaching at Harvard. That summer it was discovered that he was seriously ill, and he died in Boston on 11 September 1896.

In a sense, Child's lifetime of scholarly achievements may be seen as logically proceeding from his first publication, or at least being anticipated by it. As a result of editing *Four Old Plays* in 1848, Child was offered upon his return to America the opportunity to serve as general editor for a series on British poets. Beginning in 1853 and for a number of years thereafter, Child helped to supervise the publication of the series, which eventually extended to over 150 volumes. One of the first contributions in the series was Child's own *The Poetical Works of Edmund Spenser* (1855), which ran to five volumes. Child provided extensive philological and biographical information for the edition. Subsequently, he produced for the same series an eight-volume edition of English and Scottish ballads (1857-1858), which he culled from available printed sources. Through his work on the series in general, and on the volumes he himself compiled in particular, Child fulfilled his calling to be a consummate editor, painstakingly preparing and intelligently assessing manuscripts in order to place them in their proper context for his audiences.

The British Poets series next led Child to Chaucer, whose works had been selected for a potential revised edition. However, upon further investigation and acquisition of Thomas Wright's

Caricature of Child by William James (James Papers, Harvard College Library)

The Canterbury Tales of Geoffrey Chaucer (1847-1851), Child thought better of producing another Chaucer edition and opted instead for a philological treatise on the manuscript in hand. In *Observations on the Language of Chaucer*, Child presented a linguistic analysis of the number of syllables in the words employed by Chaucer in order to determine when the final *e* was or was not pronounced. It was an unresolved and thorny question until Child produced his exacting examination of the various cases and inflections of these words. He grouped them according to their source of origin (such as Anglo-Saxon or French) and then analyzed their use as nouns, adjectives, pronouns, verbs, and adverbs in their masculine and feminine forms, as well as considering the influence of accents, caesuras, contractions, negatives, and ellipses in order to understand the pattern of spelling and pronunciation employed by the author. He offered an approach that was logical, practical, and that produced concretely valuable results.

In 1868 Child applied the same approach to Gower's *Confessio Amantis*. Though first published in book form, both of these studies appeared in the *Memoirs of the American Academy of Arts and Sciences* after their oral presentations to that body. They were subsequently rearranged and reprinted as a single essay entitled "Observations on the language of Chaucer and Gower" by Alexander John Ellis in his five-volume study *On Early English Pronounciation* (1869-1889). Ultimately, Child's exacting and methodical charting of the grammatical logic underlying Chaucer's and Gower's use of these words helped to settle the question of the proper scansion of their poetry.

As his scholarly accomplishments indicate, Child's intellectual interests ranged broadly, from textual to linguistic to folkloric analysis, and throughout his career he maintained his involve-

Child as a student in Germany. Child gave this drawing to Joseph T. Atkinson, a fellow student at the University of Göttingen in 1850-1851 (Harvard University Archives).

ment in these disparate areas. However, in the latter half of his career his critical attention focused on producing a comprehensive and accurate edition of every extant English and Scottish ballad. This project was no small undertaking, and it became the chief goal of the rest of his life and his most noteworthy and remarkable accomplishment. Once again, it grew out of his involvement with the British Poets series, since it began as a revision of his earlier edition of ballads. However, the revision entirely superseded the previous work because Child determined that he would work from manuscripts and not from other printed texts.

This decision increased incalculably the difficulty of the project, but it also transformed it into a monumental scholarly achievement. Not only did Child conscientiously collect authentic versions of extant ballads in manuscript, but he also determined to collect and compare as many versions as possible. The key to Child's most en-

during scholarly achievement is his insistence upon a thoroughly comparative method. This comprehensive approach to the study of ballads anticipated the Finnish comparativists who later began to study folktales in the same way, diligently tracking down all authentic versions that were available. The clear-sightedness and common sense of this method yielded valuable results for its users. Thus, Child became one of the first scholars to implement the comparative approach to folklore research, which was later to become recognized as the cornerstone of that field of study.

Not only did Child's approach lead the way for modern folklore research, it also produced eye-opening results for ballad scholarship. As part of his endeavors, Child tirelessly appealed to the owners of the crucial Percy manuscript (which had belonged to Thomas Percy, Bishop of Dromore) to allow its publication. The appeals began in 1860, and finally in 1867-1868 the folio was made available. This verbatim publication of the manuscript (edited by J. W. Hales and Frederick James Furnivall) revealed to what a great extent Bishop Percy had taken liberties with popular tradition, modifying his manuscript considerably for its original publication. Child's dedication to the comparative method increased, and he perseveringly tracked down other manuscripts to expand his collection. He ultimately amassed multiple versions (frequently in double figures) of 305 ballads, which constituted essentially the full canon of extant ballads. Child proceeded to provide as full a history as possible for each ballad, indicating its manuscript sources and examining its appearance in other European countries.

In his commentaries upon the ballads, Child propounded some basic theoretical concepts about that folkloric genre which were subsequently accepted by most ballad scholars as establishing the foundation of ballad research. Child argued that ballads were the product of an early stage of human culture, appeared before the widespread use of print, and were thus entirely the creation of oral tradition. He distinguished them from the later imitative broadsides, which he considered products of a low kind of art in comparison to the earlier ballads. He emphasized that ballads were generally subject to modification, especially at the hands of professional minstrels and, even more so, literary editors. He believed the ballad to be best preserved in the oral literature of the people. Child attributed the proclivity toward recurring motifs and plots in different ballads from various nations to diffusion and communality of topic—"we have only to remember that tales and songs were the chief social amusement of all classes of people in all the nations of Europe during the Middle Ages, and that new stories would be eagerly sought for by those whose business it was to furnish this amusement, and be rapidly spread among the fraternity."

Child provided considerable illumination of the ballad's place in oral tradition. As Walter M. Hart reports in his essay "Professor Child and the Ballad," Child believed that "The author counts for nothing," since the ballad was essentially a product of oral tradition. He pointed out that even in the case of ballads influenced by literature, subsequent oral versions continued to alter the literary versions until they were "purged, in the process of oral transmission, of what was not to the popular taste." Child detailed carefully the numerous kinds of transformations that oral tradition was prone to impose upon ballads. For example, he noted that the nationality of the hero may be changed, the locality may be moved, and verses may be altered. All of his insights are amply illustrated in his discussions of the various ballads.

Finally, Child's analysis of the ballad produced an outline of its general characteristics that defined its essence. He believed that the ballad should tell a story, generally in an elliptical fashion, leaving something to the imagination of the listener. He felt that true ballads inclined toward brevity, and he observed that their style was prone to be simple and homely but with a lyrical quality. Child was most skillful in employing these various criteria of oral authenticity to assess the manuscripts that he so assiduously collected, providing thereby a critical edition of the ballad genre.

Francis James Child collected and edited the most comprehensive edition of English and Scottish ballads ever published. Rarely has an entire field, especially one as complex and extensive as the ballad, been defined quite so single-handedly by one individual. Of course, there were others in the field: Svend Hersleb Grundtvig preceded Child and guided him considerably, as their correspondence indicates; George Lyman Kittredge, Sigurd Bernhard Hustvedt, Gordon Hall Gerould, Francis Barton Gummere, Walter M. Hart, Louise Pound, and Bertrard Harris Bronson are some of the many who followed him and who acknowledged and expanded upon his contribution. However, the combination of

Child reading on the porch of his house in Cambridge, Mass. (Harvard University Archives)

Child's method, his dedication, and his productivity yielded a scholarly bounty that has no equal in his field.

It should also be noted that Child was not just an outstanding scholar, he was a remarkable person as well. The richness of Child's influence is perhaps best illustrated by his impression on the James brothers, Henry and William, who were no small luminaries in their own right. Henry described Child as a "delightful man, rounded character, above all humanist and humorist." William was even more favorably inclined and said of Child, "He had a moral delicacy and a richness of heart that I never saw and never expect to see equalled . . . I loved Child more than any man I know." It seems appropriate that after a lifetime of dedication to teaching (his former students recalled fondly old Stubby Child) and commitment to editing and analyzing literature so that others might enjoy it better, Child should be remembered not just for his abundant intellect and academic industry, but also for his warmth of character and personal charm.

Letters:

A Scholar's Letters to a Young Lady; Passages from the Later Correspondence of Francis James Child, edited, with a biographical introduction, by M. A. DeWolfe Howe (Boston: Atlantic Monthly Press, 1920 [limited edition]; Westport, Conn.: Greenwood Press, 1970);

"Appendix A. The Grundtvig-Child Correspondence," edited by Sigurd Bernhard Hustvedt, in his *Ballad Books and Ballad Men* (Cambridge: Harvard University Press, 1930), pp. 241-299;

Letters on Scottish Ballads, from Professor Francis J. Child to W. W. Aberdeen (Aberdeen: Bon Accord Press, 1930 [privately printed]; facsimile edition, Darby, Pa.: Norwood Editions, 1972);

The Scholar Friends: Letters of Francis James Child and James Russell Lowell, edited by Howe and G. W. Cottrell, Jr. (Cambridge: Harvard University Press, 1952).

References:

Gamaliel Bradford, "Portrait of a Scholar: Francis James Child," in *As God Made Them* (Boston: Houghton Mifflin, 1929), pp. 203-236;

Gordon Hall Gerould, *The Ballad of Tradition* (Oxford: Clarendon Press, 1932);

Francis Barton Gummere, *The Popular Ballad* (Boston: Houghton Mifflin, 1907);

Walter M. Hart, *Ballad and Epic; a Study in the Development of the Narrative Art* (Boston: Ginn, 1907);

Hart, "Professor Child and the Ballad," *PMLA,* 21 (1906): 755-807;

Sigurd Bernhard Hustvedt, *Ballad Books and Ballad Men: Raids and Rescues in Britain, America, and the Scandinavian North Since 1800* (Cambridge: Harvard University Press, 1930);

Hustvedt, *Ballad Criticism in Scandinavia and Great Britain During the Eighteenth Century* (New York: American-Scandinavian Foundation, 1916);

George Lyman Kittredge, "Francis James Child," in *The English and Scottish Popular Ballads* (Boston & New York: Houghton, Mifflin, 1883-1898), pp. xxiii-xxxi;

Kittredge, "Professor Child," *Atlantic Monthly,* 78 (December 1896): 737-742;

Charles Eliot Norton, "Francis James Child," *Harvard Graduate's Magazine,* 6 (December 1897): 161-169;

Louise Pound, *Poetic Origins and the Ballad* (New York: Macmillan, 1921).

Papers:

The *Child MSS,* 30 volumes, arranged and indexed by George Lyman Kittredge, are housed in the Harvard College Library.

Lewis Gaylord Clark

(5 October 1808-3 November 1873)

Bette S. Weidman

Queens College, City University of New York

See also the Clark entry in *DLB 3, Antebellum Writers in New York and the South.*

BOOK: *Knick-Knacks from an Editor's Table* (New York: Appleton, 1852).

OTHER: *The Literary Remains of the Late Willis Gaylord Clark. Including the Ollapodiana Papers, The Spirit of Life, and a Selection from his Various Prose and Poetical Writings*, edited by Clark (New York: Burgess, Stringer, 1844);

The Knickerbocker Sketch-Book: A Library of Select Literature, edited by Clark (New York: Burgess, Stringer, 1845);

The Lover's Gift; and Friendship's Token, edited by Clark (Auburn, N.Y.: Derby, 1848);

The Life and Eulogy of Daniel Webster, edited by Clark (Rochester: Hayward/New York: De-Witt & Davenport, 1853); enlarged and republished as *The Life, Eulogy, and Great Orations of Daniel Webster* (New York: McKee, 1855).

Lewis Gaylord Clark earned a significant place in American literary criticism by editing the *Knickerbocker Magazine, or New York Monthly* from 1834 to 1861. During this crucial period in the development of American literature, it was an achievement in itself to sustain a serious periodical that paid contributors for original papers despite the lack of international copyright legislation. Clark exerted the multiple influences of a strong editor and hardworking journalist: he shaped the literary careers of those whose work he chose to print; he influenced readers through his own reviews and those he assigned; and he contributed directly to the development of taste in his brief essays on writers and contemporary literary life and his humorous and touching anecdotes and clever parodies.

While he did not pause, in a life of literary labor, to elaborate a theory of literary criticism, his interests and principles emerge from a study of his magazine, which, in its time, was roughly the equivalent of the modern *New Yorker* sans cartoons and glossy advertisements. It was addressed to an educated general audience and identified itself with New York, which meant then, as it still does, cosmopolitan culture; and it printed fiction and especially serious nonfiction prose, a bit of poetry, reviews of books, plays, art, and musical events. Each month ample space was reserved for Clark's innovation, "The Editor's Table," a column of personal commentary like the *New Yorker*'s "Talk of the Town," in which the editor reported news from correspondents and described his own social and literary enthusiasms and encounters.

Born in Otisco, New York, on 5 October 1808 to Lucy Driggs Clark and Capt. Eleakim Clark, Lewis and his twin brother, Willis Gaylord, derived their interest in journalism from a cousin, Willis Gaylord, editor of the *Genessee Farmer and Albany Cultivator.* Willis Clark left home for Philadelphia in 1829, first working on the *Columbian Star,* a religious and literary magazine; in 1834 he became editor of the *Philadelphia Daily Inquirer.* Before he died of tuberculosis in 1841, he wrote quantities of lyric poetry and informal prose, much of it sent to fill the pages of the *Knickerbocker.* Lewis, leaving home in 1832, addressed *his* ambitions to New York. When the *Knickerbocker,* founded in 1833 by Samuel Langtree, a New York physician, was about to fail in 1834, Clark and an Otisco friend, Clement M. Edson, purchased the controlling interest. In the uncertain financial world of antebellum New York, where literary life was far from established, Clark kept his monthly going for twenty-seven years by carefully cultivating contributors like Washington Irving (after whose famous pseudonym the magazine was named), Henry Wadsworth Longfellow, James Fenimore Cooper, Nathaniel Hawthorne, William Cullen Bryant, John Greenleaf Whittier, and Francis Parkman.

He described his work on the *Knickerbocker* as "unremitting toil . . . the last three weeks of every month until 1 o'clock in the morning." He was repaid by the pleasure of participating in the social aspects of literary life more than by financial reward; at the end of his life, when the magazine finally foundered during the Civil War, he was left without the resources to support himself. He worked in the Custom House, like Herman Melville, until his loyal former contributors made up a volume called *The Knickerbocker Gallery* (1855), to be sold for his benefit; on the proceeds he retired to a small cottage on the Hudson at Piermont.

Before Clark took over the editorship of the *Knickerbocker,* Langtree and his editors, Charles Fenno Hoffman and Timothy Flint, had established the magazine's design and policy, which he maintained. They promised to promote American literature in place of "the absurd trash of driveling sentimentality and pseudo-fashion with which the shelves of our circulating libraries are filled from the London press." Resisting the "second hand," the first number of the *Knickerbocker*

offered articles on the gypsies of Granada, Esquimaux literature, Italian opera, and political economy, along with prose by James Kirke Paulding and poetry by William Cullen Bryant.

In Clark's first issue (May 1834) he continued this policy of offering original papers on various subjects, and he added the first "Editor's Table." He presented essays on Talleyrand, peace societies, and cats; in following issues, he ran readable essays on Ottoman institutions and American poets and their critics; he offered Icelandic legends, African anecdotes, and a particularly skillful memoir of the Revolutionary War period slave poet, Phillis Wheatley. A reader of these volumes today is likely not only to find them interesting, but to be struck by the range of the material.

By 1839 Clark was confident enough to offer Washington Irving $2,000 a year, a tremendous sum in the budget of the young magazine, for the writings of "Geoffrey Crayon." He thus insured contributions in the style he most valued—charming, sophisticated, light-hearted. Dedicated to developing an urbane tone for his journal, Clark preferred the "Lamblike" sketches of Hawthorne to his darker tales; he resisted the transcendentalism of Emerson and Thoreau and objected to Melville's *Typee.* He had better taste in prose than in poetry; beyond Longfellow, Bryant, and Halleck, his selections in verse run to the work of his brother, such as "Death of the First Born," or Mrs. C. E. DaPonte, who provided the predictable "An Indian Legend." In poetry, Clark ratified the accepted; in prose his range was broader, and he included reviews of *Naval Stories* by William Leggett and "My First and Last Flogging," which young Melville probably read with interest. He also grasped the importance of essays on native American culture by Henry Rowe Schoolcraft and included work by Oliver Wendell Holmes and Park Benjamin.

A study of his reviews produces evidence of consistent critical thinking in support of his choices. He valued "semblance to reality" in fiction, writing rich in "moral and religious inculcation," avoidance of egotism and pretension. In December 1834 he printed, with great enthusiasm, an "Original Letter from Florence," written by a young American girl abroad, remarking that it pointed out "an important moral to that class of females, who, sated with the amusements of their own happy country, sigh for the fancied Elysium of Europe." The writer of the letter informs the reader that her father has failed in "the codfish and turpentine line" and recalled his

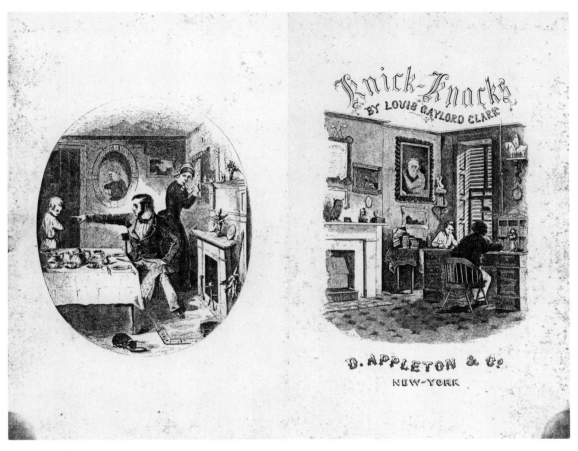

Frontispiece and engraved title page for Clark's only book, an anthology of essays and anecdotes reprinted from his column "The Editor's Table." The title page shows a variant spelling of Clark's first name.

family from their European wandering. She sounds like an antebellum Daisy Miller as she remarks, with Clark's evident approval, "For my part, though I lament the misfortune of poor papa, I am rejoiced at the idea of returning to a country where I shall again be somebody."

In art as well as literary criticism, Clark praises what he calls "naturalness." He wrote, "We know that in literature, as in politics, he who undertakes to lead or guide should be able to satisfactorily answer two questions. . . . Is he honest? Is he capable?" In his call for "local and metropolitan pictures," celebrating the beauties of the near, Clark is not so different from his younger contemporary, Thoreau, but he also called for historical fiction, a taste the Transcendentalists found frivolous. Clark further differed from the radical New Englanders by acknowledging the importance of public approval, calling the public, rather than the individual, the "umpire of taste."

To promote the health of an American literature, Clark wrote on behalf of copyright legisla-

tion and praised work that made use of American scenes and historical events. Advertising his thirteenth volume (January 1839), he reflected on his achievement in having published serious essays on sixty subjects: "The Magazine has aimed to reach nearly every division of general literature and to comprehend, in its ample though transient survey, amusement and instruction."

Clark's own writing contributed to the development of the memoir, the brief essay, the witty anecdote, the sustained parody. In his first noneditorial contribution to the magazine, "A Contrasted Picture" (April 1834), he presents a brilliant portrait of the city and "the buoyant newness of feeling and excitement which it wakened in me." At the beginning of his sixteenth year of tenure Clark began a series of memoirs he called "Editorial Narrative-History of the Knickerbocker Magazine." The narrative includes reminiscences, now doubly valuable, of New Yorkers such as Charles King and Judge Riker. Riker's name has become so much a part of New York geography we forget it was once attached to a "bald head [that] shone like a greased ostrich egg."

In the narrative, Clark emphasizes that his original intention to include political commentary had been discouraged by reviews of his early issues, and that he had retreated to "a broad and neutral literary ground, in which all parties in politics, and men of all creeds in religion, might meet like brothers." This disclaimer of political intention is contested by Perry Miller, who has observed that Clark's neutrality concealed a bias toward High Church Episcopalianism and Whig politics; Clark's biographical sketch of Daniel Webster (*The Life and Eulogy of Daniel Webster*, 1853) supports this position. Yet the narrative also supports Clark's claim to neutrality in its April 1859 publication of long quotations from Timothy Flint's 1834 description of the horrors of war.
25   The narrative includes many indications of Clark's principles and tastes—his demand that a critic be also a productive writer, his affection for Robert Burns and active participation in the Burns Society, his preference for folk song over opera, his interest in scientific theory. The "Editorial Narrative" series deserves republication and attention as a portrait of the intellectual and social life of a literary man on the eve of the Civil War. With its publication of readers' letters from as far away as Corpus Christi, Texas; its appreciative description of local sights such as the Cedar-Ware Manufactory at Nyack; its humorous sketch of the village of Waterproof, Louisiana, with its Hardshell Baptist preacher, Brother Zeke; and its advice to parents on dangerous toys for children, it is an American classic.

Clark's continued readability has been remarked in a recent essay by Peter Turner, "Photographs—Demands and Expectations," included in the volume *Reading Photographs: Understanding the Aesthetics of Photography* (1977), edited by Jonathan Bayer. Turner quotes at length from remarks Clark made in the December 1839 "Editor's Table" concerning daguerreotypes taken in Paris. Clark reported his admiration of their "exquisite perfection": "There is not a shadow in the whole that is not *nature itself*. . . . The shade of a shadow is frequently reflected in the river, and the very trees are taken with the shimmer created by the breeze." Turner remarks that "Clark's recognition of the significance of fact within a photograph is an excellent point to begin the journey toward its meaning."

Less easy to appreciate today, but as important in grasping Clark's aesthetic principles, is his series of parodies of American newspapers, entitled "*The Bunkumville Flagstaff* and *Independent Echo*." Replete with topical humor and dialect, the *Bunkumville Flagstaff* attacks the principles of its rival, the *Bunkumville Chronicle*, offers comments on cultural events, satirizes music and book reviews, and even includes a section of humorous advertisements. The exuberance of American humor is well represented in Clark's extended satirical sally, and while some of it is dense to the modern reader, other sentences emerge from the page with all the gusto of an early Mark Twain; for example, this passage from the July 1849 *Knickerbocker*: "We like to see a strong-headed, lion-hearted, bushy headed individual, with a chin like a nose sticking out like a promontory into the great ocean of air, say somethin' or 'nother just as nobody else can say it." While his *Bunkumville Flagstaff* made fun of raw American ignorance (in a review of Sir Walter Scott Bart. referring to Mr. Bart!), it also comically but effectively raises the flag by demonstrating a new kind of cultural self-confidence.

In his later years, Clark was often asked to contribute literary reminiscences to contemporary periodicals. Among these works are essays on Washington Irving and Noah Webster for *Lippincott's* (May 1869 and April 1870) and a memoir of Charles Dickens for *Harper's New Monthly Magazine* (August 1862). The Dickens article offers a good example of Clark's strengths as a critic. He wrote about Dickens from the vantage point of one who knew him personally, but without an intrusive "I." The essay begins with an account of a dinner party Clark himself gave in Dickens's honor; it focuses on the English guest's manner, appearance, and conversation, reporting at length anecdotes offered by Dickens and Washington Irving. Clark describes the quality of Dickens's correspondence, quoting sentences on copyright, American culture, and the novelist's method of working. The essay provides a sense of Dickens's impact on literary New York from a primary source whose capacity to compress meaning into the well-told anecdote rivals that of the writer he means to praise.

Clark's confidence in the revealing anecdote, in the power of a brief story, is underlined by the work he chose to publish in his sole anthology, *Knick-Knacks from an Editor's Table* (1852). He addressed his collection to that audience he al-

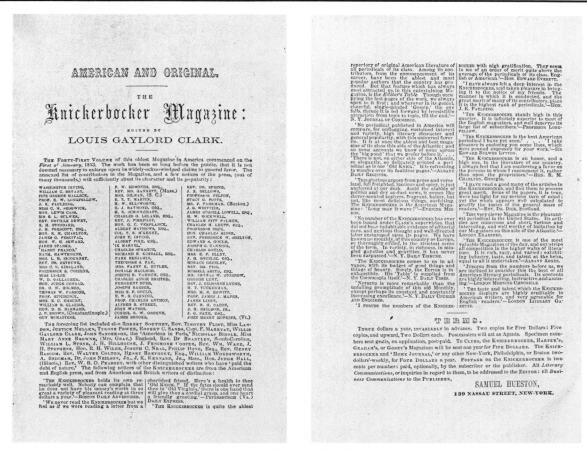

Advertisement with testimonials for the magazine Clark edited from 1834 to 1861

ways venerated: "any one man who feels and enjoys—who can neither resist laughter nor forbid tears that must have out and will have vent—is in some sort an epitome of the public." He reprints pieces from his column that offer a view of the city from a house in Hoboken, a childhood memory of losing a kite, a visit to Sing Sing; he tells of an old horse who returned to his New York owner from the West Indies. He treats childhood with special tenderness; he celebrates the beauty of earth, rather than heaven; he foreshadows the sarcasm of Twain's *Pudd'nhead Wilson* in a tale about a lobster and a dog. If there is a touch of morbidity in the frequency of deathbed scenes it must be attributed to harsh experience; the mawkishness of a tale about a hero whose only comment on losing his arm is "how shall I tell my sister?" is more than balanced by Clark's humor, his interest in local dialects, his pride in his adopted home—"the great metropolis of our native state." New York City made it possible for Clark to lead a literary life, and he, in turn, defined its hopeful nineteenth-century outlook: "What a city we shall be by and by!"

Letters:

The Letters of Willis Gaylord and Lewis Gaylord Clark, edited by Leslie W. Dunlap (New York: New York Public Library, 1940).

References:

Perry Miller, *The Raven and the Whale: The War of Words and Wits in the Era of Poe and Melville* (New York: Harcourt, Brace, 1956);

Frank Luther Mott, *A History of American Magazines 1791-1850* (New York: Appleton, 1930), pp. 604-614;

John W. Rathbun, *American Literary Criticism 1800-1860* (Boston: G. K. Hall, 1979);

Benjamin T. Spencer, "A National Literature, 1837-1855," *American Literature,* 8 (1936): 125-159;

Thomas Bangs Thorpe, "Lewis Gaylord Clark," *Harper's New Monthly Magazine,* 48 (March 1874): 587-592.

Samuel Langhorne Clemens
(Mark Twain)
(30 November 1835-21 April 1910)

Howard G. Baetzhold
Butler University

See also the Clemens entries in *DLB 11, American Humorists, 1800-1950; DLB 12, American Realists and Naturalists;* and *DLB 23, American Newspaper Journalists, 1873-1900.*

SELECTED BOOKS: *The Celebrated Jumping Frog of Calaveras County, and Other Sketches* (New York: C. H. Webb, 1867; London: Routledge, 1867);

The Innocents Abroad, or The New Pilgrims' Progress (Hartford, Conn.: American Publishing Company, 1869); republished in 2 volumes as *The Innocents Abroad* and *The New Pilgrims' Progress* (London: Hotten, 1870);

Mark Twain's (Burlesque) Autobiography and First Romance (New York: Sheldon, 1871; London: Hotten, 1871);

"Roughing It" (London: Routledge, 1872);

The Innocents at Home (London: Routledge, 1872);

Roughing It, augmented edition (Hartford, Conn.: American Publishing Company, 1872)—comprises *"Roughing It"* and *The Innocents at Home;*

A Curious Dream; and Other Sketches (London: Routledge, 1872);

The Gilded Age: A Tale of Today, by Twain and Charles Dudley Warner (Hartford, Conn.: American Publishing Company, 1873; 3 volumes, London: Routledge, 1874);

Mark Twain's Sketches, New and Old (Hartford, Conn.: American Publishing Company, 1875);

The Adventures of Tom Sawyer (London: Chatto & Windus, 1876; Hartford, Conn.: American Publishing Company, 1876);

Old Times on the Mississippi (Toronto: Belford, 1876); republished as *The Mississippi Pilot* (London: Ward, Lock & Tyler, 1877); expanded as *Life on the Mississippi* (London: Chatto & Windus, 1883; Boston: Osgood, 1883);

Samuel Langhorne Clemens in 1880

An Idle Excursion (Toronto: Rose-Belford, 1878); expanded as *Punch, Brothers, Punch! and Other Sketches* (New York: Slote, Woodman, 1878);

A Tramp Abroad (London: Chatto & Windus / Hartford, Conn.: American Publishing Company, 1880);

"1601" Conversation, As It Was by the Social Fireside, in the Time of the Tudors (Cleveland, 1880);

The Prince and the Pauper (London: Chatto & Windus, 1881; Boston: Osgood, 1882);

The Stolen White Elephant (London: Chatto & Windus, 1882); republished as *The Stolen White Elephant, Etc.* (Boston: Osgood, 1882);

The Adventures of Huckleberry Finn (London: Chatto & Windus, 1884); republished as *Adventures of Huckleberry Finn* (New York: Webster, 1885);

A Connecticut Yankee in King Arthur's Court (New York: Webster, 1889); republished as *A Yankee at the Court of King Arthur* (London: Chatto & Windus, 1889);

The American Claimant (New York: Webster, 1892; London: Chatto & Windus, 1892);

Merry Tales (New York: Webster, 1892);

The £1,000,000 Bank-Note and Other New Stories (New York: Webster, 1893; London: Chatto & Windus, 1893);

Tom Sawyer Abroad by Huck Finn (New York: Webster, 1894; London: Chatto & Windus, 1894);

Pudd'nhead Wilson, A Tale (London: Chatto & Windus, 1894); augmented as *The Tragedy of Pudd'nhead Wilson and the Comedy of Those Extraordinary Twins* (Hartford, Conn.: American Publishing Company, 1894);

Personal Recollections of Joan of Arc by the Sieur Louis de Conte (New York: Harper, 1896; London: Chatto & Windus, 1896);

Tom Sawyer Abroad, Tom Sawyer, Detective, and Other Stories (New York: Harper, 1896);

Tom Sawyer, Detective, as told by Huck Finn, and Other Stories (London: Chatto & Windus, 1896);

How to Tell a Story and Other Essays (New York: Harper, 1897);

Following the Equator (Hartford, Conn.: American Publishing Company, 1897); republished as *More Tramps Abroad* (London: Chatto & Windus, 1897);

The Man That Corrupted Hadleyburg and Other Stories and Essays (New York & London: Harper, 1900); enlarged and republished as *The Man That Corrupted Hadleyburg and Other Stories and Sketches* (London: Chatto & Windus, 1900);

A Double Barrelled Detective Story (New York & London: Harper, 1902);

A Dog's Tale (New York & London: Harper, 1904);

King Leopold's Soliloquy: A Defense of His Congo Rule (Boston: P. R. Warren, 1905);

Eve's Diary Translated from the Original Ms (London & New York: Harper, 1906);

What Is Man? (New York: De Vinne Press, 1906); enlarged and republished as *What Is Man? and Other Essays* (New York & London: Harper, 1917);

The $30,000 Bequest and Other Stories (New York & London: Harper, 1906);

Christian Science with Notes Containing Corrections to Date (New York & London: Harper, 1907);

A Horse's Tale (New York & London: Harper, 1907);

Is Shakespeare Dead? (New York & London: Harper, 1909);

Extract from Captain Stormfield's Visit to Heaven (New York & London: Harper, 1909);

Mark Twain's Speeches, compiled by F. A. Nast (New York & London: Harper, 1910);

The Mysterious Stranger, a Romance, edited by Albert Bigelow Paine and Frederick A. Duneka (New York & London: Harper, 1916); enlarged and republished as *The Mysterious Stranger and Other Stories*, edited by Paine (New York & London: Harper, 1922);

The Curious Republic of Gondour and Other Whimsical Sketches (New York: Boni & Liveright, 1919);

Mark Twain's Speeches, edited by Paine (New York & London: Harper, 1923);

Europe and Elsewhere, edited by Paine (New York & London: Harper, 1923);

Mark Twain's Autobiography, edited by Paine, 2 volumes (New York & London: Harper, 1924);

Sketches of the Sixties, by Twain and Bret Harte (San Francisco: Howell, 1926);

The Adventures of Thomas Jefferson Snodgrass, edited by Charles Honce (Chicago: Pascal Covici, 1928);

Mark Twain's Notebook, edited by Paine (New York & London: Harper, 1935);

Letters from the Sandwich Islands Written for the Sacramento Union, edited by G. Ezra Dane (San Francisco: Grabhorn, 1937);

The Washoe Giant in San Francisco, edited by Franklin Walker (San Francisco: Fields, 1938);

Mark Twain's Travels With Mr. Brown, edited by Walker and Dane (New York: Knopf, 1940);

Mark Twain in Eruption, edited by Bernard DeVoto (New York & London: Harper, 1940);

Mark Twain at Work, edited by DeVoto (Cambridge: Harvard University Press, 1942);

Mark Twain, Business Man, edited by Samuel Charles Webster (Boston: Little, Brown, 1946);

Mark Twain of the ENTERPRISE, edited by Henry Nash Smith (Berkeley: University of California Press, 1957);

Traveling with the Innocents Abroad: Mark Twain's Original Reports from Europe and the Holy Land, edited by Daniel Morley McKeithan

(Norman: University of Oklahoma Press, 1958);

Contributions to the Galaxy, 1868-1871, by Mark Twain, edited by Bruce R. McElderry, Jr. (Gainesville, Fla.: Scholars' Facsimiles & Reprints, 1961);

Letters from the Earth, edited by DeVoto (New York: Harper & Row, 1962);

Mark Twain's "Which was the Dream" and Other Symbolic Writings of the Later Years, edited by John S. Tuckey (Berkeley: University of California Press, 1967);

Mark Twain's Satires and Burlesques, edited by Franklin R. Rogers (Berkeley: University of California Press, 1967);

Clemens of the "Call": Mark Twain in San Francisco, edited by Edgar M. Branch (Berkeley: University of California Press, 1969);

Mark Twain's "Mysterious Stranger" Manuscripts, edited by William M. Gibson (Berkeley: University of California Press, 1969);

Mark Twain's Hannibal, Huck, and Tom, edited by Walter Blair (Berkeley: University of California Press, 1969);

Mark Twain's Fables of Man, edited by Tuckey (Berkeley: University of California Press, 1972);

Mark Twain's Notebooks and Journals, volume 1, 1855-1873, edited by Frederick Anderson, Michael B. Frank, and Kenneth M. Sanderson; volume 2, 1877-1883, edited by Anderson, Lin Salamo, and Bernard L. Stein; volume 3, 1883-1891, edited by Robert Pack Browning, Frank, and Salamo (Berkeley: University of California Press, 1975, 1979);

Mark Twain Speaking, edited by Paul Fatout (Iowa City: University of Iowa Press, 1976);

Mark Twain Speaks for Himself, edited by Fatout (West Lafayette: Purdue University Press, 1978);

The Devil's Race-Track: Mark Twain's "Great Dark" Writings, edited by Tuckey (Berkeley: University of California Press, 1979);

The Adventures of Tom Sawyer by Mark Twain: A Facsimile of the Author's Holograph Manuscript, 2 volumes (Frederick, Md.: University Publications of America / Washington, D.C.: Georgetown University Library, 1982);

Adventures of Huckleberry Finn (Tom Sawyer's Comrade) by Mark Twain: A Facsimile of the Manuscript, 2 volumes (Detroit: Gale Research, 1983).

Collections: *The Writings of Mark Twain,* Autograph Edition, 25 volumes (Hartford, Conn.: American Publishing Company, 1899-1907);

The Writings of Mark Twain, Author's National Edition, 25 volumes, (New York & London: Harper, 1899-1917);

The Writings of Mark Twain, Definitive Edition, 37 volumes, edited by Paine (New York: Wells, 1922-1925).

Editions prepared by the University of California Press for the Iowa Center for Textual Studies: *Roughing It,* edited by Franklin R. Rogers (Berkeley: University of California Press, 1972);

"What Is Man?" and Other Philosophical Writings, edited by Paul Baender (Berkeley: University of California Press, 1973);

A Connecticut Yankee in King Arthur's Court, edited by Bernard L. Stein (Berkeley: University of California Press, 1979);

The Prince and the Pauper, edited by Victor Fischer and Lin. Salamo (Berkeley: University of California Press, 1979);

Early Tales & Sketches, volume 1 (1851-1864), volume 2 (1864-1865), edited by Edgar M. Branch and Robert H. Hirst (Berkeley: University of California Press, 1979, 1981);

The Adventures of Tom Sawyer; Tom Sawyer Abroad; Tom Sawyer, Detective, edited by John C. Gerber, Baender, and Terry Firkins (Berkeley: University of California Press, 1980).

OTHER: Letter to Edgar W. Howe (1884), in C. E. Schorer's "Mark Twain's Criticism of *The Story of a Country Town,*" *American Literature,* 27 (March 1955): 109-112.

PERIODICAL PUBLICATIONS: "Report to the Buffalo Female Academy," *Buffalo Express,* 18 June 1870; republished in *Mark Twain on the Art of Writing,* edited by Martin B. Fried (Buffalo, N.Y.: Salisbury Club, 1961);

"Post Mortem Poetry," *Galaxy* (June 1870);

"About Magnanimous Incident Literature," *Atlantic Monthly* (May 1878);

"Unlearnable Things," anonymous, *Atlantic Monthly* (June 1880): 145-180;

"English as She is Taught," *Century* (April 1887);

"Private History of the 'Jumping Frog' Story," *North American Review* (April 1894);

"In Defence of Harriet Shelley," *North American Review* (July-September 1894);

"What Paul Bourget Thinks of Us," *North American Review* (January 1895);

"Fenimore Cooper's Literary Offences," *North American Review* (April 1895);

"How to Tell a Story," *Youth's Companion* (3 October 1895);

"About Play-Acting," *Forum* (October 1898);

"My Boyhood Dreams," *McClure's* (January 1900);

"Italian without a Master," *Harper's Weekly* (2 January 1904);

"Italian with Grammar," *Harper's Monthly* (August 1904);

"William Dean Howells," *Harper's Monthly* (July 1906);

"A Fable," *Harper's Monthly* (December 1909).

When one considers Samuel Langhorne Clemens's life and writings, the role of literary critic is hardly the first category that comes to mind. Yet in the course of his career he compiled a large body of comment—in essays, sketches, reviews, and informal statements on language and literature. In addition, Clemens's comments on literature abound in interviews, letters, and, both explicitly and implicitly, in his works themselves.

Allied with those who have been called "Critical Realists," Clemens derived his literary opinions primarily from his own actual practice and from his reactions to what he read, rather than from any formal theoretical or philosophical basis. He presented his critical judgments less fully or formally than his fellow authors William Dean Howells and Henry James, the two other major voices of nineteenth-century American literary realism. Intellectually a realist, he was also a romantic. In his best works he looked nostalgically back—not to the long ago and far away, and certainly not to the glamour of medieval chivalry—but to the days of his youth along the Mississippi. At the same time he insisted on realistic detail, accuracy of diction, probability of motive, possibility of situation and action, and often attacked, either directly or indirectly, those authors whose works seemed to violate those principles.

The development of Clemens's critical sense began during his early experience in printing offices. As he said years later in "The Turning-Point of My Life" (included in *What Is Man? and Other Essays*, 1917), "One isn't a printer ten years without setting up acres of good and bad literature, and learning—unconsciously at first, consciously later—to discriminate between the two, within his mental limitations. . . ." Travel letters and various humorous sketches for his brother

Clemens in Constantinople in 1867, during his excursion aboard the Quaker City *(photograph by Abdulah Frères, courtesy of the Mark Twain Papers, Bancroft Library, University of California, Berkeley)*

Orion's newspapers were products of his printing days. The full development of his writing skills really began in the West during successive posts on the *Virginia City Territorial Enterprise* (where he first adopted the name "Mark Twain" in the winter of 1862-1863) and in San Francisco on the *Daily Call* and the *Californian*. There, in addition to straight reporting, he forged his own unique style, experimenting with hoaxes, burlesques, and imaginative sketches, and with various poses in the guise of "Mark Twain" and through other personae like "Simon Wheeler," of the famous jumping frog story.

His literary criticism first took the form of burlesque, a staple of newspaper and magazine humor of the day. Burlesque does not necessarily reflect a real distaste for the object of its ridicule, and doubtless Clemens was more intent on amusing his readers than on seeking to reform literary taste and expression. Yet his treatment reveals an underlying critical position that he maintained throughout his career. Often presenting the narrator in the guise of a fool, or an innocent, puzzled by departures from the rational or the believable, the burlesques also reveal a concern for realism, an antipathy toward affected diction, overwrought striving for emotional effects, and romantic excesses in general.

Besides giving him an outlet for his more imaginative writings, Clemens's association with the *Californian* provided further instruction in the art of literary burlesque. His targets were sentimentalism, extravagant action and rhetoric, and the unreality of moral stances that did not recognize the realities of human nature. During the next several years he would continue to burlesque these qualities in his letters to the *Sacramento Union* from Hawaii (then known as the Sandwich Islands), in which the comments of a rather vulgar "Mr. Brown" deflated "Mr. Twain's" rhapsodizings over the beauties of the islands, and in the letters to the *Alta California* during his excursion to the Mediterranean and the Holy Land on the steamship *Quaker City*, which ultimately became his first highly successful book, *The Innocents Abroad, or The New Pilgrims' Progress* (1869).

After returning to California from Hawaii in 1866 Clemens also initiated a long and profitable career on the lecture circuit. The platform experiences were of utmost importance to the development of his literary style. They sharpened his critical faculties, taught him to analyze his audience so as to exploit the full possibilities of oral presentation, and in turn, enhanced his ability to transfer speech rhythms to the printed page. He would later analyze the elements of the method he developed in an essay entitled "How to Tell a Story" (*Youth's Companion*, 3 October 1895).

Following the *Quaker City* voyage, and his marriage to Olivia Langdon of Elmira, New York, in February 1870, Clemens continued many of the same sorts of burlesques in the *Buffalo Express*, in which he had purchased part ownership, in the *Galaxy* magazine, and in his next book, *Roughing It* (1872).

Also during the 1870s he began occasionally to comment directly on matters of style and literary practices. In the spring of 1870 his "Report to the Buffalo Female Academy" (*Buffalo Express*, 18 June 1870) explained his criteria for awarding prizes in the academy's annual writing contest. Though applied to school compositions, the guidelines reveal principles that he would continue to apply to literature in general. The essays chosen were, he said, "the least ambitious . . . , the least

showy . . . , the least artificial, the least labored, the clearest and shapeliest, and the best carried out." Avoiding any sermonizing and "instinct with naturalness," they told their story "in unpretentious language" and apt and accurate diction. Clemens then went on to deplore the "dead weight of custom and tradition" perpetuated by schoolteachers and the "unspeakably execrable models which young people are defrauded into accepting as fine literary composition. . . ."

It was probably in the late 1860s and early 1870s, too, that Clemens's concept of what literature should be and do received its first theoretical underpinnings, again perhaps "unconsciously," from his reading in two of his favorite authors, Thomas Babington Macaulay and W. E. H. Lecky, both historians. Complimentary references to Macaulay's "stately sentences," and "glittering pageantry" in *The Innocents Abroad* (1869) and in a letter to Olivia Clemens during the winter of 1868-1869 suggest that he first read Macaulay's *History of England from the Accession of James II* (1849-1861) in the late 1860s. Thoroughly enchanted by the historian's vivid recreation of the life of the times, he would often return to it and to Macaulay's other works. Even more important, Lecky's *History of European Morals from Augustus to Charlemagne* (1869), after a first reading in 1874, became a major stimulus to Clemens's thought in general and an influence on successive works.

What apparently appealed to him most, and thus influenced his criticism, was the emphasis of both authors on re-creating history so that the reader might "realize" it, actually experience it as life. Lecky, in particular, early in his book, stressed the interrelationship of imagination (which he defined as "the power of realization") and compassion, and the influence of education upon both. Lecky argued that men pity suffering only when they "realize" it, and that the intensity of their compassion is directly proportional to the extent of that "realization."

Both Macaulay and Lecky probably fortified Clemens's own sense of the importance of achieving imaginative vitalization of the past—realism in an "exalted sense (over and above authenticity of details and the faithful representation of experience)," as S. J. Krause put it in his *Mark Twain as Critic* (1967). And from the 1870s on, in one way or another, many of Clemens's critical pronouncements would reflect this concern with "realization."

Concern for the actuality that could re-create experience for the reader dominated

From Mark Twain.
· W.D.H. Dec. 3. 1874

My Dear Howells:

Let us change the heading to "Piloting on the Miss in the Old Times" — or to "Steamboating on the M in the Old Times" — or to "Personal Old Times on the Miss." — We could change it for Feb. if now too late for Jan. —

I suggest it because the present heading is too pretentious, too broad & general. It seems to command me to deliver a Second Book of Revelation to the world, & cover all the Old Times the Mississippi (darn that word, it is worse than Type or Egypt) Ever saw —— whereas here I have finished Article No. III + a——

A page from Clemens's letter to William Dean Howells in which he discusses his wish to change the title of his "Old Times on the Missis-
sippi" series in the January through July 1875 Atlantic Monthly *(courtesy of the Mark Twain Papers, Bancroft Library, Univer-*
sity of California, Berkeley, and the Mark Twain Foundation)

Thomas Nast cartoon depicting Clemens's November 1881 trip to Canada to protect his copyright for The Prince and the Pauper *(1881). An author, or his publisher, was required by the law of that time to cross the border of the country in which he wished to secure his copyright.*

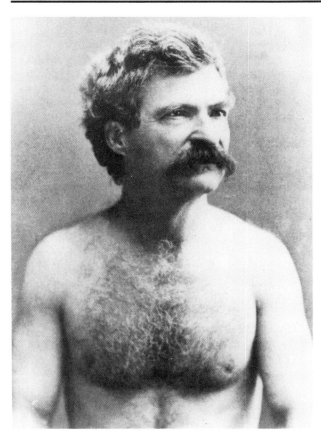

Clemens in an 1885 photograph taken to celebrate his 50th birthday and included in his letters to friends (Mark Twain Memorial)

Clemens's reactions in the late 1870s and early 1880s to works of his one-time mentor, Bret Harte. Primarily in the margins of his copies of Harte's books and in one unsigned essay in the June 1880 *Atlantic Monthly*'s "Contributors Club" column ("Unlearnable Things"), he praised Harte's California settings, but castigated his faulty observation, excessive sentiment, and especially his use of inaccurate dialect.

Clemens also charged that Harte had not sufficiently experienced or even really observed the life he wrote about—especially life among the miners—to make it truly believable. As he later expressed it to a British correspondent in 1890, he considered personal experience "the most valuable capital, or culture, or education usable in the building of novels." And in a January 1895 *North American Review* essay, "What Paul Bourget Thinks of Us," he would argue that "almost the whole capital of the novelist is the slow accumulation of *unconscious* observation—absorption."

Moreover, in his concern with false sentimen-

tality and other violations of actuality, there is evidence of a strong moral element, a quality he shared with other Critical Realists, especially his friend Howells. There was a Victorian streak, to be sure, which led Clemens on several occasions to cite the works of Fielding, Smollett, and others as "indecent" or even "disgusting." But a more basic element involved the power of literature to instruct by revealing the reality behind appearances.

Though his early work consisted primarily of humor for its own sake, he had soon become known not only as "The Wild Humorist of the Sagebrush Hills" but also as "The Moralist of the Main." Perhaps enhanced by his observations of the injustices and human frailties as a reporter and by the moral emphasis he encountered in both Macaulay and Lecky, an underlying morality was part of his basic equipment as a humorist. When Yale University awarded him an honorary Master of Arts degree in 1888, his letter of acceptance, though referring specifically to humor, contained elements that he elsewhere applied to fiction in general. Humor, he said, "has one serious purpose, one aim, one speciality . . . , the deriding of shams, the exposure of pretentious falsities, the laughing of superstitions out of existence" (*Hartford Courant*, 22 June 1888). More broadly applied, that statement—along with Clemens's observation in "What Paul Bourget Thinks of Us" that, taken together, the works of native novelists might get at "the soul of a nation"—suggests that it is the novelist's duty to reveal life as it really is and that the falsification of reality is harmful to cultural progress.

This attitude formed an essential element of his judgment of Sir Walter Scott in *Life on the Mississippi* (1883). Whereas he was critical of Bret Harte, an avowed realist, for his falsification of realism, he blasted Scott for glamorizing false ideals, which, in turn, infected his doting readers, especially in the American South. Earlier he had criticized Scott's awkwardness and wordiness; now he charged that the "Sir Walter disease" was responsible for the South's failure to keep pace with nineteenth-century progress, listing as its symptoms a "jejeune romanticism" reflected in the "pathetic shams" of southern architecture, the "wordy, windy eloquence" of southern literature, especially the gushing verbosity of its journalists, and the deplorable attachment to traditions long abandoned by the rest of the world. Finally, though he termed the proposition "a wild one," he suggested that the values inculcated by

*Clemens and his daughter Susy as Hero and Leander at the
Onteora Club, 1890 (Mark Twain Memorial)*

"Scottism" and its "chivalry-silliness" had caused
the Civil War.

At this time Clemens's major thrust was
aimed at the South's backwardness in clinging to
the outworn ideals. Later he would examine several of Scott's novels themselves, again criticizing
Scott's diction but also his failure to create characters whose speech and actions were faithful to
their natures and social position.

On reading Emile Zola's *La Terre* (1887),
probably during the winter of 1887-1888, Clemens expressed his combined shock, fascination,
and final approval in an essay that remained unpublished until Bernard De Voto included it in *Letters from the Earth* (1962). At first Clemens's
Victorian sensibilities must have suffered repeatedly as Zola's "fearful book" unrolled its tale of
greed, bestiality, betrayal, rape, torture, and murder. But though chapter after chapter at first
seemed "only crazy inventions of an obscene
mind," he finally found himself convinced that
this was "no dream, but reality, and a picture of
phases of life to be found here and there in *all*
Christian lands," that the story was "true, absolutely true, photographically true. . . ."

Why he did not submit the essay for publication probably reflects both his Victorian reticence
and his expedient reluctance to publish opinions
that might offend his middle-class reading public. He himself would express that reluctance in
an autobiographical dictation printed in *Mark
Twain in Eruption* (1940), commenting upon his
conversation in 1907 with British novelist Elinor
Glyn, whose recent best-selling novel, *Three Weeks,*
had caused a sensation. Though he discussed
very frankly the sexual content of her book and
agreed that she had truly and effectively portrayed human nature and the operation of natural law that had governed the young lovers in the
grip of a passion that neither could control, he
was unwilling to grant Glyn's request for a public
endorsement of her book because such a statement "would damn me before my time and I
didn't wish to be useful to the world on such expensive conditions."

Most of Clemens's formal essays directly related to literature and its makers were products
of the 1890s. At this time, because of the declin-
ing fortunes and the final failure of his Charles
L. Webster Publishing Company and the Paige
typesetting machine, he was writing almost franti-
cally. From 1891 to 1895, in addition to essays on
numerous subjects, he produced five novels and
many short stories and essays. Among the literary
essays, several are skillful works of art, and all of
them further reveal his statement that his literary
taste and writing methods had developed "unconsciously" to be greatly exaggerated.

"How to Tell a Story" particularly unveils a
deep sense of literary craftsmanship in its detailed description of the specific techniques of
the American humorous story and the manner of
its telling. In implicitly arguing that the effective-
ness of a story depends greatly on the proper
choice of narrator, Clemens here dealt with a primary concern in his later fiction—"point of view."

As for his literary criticism as such, an otherwise undistinguished piece, "A Cure for the
Blues," which appeared in *The £1,000,000 Bank-
Note and Other New Stories* (1893), listed for the
first time in a published essay the weaknesses of romantic and sentimental fiction and identified by
contrast the elements which "good literature"
should embody. Commenting on S. Watson
Royston's *The Enemy Conquered; or Love Trium-
phant* (1845)—one of the specimens of literary "hog-
wash" which he found "delicious" in its very
badness—Clemens cautioned the reader about expecting the book to display any "wisdom, brilliancy, fertility of invention, ingenuity of
construction, excellence of form, purity of style,
perfection of imagery, truth to nature, clearness

Clemens having breakfast in his hotel room, Olympia, Washington. Clemens was in Olympia 10 and 11 August 1895 on a stop for his around-the-world lecture tour which opened in Cleveland, Ohio, 15 July

of statement, humanly possible situations, humanly possible people, fluent narrative, connected sequence of events—or philosophy, or logic, or sense. . . ." As for style, Clemens felt that the author consistently emulated the inflated rhetoric of the southern authors of his day, with his "big words, fine words, grand words, rumbling, thundering, reverberating words; with sense attaching if it could be got in without marring the sound, but not otherwise."

Among the more important essays, "In Defence of Harriet Shelley" (*North American Review*, July-September 1894) attacked Edward Dowden's biography of Percy Bysshe Shelley, not only for its unflattering and biased treatment of Harriet, the poet's first wife, but for the extravagant stylis-

tic embellishments, a posing and preening that made the book a "literary cake-walk." Clemens's moral stance also emerged in this essay, not merely as a Victorian defense of the purity of women, but in his detailed analysis of Dowden's faulty logic and unfair conclusions.

These years also produced perhaps the best known of Clemens's critical pieces, "Fenimore Cooper's Literary Offences" (*North American Review*, April 1895). Unfair as it is to Cooper's accomplishments as America's first major novelist, primarily because of Clemens's application of strictly contemporary standards to the fiction of older times, the analysis is effective; in fact, many readers have found it difficult to appreciate Cooper after reading it.

Clemens after the conclusion in May 1896 of his lecture tour
(Mark Twain's Letters, *edited by Albert Bigelow Paine, 1917*)

In this masterfully crafted essay, Clemens embodied the elements of his "Cure for the Blues" list in a set of "rules governing literary art in the domain of romantic fiction" and demonstrated in detail, with devastating humor, how Cooper violates them. The rules and discussion systematically cover plot, character, and style. Among major flaws, Clemens charges Cooper with poverty of invention, inaccurate observation, and "a word sense that was singularly dull" and concludes his essay with a list of failings represented by *The Deerslayer* (1841): "It has no invention; it has no order, system, sequence, or result; it has no lifelikeness, no thrill, no stir, no seeming of reality; its characters are confusedly drawn, and by their acts and words they prove that they are not the sort of people the author claims that they are; its humor is pathetic; its pathos is funny; its conversations are—oh! indescribable; its love-scenes odious; its English a crime against the language. . . ." Clemens completes his dissection with a final razor-cut of ironic understatement: "Counting these out, what is left is Art. I think we all must admit that." About this

same time Clemens repeated many of these charges and analyzed specific passages in another essay, first published as "Fenimore Cooper's Further Literary Offenses" in the September 1946 *New England Quarterly* and collected by DeVoto in *Letters from the Earth*. And he would make many of the same points in 1903 in two letters to Brander Matthews about his renewed attempt to read his old enemy Scott.

Clemens's other major essay of the 1890s, "About Play-Acting" (*Forum*, October 1898), featured a discussion of Adolph Wilbrandt's *Der Meister von Palmyra*, which he saw in Vienna's Burg Theater. His comments revealed, as did the essay on Zola, that he could appreciate experimental literature—in this case a mystical drama complete with metempsychosis and a protagonist who had been granted eternal life—provided the characterization and action were convincing. Written in 1898 at the time of perhaps his deepest pessimism—following the death of his daughter Susy and during the writing of works like *What Is Man?* (1906), "The Man that Corrupted Hadleyburg" (1899), "The Chronicle of Young Satan," the first and best known of the "Mysterious Stranger Manuscripts," and speculations about "dream selves" as parts of the human personality—his act-by-act review stressed the power of drama, unreal though its elements might seem, to reveal basic truths of human existence.

To close his essay, Clemens proposed the establishment of a theater in New York devoted entirely to tragedy, which could provide a refreshing tonic for the "disease of the intellect" that lets one believe life is a comedy. All human beings would benefit from "an occasional climb among the intellectual snow-summits" built by Shakespeare and other tragedians and, in realizing the basic tragedy of existence, be able to enjoy more fully the occasional happy times in life.

Seven years later in *Harper's Monthly* (July 1906), Clemens paid tribute to his old friend William Dean Howells with an essay as artfully constructed as the Cooper piece. One of the best discussions of Howells's style available, the essay once again revealed the literary characteristics Clemens deemed most important. Praising Howells for his "sustained exhibition" over forty years of the "great qualities" of "clearness, compression, verbal exactness, and . . . seemingly unconscious felicity of phrasing," he cited as vital to that accomplishment his friend's ability to find "that elusive and shifty grain of gold, the *right*

Olivia and Samuel Clemens, circa 1900 (Yale University Library)

word." The style itself he found distinguished by an "easy and effortless flow," a "cadenced and undulating rhythm," and "architectural felicities of construction." After comparing in detail passages from *Venetian Life* (1866) and a recent essay on Machiavelli written some forty years apart, he seems again to invoke the principle of "realization" by stressing Howells's expertise in "concretizing abstractions" so that the reader can truly experience the place and time.

Clemens also implicitly praised Howells for the skill which he himself had earlier defined as the essence of the American humorous story, crediting him with being better than anyone at playing with "humorous fancies, so gracefully, and delicately and deliciously," as if he were not aware of the humor involved. And related to the importance of the right word, he paid tribute to Howells's skill in devising "stage directions" which contribute to the "naturalness" of the scene and conversation and hence to the reader's understanding. Finally, having begun his essay with the premise that if man's mental powers decline after forty, Howells's career is the exception

that proves the rule, he returned to his point by concluding: "I know by the number of . . . years that Howells is old, but his heart isn't, nor his pen; and years do not count."

Samuel Clemens was not a literary critic in the true sense, nor did he think of himself as one, but he read closely and thoughtfully, absorbed what he found pleasing, and attacked what to him did not ring true. As Krause has said, "He could tolerate no substitute for the texture of experience accurately perceived, no subjective faking where the sense of actuality is concerned; and he enjoined severe practice on those who would master the art of representing honestly what they had trained themselves to know." Both William Dean Howells and Brander Matthews, noted critics in their own right, attested to the excellences of his insights, and though his criticisms sometimes dealt with insignificant works, their range and scope were impressive, especially in view of the fact that they derived only minimally, if at all, from a philosophical basis or formal theory.

Clemens provided a sort of "last word" about literary criticism in "A Fable," published in the December 1909 *Harper's Monthly*, some four months before his death. Its "Moral" serves as a fundamental admonition to all who aspire to the role of critic: "You can find in a text whatever you bring, if you will stand between it and the mirror of your imagination."

Letters:
Mark Twain's Letters, 2 volumes, edited by Albert Bigelow Paine (New York: Harper, 1917);
Mark Twain the Letter Writer, edited by Cyril Clemens (Boston: Meador, 1932);
Mark Twain's Letters to Will Bowen, edited by Theodore Hornberger (Austin: University of Texas Press, 1941);
The Love Letters of Mark Twain, edited by Dixon Wecter (New York: Harper, 1949);
Mark Twain to Mrs. Fairbanks, edited by Wecter (San Marino: Huntington Library, 1949);
Mark Twain-Howells Letters, 2 volumes, edited by Henry Nash Smith and William M. Gibson (Cambridge: Harvard University Press, 1960);
Mark Twain's Letters to Mary, edited by Lewis Leary (New York: Columbia University Press, 1961);
Mark Twain's Letters to His Publishers, edited by Hamlin Hill (Berkeley: University of California Press, 1967);

Clemens at Oxford University, 26 June 1907, in procession to receive his honorary Doctor of Literature degree (Clara Clemens, My Father: Mark Twain, *1931)*

Mark Twain's Correspondence with Henry Huttleston Rogers, edited by Leary (Berkeley: University of California Press, 1969).

Bibliographies:

Merle Johnson, *A Bibliography of the Works of Mark Twain,* revised and enlarged edition (New York & London: Harper, 1935);

Thomas Asa Tenney, *Mark Twain, A Reference Guide* (Boston: G. K. Hall, 1977);

Alan Gribben, "Removing Mark Twain's Mask: A Decade of Criticism and Scholarship," *ESQ: Journal of the American Renaissance,* 26 (1980): 100-108, 149-171;

William B. McBride, *Mark Twain: A Bibliography of the Collections of the Mark Twain Memorial and the Stowe-Day Foundation* (Hartford, Conn.: McBride / Publisher, 1984).

Biographies:

William Dean Howells, *My Mark Twain* (New York & London: Harper, 1910);

Albert Bigelow Paine, *Mark Twain, A Biography,* 3 volumes (New York & London: Harper, 1912);

Bernard DeVoto, *Mark Twain's America* (Boston: Little, Brown, 1932);

Minnie M. Brashear, *Mark Twain, Son of Missouri* (Chapel Hill: University of North Carolina Press, 1934);

Ivan Benson, *Mark Twain's Western Years* (Stanford: Stanford University Press, 1938);

DeLancey Ferguson, *Mark Twain: Man and Legend* (Indianapolis & New York: Bobbs-Merrill, 1943);

Kenneth Andrews, *Nook Farm: Mark Twain's Hartford Circle* (Cambridge: Harvard University Press, 1950);

Dixon Wecter, *Sam Clemens of Hannibal* (Boston: Houghton Mifflin, 1952);

Paul Fatout, *Mark Twain in Virginia City* (Bloomington: Indiana University Press, 1964);

Edith Colgate Salsbury, *Susy and Mark Twain* (New York: Harper & Row, 1965);

Justin Kaplan, *Mr. Clemens and Mark Twain* (New York: Simon & Schuster, 1966);

Hamlin Hill, *Mark Twain: God's Fool* (New York: Harper & Row, 1973).

References:

Howard G. Baetzhold, *Mark Twain and John Bull* (Bloomington: Indiana University Press, 1970);

Gladys Bellamy, *Mark Twain as a Literary Artist* (Norman: University of Oklahoma Press, 1950);

Walter Blair, *Mark Twain & Huck Finn* (Berkeley: University of California Press, 1960);

Edgar M. Branch, *The Literary Apprenticeship of Mark Twain* (Urbana: University of Illinois Press, 1950);

Van Wyck Brooks, *The Ordeal of Mark Twain* (New York: Dutton, 1923; revised, 1933);

Louis J. Budd, *Interviews with Samuel L. Clemens, 1874-1910* (Arlington: University of Texas at Arlington, 1977);

Budd, *Mark Twain, Social Philosopher* (Bloomington: Indiana University Press, 1962);

Budd, *Our Mark Twain* (Philadelphia: University of Pennsylvania Press, 1983);

James M. Cox, *Mark Twain, The Fate of Humor* (Princeton: Princeton University Press, 1966);

Everett Emerson, *The Authentic Mark Twain* (Philadelphia: University of Pennsylvania Press, 1984);

Paul Fatout, *Mark Twain on the Lecture Circuit* (Bloomington: Indiana University Press, 1960);

Robert L. Gale, *Plots and Characters in the Works of Mark Twain*, 2 volumes (Hamden, Conn.: Archon Books, 1973);

William M. Gibson, *The Art of Mark Twain* (New York: Oxford University Press, 1976);

Alan Gribben, *Mark Twain's Library: A Reconstruction*, 2 volumes (Boston: G. K. Hall, 1980);

S. J. Krause, *Mark Twain as Critic* (Baltimore: Johns Hopkins University Press, 1967);

Robert L. Ramsay and Frances G. Emberson, *A Mark Twain Lexicon* (Columbia: University of Missouri Press, 1938; New York: Russell & Russell, 1963);

Franklin R. Rogers, *Mark Twain's Burlesque Patterns* (Dallas: Southern Methodist University Press, 1960);

Arthur L. Scott, *On the Poetry of Mark Twain with Selections from His Verse* (Urbana: University of Illinois Press, 1966);

David E. E. Sloane, *Mark Twain as a Literary Comedian* (Baton Rouge: Louisiana State University Press, 1979);

Henry Nash Smith, *Mark Twain, The Development of a Writer* (Cambridge: Harvard University Press, 1962);

Albert E. Stone, *The Innocent Eye, Childhood in Mark Twain's Fiction* (New Haven: Yale University Press, 1961).

Papers:

The major collection of Samuel Clemens's papers is at the Bancroft Library, University of California, Berkeley. Other major collections are at Yale University Library, the Henry W. and Albert A. Berg Collection of the New York Public Library, Vassar College, and the Alderman Library of the University of Virginia.

Evert Augustus Duyckinck

(23 November 1816-18 August 1878)

Heyward Ehrlich
Rutgers University, Newark

See also the Duyckinck entry in *DLB 3, Antebellum Writers in New York and the South.*

BOOKS: *Cyclopædia of American Literature,* 2 volumes, by Duyckinck and George L. Duyckinck (New York: Scribners, 1855; revised and enlarged, 1866; revised again, Philadelphia: Zell, 1875);

Irvingiana: A Memorial of Washington Irving (New York: Richardson, 1860);

National History of the War for the Union: Civil, Military, and Naval, 3 volumes (New York: Johnson, Fry, 1861-1865);

National Portrait Gallery of Eminent Americans, 2 volumes (New York: Johnson, Fry, 1862);

Lives and Portraits of the Presidents of the United States, from Washington to Johnson, 2 volumes (New York: Johnson, Fry, 1865); enlarged as *Lives and Portraits of the Presidents of the United States, from Washington to Grant,* 2 volumes (New York: Johnson, Wilson, 1873); enlarged as *Lives and Portraits of the Presidents of the United States from Washington to Arthur,* 2 volumes (New York: Johnson, 1881);

Portrait Gallery of Eminent Men and Women of Europe and America, 2 volumes (New York: Johnson, Fry, 1873).

OTHER: William Makepeace Thackeray, *The Confessions of Fitz-Boodle; and Some Passages in the Life of Major Gahagan,* edited by Duyckinck (New York: Appleton, 1852);

Wit and Wisdom of the Rev. Sydney Smith: Being Selections from his Writings and Passages of his Letters and Table Talk, edited by Duyckinck (New York: Redfield, 1856);

The Poets of the Nineteenth Century: Selected and Edited by the Rev. Robert Aris Willmott, with English and American Additions Arranged by Evert A. Duyckinck (New York: Harper, 1860);

William Irving, James Kirke Paulding, and Washington Irving, *Salmagundi; or, The Whim-*

Evert A. Duyckinck (Prints Division, New York Public Library, Astor, Lenox and Tilden Foundations)

whams and Opinions of Launcelot Langstaff, esq., and Others, edited by Duyckinck (New York: Putnam's, 1860);

Philip Freneau, *Poems Relating to the American Revolution,* edited by Duyckinck (New York: Widdleton, 1865);

History of the World: From the Earliest Period to the Present Time, 4 volumes, compiled by Duyckinck (New York: Johnson, Fry, 1869);

A Memorial of Fitz-Greene Halleck: A Description of the Dedication of the Monument Erected to his Memory at Guilford, Connecticut, edited by

Duyckinck (New York: Printed for the Committee by Amerman & Wilson, 1877);

The Complete Works of Shakespeare, edited by William Cullen Bryant, assisted by Duyckinck (New York: Amies, 1888).

Evert A. Duyckinck was the most important American literary critic in New York during the two decades before the Civil War. He was a principal figure in the Young America movement of literary nationalists in the 1840s, the chief editor for Wiley and Putnam's Library of American Books (1845-1848), the founder of the weekly *Literary World* (1847-1853), a major literary diarist and correspondent, the principal compiler of the landmark *Cyclopædia of American Literature* (1855), and the donor of a major founding collection of books to the New York Public Library. Best known for his friendship with and influence upon Herman Melville, Duyckinck was also a significant figure in the careers of Nathaniel Hawthorne, Edgar Allan Poe, William Gilmore Simms, and, to a lesser degree, Margaret Fuller, Henry David Thoreau, James Russell Lowell, Ralph Waldo Emerson, and Washington Irving.

Although Duyckinck's periodical publications were frequently a mixture of practical and descriptive rather than analytic or legislative criticism, he is best known for his early radical pronouncements and later conservative criticism. In the 1840s he agitated in support of the literary theories of the nationalistic Young America movement, but in 1855 he established the first canons of American literary achievement in the encyclopedia he produced with the aid of his brother, George L. Duyckinck.

Born on 23 November 1816, Duyckinck was a graduate of Columbia College and was trained as a lawyer, but he soon abandoned the practice of law and made an unsuccessful attempt to obtain a professorship at New York University (to fill the post vacated by the death of Lorenzo da Ponte, better known to Viennese music than American literature as the author of two Mozart libretti). As an heir to the earlier Knickerbockers Duyckinck's credentials were unexcelled: he was the son of Harriet Jane and Evert Duyckinck, a New York bookseller of Dutch extraction immortalized in Irving's *Knickerbocker History* (1809) by the pun "Ever Duckings" and then glorified in Irving's remark that he wished the father had been the publisher of the book. The son took up the appreciation of books, their custodianship, and the assembly of what was to become the larg-

est and most select private literary library in New York. According to Perry Miller, he once confessed to his younger brother George that he deeply loved books but felt "no morbid desire to manufacture them myself."

The Young America movement began modestly in 1836 the year of Emerson's Transcendental Club, as the social circle of four young New Yorkers with a literary turn of mind who called themselves the Tetractys. The group attracted several steady visitors who raised the number from four to eight, but there were only three active members: Duyckinck, William A. Jones, and Cornelius Mathews. On 22 September 1836 Mathews in a Rabelaisian quip asked whether the group, since it liked to put its nose "(like the snipe) into muddy waters such as metaphysics, political economy and theology," might not be better named "the Teterass society." The dabbling was largely political; metaphysics and theology, suggesting transcendentalism, were less welcome. Yet Duyckinck felt that his education was incomplete until he completed his European sojourn in 1838-1839 to validate his reading. He felt the permanent imprint on his mind of Goethe, Herder, and Richter from Germany, of Voltaire and George Sand from France, and of Bulwer from Britain.

Duyckinck's first writings appeared in the *New York Review,* an Episcopalian journal. Although a devout adherent of the High Church and a vestryman in St. Thomas's, religious editors thought him too liberal and too literary. Later, writers such as Melville and Whitman were to think he was sometimes too clerical. He saw Young America as a "politico-literary system," to use Longfellow's phrase, part of the Locofoco Young Hickory or Jacksonian faction of the Democratic party between the conservative Old Hunkers on the right and the abolitionist Barnburners on the left. Young America followed Shelley more than Coleridge as its critical theoretician; it assumed that America's republic, its democratic society, and its undeveloped continent required critical standards and literary subjects and forms unlike anything from the past.

In 1840 Mathews and Duyckinck, in want of a navigational star, launched the magazine *Arcturus.* Lowell, Hawthorne, and Longfellow were among the contributors. Although the monthly lasted only eighteen issues, it achieved the distinction, as Lowell put it, of being "as transcendental as Gotham can be." The partnership of Duyckinck and Mathews was a wedding of oppo-

Page from Duyckinck's notebook entitled "Books Lent," noting his loan to Herman Melville in 1848 of volume 2 of Rabelais's
Works *and Capt. Charles H. Barnard's* A Narrative of the Sufferings and Adventures of Capt. Charles H. Barnard, in
a Voyage round the World *(Duyckinck Collection, Manuscript and Archives Division, New York Public Library, Astor, Lenox
and Tilden Foundations)*

sites. In keeping with his public sense of literature, Mathews, also a lawyer, taught himself to be a playwright. The title of his closet drama, *The Politicians* (1840), indicated his purpose. Duyckinck's circle needed practicing writers—playwrights, novelists, poets, theorists, lobbyists, critics, and pamphleteers—but it is doubtful that anyone expected one person would try to be all these things, as did Mathews.

In 1842 the visit to New York of Charles Dickens gave Young America an opportunity to dramatize the issue of the lack of an international copyright law in the United States. Since 1790 American copyright law had exempted foreign citizens from all protection; as a consequence, international piracy was entirely legal in American publishing (and was to remain so until 1891). Economically, the system debased the value of foreign authors and made domestic writing virtually worthless. To dramatize the issue Mathews made an unscheduled and impassioned copyright speech at a dinner held in Dickens's honor. While few disagreed with the content of the speech, only Mathews's friends and allies approved of its timing. Thus Mathews changed the issue from the rightness of home rule to the politics of who would rule at home. As Simms summed it up in a letter a quarter-century later, "Mathews would not permit himself to be a gentleman in his passion to be an author."

By 1843 the Whigs began to line themselves up against Mathews and Duyckinck. They were cosmopolitan, traditional, and arbiters of style and taste: Mathews stood for nationality, even provinciality, for works judged by a belief in their manifest destiny. Mathews's mission in American literature was to create an egalitarian Jacksonian culture of all classes, all professions, all races, a melting pot, as it were, of styles and genres. Mathews for the next decade created work after work, each a manifesto of the future American political art. To the smug Whig satirists, ever keen for a deviation from the Knickerbocker norm, Mathews's poems celebrating all workingmen's occupations, his myths of land behemoths of American prehistory, his visions of the pluralistic cultures of Dutch, Indian, and white New York, and above all his faith in the equality or supremacy of American literature to British literature, of contemporary writers to classic writers, of the future standards of New York criticism and readership to past standards of the London literary scene, were simply ridiculous. The Whig journals, led by the *Knickerbocker* and followed by the

American Whig Review, began to take open shots at Mathews and Duyckinck; Young America was a "Mutual Admiration Society"; Mathews was "the Behemoth," and Duyckinck was only "Mr. Shadow."

Despite the advice of all who knew him, Duyckinck refused to abandon Mathews. Poe, in "The Literati of New York" (1846), described Duyckinck's two main traits as "*bonhomie*" and a "Quixotic loyalty to his friends." Simms, writing to Duyckinck on 7 August 1895, agreed in principle: "To be great & successful, we must fling *conventional* to the dogs, & how many Americans do you know prepared for this?"—yet he insisted that Mathews was not the man he had in mind: he reminded Duyckinck in a letter dated 13 November 1895 that Mathews was his "*questio vexata* in New York."

In 1845 Duyckinck began to supervise the production of a library of American books for Wiley and Putnam. Duyckinck's feat was extraordinary. In a few years he assembled the first critical mass of American writing, including Melville's *Typee*, Hawthorne's *Mosses from an Old Manse*, Poe's *The Raven* and *Tales*, Margaret Fuller's *Papers on Literature and Art*, Simms's *The Wigwam and the Cabin* and *Views and Reviews*, Bayard Taylor's *Views A-Foot*, and Whittier's *Supernaturalism of New England*. For the first time there was an American equivalent of the Everyman's Library, and while not profitable, it was a turning point in American book publishing.

The Wiley and Putnam series also enabled Duyckinck to establish himself professionally. In *A Fable for Critics* (1848), Lowell called him a sound scholar and a good social critic who managed to carry through the literary Grub Street of New York "the soul of a gentleman." Duyckinck was the one person in literary New York who was acceptable to both New Englanders and southerners. When Emerson in 1845 described his "friendly correspondence" with Duyckinck, he meant that he hoped for a favorable publishing contract for a book. For his known conservatism—threefold on account of his religious, political, and economic beliefs—Duyckinck was often able to represent both the publisher as his editor and the author as his literary agent, and then go on to write and print the reviews of the book.

In 1846 Young America launched *Yankee Doodle*, its version of the English magazine *Punch*, a topical weekly of political satire. The assignment to do a series on General Zachary Taylor was given to a young man who had all the requisite

Letter from Melville to Duyckinck, 26 March 1851 (Melville Papers, Duyckinck Collection, Manuscript and Archives Division, New York Public Library, Astor, Lenox and Tilden Foundations)

qualifications: he had two grandfathers who had distinguished themselves in the American Revolution, one brother who had been a brilliant orator for the Democrats in 1844, another who was a Wall Street lawyer of conservative Democratic stamp, and, moreover, had himself just published a best-selling book on the South Seas. The book, originally endorsed in manuscript in London by Washington Irving, was brought out in New York by Wiley and Putnam; in turn, Duyckinck brought it to Hawthorne's attention, calling it "a Frenchy coloured picture of the Marquesa islanders." It was *Typee*, Herman Melville's first book.

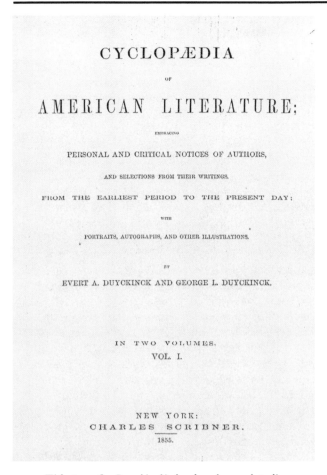

CYCLOPÆDIA

OF

AMERICAN LITERATURE;

EMBRACING

PERSONAL AND CRITICAL NOTICES OF AUTHORS,

AND SELECTIONS FROM THEIR WRITINGS.

FROM THE EARLIEST PERIOD TO THE PRESENT DAY;

WITH

PORTRAITS, AUTOGRAPHS, AND OTHER ILLUSTRATIONS.

BY

EVERT A. DUYCKINCK AND GEORGE L. DUYCKINCK.

IN TWO VOLUMES.
VOL. I.

NEW YORK:
CHARLES SCRIBNER.
1855.

Title page for Duyckinck's landmark encyclopedia

No adequate term exists to describe New York literature as Melville found it in Duyckinck's era–after the close of the Knickerbocker period in 1837 and before the outbreak of the Civil War in 1861. One brilliant contemporary assessment of the critical wars of the period, Lowell's *Fable for Critics*, begins with a portrait of Duyckinck as the first manifestation of "Our Hero." A fortunate literary visitor to New York would find his way to the Duyckinck salon in the basement at 20 Clinton Place near Washington Square and enjoy cigars, champagne or punch, a good deal of literary talk, and even choice gossip.

But the newcomer would also find the unexpected. Duyckinck's private library (from which Melville borrowed frequently) contained not just the standard British authors–from Shakespeare to Milton to the satirists, novelists, and essayists of the eighteenth and nineteenth century–but also his specialties, including the seventeenth-century authors Sir Thomas Browne, George Herbert, Andrew Marvell, and the Jacobean

dramatists. Duyckinck's library was well stocked with the latest American editions and imports of the German authors Goethe, Herder, and Richter, and the Germanicized and transcendentalized Britons and Americans, including Carlyle, Emerson, Thoreau, and Sylvester Judd. But Duyckinck did not approve of transcendentalism in public; he denied Emerson's request to publish a book by Thoreau, even though he did collect the periodical work of the controversial Margaret Fuller in the Wiley and Putnam series as *Papers on Literature and Art* (1846). Because of his solid footing in the literary establishment of New York, Duyckinck's ideological associations with such activists, revolutionists, and propagandists as Mathews, Fuller, and John L. O'Sullivan were all the more telling. He was one of the few editors whose word could be a guarantee of admission, as Lowell quipped in *A Fable for Critics*, to the pages of O'Sullivan's *Democratic Review*.

In 1847 Duyckinck and Mathews turned to a new venture. Duyckinck was aware that many of the Wiley and Putnam books were reprints from magazines. A strong publishing industry would need healthy periodicals for some time to come. They decided to launch the *Literary World* as the first serious weekly in the United States devoted entirely to books. It ran for six years and achieved new heights of excellence. Evidently Duyckinck believed that there were some things more sacred than contracts because in the first few months he was temporarily ousted as editor for violating his agreement not to employ the outcast Mathews as a contributor.

Gradually a new professionalism was eclipsing the old town spirit of earlier Knickerbocker literature. Poe's "Literati of New York" had opened the way to a less-polite form of satire. Thomas Dunn English ("done brown" according to Poe) replied with a newspaper serial depicting Poe as Marmaduke Hammerhead. In 1847 Charles Frederick Briggs, Poe's ex-partner on the *Broadway Journal*, began to serialize a novel, *Tom Pepper*, in which he ridiculed Poe as Austin Wicks, savaged Mathews for grandiose theories of literary nationality as a character named Ferocious, and painted Duyckinck as Tibbings, the ineffectual sycophant of Ferocious. Meanwhile, Briggs was receiving private installments of yet another satire written for him by Lowell.

When it appeared in 1848 Lowell's *Fable for Critics* made strange bedfellows of Mathews and Margaret Fuller. When Duyckinck compiled her *Papers on Literature and Art* he added to her contri-

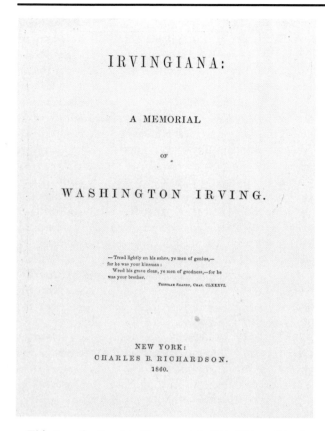

IRVINGIANA:

A MEMORIAL

OF

WASHINGTON IRVING.

—Tread lightly on his ashes, ye men of genius,—
for he was your kinsman :
Weed his grave clean, ye men of goodness,—for he
was your brother,
TRISTRAM SHANDY, CHAP. CLXXXVI.

NEW YORK:
CHARLES B. RICHARDSON.
1860.

Title page for Duyckinck's memorial of his lifelong friend

butions from the *Dial* and *New York Tribune* a new article which turned the history of American literature into a puff for Mathews's latest play, *Witchcraft* (1852). Lowell's satire depicts Margaret Fuller as Miranda, who raised the radical issue of whether or not ideological criticism can be greater than art. Everywhere Mathews is a secondary target. The *Knickerbocker*, leaving no room for doubt as to what mattered in New York, reprinted the passages on Duyckinck and Mathews. By 1849 so many literary satires had appeared against Mathews that the *Literary World* wondered if a single American novel had appeared in the last five years without some portrait of him.

Young America needed someone to write a reply, and it could not be Mathews. For the time being Duyckinck still doubted the originality of the Melville he had seen in *Yankee Doodle;* moreover, Duyckinck had a vision of an entire shelf of the Everyman's Library: "Novels rewritten by Melville." To cure this, Duyckinck encouraged Melville to follow Mathews into the cult of originality. In a letter to his brother George, Duyckinck expressed his belief that the drafts of *Mardi* (1849) were far ahead of *Typee* (1846) and

Omoo (1847) "in the poetry and the wildness of the thing." Hawthorne agreed, finding *Mardi* "a rich book with depths here and there that force a reader to swim for his life." However, a decade later in the *Cyclopædia of American Literature* Duyckinck was to complain that in *Mardi* Melville "wanders without chart or compass in the wildest regions of doubt and scepticism."

Nevertheless in 1849 Duyckinck was still encouraging Melville to spread his wings for flight. Melville took the cue, punning imaginatively in a letter to Duyckinck dated 3 March 1849 on the names Duyckinck and *Literary World* and on punch in the Duyckinck cellar: "I love all men who *dive*," if not the "great whale" who can reach the bottom, then "the whole corps of thought-divers, that have been diving & coming up again with bloodshot eyes since the world began." Melville's response was greater than what Duyckinck expected whenever his humor followed Carlyle more than Irving. Surely Duyckinck was equally nonplussed by Melville's spontaneity. In a letter to George dated 12 September 1849 he stated, "Melville put me all in a flutter the other evening by proposing that I should go to Europe with him on a cheap adventurous flying tour of eight months, compassing Rome!"

Knickerbocker humor changed its tone in the late 1840s. It was ill-equipped to deal with the foreign and domestic upheavals and changes after the revolutions of 1848. Young America assumed the millennium would be Jacksonian, not Barnburner or Fourierite. On occasion literary politics mixed with issues of class and nationalism. After a nativist mob on 7 May 1849 stopped the Shakespearean performance of an English tragedian, Duyckinck helped to organize the Macready petition, duly signed by Mathews, Melville, Irving, and others. They took the principled position of defending the right of the English actor Macready to introduce *Macbeth* at the Astor Place Opera House–even though it competed with the *Macbeth* currently performed at another theater by their American favorite, Edwin Forrest. Assured by the prestigious support of Duyckinck and others, the Englishman resumed his performances. James Fenimore Cooper, who understood the explosiveness of the situation, refused to sign.

On 10 May the clash took place outside the Astor Place Opera House: the nativists' paving stones skinned a few militiamen, but the firearms of the militia killed twenty-two persons and wounded thirty more. The size of the public uprising was estimated at 25,000. The following year, Melville, remembering these events in town from his sanctuary in the Berkshires, heaped irony upon irony when he asked Duyckinck whether he and Mathews still played ball by pitching paving stones in the evening in Astor Place.

Until 1850 Duyckinck remained the most important personal influence on Melville's career; then the novelist moved from New York City to the Berkshires and discovered Hawthorne. That August Duyckinck and Mathews left New York City to join Melville, Hawthorne, Oliver Wendell Holmes, and others in the most famous picnic in American literary history. Afterwards, Duyckinck introduced Melville to the inmost Hawthorne circle by giving him a package to deliver; the contents, as Melville did not guess, were a set of his own works, which Hawthorne promptly took to the barn to read. In the same month Duyckinck gave Melville Hawthorne's *Mosses from an Old Manse* (1846) to review for the *Literary World*. The result was Melville's emotionally powerful manifesto on behalf of Young America, the essay "Hawthorne and his Mosses."

Just what state Melville's most recent book manuscript was in during this critical month of August 1850 is a matter of debate. What is not in dispute is that it was a draft of *Moby-Dick* and that its godfather was still Duyckinck, who noted in a letter to George: "Melville has a new book mostly done—a romantic, fanciful & literal & most enjoyable presentment of the Whale Fishery—something quite new." In the final revision, however, Melville recast the work in the Hawthorne manner and dedicated the book to him.

In reviewing *Moby-Dick* for the *Literary World* on 22 November 1851, Duyckinck wrote what still remains one of the soundest, fairest, and most useful essays on the novel; yet he complained of discomfort at Melville's "piratical running down of creeds and opinions, the conceited indifferentism of Emerson, or the run-a-muck style of Carlyle," and what bothered him most of all was to see "the most sacred associations of life violated and defaced." For his part, Duyckinck was a staunch Episcopalian always ready to take up his pen to defend Christianity, its churches, and especially its High Church. When Duyckinck's religion came into conflict with his political and literary judgments, as it did in considering Melville's questings, the Episcopalian, the Democrat, and the Young American in him wrestled until the Episcopalian prevailed. Even Haw-

thorne complained of this, writing to Duyckinck in early December: "What a book Melville has written! It gives me an idea of much greater power than his preceding ones. It hardly seemed to me that the review of it, in the Literary World, did justice to its best points."

In 1852 Melville and Duyckinck cooled in their friendship for reasons unknown. After five years of participation in the *Literary World* as a contributor, sympathizer, and reader, Melville cancelled his subscription. Since 1850 the *Literary World* had assumed an antirevolutionary editorial position: the issue was not revolution in France and Germany but rather the way in which New York had become a national center for utopian agitation after the close of Brook Farm in 1847. For Duyckinck literary style and politics had become connected. On 9 April 1851 the magazinist George W. Curtis wrote to Charles Eliot Norton to report a conversation with Duyckinck about style: " 'I see that you have been experimenting in style.—It's rather dangerous--' !!!!!!!!!!!!! I feel convinced that Evert will never be blown up by any such rash experimenting."

Meanwhile, Melville, working on a rural domestic philosophical romance with deep paradoxes called *Pierre; or The Ambiguities* (1852), suddenly felt the need to change course. He moved the action of the novel to the literary-political life of New York City and wrote chapter after chapter of satire in the Irving-Briggs-Lowell manner on New York as Grub Street, as bohemia, as headquarters for Utopian agitation. Duyckinck appears as the inoffensive man with the cigar. Replying to Duyckinck's chiding of his speculations in *Moby-Dick*, Melville returned fire for fire, and borrowing Irving's Knickerbocker weapon, the name pun, attributed "diving and ducking moralities" to Duyckinck. The *Literary World* of 21 August 1852 complained of the "immoral *moral*" of Melville's paradoxes and his allowing "his mind to run riot amid remote analogies." Afterwards, it is possible that Duyckinck—the ultimate literary gentleman in New York, good humored, well intentioned, tolerant, liberal, no foe of business, highly literate but innocent of the blackness in Melville's world—was a starting point for the series of related narrators, characters, and themes of this cast in Melville's writing from "Bartleby the Scrivener" (1853) to *Billy Budd, Sailor* (completed in 1891 but not published until 1924).

After the demise of the *Literary World* in 1853, the prospects for Young America had

Evert Duyckinck

changed: Jackson, Oregon, and Texas had become words from the past; moreover, Duyckinck's original hopes for national magazines, national writers, and national books had been partly realized. The Duyckinck brothers turned to the production of a monument to national literature, the *Cyclopædia of American Literature*. Between 1847, when Duyckinck launched the *Literary World*, and 1855, when he published the first edition of the *Cyclopædia*, American literature finally came of age: the miraculous early 1850s had produced Hawthorne's *The Scarlet Letter* (1850), Emerson's *Representative Men* (1850), Melville's *Moby-Dick* (1851), Thoreau's *Walden* (1854), and Whitman's *Leaves of Grass* (1855).

The *Cyclopædia of American Literature* contains estimates that are of surprising durability. It has the first recognition of Thoreau during his lifetime. Duyckinck forgave Lowell for his *Fable for Critics* as "a series of sharply drawn portraits drawn in felicitous verse." The deceased Margaret Fuller, satirized by Hawthorne as Zenobia in *The Blithedale Romance* (1852), was "an intellectual, sympathetic, kind, generous, noble-hearted woman." Emerson's works displayed "a species of

philosophical indifferentism tending to license in practice, which . . . he would be the last to avail himself of." Had Poe possessed a moral sense "he would have been in the first rank of critics." This was no place or time to raise the old issues surrounding Mathews, who merely "has chosen new subjects, and treated them in a way of his own." Melville himself might still be reached in his isolation in Berkshire with an appeal to his old Knickerbocker sociality: "In this comparative retirement will be found the secret of much of the speculative character engrafted upon his writings." The old firebrand views of Young America and the conservative views of their opponents became indistinguishable in the view of Longfellow's Epicurianism as a treatment for excess: he was after all "not a bad corrective of ultraism, Fourierism, transcendentalism, and other morbidities."

On 1 October 1856 Duyckinck noted in his diary a lusty visit from Melville, the talk full of "sailor metaphysics and jargon of things unknowable," with stories worthy of the Decameron about female convicts at Sing Sing, in all "an orgie of indecency and blasphemy." The difference of opinion between Melville and Duyckinck on the matter of religious orthodoxy remained unbridgeable, but their friendship revived in common hostility to Emersonian transcendentalism, one subject of Melville's satire in *The Confidence Man* (1857). Duyckinck, writing to George in 1857, looked forward to see "what the sea dog philosophy of Typee makes of it" when applying the methods of Swift or Voltaire to such "an original American idea" for satire.

In the final twenty years of his life Duyckinck produced many historical compilations and personal memorials, but the old critical wars were over. The effects of Young America could be seen on nearly every American writer at mid century except Poe. Yet the most complete justification for Young America was not in Mathews but in the revolutionary manifestos and wholly new poetry of still another veteran of the Democratic party journalism of the 1840s, Walt Whitman. Ironically, Whitman did not appear in the original *Cyclopædia of American History*, and he was disappointed that he never was added to subsequent editions.

Upon Irving's death in 1860 Duyckinck produced a memorial volume, *Irvingiana: A Memorial of Washington Irving* (1860). In Duyckinck's last years, Melville's personal visits became increasingly frequent and regular. Upon Duyckinck's death on 18 August 1878 he was buried in

Sleepy Hollow, where he and Irving had selected sites together years before. His memorialist Samuel Osgood summed up the Duyckinck era: it was the "American Renaissance."

References:

Merrell R. Davis and William H. Gilman, *The Letters of Herman Melville* (New Haven: Yale University Press, 1960);

Jay Leyda, *The Melville Log*, 2 volumes (New York: Harcourt, Brace, 1951);

Perry Miller, *The Raven and the Whale: the War of Words and Wits in the Era of Poe and Melville* (New York: Harcourt, Brace, 1956);

Mary C. Simms Oliphant and others, *The Letters of William Gilmore Simms*, 5 volumes (Columbia: University of South Carolina, 1952);

Samuel Osgood, *Evert Duyckinck, His Life, Writings, and Influence: A Memoir* (Boston: David Clapp, 1879);

John Stafford, *The Literary Criticism of " Young America"* (Berkeley: University of California Press, 1952);

Donald Yanella and Kathleen Malone Yanella, "Evert A. Duyckinck's Diary: May 29-November 8, 1847," in *Studies in the American Renaissance 1978*, edited by Joel Myerson (Boston: Twayne, 1978), pp. 207-258.

Papers:
Evert A. Duyckinck's papers are located in the Duyckinck manuscripts division of the New York Public Library.

John Fiske

(30 March 1842-4 July 1901)

George P. Winston
Nichols College

See also the Fiske entry in *DLB 47, American Historians, 1866-1912.*

SELECTED BOOKS: *Tobacco and Alcohol* (New York: Leypoldt & Holt, 1869);

Myths and Myth-Makers: Old Tales and Superstitions Interpreted by Comparative Mythology (Boston: Osgood, 1872);

Outlines of Cosmic Philosophy, Based on the Doctrine of Evolution, With Criticisms on the Positive Philosophy, 2 volumes (Boston: Osgood, 1874; London: Macmillan, 1874);

The Unseen World, and Other Essays (Boston: Osgood, 1876);

Darwinism and Other Essays (London & New York: Macmillan, 1879; revised and enlarged edition, Boston & New York: Houghton, Mifflin, 1885);

Excursions of an Evolutionist (Boston: Houghton, Mifflin, 1884; London: Macmillan, 1884);

The Destiny of Man Viewed in the Light of His Origin (Boston: Houghton, Mifflin, 1884; London: Macmillan, 1884);

American Political Ideas Viewed from the Standpoint of Universal History: Three Lectures Delivered at the Royal Institution of Great Britain in May 1880 (New York: Harper, 1885; London: Macmillan, 1885);

The Idea of God as Affected by Modern Knowledge (Boston & New York: Houghton, Mifflin, 1885; London: Macmillan, 1885);

The Critical Period of American History, 1783-1789 (Boston & New York: Houghton, Mifflin, 1888; London: Macmillan, 1888; revised edition, Boston & New York: Houghton, Mifflin, 1898);

The Beginnings of New England; or, The Puritan Theocracy in Its Relations to Civil and Religious Liberty (Boston & New York: Houghton, Mifflin, 1889; London: Macmillan, 1889; revised edition, Boston & New York: Houghton, Mifflin, 1898);

The War of Independence (Boston & New York: Houghton, Mifflin, 1889);

Civil Government in the United States Considered with Some Reference to Its Origins (Boston & New

York: Houghton, Mifflin, 1890; London: Macmillan, 1890);

The American Revolution, 2 volumes (Boston & New York: Houghton, Mifflin, 1891; London: Macmillan, 1891; revised edition, Boston & New York: Houghton, Mifflin, 1896; London: Gay & Bird, 1897);

The Discovery of America, with Some Account of Ancient America and the Spanish Conquest, 2 volumes (Boston & New York: Houghton, Mifflin, 1892; London: Macmillan, 1892);

Edward Livingston Youmans, Interpreter of Science for the People: A Sketch of His Life With Selections from His Published Writings and Extracts from His Correspondence with Spencer, Huxley, Tyndall and Others (New York: Appleton, 1894);

A History of the United States for Schools (Boston, New York & Chicago: Houghton, Mifflin, 1894; London: Clarke, 1894);

Old Virginia and Her Neighbors, 2 volumes (Boston & New York: Houghton, Mifflin, 1897; London: Macmillan, 1897);

Through Nature to God (Boston & New York: Houghton, Mifflin, 1899; London: Macmillan, 1899);

The Dutch and Quaker Colonies in America, 2 volumes (Boston & New York: Houghton, Mifflin, 1899; London: Macmillan, 1899);

A Century of Science and Other Essays (Boston & New York: Houghton, Mifflin, 1899; London: Macmillan, 1900);

The Mississippi Valley in the Civil War (Boston & New York: Houghton, Mifflin, 1900);

Life Everlasting (Boston & New York: Houghton, Mifflin, 1901; London: Macmillan, 1902);

Colonization of the New World (Philadelphia & New York: Lea, 1902);

Independence of the New World (Philadelphia & New York: Lea, 1902);

Modern Development of the New World, completed by John Bach McMaster (Philadelphia & New York: Lea, 1902);

New France and New England (Boston: Houghton, Mifflin, 1902; London: Macmillan, 1902);

Essays Historical and Literary, 2 volumes (New York & London: Macmillan, 1902).

OTHER: H. A. Taine, *The Classroom Taine*, translated by H. Van Laun, abridged and edited by Fiske (New York: Holt & Williams, 1872);

H. W. Smith, *The Presidents of America: A Series of Original Steel Engravings Taken From Paintings and Photographs by Distinguished Artists*, introduction and biographical sketches by Fiske (Boston & New York: Thayer, 1879);

Appleton's Cyclopedia of American Biography, 6 volumes, edited by James Grant Wilson and Fiske (New York: Appleton, 1887-1889).

During his lifetime and well into the twentieth century John Fiske was regarded as an eminent scholar. He had numerous connections in the academic world–particularly at Harvard University where he was assistant librarian and occasional faculty member. Among his friends and associates were such notables as Henry Wadsworth Longfellow, William Dean Howells, Francis Parkman, Henry Adams, Charles Eliot, T. H. Huxley, Charles Darwin, and George Eliot. There were some who found Fiske's scholarship superficial; most negative criticism focused, however, on his handling of controversial themes, especially the importance of evolutionary theory and its relationship to religion.

Fiske's major achievement was to reconcile evolutionary science and religion in such a way as to appeal to a large audience. Whatever his subject, the underlying pattern which Fiske consistently evoked was evolution, both as the most rational explanation of human knowledge and the best perspective for guiding human inquiry. This view did not endear him to those who believed in divine creation. He was deeply religious, but he was anything but orthodox. Fiske served for a time as a reviewer for the *World,* the *North American Review,* the *Atlantic Monthly,* and the *Christian Examiner.* His friends and early biographers tended to think of him primarily as a literary man, a man of letters. A key to the kind of person Fiske was and to the niche he occupied in American scholarship is seen in his relationship to Ralph Waldo Emerson. As a college sophomore he had the opportunity to visit Emerson at home. Completely impressed, he wrote to his family, "I thought him the greatest man I ever saw." The impression lasted a lifetime. John Spencer Clark reports in *The Life and Letters of John Fiske* (1917) that many years later Fiske was still reading Emerson with a focus on the latter's anticipation of evolutionary theory.

John Fiske was born Edmund Fisk Green on 30 March 1842 in Middletown, Connecticut. From birth he grew up largely in the household of his maternal grandmother. His father, Edmund Brewster Green, died while on a trip to Panama in 1852. Three years later his mother, Mary Fisk Bound Green, married Edwin Wallace Stoughton, a well-known lawyer, and the boy legally adopted the name of his great-grandfather, John Fisk, at his grandmother's request. The final *e* was added in 1860, though the change was never legalized. Middletown was a rural community with such activities as nutting and fishing of prime interest to a boy; the atmosphere within the home was genteel and strongly feminine; and from an early period Fiske had difficulties with orthodox religion. The classic example of the last was his public admonition and near suspension from Harvard for reading in chapel. His polite but firm refusal to compromise put him in a position which was to haunt him for the rest of his career (it no doubt cost him a much-desired professorship at Harvard); however, this characteristic was one reason for the admiration and support he won from the less orthodox.

Within six years of his graduation from Harvard in 1863, Fiske published his first book. During the interim he had gone through law courses, been admitted to the Massachusetts bar, and made a stab at a career in law. He had also married Abby Morgan Brooks of Petersham, Massachusetts, and had begun to raise a family. As a

reviewer for various periodicals, Fiske was sent copies of many books; among these appeared *Smoking and Drinking* by James Parton. Parton argued that these habits would be abandoned as not only unhealthful but morally unsound. Annoyed to find the question treated as a moral issue, the young scholar shifted the question to the medical area and what was to have been a review became a book, *Tobacco and Alcohol* (1869). All of the paraphernalia of footnotes and references are included, as scientists and doctors are cited in support of the idea that these practices are not injurious to health. The book shows the young critic's tendency toward teaching (or even preaching). Later Fiske wrote that he could not regard *Tobacco and Alcohol,* as one critic did, "a wonderful mosaic of learning"; nevertheless today it is of prime interest for the barrage of scholarship he brought to bear on the issue.

The approach in Fiske's second book, *Myths and Myth-makers* (1872), is synthesis: in the preface Fiske acknowledges that he has freely used Jacob Grimm, Max Muller, Adalbert Kuhn, Michel Bréal, Sir George Dasen, and Edward Taylor; he has also synthesized by interweaving previously published essays of his own. Attempting to present scholarly materials in such a way as to arouse general interest, Fiske traces the evolution of various myths back to common sources which in general present prescientific attempts to explain nature. Myths "are the earliest recorded utterances of men concerning the visible phenomena of the world into which they were born." It may be a long jump, for example, from William Tell to primitive explanations of the sun's path or the lightning bolt; but Fiske's argument makes the connection convincing. First he cites historical record to prove that the story of Tell was not an actual historical event; then he demonstrates its origin through a number of parallel stories, all of which he traces back to related explanations of natural phenomena. This first major work, dedicated to "my friend William Dean Howells, in remembrance of pleasant autumn evenings spent among werewolves and trolls and nixies," already shows Fiske's talent for making a subject readable. It also demonstrates the point on which more solemn scholars were to attack him regularly. They regarded his prefatory statement that "in dealing with a subject which depends on philology almost as much as astronomy depends on mathematics, I have omitted philosophical considerations wherever it has been possible to do so" as far too cavalier to be accepted as sound scholarship.

Fiske wrote a good deal of literary criticism, including essays on such figures as Howells, George Eliot, and Oliver Wendell Holmes. While his letters and works are filled with observations about poets, novelists, and other creative writers, most of his essays on literary subjects remain buried in the periodicals for which they were first written. The two volumes labeled *Essays Historical and Literary* (collected by Abby Morgan Fiske, 1902) contain but one essay devoted to a literary figure, John Milton. This essay, in the vein of Sainte-Beuve, is largely biographical narrative but presents the idea that Milton's classical and Renaissance qualities are perhaps more important than his Puritan outlook. Fiske maintains that in a listing of major writers Milton must come after Homer, Dante, and Shakespeare, or at least share fourth place with Aeschylus, Sophocles, Lucretius, Virgil, and Goethe.

Fiske considered the writing of history a literary task. "Old and New Ways of Treating History" (*Essays*, volume 2), which to some extent is reminiscent of Hippolyte Taine in the *History of English Literature*, offers principles which Fiske also applied to his literary criticism. In summary, the aims of the new way of writing history are: accuracy based on the study of original sources such as statutes, debates in councils, memoirs, diaries, and newspapers, rather than on previous histories; avoidance of preference or bias; a focus no longer on kings and battles but on a spectrum broad enough to include art, literature, and daily life as well as commerce, finance, and politics; a full attention to periods outside conventional frames of study; and finally as a capstone, appreciation of the native genius of the old masters. Without this last, all the scientific care in the world will not produce a great historian like Herodotus, Thucydides, or Gibbon.

By the early 1870s Fiske had become a major lecturer on the public circuit and at Harvard. He was much involved in the academic and political life of the university, giving support to those who were demanding educational reform. A Fiske article, requested by James Russell Lowell and E. L. Godkin for the *Nation,* was influential in the appointment of Charles W. Eliot as president of Harvard. Eliot later did much to further Fiske's career. The main thrust of Fiske's earliest lecture series had been to defend and interpret Herbert Spencer's philosophy. Expanding the project required a voyage to England to consult with Spencer. With financial assistance from a patron, Mrs. Mary Hemenway, and his brother-in-law, James Brooks, Fiske was able to sail for Europe on 12 August 1873. The resulting two-volume work, *Outlines of Cosmic Philosophy,* was published simultaneously in Britain and the United States in 1874.

Designed as an explication of Spencer, *Outlines of Cosmic Philosophy* nevertheless has a focus which is entirely Fiske: to prove to his readers that because of and not in spite of evolutionary doctrine they could perceive that God is in his heaven and all is right with the world. The extent to which this is not exactly Spencer's intent is shown by the dispute the two men had over the title: Spencer wished it to be "Synthetic Philosophy" while Fiske insisted on "Cosmic Philosophy," thus emphasizing a religious implication that Spencer was not prepared to support. In fact Fiske gained acceptance of his title only by including a graceful prefatory note acknowledging the difference of opinion.

Reaction to *Outlines of Cosmic Philosophy* was sharply divided along predictable lines, with the religious press acridly opposed. Fiske had quoted Spencer as saying that man was not moved by ideas but by feelings, so that emotion was at the base of the critical comment. Clergymen were incensed by the continued denial of special creation. Some of their objections, especially in cartoons, bordered on a sarcasm that suggests a sense they were losing ground in the debate. On the opposite side, the most notable commendation came from Darwin, who had earlier confessed that he had not understood Spencer until Fiske had explicated him. By the time the critical pros and cons appeared, Fiske had returned to family life and to work at the Harvard Library, but most important, he had begun to focus more on historical works than on philosophical ones.

It is impractical to follow a strict chronology in considering Fiske's works. Once he had established himself as a lecturer, he regularly reworked lectures into book form and did not hesitate to include materials that had earlier been published in various periodicals or to mine other works that proved relevant. Most of the later philosophical collections follow this pattern. Among these, two are worthy of special note: *The Destiny of Man Viewed in the Light of His Origin* (1884) and *The Idea of God as Affected by Modern Knowledge* (1885). In 1884 Bronson Alcott's Concord School of Philosophy invited Fiske to take part in a symposium considering man's immortality from various

Abby Morgan Brooks at the time of her engagement to Fiske, 1862

philosophical and theological viewpoints. *The Destiny of Man Viewed in the Light of His Origin* is a description of the universe as seen by modern science. The difference between this book and *Outlines of Cosmic Philosophy* is of degree and tone rather than of kind. Fiske continues to point out the immeasurable vastness and variety of the universe, but the emphasis here is on unity and order in accordance with immutable law. The book ends with a statement which Fiske had never before made so directly: "It is Darwinism which has placed Humanity upon a higher pinnacle than ever. . . . The dream of poets, the lesson of priest and prophet, the inspiration of the great musician, is confirmed in the light of modern knowledge."

The reception of both lecture and book was so notable that Fiske was asked to return to the program in 1885. The second lecture and subsequent book, *The Idea of God as Affected by Modern Knowledge,* were sequels to the first. As Fiske stated in the preface, "The two books taken together contain the bare outlines of a theory of reli-

gion." Fiske's main concern here is the rapidly accelerating course of progress. He considers the nineteenth century to be in the midst of a mighty revolution in human thought. In a series of illustrations he graphically sketches the increasing rate of material progress, noting that the minds of his readers have become so adjusted to the actual changes that his examples have an air of triteness. Having surveyed the concepts of God through the ages he finds most drastic changes occurring in the nineteenth century because of the overwhelming increase in the area of human knowledge, which he says since the dawn of consciousness has been advancing in geometric progression.

Early in 1878 Fiske was invited to give a series of lectures in Boston to aid in saving the Old South Church, a series called "America's Place in History." This venture was to shift the entire focus of his career. The moment was propitious for such a scheme: his audience was the kind he most appealed to; his theme was one they were eager to hear. Regularly Americans were being told of their shortcomings by European visitors. Setting such criticism aside, Fiske insisted that America was the culmination of Western civilization, its goal and its intent. Urged by Mrs. Hemenway, he contacted friends in England offering to give the series there. He sailed in May 1879 for a second trip abroad, once again with financial sponsorship. In a letter reporting his success, he reminds Abby to relay the news to "my fairy godmother, Mrs. Hemenway."

Though he never became a full-time member of the Harvard faculty, in June 1879 Fiske was appointed to the university's Board of Overseers. By this time he was caught up in his historical lectures, offered widely in the United States and England. One such notable occasion was the series at the Royal Institution in 1880. These activities led to an agreement with Harper to produce a "Short History of the American People"–an agreement which became something of an albatross. Fiske was not adept at summaries; he was prone to explore background, foreground, and middle distance, and like the artists of his day he needed a large canvas.

Nevertheless the two projects of the lectures and the history began to intertwine and emerge as a series of books beginning with *American Political Ideas Viewed from the Standpoint of Universal History* in 1885. Events of this same year brought about a change in his lecturing procedure which is important to an understanding of Fiske's position as a scholar and lecturer. After attending one of these lectures, Henry Ward Beecher told him, "you need a good manager to make engagements for you. Let me send you my manager, Major J. B. Pond, and you will find that what he doesn't know about managing isn't worth knowing." Pond was perceptive: he pointed out that Fiske's lectures were too "highbrow" for a popular audience. In light of Pond's observation, the modern evaluation of Fiske as "popularizer" must be understood to mean that he was an interpreter and teacher rather than an original thinker. It must not be taken to mean one who cheapens ideas in the service of "popular culture."

In accordance with Pond's suggestions Fiske proposed a series of lectures on great campaigns of the Civil War, illustrated with the aid of a stereopticon with maps, diagrams, portraits, and the like. However, as the *Boston Advertiser* had already noted, "Mr. Fiske makes no gestures and indulges in no high-flown rhetoric. . . . Part of the effect is due to the surpassing beauty of his language." For a low-key man like Fiske, Major Pond's legitimate but theatrical ideas were too taxing. Their association might have been successful if it had not exhausted Fiske physically. The price for gaining the freedom of time to write was too high to pay and he soon returned to his own methods of presentation.

The lectures were the germs for the books which were to follow, perhaps even the drafts from which the books grew. Both were intentionally "literary." In commenting on fellow historians like Francis Parkman and W. H. Prescott, Fiske focused on their ability to carry the narrative forward, to be poetic. *American Political Ideas Viewed from the Standpoint of Universal History* became the cornerstone for the whole project; here he demonstrates the application of his evolutionary philosophy to the interpretation of history. The intent of the book is to set forth the relationship between some fundamental ideas of American politics and the general history of mankind. Fiske focused on the meaning of the town meeting, traced its origins to village assemblies of early Aryans, showed its relationship to the federal union, and finally offered his dream of manifest destiny. Fiske's evolutionary concept is well-suited to his love of narrative since it insists upon a linear progression and is a constant marker that American history should be measured not in a vacuum but against the backdrop of all world history.

Fiske in 1867, the year he moved to Cambridge

Despite this broad view, Fiske's historical writings provoked criticism, both in his own time and later, such as Vernon Louis Parrington's observation that only a New Englander could have revealed such provincialism as to regard the town meeting as a "germinal source of American democracy." But the limitations were as much of the era as of Fiske personally: Henry Adams came under fire for similar provincial myopia. Writers of Parrington's generation, many of them from other parts of the country, were particularly sensitive to the "New England" orientation of their literary predecessors. Were the process as scientific as Fiske supposed, he would not have been led into prophecies as grimly amusing as time has made them. To Fiske, the world had become completely Anglo-Americanized, led by these two nations to Tennyson's "parliament of man and federation of the world" or to the point of "peaceful concerted action throughout the Whole."

The publication of *American Political Ideas Viewed from the Standpoint of Universal History* underlined Fiske's inability to produce a short history. By mutual consent the agreement with Harper was cancelled. It was replaced by a remarkable contract with Henry Houghton, who must have been both a true patron of the arts and a shrewd businessman. He was willing to take a risk in the hope of publishing works of high cultural value and long-term marketability. In effect the agreement put Fiske on a regular salary so that, as Clark has noted, he might be "placed at ease for the preparation of the fundamental works of his scheme, which required some years of patient research-study."

The first book under this agreement, *The Critical Period of American History, 1783-1789*, was published in 1888. It is a detailed examination of the period of American history which saw the slow and sometimes doubtful growth of the concept of a constitutional federal government whose powers superseded those of the states. Fiske's thesis has attracted a good deal of scholarly attention and has been equally refuted and defended. The book considers such major issues and events as the Constitutional Convention and Shay's Rebellion. Aware of the vital role of transportation and communication in the development of the country, Fiske underlines how fortunate it was for later periods that attention was given to those areas early on. Apropos of the system of checks and balances, he heavily criticizes the tyranny of democracy. It is a great relief to him to know that the independence of the executive branch can protect the citizenry "from the knavery and folly of our representatives."

The year 1889 saw the publication of a major work in the series, *The Beginnings of New England; or, The Puritan Theocracy and Its Relations to Civil and Religious Liberty*, essentially an expansion and illustration of the thesis in *American Political Ideas Viewed from the Standpoint of Universal History*. Fiske opens with a long prefatory chapter, "The Roman Idea and the English Idea," in which he traces the three main approaches used by a people in "nation-making": the Oriental method of conquest without incorporation, the Roman method of conquest with incorporation but without representation, and the English method of conquest with representaiton. From this overview he moves on to how vital Puritanism was in keeping alive the last and highest of these approaches. Puritan theology as it created certain philosophical and political ways of thinking is then taken to be the deciding thread in the growth of New England and hence in the development of the United States.

The early years of the 1890s found Fiske a very busy man. He published two textbooks for schools; in May of 1892 he went west to be ora-

tor at the centennial of the discovery and naming of the Columbia River; and he published *The Discovery of America, with Some Account of Ancient America and the Spanish Conquest* (1892), a work which filled a notable gap in his historical sequence. Most exciting was a meeting in San Francisco with John Muir, who persuaded Fiske to take a vacation in Alaska before returning home.

The Discovery of America is a two-volume project which discusses the separate but soon to be intermingled histories of the European world of Columbus's time and the American world to the west that lay virtually unknown. A good portion of the first volume is devoted to the western hemisphere before 1492. Fiske was remarkably alert to the need for Indian studies and among the first to recognize Major John Powell and George Catlin as leaders in this area. Many observers realized that the theme of the vanishing red man was not a mere romantic notion; but few scholars noted "that no time should be lost in gathering and putting on record all that can be learned of the speech and the arts, the customs and beliefs, everything that goes into the philology and anthropology of the red man."

As usual, Fiske's scholarship was wide-ranging. He used some highly dependable sources, such as Bartolomé de Las Casas, and others which were often secondary and, like Washington Irving, more literary than historical. Other historians, such as Edward Freeman (to whom this work was dedicated) and Sir Henry Maine, were also propounding the evolutionary view. However, as a favorable review in the *New York Sun* pointed out, no one else had so consistently tried to synthesize the American story. Irving had written a life of Columbus; Prescott the conquest of Mexico and Peru; and others had concerned themselves with other aspects; but Fiske swept the whole canvas.

In the late 1890s Fiske completed his picture of the colonial period with *Old Virginia and Her Neighbors* (1897) and *The Dutch and Quaker Colonies in America* (1899). Some critics again objected that Fiske, as well as other New England historians, tended to distort the facts, but in his preface to *Old Virginia and Her Neighbors* he states that he does not intend to write a history of these colonies but to "follow the main stream of causation from the time of Raleigh to the time of Dinwiddie, from its source to its absorption in the mightier stream." By choosing to begin in the Elizabethan age, Fiske allows his developmental theme to dominate so that Virginia gets the bulk

Fiske in the library of his Cambridge home, 1887

of attention and Georgia a mere mention. The focus is on the growth and development of political institutions and the implications of evolution that Fiske reads into this development. "In the unfolding of these events there is a poetic beauty and grandeur as the purpose of the infinite wisdom reveals itself in its cosmic process, slowly but inexorably, hasting but resting not, heedless of the clashing aims and discordant cries of short-sighted mortals, sweeping their tiny efforts into its majestic current, and making all contribute to the fulfillment of God's will."

Fiske acknowledges that earlier historians have failed to give due consideration to non-English founders of colonies. On the other hand, he argues, nearly all the constitutions of the world have been closely modeled on British concepts or on the federal and state consitutions of the United States during the nineteenth century, which proves that England had been preeminent as a colonizer. In "Mr. Fiske and the History of New York" (*North American Review*, August 1901), Mrs. Schuyler Van Rensselaer objects that "He identified the love and enjoyment of liberty too closely with the character of current political

instituitons." These volumes also have stylistic problems. In discussing the development of New York, for example, Fiske uses Irving's Knickerbocker history as a legitimate historical source. Concerned with creative color and poetry, he tends to forget that Irving was writing burlesque. As an avid reader of Dickens, Scott, and George Eliot, Fiske liked to turn to the creative writers and often found them closer to the truth than those he called "dry-as-dust historians." While he did not hesitate to criticize the poet who was inaccurate, he could still say that he had "known the conscientious poet to set public opinion right on a matter of history."

Turning to Pennsylvania, Fiske reveals his strong Federalist views. Though William Penn was remarkably democratic in his thinking, Fiske wrote, he thought of himself as a "kind of patriarch who knew much better what was good for his little sylvan community than the people themselves. In this assumption he was very likely correct." Fiske adds caustically: "But it is one of the features of a thorough-going democracy that those who don't know what is best should have a much greater part in government than those who do since they are more numerous." Penn was a born leader and his people were sensible enough to realize it.

The turn of the century found Fiske engaged in a number of projects. Some of the time was spent in revising his Civil War lectures for a volume called *The Mississippi Valley in the Civil War,* published in 1900. In the same year he received an invitation from the committee for the millennial celebration in honor of King Alfred to be held in Winchester in September 1901. His lectures before the Royal Institution in 1880 had made him so well known to the historians of England that he was unanimously chosen as best qualified to represent the Western world. He accepted the invitation and chose as his subject "The Beginnings of Federalism in New England, as related to the expansion of Alfred's World."

All of this was apparently carried on concurrently with a great deal of work on one more volume related to the colonial period, *New France and New England,* which was published posthumously in 1902. Though unfinished, it makes an interesting addition to the series by further demonstrating Fiske's colonization theory. France had long been Fiske's classic example of contemporary modifications of the Roman method, the approach used by absolute monarchy. The contrast is made between the more or less independent British colonies and the overprotective, overlegislative actions of the French kings. The book is finally a tribute to his friend Francis Parkman, a tribute made evident by heavy borrowings rather than by stated acknowledgment. Since this portion was all but finished, it is doubtful that Fiske would have done much to make it more his own—the work of other historians had more than once been woven in without apology when it met with his needs and his approval.

John Fiske died on 4 July 1901 in Gloucester, Massachusetts, and was buried in his beloved Petersham, where the Fiske family frequently spent their summers. The years between 1902 and 1909 saw the publication of Standard Library Editions of his works and other collections and reprints. The first major biography was John Spencer Clark's *The Life and Letters of John Fiske* in 1917. Though Fiske has not retained the reputation that he held in his lifetime, there has been a small but steady stream of scholarly interest during the twentieth century. Essentially he remains an important figure for historical reasons, for the role he played in the development of American intellectual and cultural history. Nevertheless

many of his works are still worth reading because of their lucidity, breadth of scope, and rare aptitude for making things concrete. The histories and letters particularly help present-day readers to recapture the sweep, excitement, and romance of the American past.

Letters:

The Personal Letters of John Fiske (Cedar Rapids, Iowa: Printed for the Bibliophile Society by Torch Press, 1939);

Ethel F. Fisk, ed., *The Letters of John Fiske* (New York: Macmillan, 1940).

Biographies:

Thomas S. Perry, *John Fiske* (Boston: Small, Maynard, 1906);

John Spencer Clark, *The Life and Letters of John Fiske* (Boston & New York: Houghton Mifflin, 1917);

Milton Berman, *John Fiske: The Evolution of a Popularizer* (Cambridge: Harvard University Press, 1961).

References:

Henry S. Commager, "John Fiske: An Interpretation," *Proceedings of the Massachusetts Historical Society,* 66 (1942): 332-345;

Albert B. Hart, "The Historical Service of John Fiske," *Connecticut Magazine,* 7 (1902-1903): 611-617;

James K. Hosmer, "Giants of Yesterday," *Boston Transcript,* 11 June 1911;

Russel B. Nye, "John Fiske and His Cosmic Philosophy," *Papers of the Michigan Academy of Science, Arts, and Letters,* 28 (1943): 685-698;

Josiah Royce, "John Fiske," *Unpopular Review,* 10 (1918): 160-189;

Royce, "John Fiske as Thinker," *Harvard Graduates' Magazine,* 10 (1901): 23-33;

J. B. Sanders, "John Fiske," *Mississippi Valley Historical Review,* 27 (1930): 264-277;

George P. Winston, *John Fiske* (New York: Twayne, 1972).

Papers:

A large collection of John Fiske's papers is in the Harvard College Library. Others are in the Princeton University Library, and there is also a notable collection in the Henry L. Huntington Library and Art Gallery in San Marino, California.

Horace Howard Furness
(2 November 1833-13 August 1912)

David Laird
California State University, Los Angeles

WORKS: *Prospectus of the First Volume, Containing Romeo and Juliet, of a Proposed New Variorum Edition of Shakespeare* (Philadelphia: Lippincott, 1870);

A New Variorum Edition of Shakespeare, volumes 1-15, 18, edited by Furness (Philadelphia & London: Lippincott, 1871-1913);

The Sacred Books of the Old and New Testaments: A New English Translation, edited by Paul Haupt with the assistance of Furness, 6 volumes (New York: Dodd, Mead, 1898-1899; London: Clarke, 1898-1899);

Records of a Lifelong Friendship, 1807-1882. Ralph Waldo Emerson and William Henry Furness, edited by Furness (Boston & New York: Houghton Mifflin, 1910).

Horace Howard Furness launched and guided the New Variorum Edition of Shakespeare, considered by many critics to have been the single most important project in Shakespearean scholarship and criticism in America in the nineteenth century, and one which, in this century, is rivaled only by Charlton Hinman's 1968 facsimile reproduction of the First Folio. The New Variorum Edition brought to American scholarship international recognition and commendation. By 1869 Furness had completed plans for the edition, which was designed to bring together the results of critical and textual commentary spanning a range of 300 years. The New Variorum thus would make available in one edition the best interpretative comments on each play, including those originally printed in English and translations into English of what had appeared in other languages, most notably in German and French

For the next forty-three years Furness devoted himself with unceasing energy to the monumental task of editing and publishing no fewer than fourteen plays and virtually completing another, *Cymbeline,* published with the assistance of his son, Horace H. Furness, Jr., in 1913. He undertook to reproduce the most nearly accurate play

Horace Howard Furness

texts that scholarship could provide together with the remarks of various commentators on the text and on the interpretation and valuation of individual plays. Each volume includes a systematic record of every textual variant in all the early editions (the Quartos and the four Folios) and in the important editions as well. The importance with which the New Variorium was viewed by British scholars and critics is indicated in a review appearing in *Blackwood's Magazine* in 1890: "In what is called 'The Variorum Edition of Shakespeare,' America has the honor of having produced the very best and most complete edition, so far as it has gone, of our great national poet."

In 1871, at the outset of the project, Furness wrote to William Aldis Wright, one of the editors of the Old Cambridge Shakespeare. He confessed to being worn down by the inevitable strains and frustrations of his editorship: "Is there anything on earth better calculated to teach self-distrust than the attempt to collate old editions or to reprint a Quarto? I am lost in wonder at the moderation of our ancestors in restricting to printers' boys the soubriquet of *devil,* and in not applying it to every member of the establishment. No one will more readily than yourself credit the laborious pains with which I collated Ashbee's Facsimile and your Reprint (which, you rightly conjectured, I used to print from). I fairly rubbed my nose over every word, and glared at every comma, and repeated the same process over the proof-sheets, and yet, out of that list that you kindly sent me, eighteen unpruned, unlettered, untrained, unconformed misprints seared my eyeballs!" But Furness persisted. The first of the series, *Romeo and Juliet,* appeared in 1871, the year he had written to Wright. Upon his death in 1912, the series was continued under the editorship of Furness's son, who edited and published the texts of five plays from 1908 to 1928. He, in turn, was succeeded by editors and scholars working under the auspices of the Modern Language Association of America which began its sponsorship in 1933 and continues in that role. The series is presently directed by the Committee on the New Variorum Edition with Robert K. Turner, Jr., serving as its general editor. The most recent publication is Mark Eccles's edition of *Measure for Measure* (1980).

The earlier volumes in the series are based on the text of the Old Cambridge Shakespeare edited from 1863 to 1866 by Wright, John Glover, and William George Clark. This nine-volume edition gained widespread recognition as the most authoritative of the "eclectic" or critical editions. Its value was more than scholarly; it formed the basis of the one-volume "Globe" Shakespeare (1864), intended for the popular market, which became the established text for most readers in the English-speaking world. In his edition of *Romeo and Juliet,* Furness drew upon the Cambridge Shakespeare as his primary text. Line, scene, and act numbering is that of the Cambridge edition. The Furness edition, however, includes a more complete record of textual variants and emendations and locates that record just below the printed text to which it refers. Though there is detailed acknowledgement of the text he chose to re-

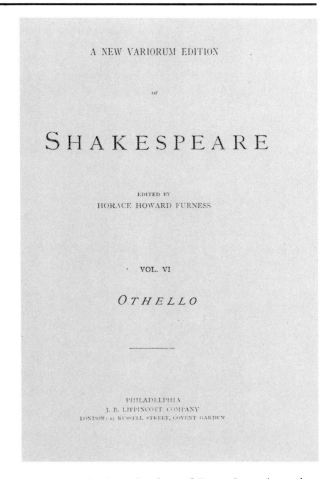

A NEW VARIORUM EDITION

OF

SHAKESPEARE

EDITED BY
HORACE HOWARD FURNESS

· VOL. VI

OTHELLO

PHILADELPHIA
J. B. LIPPINCOTT COMPANY
LONDON: 13 RUSSELL STREET, COVENT GARDEN

Title page for the sixth volume of Furness's massive and ambitious project

produce, Furness was nonetheless called upon to defend himself against a charge of plagiarism. In 1870 he produced the *Prospectus of the First Volume, Containing* Romeo and Juliet, *of a Proposed New Variorum Edition of Shakespeare,* in which he locates the distinctiveness of his edition in the collation of his primary text with all variant readings found in the four Folios, four out of five Quartos, and the texts of thirty-five later editions. The text in which each variant occurs is identified; the emendations of later editors are made clear and in some instances commented upon. No comparable sense of the critical history of the text is available to readers of the Cambridge Shakespeare. "In disputed passages," Furness wrote, "it is of great interest to see at a glance on which side lies the weight of authority."

Romeo and Juliet (1871), *Macbeth* (1873), *Hamlet* (two volumes, 1877), and *King Lear* (1880) all rely on the Cambridge Shakespeare. With *Othello* (1886) Furness significantly modified his editorial

Furness in his library (Furness Memorial Library, University of Pennsylvania)

practice, reproducing the text from his own copy of the First Folio. Even grant that "the First Folio is, as has been asserted, one of the most carelessly printed books ever issued from the press, it is, nevertheless, the only text that we have for at least sixteen of the plays, and condemn it as we may, 'still is its name in great account, it still hath power to charm.' " While Furness acknowledged the very considerable problems posed by the Folio text, he justified the decision to reproduce it on the grounds that by doing so he could remove himself from between reader and text. Thus the reader gains unmediated access to the single most important printed version of the plays, a version sponsored and overseen by Shakespeare's contemporaries. But the decision did not sit well with some critics. The eleventh edition of the *Encyclopaedia Britannica* (1910-1911), for example, notes that while the Variorum "has been generally accepted as a thorough and scholarly piece of work, its chief fault is that, beginning with Othello (1886), the editor used the First Folio text as his basis."

The edition does have a different look than that of its predecessors, reproducing as it does features of Jacobean typography including the long *s*, and thus constituting something of a challenge to readers unfamiliar with print-shop practice. It was a bold decision and Furness was under no illusion about the consequences. Of the project in general he wrote in his introduction to *Hamlet*: "I do not flatter myself that this is an enjoyable edition of Shakespeare. I regard it rather as a necessary evil." In 1877 he wrote to A. H. Dooley: "For the general 'everyday' reader the text of all the various editions does not differ enough to make it any matter which edition he uses. Choose, therefore, some edition in good legible type and on good paper and experience the purest delight that the drama can give." Yet for those devoted to the study of Shakespeare's text as well as to its enjoyment, Furness remained firm in his advocacy of the Folio text: "Who am I that I should thrust myself in between the student and the text, as though in me resided the power to restore Shakespeare's own words?" More recent scholarship has in large measure vindicated Furness's decision to follow the Folio text which, as Charlton Hinman puts it, is "the most authoritative surviving text for most, though not for all, of Shakespeare's plays." It is, perhaps, noteworthy that in the New Variorum Edition of *Measure for Measure* (1980), Eccles also reproduced the First Folio as his primary text. According to Georgianna Ziegler, the curator of the Furness Memorial Library at the University of Pennsylvania, Furness "foreshadowed the current scholarship which reconsiders the importance of the earliest versions of Shakespeare's texts."

Furness was able to have the text of *Othello* set from his own copy of the Folio. In the course of his labors he had built an extensive collection of Elizabethan and Jacobean printed texts (a set of the Folios and no fewer than twenty-two Quartos) together with works of textual criticism and interpretive commentary. The collection, some 7,000 volumes in Furness's time and now numbering over 25,000 volumes, resides in the Furness Memorial Library. It constitutes one of the first major collections of Shakespeareana in the United States and is the more remarkable for having come into being well before Shakespeare entered the academic curriculum or was held to be an appropriate subject for research at the university or college level. The earliest reference to Shakespeare in a college or university catalogue is that of 1855 at the University of Virginia. Harvard's first offerings in English literature (in 1872-1873) included a course in philology based on Chaucer and Shakespeare and another in composition in which *Hamlet* was one of the assigned texts.

If the study of Shakespeare found little in the way of institutional support, it was still possible for those wishing to pursue that study to do so in concert with others in reading groups and societies. Of major importance to Furness was the Shakspere Society of Philadelphia, founded in 1851 by four young men, three of whom were then engaged in the practice of law. The society (originally called Shakspere Apostles) has the distinction of being the oldest continuing group devoted to the study of Shakespeare. Furness was elected to membership in 1860 and served as its presiding officer or "dean" from 1879 to 1912. It is reported that he used to ask his fellow members their views on the verbal cruces in the lines of the play they were reading, or their interpretation of one of its scenes or situations, and furthermore, "a number of the matters mooted by his

questions were thrashed out into the fine wheat of the Variorum notes." Indeed, there is reason to believe that his association with the Shakspere Society sparked the plan for his monumental research project. He is on record as having been frustrated by the discrepancies and inaccuracies of the various editions in use by members of the society.

Throughout his life, Furness was sustained in his solitary labors by an extraordinary range of friendships and by a network of social and domestic relationships. The Furness household was a center of intellectual and artistic activity, dominated for a time at least by the enlivening presence of Furness's father, the Reverend William H. Furness, of whom Emerson wrote: "He had a face like a benediction, and a speech like a benefaction, and his stories more curative than the Philadelphia Faculty of Medicine." Emerson and the elder Furness maintained a regular correspondence, collected and published in 1910 by Horace Howard Furness as *Records of a Lifelong Friendship, 1807-1882. Ralph Waldo Emerson and William Henry Furness*. A striking feature of that correspondence is the repeated plea to Emerson to become more actively engaged in the antislavery movement. Joining the household in 1860 and destined to become a sustaining influence was Furness's wife, Helen Kate Furness (1837-1883), who gained scholarly acclaim in her own right by compiling *A Concordance to the Poems of Shakespeare* (1872). It was a distinguished intellectual family and not ashamed to be so.

In addition to his scholarly pursuits and activities shared with his immediate family and friends, Furness carried on a flourishing exchange of ideas with a wide range of acquaintances in this country and abroad, including active Shakespeareans in England, France, and Germany. He was first drawn to Shakespeare when at the age of fourteen he heard Fanny Kemble read from the plays, and among his close friends in later years were leading actors and actresses who possessed a familiarity with Shakespeare in performance which he eagerly sought. He was himself a gifted reader; it was said that he possessed the power to lose himself past finding in every character he portrayed, including Cleopatra.

The honorary degree of Ph.D. was conferred upon him by the University of Halle in 1878, that of LL.D. by the University of Pennsylvania in 1879, by Harvard in 1894, and by Yale in 1901. Cambridge University conferred the Litt.D.

in 1899. In an address delivered in the name of the American Philosophical Society in May 1913, J. J. Jusserand, editor of *Piers Plowman* (1894), author of the *History of the Literature of the English People* (1895-1909), and, at the time, the Ambassador of France to the United States, paid yet another tribute to this tireless citizen of the republic of letters: "But so far as anything in this fleeting world may be held to remain, so long as mankind shall be able to appreciate honest work honestly done, the name of Furness will not pass away, but live enshrined in every scholar's grateful memory."

References:

James M. Gibson, "Horace Howard Furness: Book Collector and Library Builder," in *Shakespeare Study Today: The Horace Howard Furness Memorial Lectures,* edited by Georgianna Ziegler (New York: AMS Press, 1986);

J. J. Jusserand, "Horace Howard Furness," in his *With Americans of Past and Present Days* (New York: Scribners, 1916);

James G. McManaway, "Shakespeare in the United States," in *Studies in Shakespeare, Bibliography and Theater* (New York: Shakespeare Association of America, 1969);

Joseph G. Price, "The Cultural Phenomenon of Shakespeare," in *William Shakespeare: His World, His Work, His Influence,* edited by John F. Andrews (New York: Scribners, 1985);

Agnes Repplier, "Horace Howard Furness," *Atlantic Monthly,* 110 (1912): 624-628;

Henry L. Savage, "The Shakespeare Society of Philadelphia," *Shakespeare Quarterly,* 3 (1952): 341-352;

George Walton Williams, "The Publishing and Editing of Shakespeare's Plays," in *William Shakespeare: His World, His Work, His Influence,* edited by Andrews (New York: Scribners, 1985);

Talcott Williams, "Our Great Shakspere Critic—Horace Howard Furness," *Century,* 85, new series 63 (1912): 109-115;

Owen Wister, "Horace Howard Furness: A Short Memoir," *Harvard Graduates' Magazine,* 21 (1912): 201-210;

Georgianna Ziegler, "The Horace Howard Furness Memorial Library," *Jahrbuch der Deutschen Shakespeare-Gesellschaft West* (Bochum, West Germany, 1985);

Ziegler, Introduction to *Shakespeare Study Today: The Horace Howard Furness Memorial Lectures* (New York: AMS Press, 1986).

Papers:

The Horace Howard Furness Memorial Library quartered in the Van Pelt Library of the University of Pennsylvania contains unpublished letters, notebooks, and journals. The Henry E. Huntington Library, San Marino, California, has unpublished letters by Furness including those in the Annie Adams Fields and James Thomas Fields collection. There are also unpublished Furness letters at the Folger Shakespeare Library, Washington, D.C.

Richard Watson Gilder

(8 February 1844-18 November 1909)

Herbert F. Smith
University of Victoria

BOOKS: *The New Day: A Poem in Songs and Sonnets* (New York: Scribner, Armstrong, 1876);
The Poet and His Master and Other Poems (New York: Scribners, 1878);
Lyrics and Other Poems (New York: Scribners, 1885; London: Hutt, 1886)–includes *The New Day* and *The Poet and His Master;*
The Celestial Passion (New York: Century, 1887);
Two Worlds and Other Poems (New York: Century, 1891; London: Unwin, 1891);
The Great Remembrance and Other Poems (New York: Century, 1893);
In Palestine and Other Poems (New York: Century, 1898);
Poems and Inscriptions (New York: Century, 1901);
"In the Heights" (New York: Century, 1905);
The Fire Divine (New York: Century, 1907);
Lincoln the Leader and Lincoln's Genius for Expression (Boston & New York: Houghton Mifflin, 1909);
Grover Cleveland: A Record of Friendship (New York: Century, 1910).

PERIODICAL PUBLICATIONS: "Certain Tendencies in Current Literature," *New Princeton Review,* 4 (July 1887): 1-20;
"Journalism and American Literature," *The Critic,* new series 15 (7 February 1891): 71;
"An 'Open Letter' about Editing," *Independent,* 48 (10 December 1896): 1669-1670;
"The Newspaper, the Magazine, and the Public," *Outlook,* 61 (4 February 1899): 317-321.

For thirty-nine of the most eventful years in American literature (1870-1909) Richard Watson Gilder controlled or helped to control the fortunes of one of the most influential magazines in America. As assistant editor of *Scribner's Monthly Magazine* and as editor-in-chief of its successor, the *Century Monthly Magazine,* his power as an editor was second to none. But his critical writings per se, many of them never published at all and the rest confined to ephemeral publications or unindexed in his own magazines, do not provide

Gilder at his desk in the Century Monthly Magazine *office*

the kind of canon one usually associates with a significant critic. An editor, from one point of view at least, may be no more obtrusively present in the literature of his time than the midwife who presides at the birth of a great man may be in his biography. Yet, from another and a more profound point of view, an editor may do more to shape the literature of a period than any single writer–novelist, poet, or critic–could possibly do. An editor is by his very nature a critic, performs all the functions of a critic, and is, in fact, more powerful than a critic in his efforts upon literature because his critical judgments are not delivered ex post facto. Thus a true perception of

Gilder the literary critic requires at least some consideration of Gilder the magazine editor.

Gilder was born on 8 February 1844 in Bordentown, New Jersey, where his father, the Reverend William Henry Gilder, was a Methodist minister and headmaster of a girls' school. After acquiring the consent of his mother, Jane Nutt Gilder, he enlisted in the First Philadelphia Artillery in 1863 but saw little action during the Civil War. In 1864 he took a job as paymaster on the Camden and Amboy Railroad, and he began working for various newspapers shortly after the war. His first literary effort was an edition of the poems of Ellen Clementine Howarth, for which he wrote an eight-page introduction in 1867. In 1869, while working as a reporter on the *Newark Morning Register*, he joined the staff of a moribund monthly, *Hours at Home*, as a second job. When that magazine was reorganized to create the new *Scribner's Monthly*, he became assistant editor under Josiah Gilbert Holland. His career was tied to that magazine and the magazine it became, the *Century*, for the rest of his life.

Gilder's earliest literary interest was poetry, and he published "slender volumes" with titles like *The New Day: A Poem in Songs and Sonnets* (1876; in conscious imitation of Dante's *Vita Nuova*) and *The Poet and His Master and Other Poems* (1878) throughout his lifetime. Though his poetry is considered undistinguished today, his literary influence was such that he was chosen by Houghton Mifflin in 1908 to be the first living poet in a projected series of "American Household Poets." The vision of Gilder's poems among the pots and pans, as it were, is ludicrous now, but in 1908 it was a singular honor to be chosen for a series that was to include Bryant, Longfellow, Lowell, and Whittier.

However, Gilder's "success" as a poet probably reflects more on his power as a critic than on his artistry. As editor of one of the most influential American monthlies, he held the keys to access to the public for any poet with ambition. For a poet to be published in the *Century* in the 1890s meant for his career about what it means for a contemporary poet to appear in the *New Yorker*. In general it was a closed shop, available only to poets who were willing to submit to "editing" to a standard of poetic excellence that was really a measure of submission to what is now called the Genteel Tradition. The result was a predictable gush of sameness that Gilder was aware enough of to permit a parody in this satire by R. K. Munkittrick published in the *Century* in 1890:

Gilder and Helena deKay at the time of their marriage, 1874

> 'T is Ever Thus,
> Ad Astra, De Profundis,
>   Keats, Bacchus, Sophocles;
> Ars Longa, Euthanasia
>   Spring, The Eumenides.
> ....
> Dum Vivimus, Vivamus,
>   Sleep, Palingenesis;
> Salvini, Sursum Corda,
>   At Mt. Desert, To Miss——.
>
> These are part of the contents
>   Of "Violets of Song,"
> The first poetic volume
>   Of Susan Mary Strong.

For all his acceptance of the poetic standards of his time, Gilder was not incapable, when the occasion arose, of recognizing poetic genius. He shared with his friend Arthur Stedman an enthusiasm for the late poems of Herman Melville and published a memorial tribute upon Melville's death in the *Century*, consisting of five of these poems and a preface by Stedman. But his most significant deviation from the tradition of mediocrity prevalent with regard to the poetry of his day is undoubtedly his espousal of the cause of Walt Whitman. His treatment of Whitman is the more unusual because their first contacts were anything but propitious. Whitman submitted some poems to *Scribner's Monthly* while Holland was the editor which were rejected, Whitman noted, "not . . . mildly, noncommittedly, in the customary manner, but with a note of the most offensive character." To Holland, Whitman was an "old wretch" whose writings were full of "smut" and whose art was "a monster or a bastard, and will have no progeny." For Whitman, Holland "was a man of his time, not possessed of the slightest forereach. . . . The style of man . . . who can tell the difference between a dime and a fifty cent piece— but is useless for occasions of more serious moment."

Gilder defied his boss on this issue, insisting that Whitman be included in a series of articles on American poets planned for the magazine. "No review of the American poets," he argued, "could ignore a man who made himself so much talked-of at home and abroad." Gilder won the point, and Holland gave his grudging assent. From the first time he had looked into *Leaves of Grass* (1855) Gilder recognized Whitman's genius. He often carried around with him a battered copy of Whitman's poem and collared surprised bystanders to read passages from it and demand that they acknowledge its greatness. When Holland left the magazine, its treatment of Whitman changed instantly. Just a few months before his death, Whitman acknowledged that Gilder, in accepting everything he submitted and "never interjecting a single word of petty criticism," provided him with the kind of treatment "no other magazine editor in America" had given him.

Gilder's admiration for Whitman's poetry led him to give the keynote address at Whitman's seventieth birthday celebration on 31 May 1889. He used the occasion for careful criticism of the poet's work as well as for the type of praise such an occasion demanded. He surprised everyone by concentrating on Whitman's form, an aspect of his writing for which Gilder had a good deal of empathy because he had tried himself to use open form in some poems, without noticeable success. He remarked that all who tried to imitate Whitman's style had failed; he had certainly adequate experience of reading free-verse submissions to the *Century* to make that judgment (although it should be noted that Gilder was open to Ernest Fenollosa's Whitmanesque experi-

ments in Oriental poetry). His conclusions concerning Whitman's oeuvre were that its sensuality was a necessary part, that "because he covers both the flesh and the spirit . . . Whitman reaches some of the loftiest minds of our day."

However, full sympathy with Whitman was beyond Gilder's capability. Much later, in a letter to Bliss Perry dated 21 October 1906, he revealed that he believed Whitman suffered from what Gilder called "the defect of the quality"— that is, his unconventionality was needed to make him a great poet, but it led him to go too far in his rediscovery of the sensual. Gilder could recognize the virtue of defamiliarization but needed limits on its application.

Gilder's own ambition was to be a poet, and poetic theory commanded much of his attention; but he lived and worked in an age of prose, and his major critical contributions were to prose fiction. Perhaps the most important movement of this period was the southern renaissance after the Civil War. Gilder was in a fortunate position as the editor of the magazine that set out to reconcile the North and South as a matter of editorial policy. Gilder contributed to that policy by encouraging southern writers, by aiding them with practical critical and editorial advice, and by providing them with a theory of literature which served virtually as a raison d'être. Gilder's encouragement of writing in the South ranged from seeking out new talent (he sent Edward King through the South on such an errand and was rewarded with the discovery of George Washington Cable) to nourishing their tropical blooms in the frigid North (Joel Chandler Harris, in particular, was so shy and sensitive that Gilder threw out the rule book for the treatment of writers just to insure that Harris's self-confidence was never shaken).

Harris and many other southern writers (like Thomas Nelson Page and Cable) needed extensive help in structuring their fictions and especially in resisting the temptation to provide inartistic didactic conclusions. In his editorial letters to southern writers in particular, Gilder frequently pointed out the need to let the story point the moral or the message. In the case of Cable, Gilder went so far as to encourage him to come north to avoid the persecution he was suffering at the hands of his neighbors but warned him that an "untrained or misapplied conscience" could ruin his career. "You and I do not object," he wrote, "to the patriotism and philanthropy of Tourguenieff . . . because the form is always artis-

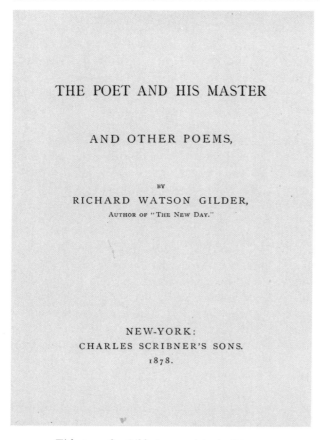

THE POET AND HIS MASTER

AND OTHER POEMS,

BY
RICHARD WATSON GILDER,
AUTHOR OF "THE NEW DAY."

NEW-YORK:
CHARLES SCRIBNER'S SONS.
1878.

Title page for Gilder's second book of poems

tic." It is extremely doubtful that many of the writers Gilder encouraged could have succeeded without the delicate editorial touch that he provided them.

Gilder's theoretical contribution to the rebirth of southern literature appears in a speech entitled "The Development of Southern Literature," which he wrote about 1880 and gave on numerous occasions during the following two decades. "It is of the essence of literature," he wrote, ignoring the examples of Greece and Rome, "that it should be free. It must criticize life without reserve." From that basis he argued that emancipation had freed southern writing no less than the Negro. Only after the South had given up its "peculiar institution" could its writers consider freely and honestly the problems of human relationship. Pre-Civil War writers, he believed, had either written polemics or had fallen back on an escapist's romanticism that was only "the second fiddle to Cooper's second fiddle of Scott." The theory had its flaws, but it served as an invitation to a generation of southern writers to develop and prosper from their craft.

Gilder did not serve quite such an elementary purpose for most of the other writers he edited; the *Century* was not as important a publishing resource for the American West as it was for the South, and the *Atlantic Monthly* retained its cachet as *the* intellectual monthly compared to the more popular *Century*. Nevertheless, Gilder was an important force in the literary development of the three most important writers of fiction of his day: William Dean Howells, Henry James, and Mark Twain.

When Howells quit his editorial position with the *Atlantic Monthly* to devote himself full-time to his fiction, he very possibly did so because he knew he could place virtually everything he wrote with the *Century*. He had his pick of American magazines during the years 1880 to 1885, but fifteen of his subsequent twenty-nine periodical contributions, including serializations of four of his five novels written during this period, went to the *Century*. Gilder's letters to Howells are written with an assumption of congruence of critical opinions that allows for a kind of shorthand. In a letter dated 16 December 1882 he stated that "The modern novel . . . is getting a pretty thorough overhauling. . . . The new novel . . . will add fuel to the fire. . . . Gosse was frightened at first . . . but he now feels that the Channel waters are not going to swamp us." Such correspondence gives the reader the sense of an exhilarating conspiracy to make over the modern novel into a form perfected from American realism, thumbing their noses at the reservations of the more conservative English, building instead from the standards of the great continental examples: Tolstoy, Turgenev, Maupassant.

Nonetheless, Gilder was a practical editor, and in 1883 he had to begin discouraging Howells from placing his fiction in the *Century*. Howells had appeared in twenty-two of twenty-four issues of the magazine and had commitments for serialization of two more novels (*A Woman's Reason*, 1883; and *The Rise of Silas Lapham*, 1885) plus some travel sketches. Gilder's refusal to commit the magazine to more of Howells's output was certainly justified by the realities of magazine publishing, but it was such a blow to Howells's plans to continue independently as a novelist that he soon returned to editing, accepting a position with *Harper's Monthly*.

Gilder's influence on Henry James's career was also first positive and then frustrating. Gilder cultivated James as a contributor of the same kind of New Realism that Howells espoused, but

Gilder, circa 1880, in a studio portrait by G. C. Cox

never again sought to publish any of James's later work.

Gilder's relationship with Mark Twain was more complex than with any of the other major writers of his day. He had his position, with Joseph Hopkins Twichell and Howells, among those Twain liked to scandalize, and he deserved a place in Van Wyck Brooks's *The Ordeal of Mark Twain* (1923), although he was never mentioned there. He was mentioned, as a bowdlerizer of Twain's work, in Bernard DeVoto's reply to Brooks's work, *Mark Twain's America* (1932). The basis of the accusation lies mainly in the prepublication of three excerpts from *Huckleberry Finn* between December 1884 and February 1885 in the *Century*. By failing to consider that the excerpts were not intended to be anything more than prepublication advertising for the work, DeVoto and those who followed him blithely assumed that Gilder's cuts in the text were to censor it, when they were actually only made because of the limitations of space. Gilder himself admitted that some of the cuts were made with "regard for our audience" but added in a letter to Twain dated 10 October 1884 that he had a "'robustuous taste' (for a pharisaical dude)" and would not mutilate his work. Much more to the point, the *Century* later published a promotional excerpt from *A Connecticut Yankee in King Arthur's Court* (1889) that included details that were censored from the novel and a serialization of *Pudd'nhead Wilson* (1894) that was not expurgated at all. Far from being a bowdlerizer, Gilder was the only editor in America who consistently supported Twain's not always popular genius.

Of course, the great limitation upon Gilder's career as editor or critic was his genteel taste with regard to things sexual. He was no more prudish than other editors of his period, but he was also no less. Moreover, he was not averse to explaining in print why he felt a need to be on guard against "salaciousness and gross sensationalism." "There are many who believe that America has the purest society in the world," he wrote. "Is not this purity worth paying for with a little prudery?" He believed sincerely that it was the duty of the "best and honorablest" to set an example for those who were less fully evolved, and he believed absolutely in "not preaching letting loose." However, as can be seen by his treatment of the works of Twain and Howells, he was always willing to make exceptions in the case of genius. He also believed in a "free market" philosophy of publication: that "works of real art, of

their relationship foundered on the disaster of the serialization of *The Bostonians* (1886). The novel was so unsuccessful that one of the editors of the magazine only half-jokingly suggested that James and one other of the magazine's editors who had prepared it for printing were the only ones who had read it. Gilder wrote James a lengthy critique of the novel, and James did attempt to "improve" it with some revisions for book publication, but it remained the one novel with which he was most disappointed, so much so that he did not include it in the New York edition of his works. It is easy for the modern critic to see in the failure of both Gilder and James to recognize the greatness of the novel the "defect of the quality" of all critics of the period who were convinced of the revolutionary value of realism to the point that they could not imagine a literary value beyond realism. James's disappointment was so great he left America for an illusory haven in England. Gilder remained, but he too was so disillusioned by the experience that he

Gilder, second from left, speaking with Jean Clemens at the dinner held to honor Samuel Clemens on his seventieth birthday
(Museum of the City of New York)

real power" would always find some kind of publisher in America. Within these limits, Gilder strove for the improvement of American writing, always preferring the native product over the imported when he had a choice. He was one of the prime movers in America for international copyright and believed that the success of that movement (with the signing of the 1891 treaty) was the single most important step in the status of American writers–an opinion that time has modified but not rejected entirely.

The twentieth century has not been kind to Gilder. Alfred Kazin in *On Native Grounds* (1942) accused him of calling himself a "squire of poesy" and writing several volumes of verse while becoming a "perfect symbol of all that the new writers were to detest." Gilder was much more than that. As a force in the development of American literature, he is important both for his promotion of American writing by his perceptive editing and critical encouragement of thousands of American writers over a period of forty years and for the editorial genius with which he sup-

ported such writers as Whitman, Cable, Howells, and Twain. He suffered from many of the limitations of his age. He could be prudish, his critical ideas were often conservative, and he sometimes did serve as a bastion for the "genteel tradition." He was not, however, a symbol. He was an intelligent critic and editor and, what is perhaps more important, a man aware of his own limitations and the limitations of his age. Doubtless he will always be remembered as the man who found Stephen Crane's *Maggie: A Girl of the Streets* (1893) "too honest," and who told Cable to take "Posson Jone'" elsewhere–editorial miscalculations that could probably be multiplied a hundred times in his own case, and just as often for any editor who ever took blue pencil to manuscript or wrote a letter of rejection. But Gilder should also be remembered for the real services he performed for American writers and for the many instances when his judgment was correct, when his vision exceeded that of his own age, and when his courage was extended beyond his own limits.

Letters:

Letters of Richard Watson Gilder, edited by Rosamond Gilder (Boston & New York: Houghton Mifflin, 1916; London: Constable, 1917).

References:

Robert Berkleman, "Mrs. Grundy and Richard Watson Gilder," *American Quarterly,* 4 (1952): 66-72;

Samuel C. Chew, *Fruit among the Leaves* (New York: Appleton-Century-Crofts, 1950);

James L. Ford, *Forty-Odd Years in the Literary Shop* (New York: Dutton, 1921);

Carlin T. Kindilien, *American Poetry in the Eighteen-Nineties* (Providence, R.I.: Brown University Press, 1956);

Ludwig Lewisohn, *Expression in America* (New York & London: Harper, 1932);

James L. Onderdonk, *History of American Verse (1610-1897)* (Chicago: McClurg, 1901);

Arthur L. Scott, "The *Century Magazine* Edits *Huckleberry Finn,* 1884-1885," *American Literature,* 27 (November 1955): 356-362;

Herbert F. Smith, "Joel Chandler Harris's Contributions to *Scribner's Monthly* and *The Century Magazine,* 1880-1887," *Georgia Historical Quarterly,* 47 (June 1963): 169-179;

Smith, *Richard Watson Gilder* (New York: Twayne, 1970);

Smith and Michael Peinovich, "*The Bostonians:* Creation and Revision," *Bulletin of the New York Public Library,* 73 (May 1969): 298-308;

Edward C. Wagenknecht, "Richard Watson Gilder: Poet and Editor of the Transition," *Boston University Studies in English,* 1 (1955): 84-95.

Papers:

The Manuscript Division of the New York Public Library holds Richard Watson Gilder's personal papers as well as the "Gilder Letterbooks," letterpress copies of letters sent by Gilder from the Century Company offices, and the "Century Papers," the archives of the Century Company. However, these files are incomplete, as many of the letters received were separated from the archives and sold at an auction held by the Anderson Galleries, New York, 3 and 4 December 1928. The MLA *Checklist of Holdings of American Literary Manuscripts in . . . Libraries of the United States* lists forty-six libraries with holdings of manuscripts relating to Gilder.

Henry Giles

(1 November 1809-10 July 1882)

John W. Rathbun
California State University, Los Angeles

BOOKS: *Christian Thought on Life* (Boston: Ticknor, Reed & Fields, 1850; London: Whitfield, 1867);

Lectures and Essays, 2 volumes (Boston: Ticknor, Reed & Fields, 1850);

Illustrations of Genius, in Some of its Relations to Culture and Society (Boston: Ticknor & Fields, 1854);

Human Life in Shakespeare (Boston: Lee & Shepard, 1868);

Lectures and Essays on Irish and Other Subjects (New York: Sadlier, 1869);

Sketches of Celebrated Irishmen, Irish Characters, Etc. (New York: Kenedy, Excelsior Catholic Publishing House, 1896).

PERIODICAL PUBLICATIONS: "The New Exodus," *Christian Examiner*, 52 (May 1852): 361-384;

"The Growing and Perpetual Influence of Shakespeare," *Christian Examiner*, 67 (September 1859): 178-207;

"Francis Bacon," *North American Review*, 93 (July 1861): 149-178;

"The Philosophy of History," *North American Review*, 95 (July 1862): 163-188.

Henry Giles

Henry Giles was active in the Boston-area Unitarian fellowship and had a marked taste for both literature and social issues. The Common Sense orientation of the Scottish school provided him his philosophical basis. Within that theory he used a number of critical premises with liberal flexibility. His topical interests are often representative of mid-nineteenth-century America, but intellectual breadth, a sensible appreciation of literature as an art form, and a sensitive spirit save him from the flat prosiness of many of his contemporaries. The Coleridgean doctrine of imagination enabled him to view the writer as active, observant, creative, and intuitive, while Thomas de Quincey's distinction between the literature of knowledge and the literature of power sanctioned the linking of imagination and intel-

lect without compromising the idea that literature is a distinct form of communication. The Scottish doctrine of sympathy was employed in two senses: sympathy was the means by which the writer came to understand the signs of nature and to translate them into artistic signs; and when cultivated in the reader it served to spot just how these signs corresponded with one another. In his best criticism these critical premises unobtrusively inform his approach.

There is little to glean of Giles's biography. He was born in Crokford, County Wexford, Ireland. Raised a Roman Catholic, he attended the

Royal Academy at Belfast and apparently studied for the priesthood. Upon his conversion to Unitarianism he moved to Greenock, Scotland, where he preached for two years, then preached for three more in Liverpool. As a member of the Unitarian fellowship in Liverpool, he participated in the Unitarian-Episcopalian controversy of 1839, delivering four of the thirteen lectures offered in the series.

The following year he immigrated to the United States and settled in the Boston area. The resettlement improved neither his financial resources nor his persistently poor health. He likely occupied a Unitarian pulpit in one of the Boston suburbs, remained active in defending Unitarianism in sermons and pamphlets, opposed slavery while staying in the good graces of southerners, published articles on a variety of subjects in such journals as *North American Review* and *Christian Examiner,* and between 1850 and 1868 published three books that were for the most part on literary subjects. Of these, *Human Life in Shakespeare* (1868) was the most popular with his contemporaries. Just before its publication he was struck with a form of paralysis which finally so enfeebled him that he had to be cared for by the Unitarian Association. The obituary in the *Boston Evening Transcript* lists the date of death as 11 July but other sources agree on his dying 10 July 1882 in Hyde Park, Massachusetts.

Giles's first book of criticism was the two-volume edition *Lectures and Essays* (1850). About half the essays are on literature. The remainder address such matters as Irish history and character, liberty, patriotism, and music. Virtually all the literary essays are character studies, but within this approach Giles does ring some changes, and the range is wide. The study of Falstaff is the only one addressed to a fictional character and is devoted to the ways that Shakespeare's genius managed to work such a reprobate into an attractive personality with and at whom we can laugh. Oliver Goldsmith, Thomas Chatterton, Richard Savage, and Dermody are given perfunctory treatment, while the essays on George Crabbe and Thomas Carlyle are rather more interesting. The essay on Ebenezer Elliott of Corn Law fame evokes Giles's proletarian sympathies. Two essays on the moral spirit of Lord Byron's life and genius are several cuts above the rest.

Throughout the essays Giles's habitual stance is a rich appreciation of the imponderables and incongruities of life as they diverge toward either tragedy or comedy. Reference to critical "laws" and appeals to probability occur on occasion, but Giles's sensibility is moral rather than imaginative as he explores how the inward thoughts and associations of his subjects establish "archetypes" which frame and define concepts of man and society. The essay on Carlyle, for example, pays tribute to Carlyle's intellectual and critical strengths and complains that the later style is more to be borne than appreciated, but the focus of the essay is on weighing in the balance Carlyle's reactionary prejudices and the undeniable power of his social criticism.

The judicious equipoise so characteristic of Giles's approach is especially conspicuous in the essays on Byron. He accepts the fact of Byron's genius and locates it in Byron's strength of passion and of will, a facile memory, exhaustless powers of association, and a "most happy aptitude of utterance." Byron's diction and thought are seen as wholly interfused and possessed of an eloquence that moves beyond a "purely imaginative poetry" to arouse, convince, and act on the passions. Giles is more interested in the poetry as an extension of the poet, however. Byron's egocentricity exacted its price. Himself a voluptuary whose appetites soon faded into dejection, moral conflict, and disorganized vitality, the poems are so directly reflective of Byron's personality that Giles sees no chance for Byron ever to have become a dramatic poet, despite the narrative thrust of much of his verse. What helped Byron, Giles thinks, was the fortunate congruence of his psychological insurgency and the revolutionary tumult of his period. Political revolt overthrew governments, and contemporaneous literary revolt overthrew literary tradition and the conventions on which that tradition relied. The result for Byron and others was the impulse to create and invent anew. Their poetry was turbulent. It expressed the force of "the free life." It was destructive of the authority of tradition, assertive of personal and social independence. Basically a loner, Byron responded to his times, but he was neither priest nor prophet of a movement. He was, says Giles, "simply the pilgrim of the age, walking through its waste places with a solitary spirit."

Four years later Giles published *Illustrations of Genius, in Some of its Relations to Culture and Society* (1854). It is a better book, though stylistically it suffers from a propensity to string together parallel illustrative clauses for the sake of rhetorical effect. Its strengths are a reflective and wide-ranging intelligence and an appreciation of literature as a unique but logical mode of communication.

The two opening chapters on Cervantes and *Don Quixote* are workmanlike, while the chapter "Fiction" has some good things to say but obscures its points by too great a preoccupation with the habits of the popular reading public and the poor quality of much fiction. In chapters on *The Scarlet Letter,* William Wordsworth, and de Quincey, Giles hits his stride. Considering that Giles was writing on *The Scarlet Letter* less than four years after its publication, to place it on the level of artistic achievement that he does seems singular. He correctly sees how Hawthorne revitalized the creaky "machinery" of the Custom House opening; the fictional use of old documents to achieve verisimilitude had been common since the eighteenth century. And he is acute in pointing out how Hawthorne deepens the troubled vision of his novel by countering its narrative clarity with overtones of a "mystic and a mythical obscurity." As for the characters, they have a mystery about them of "peculiar and solemn destinies" which raises them to the level of the "mythical." Hester, noble rather than meek, heroic rather than penitent, is placed within the stoic rather than the Christian tradition. Circumstance does not conquer her, but neither does she conquer circumstance. Indeed, says Giles, we almost "lose sight of the sinner in the heroine." No absolution of Hawthorne is necessary: genius does not have to attend on a "formal moral."

Throughout his chapters Giles consistently views literature as an art form which provides enjoyment even while it acts upon the mind. Literature thus affords critical as well as emotional enjoyment: "every man has the witness in himself; he is at once the instrument upon which the master plays and a critic of the player." In most cases the reader can take the literary imagination for granted and simply inquire into its degree and kind. The imaginative element in literature, however, does suggest what the objective in reading should be. Reading is not a means for acquiring knowledge but rather a means for spotting and responding to wisdom. That wisdom is located in verbal contexts which Giles calls "signs." Signs serve as the meeting ground of writer and reader. "Truth lies in signs even to the most exact thinkers," says Giles, who then observes that even God uses "analogy and allegory" in speaking with man. The reference to analogy suggests that Giles has something in mind similar to Emerson's discussion of signs in *Nature* (1836).

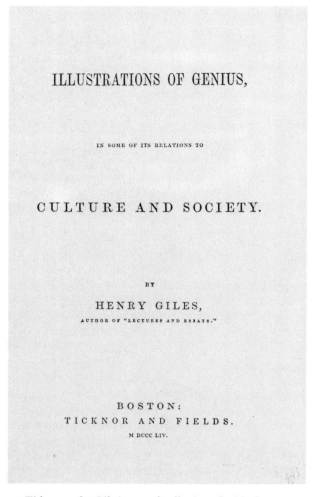

ILLUSTRATIONS OF GENIUS,

IN SOME OF ITS RELATIONS TO

CULTURE AND SOCIETY.

BY

HENRY GILES,
AUTHOR OF "LECTURES AND ESSAYS."

BOSTON:
TICKNOR AND FIELDS.
M DCCC LIV.

Title page for Giles's second collection of critical essays

But Giles actually goes beyond Emerson to anticipate Ferdinand de Saussure's idea that semiotic argument must distinguish between what signifies and what is signified.

Unfortunately Giles does not systematically apply the distinction in his criticism, but on two occasions this idea of signs does work for him. In discussing de Quincey's power and originality as a critic, Giles finds their source in the logical keenness of de Quincey's mind. De Quincey's critical mission was modest, though important: to see his subjects exactly; to remove old errors; and to restore right reading. In this activity de Quincey's mind was central, straining his diction through his consciousness and testing it by his own conceptions. The diction, therefore, is emblematic of de Quincey's intelligence, and on that level he meets his readers. "In all his communications with his readers he uses no sign which does not stand for *mind;* and, if his readers miss the mind, the fault is not in the sign, but in them."

In a quite different sense Giles uses his theory of signs to support his contention that Wordsworth was a meditative man for whom the separate and concrete existence of individuals had little significance. For Wordsworth, individuals mainly served as signs of man in the abstract, valuable only for what they could "signify." "They stand for foregone conclusions in the poet's mind; and these conclusions unfold sublime and impressive truths, if we have but sympathy and philosophy to find them out." Wordsworth's fictional Peter and John do no doubt act and suffer. The suffering and acting, however, are referentially not to them as individuals but to their usefulness as representative human beings. The distinction works for Giles, for it allows him to deny the dramatic power of Wordsworth and to play up the poet's preoccupation with the moral.

In 1868 Giles published *Human Life in Shakespeare.* The book was based on a series of Lowell Institute lectures so oversubscribed that each lecture was given twice in a 1,200-seat auditorium. The book was sufficiently popular to warrant two extra printings and to prompt a *Dial* reviewer to remark that it was a "standard" text that should be included in the top six critical books in any Shakespeare collection. For twentieth-century eyes the book is something of a disappointment. It lacks the muscular intellectuality that informs *Illustrations of Genius*, the style is even more richly and self-consciously rhetorical, and its tone is unstintingly adulatory. Giles seems to promise a study of typologies of character as found in Shakespeare, which would have had its own interest if pursued strenuously enough. However, he scarcely rises above the commonplaces of a method that matches clown to clown, heroine to heroine, tragic figure to tragic figure. Worse, he tends to remove the characters from the dramatic give and take of the actions of the plays and to vest them in a three-dimensional rather than fictional reality. On occasion there is even speculation on what they might have done under different circumstances.

Human Life in Shakespeare is mainly a tribute to the poet as complete man, his faculties in balance, imagination and wisdom in mutual support. It is this link of imagination and wisdom that Giles explores in his chapters on humor and tragedy, man and woman, and finally Shakespeare's personality. The main contention of the chapters on man and woman has a Jungian ring as Giles ascribes both masculine and feminine temperaments to the two sexes in which the appropriate temperament for each is dominant. The result is a predictably patriarchal slant on the plays: men love humor, women wit; men err consciously, women spontaneously and thoughtlessly; imagination in men is impersonal, creative, and concerned with essentials, whereas in women imagination is personal, sensitive, and impulsive. To act otherwise is to act against "nature." The chapter on Shakespeare's personality owes much to Thomas Campbell and John Payne Collier but is persuasive on Shakespeare's prudence in financial matters, the grave and temperate quality of his imagination, and the shifts in emphases in the plays as Shakespeare went through his various psychological "seasons."

On balance, Giles's criticism is disappointing, largely because he does not wholly meet his promise. He was a minister and religious disputant first and only secondarily a critic. Consequently he took shortcuts in his criticism. In lectures he fell back on overused ideas and modes of analysis, then in preparing the lectures for publication neglected the opportunity to explore his subjects in greater depth. He obviously appreciated the fictive nature of literature and the corollary notion that literature has its own manner of communication. He appreciated, too, the obligation of the reader to acknowledge the postulates set by literature and to read accordingly. With more reflection and a consistently sharper focus he might have produced some memorable criticism. As it is, one responds to his intellectual balance but asks for more.

Papers:
The Massachusetts Historical Society holds two Giles letters to Joseph Allen, both written in early 1842, but otherwise no respositories of Giles's papers can be located. There are no reference works on him.

Parke Godwin

(25 February 1816-7 January 1904)

Sterling F. Delano
Villanova University

See also the Godwin entry in *DLB 3, Antebellum Writers in New York and the South.*

BOOKS: *Democracy, Constructive and Pacific* (New York: Winchester, 1844);

A Popular View of the Doctrines of Charles Fourier (New York: Redfield, 1844);

Vala, A Mythological Tale (New York: Putnam's, 1851);

Hand-Book of Universal Biography (New York: Putnam's, 1852);

Political Essays (New York: Dix, Edwards, 1856);

The History of France, volume 1 (New York: Harper, 1860);

Out of the Past (New York: Putnam's, 1870);

A Biography of William Cullen Bryant, with Extracts from His Private Correspondence, 2 volumes (New York: Appleton, 1883);

Commemorative Addresses (New York: Harper, 1895);

Little Journeys to the Homes of American Authors (New York & London: Putnam's, 1896);

A New Study of the Sonnets of Shakespeare (New York: Putnam's, 1900).

OTHER: *Tales from the German of Heinrich Zschokke,* translated and edited by Godwin and Charles A. Dana, 2 volumes (New York: Wiley & Putnam, 1845);

The Auto-Biography of Goethe: Truth and Poetry: From My Own Life, edited and partially translated by Godwin, 2 volumes (New York: Wiley & Putnam, 1846-1847);

The Poetical Works of William Cullen Bryant, edited by Godwin, 2 volumes (New York: Appleton, 1883);

Prose Writings of William Cullen Bryant, edited by Godwin, 2 volumes (New York: Appleton, 1884).

When Parke Godwin is remembered at all today, it seems to be chiefly for the fact of his having been the son-in-law of the admired and popular nineteenth-century American poet and journalist, William Cullen Bryant. Godwin's ca-

Parke Godwin

reer as a reformer and a journalist, however, spanned the greater part of the nineteenth century, and it brought him into contact with most of the leading figures of the time, including such writers as Washington Irving and Ralph Waldo Emerson, such important journalists as Orestes Brownson of the *Democratic Review* and Horace Greeley of the *New York Tribune,* and such notable social reformers as George Ripley and William Henry Channing, both of whom were leading inspirational forces at Brook Farm, the utopian West Roxbury, Massachusetts, community. After the Civil War until the time of his death, Godwin maintained a central position in the difficult and competitive journalistic world of New York City. It was, according to one New York monthly literary magazine, Godwin's "profound understanding of the principles of democratic society [that] made, not so much the fame as the dignity and honor of New York journalism." It may be added that Godwin's faith in those principles also made the foundation of his literary and critical aesthetic. That faith, in fact, is the single most distinguishing feature of the hundreds of reviews written by the New Jersey born Princeton graduate from the beginning to the end of his distinguished and long journalistic career.

Although it is true that in 1847, relatively early in his career, Parke Godwin became the editor of the *Harbinger*–a weekly utopian socialist newspaper–and that this paper, as well as the reform movement which it represented, were outgrowths of the moral fervor known in New England in the 1830s and 1840s as transcendentalism, it needs to be remembered that Godwin was neither Boston born nor Harvard bred. He arrived independently at those social, economic, and political persuasions likewise espoused, for example, by the members of Brook Farm, perhaps the most notable of the dozens of utopian communities of the period organized around the theories of French social-scientist Charles Fourier. It is therefore important to recall that Godwin had founded his own paper, the *Pathfinder*, four years before becoming the editor of the *Harbinger*.

The *Pathfinder* was a New York City based weekly that lasted less than four months. Despite the brevity of its existence, editing the paper provided Godwin not only with valuable journalistic experience but, more importantly, with an opportunity to focus and sharpen his social and economic views, views that would increasingly have a significant bearing on the nature and substance of his literary criticism. Godwin quickly discovered that those views were very consistent with the comprehensive reform program known at the time as associationism, which was the name preferred by those American utopians who did not agree with, much less accept, all of Charles Fourier's controversial theories.

Godwin announced in the first issue (25 February 1843) that the *Pathfinder* would be an "independent political and literary publication, devoted to the cause of no particular party, sect, or man." He added, however, that, when appropriate, he would not hesitate to take the side of the Democratic party, which alone was the party of social progress and popular freedom. He promised, too, that readers would find the paper an "uncompromising friend of the liberal cause."

Godwin's interest in associationism was evident from the start of the *Pathfinder*. In only the third issue of the paper, he had occasion to refer to Charles Fourier as a "sublime genius," and, in the next issue, he provided an enthusiastic review of the Frenchman's complete works, stating at one point that he was intellectually superior to social philosophers Robert Owen and Saint Simon and, at another point, categorizing him with Francis Bacon and Sir Isaac Newton. Godwin followed this review with others no less supportive of associative doctrines, and then, in the 13 May 1843 issue he announced that he had turned over a column of the paper to associationists, whose contributions henceforth would be a regular feature of the *Pathfinder*. He stated that the column would be "wholly independent" of other parts of the paper, which, for the most part, it was. Nonetheless, one week after the announcement, Orestes Brownson, then editor of the *Democratic Review*, did not hesitate to refer to Godwin in a letter to the *Pathfinder* as a "confirmed Fourierist."

Whenever Orestes Brownson took aim, he was noted for hitting his target squarely. On this occasion, however, he missed the mark somewhat. Had the charge been that of "confirmed associationist," Godwin probably would have happily agreed. Indeed, just four years after the collapse of the *Pathfinder*, he was appointed editor of the *Harbinger*, the official organ in the United States of the American Union of Associationists. Godwin had been a contributor to the paper from its inception, though the majority of his more than one hundred articles and reviews for the journal appeared after the commencement of his editorship in 1847.

Most of the literary criticism Godwin provided for the *Harbinger* was consistent with the aims and ideals of associationism, and his reviews typically reflect the associative belief that literature should serve a high moral purpose, that it should enlighten and even liberate humanity. Since its adherents believed that associationism was a social science which had an established method of inquiry and a set of specific operating principles, it was thought that existing social problems could be substantially ameliorated. The basis of any associationist critique was therefore the extent to which other systems could similarly alleviate social ills. Reviews of most works–and, of course, authors as well–were praised or criticized accordingly.

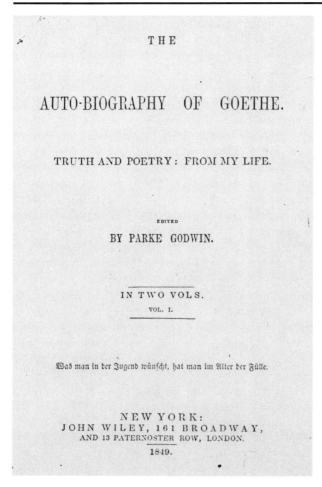

THE

AUTO-BIOGRAPHY OF GOETHE.

TRUTH AND POETRY: FROM MY LIFE.

EDITED

BY PARKE GODWIN.

IN TWO VOLS.

VOL. I.

Was man in der Jugend wünscht, hat man im Alter der Fülle.

NEW YORK:
JOHN WILEY, 161 BROADWAY,
AND 13 PATERNOSTER ROW, LONDON.
1849.

Title page for Godwin's edition of Johann Wolfgang von Goethe's Aus Meinem Leben, Dichtung und Wahrheit

Thus, for example, Godwin had mostly enthusiastic things to say about *Association and Christianity* (1845), for its author, H. H. Van Amringe, "perceives the grand truths that lie at the bottom of Fourier's scientific generalizations." Godwin's review of Alphonse Lamartine's *History of the Girondists* (1847) provided the opportunity to discuss and praise Charles Fourier. A review of a collection of lectures by the philosopher A. W. M. Schlegel was an occasion to criticize Schlegel, as well as all other German philosophers who lacked a "true perception of Man's social nature" and therefore were able to discuss man only in the abstract.

Despite the focus, however, in the associative vision of a world free from tension and disagreement, relationships in the everyday world were often anything but harmonious. Godwin must have known this well enough himself, for he seems never to have gotten along very well with George Ripley, William Henry Channing,

and John S. Dwight, three Bostonians who were among the most devoted and prominent laborers in the associative cause. In a letter to Dwight written during the early tenure of Godwin's editorship on the *Harbinger,* Ripley complained that while the Princeton graduate was "fruitful, genial, and altogether in earnest," he was not altogether "inexhaustible," and that "without a stronger infusion of the Boston element, we cannot do justice to our ideal." Several months later, with the *Harbinger* on the verge of collapse, Ripley's reservations about Godwin became substantially more pointed. He wrote to Dwight again, this time accusing Godwin of never having shown "any vital paramount interest" in the associationist journal, and charging that he did not "love it well enough to write for it without a consideration."

After the *Harbinger's* demise in 1849, it was suggested that Ripley and Godwin launch a new publication in order to continue proselytizing the cause. Ripley's response was unequivocal: he would never work on any publication with Godwin, a man who was "too much of a Caliban or Cannibal, to make cooperation with him pleasant. Indeed, I don't see ... how anyone can work under him, or over him, or with him, without extreme annoyance; and for himself he decidedly prefers to write or fight (which with him is pretty much the same thing) on his own."

The collapse of the *Harbinger* represented a fracturing of the center of the associative movement. Ripley joined Horace Greeley and became the literary critic of the *New York Tribune;* Dwight initiated *Dwight's Journal of Music;* and Channing launched the *Spirit of the Age* as a successor to the *Harbinger.* Godwin provided an infrequent contribution or two to Channing's weekly journal, but his heart was no longer in the movement. Indeed, though he would always retain his fundamental idealism, Godwin would never again devote himself as thoroughly to any special interest group as he had to the associationists. Instead, he turned his attention to the newly founded *Putnam's Monthly Magazine,* a journal that he began to edit in 1853.

Godwin's affiliation with *Putnam's Monthly Magazine* occupied much of his attention during this period though the magazine was suspended in 1857 and was not revived until 1868 as *Putnam's Monthly.* Godwin maintained close contact throughout this period with the *New York Evening Post,* and he routinely provided his father-in-law, William Cullen Bryant—who was

NOTE BY THE EDITOR.

THE Third and Fourth Parts, respectively, of this Autobiography have been translated, in the first place, by my friends, CHARLES A. DANA and JOHN S. DWIGHT, whose attainments, as scholars, ensure the general accuracy of the work. The Editor has, besides, carefully gone over every word with the original before him, in order to give uniformity to the style, as far as it might be found necessary, and to correct any errors that may have been accidentally overlooked. He believes, therefore, that the translation is at least faithful.

It was his design to have appended a series of notes, explanatory of the names and allusions that occur in the work, but after having prepared a good deal of his matter, he found that the plan, treated in any satisfactory way, would swell the book to an undesirable size.

Goethe's Life is, in the present volume, only brought down to the period of his going to reside in Weimar. It is continued, however, in other works, such as the "*Annals, or Day and Year Book*," the "*Italian Journey*," and his Correspondences with Schiller and Zelter. Should the success of this attempt warrant the undertaking, these, or some of them at least, will be presented to the public in due time.

Godwin's explanatory note at the end of volume 2 of The Auto-Biography of Goethe

chief editor of the paper—with valuable editorial assistance.

There is a striking contrast between the literary criticism Godwin wrote for the *Harbinger* with that he provided for *Putnam's*. His earlier literary responses were frequently biased by extra-literary consideration. For the *Harbinger*, Godwin often utilized the review as little more than an occasion to propagandize for associationism. However, for *Putnam's* Godwin provided discriminating critiques of writers and works ranging from the British novelist William Thackeray, to the German poet, dramatist, and critic Johann Wolfgang von Goethe, to the American essayist Ralph Waldo Emerson.

Actually, if Godwin shows any bias at all during this period, it is toward American writers. Unlike many other literary critics of the time, who frequently dismissed the contributions of American writers while deferentially bowing to the muses of England, Godwin consistently praised

and applauded native authors. As he stated in "American Authorship," one of his earliest pieces for *Putnam's*, "we allege that our younger writers abound in the unmistakable evidences of a new and vigorous direction. . . ." Of American poets, Godwin remarked in the same article that "they are more free, frank, and expansive than the modern British poets. . . ." Moreover, Godwin did not reserve his praise only for popular American writers. His continuing faith in democracy caused him to look westward beyond the Mississippi River. There, Godwin thought, the land was free from the evil of slavery, and thus from there, he believed, an expansive, free, and truly democratic literature might emerge. Several of his reviews affirm the importance of the Western literary contribution.

After leaving *Putnam's* in 1870, Godwin continued his affiliation with the *New York Evening Post*, having acquired a financial interest in the paper in 1860. When Bryant died in 1878 Godwin became the editor-in-chief, a position he held until 1881, at which time he sold his interest in the newspaper. He spent the remainder of his career editing the *New York Commercial Advertiser*, for which he provided relatively little literary criticism. Godwin's literary interests, nonetheless, remained as sincere as ever, as indicated by the publication in 1900 of *A New Study of the Sonnets of Shakespeare*. Godwin was eighty-four at the time.

By the time Parke Godwin retired in 1900, America had already witnessed the literary flowering of local-color writing and realism. Indeed, naturalism had already begun to manifest itself in the fiction of the 1890s. The romantic sensibility which had so characterized American writing before the Civil War was a thing of an increasingly distant past. Many of the literary figures with whom Godwin had been associated—in one way or another—were becoming increasingly distant too. Edgar Allan Poe had died in 1849, Henry David Thoreau in 1862, Nathaniel Hawthorne in 1864, and Ralph Waldo Emerson in 1882. Godwin's career, however, had spanned nearly seventy years, and thus he represented in 1900 one of the most important links to America's literary past. Few, if any, other critics of the time could boast of familiar acquaintanceship with Washington Irving and James Fenimore Cooper in addition to William Dean Howells and Henry James. For that reason alone Godwin's career would be worthy of note.

However, Godwin deserves attention for a reason other than his longevity and his contacts.

For he began sharpening his literary critical skills at a time when there was no established critical tradition in America. Like many of his earlier colleagues—notably Margaret Fuller and Emerson of the *Dial*—he worked in the formative years of his career in all but a critical vacuum. At the very least, then, Parke Godwin's career stands as a valuable record—if an unexamined one—of the development of the practice of literary criticism in America.

References:
Eugene Benson, "Parke Godwin, of the Evening Post," *Galaxy,* 7 (February 1869): 230-236;

Charles H. Brown, *William Cullen Bryant* (New York: Scribners, 1971);

Sterling F. Delano, *THE HARBINGER and New England Transcendentalism* (Rutherford, N.J.: Fairleigh Dickinson University Press, 1983);

Allan Nevins, *The Evening Post: A Century of Journalism* (New York: Boni & Liveright, 1922);

Charles Southeran, *Horace Greeley and Other Pioneers of American Socialism* (New York: Mitchell Kennerly, 1915).

Papers:
The Parke Godwin Papers of Princeton University contain the manuscripts of many of Godwin's works, including his history of France and his study of Shakespeare's sonnets, as well as numerous essays, addresses, and journalistic writings on such subjects as political science, economics, and science, and on such figures as Goethe, Emanuel Swedenborg, and Charles Fourier. A few short stories and some occasional poems are also contained in the collection. Significant Godwin correspondence may be found among the H. Bogart Seaman Papers (1732-1939) at the Bryant Library in Roslyn, New York; the James T. Fisher Papers (1790-1865) located at the Massachusetts Historical Society; the Bryant-Godwin Collection (1804-1913) of the New York Public Library; the Goddard-Roslyn Collection (1814-1878) of the New York Public Library; and the John Ferguson Weir Papers (1816-1939) at Yale University. The Illinois Historical Survey of the University of Illinois has microfilm holdings of many of the materials in the Bryant-Godwin Collection.

William J. Grayson

(12 November 1788-4 October 1863)

Richard J. Calhoun
Clemson University

See also the Grayson entry in *DLB 3, Antebellum Writers in New York and the South.*

BOOKS: *An Oration, Delivered in the College Chapel, Before the Clariosophic Society* (Charleston, S.C.: Miller, 1828);

Letter to His Excellency Whitemarsh B. Seabrook, Governor of the State of South-Carolina, on the Dissolution of the Union (Charleston, S.C.: Miller, 1850);

The Union, Past and Future. How It Works and How to Save It (Charleston, S.C.: Miller, 1850);

The Letters of Curtius, anonymous (Charleston, S.C.: Miller, 1851);

The Hireling and the Slave (Charleston, S.C.: Russell, 1854);

The Hireling and the Slave, Chicora, and Other Poems (Charleston, S.C.: McCarter, 1856);

The Country (Charleston, S.C.: Russell & Jones, 1858);

Marion (Charleston, S.C.: Privately printed, 1860);

Remarks on Mr. Motley's Letter in the London Times on the War in America, anonymous (Charleston, S.C.: Evans & Cogswell, 1861);

James Louis Petigru. A Biographical Sketch (New York: Harper, 1866);

Selected Poems by William J. Grayson, edited by Mrs. William H. Armstrong (New York & Washington: Neale, 1907).

PERIODICAL PUBLICATIONS: "What is Poetry?," *Russell's Magazine*, 4 (July 1857): 327-337;

"The Autobiography of William John Grayson," edited by S. G. Stoney, *South Carolina Historical and Genealogical Magazine*, 48-51 (July 1947-April 1950).

William J. Grayson, lawyer, politician, congressman, government official, Charleston man of letters, southern gentleman, and staunch defender of neoclassicism and all things that promote stability and order, was born not in Charleston, South Carolina, but in the next best

William John Grayson (courtesy of the South Carolina Historical Society)

place for entrance into South Carolina plantation society, Beaufort, South Carolina, on 12 November 1788. As a literary critic he earns a short chapter in Edd Winfield Parks's *Ante-Bellum Southern Literary Critics* (1962) under the subtitle "Neo-Classicist," as a die-hard adherent of neoclassicism in a romantic age. He appeared as a critic late in his career at a time and place where romanticism was, at long last, dominant. He might be regarded as eccentric but not unique, since the South held to neoclassical tenets longer than the North, and the Charleston professional man with literary tastes, educated in the classics and Scottish common sense philosophy, upheld these beliefs the most tenaciously. As a critic of literature, Grayson is only a minor figure, having written only one article for *Russell's Magazine* ("What is Poetry?") that is purely literary criticism. Other than that he wrote passages of literary criticism in the preface to his long poem, *The Hireling and the Slave* (1854), and in his autobiography, published serially in the *South Carolina Historical and Genealogical Magazine* from 1947 to 1950. These writings do, however, affirm his position as a staunch advocate of the classical writers and neoclassical poets and critics over the romantic poets and the new "genial" and, thereby, less judicial critics. To Grayson the best literary critic was still Horace, but the critical intelligence he felt closest to in a time when the stability of everything he valued was threatened was "that sturdy old master of vigorous common sense," Dr. Samuel Johnson.

From the perspective of Grayson's common-sense approach, romanticism fared poorly. Coleridge was cloudy philosophically; Wordsworth belied his own theory and used nature mechanically, not organically. Shelley's sentiments were empty of philosophical content. Transcendentalism in America was unrealistic about both nature and human nature. In brief, modern poetry sought the sublime but did not know how to reach it. The new literature of his time, in Grayson's view, was either unintelligible or driven by expediency.

Grayson's classicism came from his reading and from the conservative tastes of his professional class. His father, John Grayson, was a distinguished South Carolinian who served in the American artillery in the Revolutionary War. John Grayson died when William was ten, after which his mother married a wealthy planter, William Joyner, who sent him north to prepare him for Harvard. Grayson's main complaint about his schooling was that there were never enough books for him to read to satisfy his hunger for knowledge. He wrote in his autobiography, "I could have devoured a library." The consequences of his early reading of Homer, Horace, and the classical humanists Cicero and Seneca were a lifelong interest in the classics and a life devoted to an attempt to live by the ethics he found in classical humanism.

In February 1807 he entered, not Harvard, but South Carolina College, from which he was graduated with an A.B. degree in 1809. In his autobiography Grayson acknowledged that with his education there were only two pursuits open to him, that of author or schoolmaster; and he added, "the South, fifty years ago, offered no field for authorship." In 1814 he married Sarah Matilda Somersall, the daughter of a wealthy Charleston merchant and planter, and found employment as an assistant principal at Beaufort College in his hometown. When the yellow-fever epidemic in 1817 threatened Beaufort and closed the school, he abandoned teaching for the study of law, a more suitable occupation for a gentleman; but, as it turned out, of much less interest to Grayson than education had been.

Practice conflicted with the classical humanist virtues he had learned from Cicero. He found what was of primary concern to him—"Right, justice, truth"—to be "secondary considerations" in the practice of law. Consequently, Grayson turned from practice to politics, winning election as state representative from Beaufort, serving from 1822 to 1826, and then advancing to the state senate in 1826. Grayson resigned his seat in the senate to become commissioner of equity. After two years of satisfactory service in this office, he was elected in 1833 to the first of two terms in the United States Congress. On losing his seat in 1837 because he had been unwilling to stoop to the common practice of buying votes with liquor, he became collector of customs for the busy port of Charleston, a position he held for twelve years, from 1841 until he fell victim to the spoils system in 1853. The next year Grayson purchased the large Fair Lawn Plantation on the Wando River, near Charleston; and having forsaken law and politics he turned his attention to his plantation and began, belatedly, the other occupation of gentlemen of talent—entrance into the literary world.

The event that stirred Grayson's passion for book-length criticism was the publication of Harriet Beecher Stowe's *Uncle Tom's Cabin* (1852). In 1854 Grayson published his response, *The Hireling and the Slave*, which would earn him a place as a minor poet in American literary history. He went beyond literary criticism of this one antislavery novel into social and political criticism of two different societies, a defense of the southern version of the original agrarian dream and an attack on the new machine in the garden, northern industrialization. Grayson wrote his criticism as Pope and Dryden would have done, fashioning a neoclassical poem in heroic couplets, which defended slavery by picturing the unhappy lot of the "hireling," the wage earner in the industrial

North and the pastoral, idyllic life of the slave. *The Hireling and the Slave* also demonstrates his conservative literary taste as well as his agrarian politics. Grayson declared that, as a writer, he "believed in Dryden and Pope," and his poetic style, as well as his critical invective, reflected that literary discipleship.

The Hireling and the Slave achieved instant success in the Charleston area and quickly went through two printings. Today it is remembered more as antebellum proslavery rhetoric than as a poem or social criticism. It has found two modern critics who have discovered something good to say about a work that has a reputation only as a defense of a bad cause: Edmund Wilson, in *Patriotic Gore: Studies in the Literature of the Civil War* (1962); and, with less enthusiasm, the liberal historian V. L. Parrington in his *Main Currents in American Thought: An Interpretation of American Literature From the Beginnings to 1920* (1927-1930). Wilson noted that, unlike other apologists, Grayson defends slavery against its attackers but admits its imperfections and even acknowledges some of its abuses. Grayson regarded his position pragmatically as something necessary in the South. "I do not say that slavery is the best system of labor, but only that it is the best for the Negro in this country." He champions what he regards as obvious, that the agrarian way is the best way of life for this country, and if slavery is the form that this has taken in the South, then it has to be preserved. Northern industrialism is no better and is apparently even a worse alternative. When he turned to the pretensions of *Uncle Tom's Cabin* as a realistic novel, as did George Frederick Holmes in the *Southern Literary Messenger*, Grayson regarded it not as literature but as disguised rhetoric and propaganda, falsely giving its readers the impression of providing a realistic description of the South. The worse sin of writers of the Harriet Beecher Stowe ilk was that they were poor social critics, failing to recognize the evils of their own industrial wage system and failing to remember that northerners had brought the slaves to America and profited first from their sale. "They made the system and enjoy the profits. Now that they can no longer carry on the trade, they slander the slaveholder of their own making."

Grayson was an apologist, but he was by no means a fanatic. As Edmund Wilson notes, he had no desire to see more slaves added but rather to justify the rights of slaveholders to continue to hold their slaves. He tries to persuade his reader through scenes different from those in *Uncle Tom's Cabin* that cruelty and other abuses are the exceptions not actual practice, and he even interjects the hope that "in time these may be prevented." He attempts to defend the "peculiar institution" of his region by contrasting the morality of two imperfect systems, the new worse than the old. In the industrial market there is no benevolence, only the profit motive. The hireling, unlike the slave, may actually starve, and the slave, unlike the industrial hireling, may participate to a limited extent in the luxuries that his labor helps to create.

As a social critic Grayson deserves comparison with another critic of industrialism and defender of agrarianism, George Fitzhugh, who had argued this case in his *Sociology for the South*. The difference is that Grayson writes, as his models Pope and Dryden did, both literary as well as social criticism, and poetry more of their age than of his own. His most effective social criticism is his best verse, his vivid contrasting of the pastoral leisure of slaves in the South with the urban misery of wage earners in the North. His poetry is not original; it is merely imitative adaptation of neoclassical pastoral, very old-fashioned for the 1850s. His other literary talent is for invective: his denunciations of Harriet Beecher Stowe and his satirical portraits of abolitionists and their supporters, such as Horace Greeley and Charles Sumner, those who unfairly attacked the South while failing to see the vices of their own region. For all of Grayson's love for classical rationality, his critical blind spot was Harriet Beecher Stowe, in whom, in contrast to the grudging admiration given by George Frederick Holmes for what he did not like, he could find neither literary merit nor morality, only a mercenary intent.

Grayson's literary tastes were not those of his young friends Paul Hamilton Hayne and Henry Timrod, but in the vitriolic years just before conflict, when the South seemed to need rhetorical and political defenses against attacks, they needed Grayson for replies in a new periodical edited by Hayne, *Russell's Magazine*. In the first issue he replied to an attack in the influential *Edinburgh Review*. When Hayne sought a spokesman for the traditional views of Charleston literati he turned to Grayson, who produced "What is Poetry?" for the July 1857 issue of *Russell's Magazine*.

The old classicist enjoyed his opportunity to use the pages of *Russell's Magazine* to attack the romantics, now in favor in Charleston. Just as he believed that the abolitionists and their literary

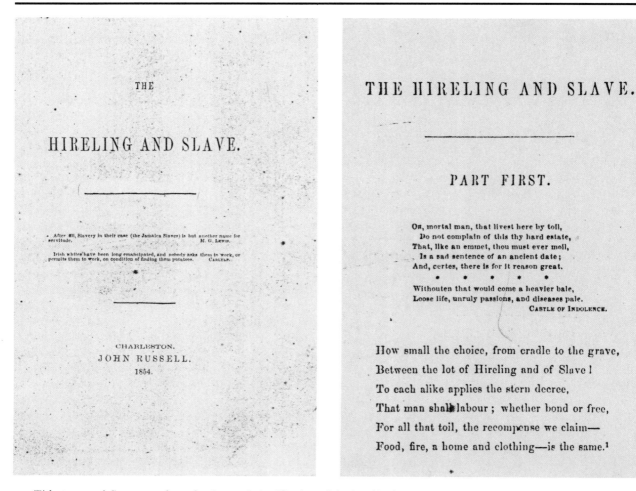

THE

HIRELING AND SLAVE.

After all, Slavery in their case (the Jamaica Slaves) is but another name for servitude.   M. G. LEWIS.

Irish whites have been long emancipated, and nobody asks them to work, or permits them to work, on condition of finding them potatoes.   CARLYLE.

CHARLESTON.
JOHN RUSSELL.
1854.

THE HIRELING AND SLAVE.

PART FIRST.

Oм, mortal man, that livest here by toil,
 Do not complain of this thy hard estate,
That, like an emmet, thou must ever moil,
 Is a sad sentence of an ancient date;
 And, certes, there is for it reason great.
    *   *   *   *   *
Withouten that would come a heavier bale,
Loose life, unruly passions, and diseases pale.
                                        CASTLE OF INDOLENCE.

How small the choice, from cradle to the grave,
Between the lot of Hireling and of Slave !
To each alike applies the stern decree,
That man shall labour ; whether bond or free,
For all that toil, the recompense we claim—
Food, fire, a home and clothing—is the same.[1]

Title page and first page of text for Grayson's justification of the South's slavery system (courtesy of the South Caroliniana Library, Columbia)

supporters posed a threat to political and social systems, he had long believed that romantic poets and critics threatened to break down generic barriers so that "Poetry becomes prose and prose becomes poetry." As for the new, more genial theories of criticism, through ignoring generic distinctions, romantic critics tended to deny poetic merit to poetry different from theirs, especially the Johnsonian style of verse that Grayson defended. Once again, he was opposed to what he believed to be unfair attacks that seemed to reserve poetry for the new romantic efforts and verse for the older style. Grayson made it clear that he saw no distinction between poetry and verse: "Poetry must be defined . . . from the form in which these words are arranged." It is "the expression by words of thought and emotion, in conformity with metrical and rhythmical laws."

As a constant spokesman against whatever seemed to threaten order and stability, Grayson was likewise staunch in his opposition to the chaos of secession. The literary critic became the political critic. He first wrote on this subject in 1850, *The Union, Past and Future. How It Works and How to Save It.* Though southern to the core, Grayson held firm to his belief that the South must stay as part of the union to fight its battles through its literature, its rhetoric, and its oratory. During the war, writing a memoir on his friend James Louis Petigru, published posthumously in 1866, he complained bitterly of those who had led the South into secession, inducing "the simple people to plunge into the volcanic vices of revolution and war." He had never believed that the South would produce better government than the union had produced, for there would always be "unprincipled demagogues" in the South, just as in the North. What he wrote in this memoir of

Petigru's opposition to secession came also from his own deeply held views. This memoir and his own autobiography were his last works, written by a man who knew his world had failed.

To his contemporaries William Grayson was one of the stars among the literati who gathered for their discussions in Russell's Bookshop in Charleston. Though a staunch defender of things southern and traditional, Grayson was never an advocate of extremism, and that was what he regarded romanticism and secession to be. He was far too much a rational neoclassicist for any sort of rebellion. He loyally supported the South's cause after the fatal break had occurred, but he did not survive the war he would have preferred to avoid, dying on 4 October 1863 in Newberry, South Carolina.

References:

Jay B. Hubbell, "William J. Grayson," in *The South in American Literature 1607-1900* (Durham: Duke University Press, 1954);

Edd Winfield Parks, "William J. Grayson: Neoclassicist," in *Ante-Bellum Southern Literary Critics* (Athens: University of Georgia Press, 1962);

Edmund Wilson, *Patriotic Gore: Studies in the Literature of the Civil War* (New York: Oxford University Press, 1962).

Papers:

The manuscripts of Grayson's autobiography and unpublished war diary are in the manuscript division of the South Caroliniana Library at the University of South Carolina.

Bret Harte
(25 August 1836-5 May 1902)

David E. E. Sloane
University of New Haven

See also the Harte entry in *DLB 12, American Realists and Naturalists.*

BOOKS: *Condensed Novels, and Other Papers* (New York: Carlton/London: Low, 1867; enlarged edition, Boston: Osgood, 1871);

The Last Galleon and Other Tales (San Francisco: Towne & Bacon, 1867);

The Luck of Roaring Camp, and Other Sketches (Boston: Fields, Osgood, 1870; enlarged, 1870);

Poems (Boston: Fields, Osgood, 1871);

East and West Poems (Boston: Osgood, 1871; London: Hotten, 1871);

Mrs. Skaggs's Husbands, and Other Sketches (London: Hotten, 1872; Boston: Osgood, 1873);

An Episode of Fiddletown and Other Sketches (London: Routledge, 1873);

M'liss. An Idyl of Red Mountain (New York: DeWitt, 1873);

Echoes of the Foot-hills (Boston: Osgood, 1875);

Tales of the Argonauts, and Other Sketches (Boston: Osgood, 1875);

Gabriel Conroy (London: Warne, 1876; Hartford, Conn.: American Publishing Company, 1876);

Two Men of Sandy Bar: A Drama (Boston: Osgood, 1876);

Thankful Blossom, a Romance of the Jerseys, 1779 (Boston: Osgood, 1877; London & New York: Routledge, 1877);

The Story of a Mine (London: Routledge, 1877; Boston: Osgood, 1878);

The Man on the Beach (London: Routledge, 1878);

"Jinny" (London: Routledge, 1878);

Drift from Two Shores (Boston: Houghton, Osgood, 1878);

The Twins of Table Mountain (London: Chatto & Windus, 1879);

The Twins of Table Mountain and Other Stories (Boston: Houghton, Osgood, 1879);

Flip and Other Stories (London: Chatto & Windus, 1882);

Flip and Found at Blazing Star (Boston: Houghton, Mifflin, 1882);

In the Carquinez Woods (London: Longmans, Green, 1883; Boston: Houghton, Mifflin, 1884);

On the Frontier (London: Longmans, Green, 1884; Boston: Houghton, Mifflin, 1884);

By Shore and Sedge (Boston: Houghton, Mifflin, 1885; London: Longmans, Green, 1885);

Bret Harte at about the time he became editor of the
Overland Monthly

Maruja (London: Chatto & Windus, 1885; Boston & New York: Houghton, Mifflin, 1885);

Snow-Bound at Eagle's (Boston & New York: Houghton, Mifflin, 1886; London: Ward & Downey, 1886);

The Queen of the Pirate Isle (London: Chatto & Windus, 1886; Boston & New York: Houghton, Mifflin, 1887);

A Millionaire of Rough-and-Ready and *Devil's Ford* (Boston & New York: Houghton, Mifflin, 1887);

Devil's Ford (London: White, 1887);

A Millionaire of Rough-and-Ready (London: White, 1887);

The Crusade of the Excelsior (Boston & New York: Houghton, Mifflin, 1887; London: White, 1887);

A Phyllis of the Sierras and A Drift from Redwood Camp (Boston & New York: Houghton, Mifflin, 1888);

The Argonauts of North Liberty (Boston & New York: Houghton, Mifflin, 1888; London: Blackett, 1888);

Cressy (London & New York: Macmillan, 1889; Boston & New York: Houghton, Mifflin, 1889; London: Macmillan, 1889);

The Heritage of Dedlow Marsh and Other Tales (Boston & New York: Houghton, Mifflin, 1889);

A Waif of the Plains (London: Chatto & Windus, 1890; Boston & New York: Houghton, Mifflin, 1890);

A Ward of the Golden Gate (London: Chatto & Windus, 1890; Boston & New York: Houghton, Mifflin, 1890);

A Sappho of Green Springs and Other Stories (London: Chatto & Windus, 1891; Boston & New York: Houghton, Mifflin, 1891);

A First Family of Tasajara (London & New York: Macmillan, 1891; Boston & New York: Houghton, Mifflin, 1892);

Colonel Starbottle's Client and Some Other People (London: Chatto & Windus, 1892; Boston & New York: Houghton, Mifflin, 1892);

Susy: A Story of the Plains (Boston & New York: Houghton, Mifflin, 1893; London: Chatto & Windus, 1893);

Sally Dows, Etc. (London: Chatto & Windus, 1893); republished as *Sally Dows and Other Stories* (Boston & New York: Houghton, Mifflin, 1893);

A Protegee of Jack Hamlin's and Other Stories (Boston & New York: Houghton, Mifflin, 1894; enlarged edition, London: Chatto & Windus, 1894);

The Bell-Ringer of Angel's and Other Stories (Boston & New York: Houghton, Mifflin, 1894; London: Chatto & Windus, 1894);

Clarence (London: Chatto & Windus, 1895; Boston & New York: Houghton, Mifflin, 1895);

In a Hollow of the Hills (London: Chapman & Hall, 1895; Boston: Houghton, Mifflin, 1895);

Barker's Luck and Other Stories (Boston & New York: Houghton, Mifflin, 1896; London: Chatto & Windus, 1896);

Three Partners or The Big Strike on Heavy Tree Hill (Boston & New York: Houghton, Mifflin, 1897; London: Chatto & Windus, 1897);

Tales of Trail and Town (Boston & New York: Houghton, Mifflin, 1898; London: Chatto & Windus, 1898);

Stories in Light and Shadow (London: Pearson, 1898; Boston & New York: Houghton, Mifflin, 1898);

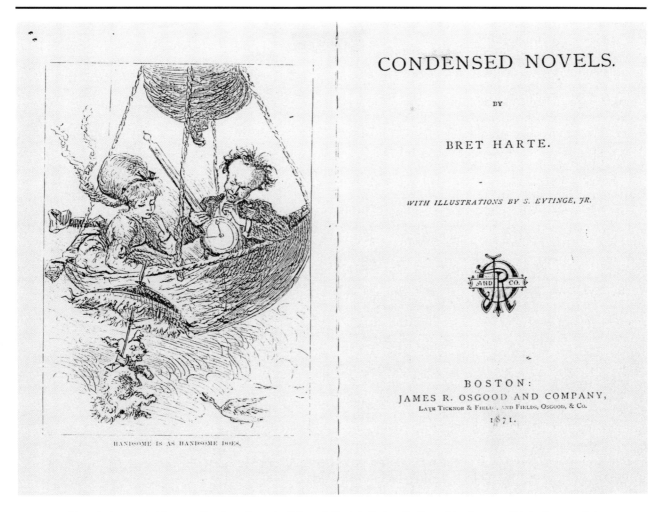

CONDENSED NOVELS.

BY

BRET HARTE.

WITH ILLUSTRATIONS BY S. EYTINGE, JR.

BOSTON:
JAMES R. OSGOOD AND COMPANY,
Late Ticknor & Fields, and Fields, Osgood, & Co.
1871.

HANDSOME IS AS HANDSOME DOES.

Frontispiece and title page for the enlarged edition of Harte's first collection of burlesques of popular novelists

Mr. Jack Hamlin's Mediation and Other Stories (Boston & New York: Houghton, Mifflin, 1899; London: Pearson, 1899);

From Sand Hill to Pine (Boston & New York: Houghton, Mifflin, 1900; London: Pearson, 1900);

Under the Redwoods (Boston & New York: Houghton, Mifflin, 1901; London: Pearson, 1901);

On the Old Trail (London: Pearson, 1902); republished as *Openings in the Old Trail* (Boston & New York: Houghton, Mifflin, 1902);

Condensed Novels, Second Series: New Burlesques (Boston & New York: Houghton, Mifflin, 1902; London: Chatto & Windus, 1902);

Sue: A Play in Three Acts, by Harte and T. Edgar Pemberton (London: Greening, 1902);

Trent's Trust and Other Stories (London: Nash,

1903; Boston & New York: Houghton, Mifflin, 1903);

Stories and Poems and Other Uncollected Writings, compiled by Charles Meeker Kozlay (Boston & New York: Houghton, Mifflin, 1914).

Collection: *The Writings of Bret Harte*, 20 volumes (Boston: Houghton, Mifflin, 1896-1914).

Bret Harte was one of the most important image makers of the Pacific slope during and immediately after the American Civil War. As such, he was important in establishing the image of the West, its concepts, and its national importance as a component in the American critical spectrum. His literary criticism, directly in his reviews for the *Overland Monthly* and indirectly through his burlesques of fiction in his two collections of "Condensed Novels," was important in stating a pragmatic western call for realistic details of "lowlife." His viewpoint helped to advance the local-color and realist fiction of the 1870s and 1880s, although that realism outgrew Harte's limited sense of its broadened subject matter by the 1890s. Harte himself hardly advanced his writing beyond the local-color fiction of "The Outcasts of Poker Flat," but other writers benefited from his critical position of advocating a fresh and descriptive literature unlimited by the formulaic.

Francis Brett Harte was the third of four children born to Elizabeth Ostrander and Henry Harte, an unsuccessful schoolteacher who died in 1845. Poverty enveloped the family until the marriage of Harte's mother to Andrew Williams, an Oakland businessman, which resulted in a move to California in 1854. Throughout his childhood Harte had been an extensive reader, especially fond of Shakespeare and Alexandre Dumas's *The Count of Monte Cristo.* In 1856 he announced his intention of undertaking a serious career in writing, using the works of Charles Dickens as a guide. He wrote first for the *Northern Californian* in 1857, then moved to the *Golden Era* in 1860. He was married in 1862 to Anna Griswold and clerked for a brief period, but he became a contributor to Charles H. Webb's *Californian* shortly thereafter and soon began publishing various burlesque "condensed novels." In 1868 he became editor of Anton Roman's *Overland Monthly,* which rapidly achieved national recognition under his editorial hand for regional color stories and incisive reviews. With its masthead of the California bear crossing a railroad, the *Overland Monthly* self-consciously intended to bring the importance of its region and its go-ahead spirit to the rest of the nation.

Harte's brief but significant tenure at the *Overland Monthly* ended in January 1871. Unfortunately, he was slow to capitalize on the success of his local-color fiction. Though he signed a lucrative one-year contract with the prestigious *Atlantic Monthly,* the quality of his submissions was such that he was not asked to renew it. Even less fortunately, he failed to capitalize on his skills as an editor and critic, giving up a chance at a promising editorship with the *Lakeside Monthly* in Chicago. For the rest of the 1870s he attempted various literary ventures: a novel; plays, including a collaboration with Mark Twain; and lectures. None of his efforts were particularly successful. He continued his output of short stories and in the 1880s supplemented that income with government posts in Europe which he handled with an integrity that

Harte in 1878

astonished other members of the consular service, but which he viewed matter-of-factly. He finally drifted into seclusion in England, maintaining his output of sentimental local-color fiction even late in his life. He died there in 1902.

Bret Harte's importance as a critic can be understood by referring to only a handful of documents, for in them he reveals the critical ideology that aligns him with the literary movement toward realism and beyond idealistic and romantic literature as practiced by his revered New England literary antecedents. In fiction the works that most easily project the "new" literary vision which Bret Harte shared with the other young writers of the 1860s and 1870s include his two most important stories—"The Luck of Roaring Camp" (1868) and "The Outcasts of Poker Flat" (1869)—his Pike County dialect ballads—"The Heathen Chinee" (1870) particularly—and his burlesque *Condensed Novels,* first and second series (1867 and 1902). Among critical reviews, his essays on Dickens, Lowell, Longfellow, and Artemus Ward—the last of which later became an essay on American humor–virtually complete what amounts to a revolutionary critical philosophy, although it is so sparely outlined that it is easy to mistake his commentaries for conventional and relatively conservative filler material. His views are overtly revealed only by a few sentences flatly advocating a "western" viewpoint.

Harte's short stories and poetry can be grouped, for their importance in understanding Harte as a critic lies in their overall tendencies. The two forms use as characters men or women who are involved not only in practical affairs but in vulgar affairs–with the word "vulgar" implying the very opposite of the pastoral, natural, or remote settings and occupations characteristic of romantic writing. Further, characters with openly degraded occupations–such as gambler and prostitute–are presented as worthy of consideration as people. In fact, their sentimentalization by Harte places them in a distinctly different category from the denizens of the popular temperance novel or didactic romance. In "The Outcasts of Poker Flat," although Oakhurst, the gambler, and his allies die, their dying is shown to be redemptive. Commonplace though such an analysis of Harte's fiction may seem, it shows Harte as accepting a range of character and behavior that would be unacceptable in established literature before the 1860s–a widened and democratized range of fictional characters–and, as opponents of democracy might well have feared, a "lowered" one. To Harte, however, it was distinctly "national" in scope–American and democratic in the highest and most noble sense.

"The Heathen Chinee" represents a similar phenomenon in verse, and this recognition helps to explain, in part, why such a hot debate developed in 1871 about the primacy of Harte's dialect poems or John Hay's *Pike County Ballads and Other Pieces.* The function of verse in America had often turned toward the satirical and political, but its treatment of vulgar subjects had been limited before Harte and Hay. Doggerel had always held its place in the humor magazines and papers, but Charles G. Leland's *Hans Breitmann's Ballads* in 1868 had advanced low Dutch into a realm of orthodoxy previously unknown–his characters were sympathetic, and they had serious philosophic underpinnings despite their vulgarity.

Harte's characters are perhaps even lower on the social scale, including cheating card players and drunken gamblers, a range of unelevated humanity that was nonetheless seen as worthy of human consideration. The literary comedians bur-

A family group, circa 1900. Standing: Bret Harte and his daughter-in-law Mrs. Francis King Bret Harte. Seated: Ethel Bret Harte, his youngest daughter, and Anna Bret Harte, his wife.

lesqued Whittier's "Maud Muller" for its falsification of human relations between poor farmers and rich gentry; Harte took a positive position by using dialect poetry to illustrate the qualities of the colorful lower caste and their worth as objects of consideration as "real" people. Where Longfellow ennobled Hiawatha, some conservative critics would see Harte degrading mankind by showing ignoble actions and actors sympathetically. Such was the nature of the realist's revolution–as begun by the literary comedians and Howells, Twain, and James in the 1860s and 1870s–of which Harte was a part. Harte's important characteristics are his choice of characters from lower ranks of the social scale, his lack of condemnation of them, his employment of their dialect and slang language, and his selection of detail and choice to elevate the criminal through plot action.

The *Condensed Novels, and Other Papers* of 1867 are a cross between fiction and criticism, for the elements burlesqued indicate the critical divergences from competing literary philosophies.

"Mr. Midshipman Breezy," for example, has a character punching the captain in the stomach and asking "How's his nibs?," for which he is flogged, and in the following chapter the line is played out that "in a few moments we were all friends." The question is borrowed from the language of New York and San Francisco shop-clerks and as such rejects the language convention of romantic literature in favor of commonplace and even slangy speech; the burlesque novel substitutes observed urban vernacular for convention. Second, the falsely easy and improbable transition in action is a second comment on commonplace life in the streets, mining camps, and other locales of the Californians Harte observed in daily life.

The analysis of "Muck-A-Muck," Harte's burlesque of Cooper, shows him handling Cooper's portrait of the Indian–a particularly sore point with Artemus Ward, Mark Twain, and virtually all western writers of the 1860s–in the same manner. Romantic "distance" is caricatured and its stilted language and simplistic development of emotional life rejected by inserting the low and vulgar for the artificially refined and therefore falsified language of the idealist. Patrick D. Morrow quite rightly describes *Condensed Novels, and Other Papers* as "an unrecognized but major event in American literature." The later *Condensed Novels, Second Series: New Burlesques* of 1902 are similar but treat a more modern-seeming group of writers. Harte's critical reviews develop these points of burlesque, and even in discussing such topics as children's literature, Harte consistently decried the tendency to lie in fiction or, alternatively, to abandon humor in favor of mannered and overly serious didactic literality.

Harte's practice as a creative writer can be translated directly into the comments which he made as reviewer and critic–the overt expressions of his critical philosophy which made him one of several influential writers in the early 1870s in the area of local-color realism. Naturally, Harte reviewed Leland's *Hans Breitmann About Town* (1869), Harriet Beecher Stowe's *Oldtown Folks* (1869), and a variety of popular literature. "Artemus Ward," which appeared in the *Golden Era* (27 December 1863), represents a starting point. Harte commented, almost negatively it seems, on Ward's lectures, although Ward was pioneering a new form of burlesque lyceum presentation mocking sentiment and publicly displayed erudition. Harte both accepts and rejects this position due to his own belief that humor should be el-evating in some overt way. He comments that Ward's humor is of a "special" type, but not the highest and most ennobling kind. Significantly, however, he also contends that Ward "has more of a national characteristic than the higher and more artistic standard."

In as little as a line, Harte thus identifies his democratic critical viewpoint. The lawlessness of Ward's humor is Harte's primary interest: "the surface of our national life, which is met in the stage, rail-car, canal and flat boat." The low subject matter is American. Harte at least partially mistakes Ward by going on to claim that his humor has no purpose to serve beyond the present joke, no moral to develop. For Harte, however, this too represents a point of critical departure, for he defends "fun without application," abandoning the necessity for moralized literature. Minstrel-show humor is identified as Ward's primary content in place of the higher truths of humorous observation as found in Lowell, Dickens, or Thomas Chandler Haliburton. Yet, even here, he concludes by hoping that Ward will use his financial success as a means to reach a higher plane of humor expressing his frank, genial nature.

Harte's position in this review supports the lowering of subject matter and the absence of the didactic while also superficially supporting the idealistic purpose of literature and its "instructive" responsibility. The essay shows Harte's ambivalence as a writer with both an interest in realistic details, as in the local colorists, and sentimentalist tendencies. His review of Mark Twain's *The Innocents Abroad* (1869) in the *Overland Monthly* (January 1870) is consistent with this attitude, and his criticisms of Twain as offering no new information on the Holy Land and lacking an elevated viewpoint need little other explanation.

Harte's other essays elaborate the points generated in his Ward review. "Railway Reading" from the *Californian* (6 June 1866) attacks the contrived action of romance fiction in a form consistent with Harte's discussion of Ward. His review of Leland's *Hans Breitmann About Town* in the *Overland Monthly* (August 1869), following a previous favorable review in September 1868 of Leland's first volume, praised Leland's poetry for its mix of humor and wisdom; Leland's Hans Breitmann in conception and realization was a garrulous German "Bummer" of an educated and philosophical sort. Harte defends Breitmann's comic dialect for its ironic creation of conflicting ideas by misspellings.

Harte in old age (courtesy of Clifton Waller Barrett)

As in the Ward essay, Harte's position—strongly advocated—is that details of speech, even vulgar ones, are appropriate when they depict clearly and add meaning to the reader's experience. Nor was Harte alone in his appreciation of Leland's dialect verse, which was greeted with enthusiasm as something genuinely new and American in both England and France at the time, two years before Harte's and Hay's dialect poems achieved book publication. Similarly, in reviewing Stowe's *Oldtown Folks* in the *Overland Monthly* (October 1869), Harte picked out "do-nothing" Sam Lawson as an honest voice and a universal one, unlike the provincial Lothrops and "negro bondsmen" that otherwise populated the book with Stowe's narrowly regional moral perceptions. Thus, Harte connected provincialism with a New England Brahmin disposition.

Harte's obituary review, "Charles Dickens," in the *Overland Monthly* (July 1870), adds the dimension of economic awareness to Harte's special mixture of sentiment and realism. His chief theme is the simplicity and directness of Dickens. However, he also praises Dickens's humor as mani-

fested in such works as *The Life and Adventures of Martin Chuzzlewit* (1842-1844), for its "delightful pantheism," what modern critics have called its "thingification" in metaphors such as door handles that "looked as if they wanted to be wound up" and drawers needing to be opened like an oyster.

Harte endorses Dickens's mode in bringing the surroundings into synchronization with events naturally, as in the death of Little Nell; "naturalness" occupies a central place in Harte's critical pantheon. A second important point, however, again consistent with Harte's own localist writings, is his contention that Dickens "brought the poor nearer to our hearts." As a democratic philosopher, Harte insists throughout his criticism that the common man be accepted and recognized. Basic to his critical philosophy is the social argument that the poor and the degraded are components of society deserving of study and having a legitimate claim on the reader's attention. In fact, his advocacy of Dumas's *The Count of Monte Cristo* (1845) in "My Favorite Novelist and His Best Book" (1894) lies in a complementary point: that the average man does not come home to read the sordid details of pathological materiality (Harte being by no means happy with the naturalism of the 1890s) but rather to be lifted out of his limited world into higher hopefulness. To Harte this was a blameless middle-class wish, if an uncritical one from a literary standpoint.

Dickens's overwhelming humanity is his greatest asset because it allows the appreciation of all levels of life, including low life, while aiming higher—the combination of "obvious philanthropic consecration" with "the exposition of some public abuse, or the portrayal of some social wrong" together with "tender and human pictures of classes on whom the world hitherto had bestowed but scant sentiment." This statement can be identified with Harte's own fictional writing, adhering as it did to the local-color formulas of the 1870s throughout his entire career. For him, the sentimentalization of details could be acceptable if the details held essential qualities of the life portrayed. As an American writer, the details of the American West allowed him his nationalism in the broadest sense used by Walt Whitman in writing to "the Americans of all nations." Harte here is an eminently "American" critic and, to the readers of the 1870s, a particularly "western" critic, even while endorsing the works of Dickens and Dumas. In fact, the critical

Last photograph of Harte, taken a few months before his death in 1902

viewpoint has an obvious consistency with his own background as well.

The independence and honesty of Harte's reviews, as noted by the *Nation* in 1870 and other sources, derive directly from his insistence on a westerner's "American" viewpoint closely related to the rambunctious regionalism that characterized San Francisco as a literary frontier, to lean on Franklin Walker's happily titled book on this period. Harte's "A Few Words About Mr. Lowell," published in the *New Review* (February 1891), recapitulated his important positions as they were demonstrated in the gamut of his writings in the 1860s and 1870s. Harte praised Lowell's early popular acceptance—showing Harte's own democratic and dollar-oriented western pragmatism at the outset—and added that Lowell's position as a controversialist made this phenomenon even more impressive. Lowell's New England details and genuine dialect—praised over the "pretty prose fancy of Sam Slick"—were chief elements in his portrayal of the "real Yankee" with a deep consciousness of a personal God accepting of "wily humanity." Harte flat-footedly

reveals his admiration of the literature depicting lower classes, stating that "It is the rude dialect of Hosea that is alone real and vital" in *The Biglow Papers* (1848).

Backing his contention with citations from "The Courtin'," Harte at this relatively late point in his own career adheres to the idea of localist detail—at the level of ruder humanity—as an author's surest mode of revelation of social vision, giving readers insight into the rougher aspects of regional life among the lower classes. In fact, the conclusion of the essay turns harshly negative on Lowell, although praising "this wonderful dialect" repeatedly, because Lowell remained a Brahman New England "Englishman," "in the broadest sense of the term." Lowell, Harte complained, recalling his own personal history, came from a family not forced by vicissitude to "go West" or change his habitat as did the "average American." Phrase by phrase, Harte reveals the layers of personal experience, regional mythos, and national philosophy underlying his critical stance. He can hardly be more damning, according to his own critical presuppositions of the California period—even though writing in England in 1891—than when he accuses New England literature and Lowell of being, like Thoreau at Walden, too much within earshot of Mr. Emerson's dinner bell. This last analytic point causes him to describe Lowell's position in regard to the whole nation as a failure in sympathetic understanding. He insists on the national writer's responsibility to portray all classes and levels of society and to urge their humane consideration.

Bret Harte's importance as a critic lies in the work he completed in a brief span of eight or nine years from 1863 through 1871. By that time he had completely demonstrated his concept of localist detail. He had accepted common and vulgar language into his own works as dialect, providing that it showed humanity and portrayed true character. He had attacked in burlesque and in explicit statement the formulaic, the overwrought, the contrived, and the devised in plot, language, and even typography. And he had soundly rejected literature which did not provide the reader with a compelling plot, providing the plot served some improving purpose as in the works of Dumas. Even in the Dumas essay, Harte manages to purposefully drop in colloquial western phrases to express the pragmatism with which he is viewing the development of an adventure plot for a reader justified in his need for escape by the confines of everyday life.

Harte's later letters and personal commentary bear out the public record. In 1890 he complained of the theatrical-seeming illustrations of his fictional miners in red woolen shirts: they wore white, as temperatures frequently reached 100°, and they did not wear woolens. Further, he noted that the forty-niners were not "rowdy" but were educated and refined men rather than laborers.

Such comments help explain why he adhered to his seemingly "sentimentalized" local-color depictions in the face of the increasing sordidness of contemporary fiction decried in the Dumas essay. Bold as his critical position was in the 1860s, the 1880s and 1890s blended a grimness of detail in their physical descriptions which exceeded Harte's willing intention. He remained an idealist according to the genteel New England pattern, even though he was not an idealist in limiting himself to sublime subject matter. For these later developments he had a limited understanding, and his criticism of Henry James's *Daisy Miller: A Study* (1878), as early as 1879, misinterprets James's development of the action. Harte declares himself unable to comprehend the "Americanness" of James's character and his symbolic treatment of European psychology through his depiction of setting.

In short, Harte remained a brilliant exponent of the western American viewpoint as it flashed in San Francisco's wits in the 1860s and in the pages of *Golden Era,* the *Californian,* and the *Overland Monthly* for the rest of America to notice for the first time. He asserted the value of dialect and of low characters because of their relevance to the truthful depiction of life and their importance in stirring worthwhile responses in the reader. Harte as editor had largely completed his review work by 1871. His most important writings were also completed by that date, and he did not expand his ability as a writer, as for example did his sometimes student Mark Twain. Nevertheless, as a spokesman for a self-consciously national viewpoint in American literature, recognizing all classes and regions, and as an advocate of vulgar detail as a means to high literary ends, his place in American criticism remains important in the early formation of the realist era.

Letters:
The Letters of Bret Harte, edited by Geoffrey Bret Harte (Boston: Houghton Mifflin, 1926).

References:
Linda D. Barnett, *Bret Harte: A Reference Guide* (Boston: G. K. Hall, 1980);

Margaret Duckett, *Mark Twain and Bret Harte* (Norman: University of Oklahoma Press, 1964);

Patrick D. Morrow, *Bret Harte Literary Critic* (Bowling Green, Ohio: Bowling Green University Popular Press, 1979);

Richard O'Connor, *Bret Harte: A Biography* (Boston: Little, Brown, 1966);

Franklin Walker, *San Francisco's Literary Frontier* (New York: Knopf, 1934).

Papers:
The Beinecke Library at Yale University and the Kozlay Collection at the Huntington Library are the major repositories of Bret Harte's manuscripts.

Paul Hamilton Hayne

(1 January 1830-6 July 1886)

Rayburn S. Moore
University of Georgia

See also the Hayne entry in *DLB 3, Antebellum Writers in New York and the South.*

BOOKS: *Poems* (Boston: Ticknor & Fields, 1855);
Sonnets, and Other Poems (Charleston, S.C.: Harper & Calvo, 1857);
Avolio; A Legend of the Island of Cos with Poems, Lyrical, Miscellaneous, and Dramatic (Boston: Ticknor & Fields, 1860);
Legends and Lyrics (Philadelphia: Lippincott, 1872);
The Mountain of the Lovers (New York: Hale, 1875);
Lives of Robert Young Hayne and Hugh Swinton Legaré (Charleston, S.C.: Walker, Evans & Cogswell, 1878);
Poems. Complete Edition (Boston: Lothrop, 1882).

OTHER: *The Poems of Henry Timrod, Edited, With a Sketch of the Poet's Life,* by Paul H. Hayne (New York: Hale & Son, 1873);
The Poems of Frank O. Ticknor, M.D., introduction by Hayne (Philadelphia: Lippincott, 1879), pp. 9-17.

PERIODICAL PUBLICATIONS: "The North British Review Upon American Poetry," *Southern Literary Gazette,* new series 2 (2 October 1852): 151-152; (9 October 1852): 163; (16 October 1852): 175-176;
"A Word of Explanation," *Southern Literary Gazette,* new series 2 (23 October 1852): 187;
"Editor's Table," *Russell's Magazine,* 3 (April 1858): 78-79;
"Literary Notices," *Russell's Magazine,* 3 (April 1858): 90-92;
"Editor's Table," *Russell's Magazine,* 3 (August 1858): 467-468;
"Editor's Table," *Russell's Magazine,* 4 (March 1859): 561-562;
Review of *Idyls of the King* by Alfred Tennyson, *Russell's Magazine,* 5 (September 1859): 542-549;
"Editor's Table," *Russell's Magazine,* 6 (January 1860): 364, 371;

Paul Hamilton Hayne.

"Editor's Table," *Russell's Magazine,* 6 (March 1860): 565, 568-569, 571-572;
"The Whittington Club, No. 10," *Southern Field and Fireside* (9 June 1860): 19;
"Literary Notices," *Southern Opinion* (7 September 1867);
"A Yankee Phenomenon," *Southern Society* (1868?);
"Our Literary Correspondence," *Rome Courier,* 10 April 1873;
"Our Literary Letter," *Wilmington Morning Star,* 1875?;

Review of *Like Unto Like* by Sherwood Bonner, *Louisville Sunday Argus,* 2 February 1879;

"Ante-Bellum Charleston," *Southern Bivouac,* new series 1 (September 1885): 193-202; (October 1885): 257-268; (November 1885): 327-336;

"Charles Gayarré," *Southern Bivouac,* new series 2 (June 1886): 28-37; (July 1886): 108-113; (August 1886): 172-176.

Paul Hamilton Hayne was the best-known southern poet and man of letters during the 1870s and 1880s. As the editor of two important antebellum magazines, the *Southern Literary Gazette* and *Russell's Magazine,* as a contributor to many important periodicals, both northern and southern, before and after the Civil War, and as an editorial writer/columnist in southern journals after the war, Hayne eventually became the chief southern spokesman on literary affairs after the death of William Gilmore Simms in 1870. His critical views, consequently, are sometimes related to his position as an unofficial laureate, though they are frequently less sectional than might be expected. On the whole, his opinions reflect a traditional and eclectic romanticism that nevertheless manages often to concern itself with contemporary writing and to express itself sometimes in a rather modern manner.

Hayne's first critical pronouncements appeared in connection with his editorial functions on the *Southern Literary Gazette* (1852-1855) and *Russell's Magazine* (1857-1860) and with contributions to other periodicals during this period. As an editor Hayne offered his views on Anglo-American and North-South literary relations, on poetry and fiction, and on such writers as Henry Wadsworth Longfellow, Oliver Wendell Holmes, William Cullen Bryant, Edgar Allan Poe, William Gilmore Simms, and Henry Timrod, among others.

In 1852 in the *Southern Literary Gazette,* for example, Hayne defended American poetry and poets from criticism by a writer in the *North British Review* and concluded that a critic who could not appreciate the merits of Longfellow's "The Psalm of Life," Bryant's "Thanatopsis," and especially Poe's "The Raven" was derelict in "the primary duties and amenities of his profession." Almost seven years later he upheld Longfellow again, this time in his editorial column in the March 1859 issue of *Russell's Magazine:* "When will 'these English' learn to know that writing in the same language ... every American author,

who, by his productions, adds anything true and permanent to the literature which belongs to us both, does as much for the glory of England, as for the glory of his own country?"

In the meantime, Hayne had published and reviewed Simms's work and had accepted Timrod's poems and essays in both magazines. He had, in 1852, also attacked Harriet Beecher Stowe's *Uncle Tom's Cabin* as "the slanderous North's publication," but in the January 1860 issue of *Russell's Magazine* he defended Bryant against an attack from a writer in the *Richmond Enquirer* who damned his poetry because of his politics. "It is," Hayne asserted, "precisely such exhibitions of narrow-minded arrogance and folly on the part of those who are presumed to speak the sentiments of our people, which give some colour to the charge of the intellectual blindness or inferiority (especially in matters of ART) of the Southern States."

At this time and throughout his career Hayne was concerned about keeping literature and politics (and personality, too, at times) apart. He maintained in *Russell's Magazine* (August 1858): "Now if there be one rule of criticism ... more clear to us than any other, it is, that where the claims of a literary man come up for adjudication, he should be considered solely in his public and artistic, not in his private and individual capacity." He was especially careful to focus his critical attention on Poe's work, not his character. Early and late, he acknowledged Poe's "moral" weaknesses and limitations but nevertheless examined and praised "The Raven," "Annabel Lee," "Ligeia," *The Narrative of Arthur Gordon Pym,* "The Philosophy of Composition," and other works. And as his letters show, in the last year of his life he still thought that "an *intellectual,* or "Art-Performance" should be judged "upon its *own* merits."

Despite such efforts to concentrate on the work instead of the writer, Hayne, on occasion, turned to ad hominem attack. He was particularly critical of Walt Whitman and George Washington Cable. Whitman, a "false, hollow, feculant [*sic*] *Eccentric*" and "tremendous charlatan," has succeeded, he asserted in 1868 in *Southern Society,* "in hoodwinking thousands of shrewd, sensible and learned men, and of imposing upon them the veriest intellectual and spiritual rubbish of the past as something possessed of a novel, incalculable value!" Whitman's "verses" he characterized as biblical in form, that is, arranged "after the style of sentences in the English versions of the

Hayne's birthplace in Charleston, South Carolina

Old and New Testament—a plan horribly incongruous, for we continually find ourselves instituting involuntary comparisons between the lofty teachings of the Book of God and the prurient assumptions of the Book of Whitman!" Years later, in 1881, Hayne concluded in a letter to Julia C. R. Dorr: "If this 'Yahoo' be in very deed a Poet; then must all established notions . . . of those high qualities and transcendent endowments which go to make up the poetic character and force be at once and forever discarded."

Cable, if anything, was more culpable than Whitman. A "Clerk & Parvenu, *a thorough Yankee in blood,* wherever, by *accident,* he was born," Cable was, for acknowledging the justice of the Union cause in *Dr. Sevier* (1884) and espousing the cause of the Negro in the 1880s, denounced as a traitor by Hayne in public and private and particularly in a sonnet entitled "The Renegade" in which "*one* traitorous Knave" (unnamed) mocked, "feigned, . . . flattered, fawned & lied" and "blithely" left a "glorious Cause" to join "the Conqueror's proud 'command'–/And–Stentor–Judas–, shouts on . . . *victory's* side" (*Independent,* 22 January 1885).

Not surprisingly, Hayne often wrote favorably about the work of authors whose characters he admired, respected, and loved, most notably Longfellow and Simms. He praised Longfellow's work in the 1850s, and by the 1870s (particularly in "The Snow-Messengers," composed in late 1879) he honored both the poet whose "songs" had "made Arcadian half the world" and the man, "the cordial prince of kindly men." When Longfellow died in 1882 Hayne was quick to respond. In "Longfellow Dead" he pictured the departed poet as "crowned and shriven" standing "amid his peers, the grand immortals." With Simms's work he was, on occasion, more forthright. A generous supporter of the elder author's productions from 1852 onward, Hayne usually acknowledged Simms's faults as man and author—haste in composition, too frequent publication, bulldog tenacity of opinion, and a tendency toward Johnsonian authoritarianism—but at the same time, he generally lauded Simms's gift with story and narrative and his courage and intelligence as critic and man.

After the war Hayne held fewer important editorial posts but he served until his death in vari-

DEDICATORY SONNET

TO EDWIN P. WHIPPLE, ESQ., OF BOSTON.

O FRIEND! between us, for long dreary years,
  Distance and Fate have raised their barriers strong;
  Yet Love, surviving, takes the wings of Song,
  And flies to greet thee; whatsoe'er appears
Of false or feeble in these various lays,
  Forgive; the heart is in them, and to thee
  The lowliest strains of true sincerity
  Rise like the music of a voice of praise.
Though thou hast searched the souls of greatest Seers,
  Shakespeare, and Spencer, Sidney, — to the core
  Of their deep natures probing o'er and o'er, —
Still not the less to humbler bards are given
  Thy faith and homage, — for the Poet's lore,
  Or great or small, is knowledge caught from
    Heaven!

Dedication page for Avolio *(1860), Hayne's third collection of verse*

Hayne in the 1870s (courtesy of Duke University Library)

ous editorial capacities with southern newspapers and magazines. In this way, and in exchanges of correspondence with literary friends and contemporaries, he expressed his critical views on most British and American literary monuments, past or present. Shakespeare and Milton were at the summit of the Anglo-American Olympus. Shakespeare he had considered his master as early as 1852, and in the last years of his life, Hayne reiterated his debt and sought to make distinctions between the accomplishments of Shakespeare and Milton. In 1884 he characterized Shakespeare a "gigantic genius" and Milton a "majestic genius." Shakespeare's "grand capacious soul took in all humanity"; Milton's verse was "truly inspired by some Titan muse at his best and grandest." Shakespeare "appears to have absorbed universal knowledge by the *pores of his skin! Milton—& I yield to none in admiration—was *after all*, but a *child* compared with Shakspeare. He had the *sharpest* limitations; the other almost no *limitations* at all."

Of the English poets of his own day Hayne judged Tennyson to be the greatest. He thought

well of the achievements of Browning, Arnold, and Swinburne (he admitted the latter's immorality, but readily acknowledged his position as an important poet); he praised the work of Wordsworth, Coleridge, Scott, Shelley, Keats, and Leigh Hunt; he was fascinated by the long poems of William Morris and the lyrics of Dante Gabriel Rossetti and other members of the Pre-Raphaelite group (after corresponding in the 1880s with Philip Bourke Marston, poet, critic, and friend of Swinburne, Rossetti, and others, Hayne's appreciation of the Pre-Raphaelites deepened). But Tennyson's name led all the rest. He was the "sovereign master of a thousand lays" whose *The Princess, In Memoriam,* and *Idyls of the King* were "wonderful works"; indeed, in a review of *Idyls of the King* in 1859, Hayne characterized it as "an almost consummate work of Art, and the *great imaginative poem of the century*" (*Russell's Magazine,* September 1859). But even Tennyson could err. In 1875 when *Queen Mary* appeared, Hayne pointed out in an essay in the *Wilmington Morning Star* that, though *Queen Mary* was "both interesting and instructive," it was "a failure" as "an artistic Historical Tragedy" when measured by "any high standard." Nevertheless, when the whole corpus was considered, he concluded that Tennyson was the great poet of the period.

As for fiction, Hayne was also romantically inclined, though he liked Defoe (*Robinson Crusoe* was always one of his favorite books), Fielding, Thackeray, Trollope, Hardy, and George Eliot. Eliot's *Middlemarch* (1872), for example, he denominated a "classic" in 1873, and he concluded that "Mrs. Lewis [*sic*]" "stands alone among the women, and indeed, so far as we know, among the ablest men of her generation!" (*Rome Courier,* 10 April 1873). His chief favorites were Scott and Dickens, and he considered story and character the two primary elements of the novel (philosophy and psychological analysis were acceptable in George Eliot's fiction, but in general might too easily impede the progress of the narrative). Scott, he thought, was the master storyteller and Dickens the master of character. As late as 1886 Hayne characterized Scott as the "Scotch Shakspeare & Chaucer *combined*" and Dickens as an "imaginative genius & artist" whose art was "steeped in the life-blood of the human heart," and chastised the new critics of the postwar period who belittled Dickens and Thackeray and who ignored or condescended to Scott.

Hayne's Georgia home, "Copse Hill," where he resided following the Civil War until his death

As for American poetry and fiction, Hayne tended to follow the same standards he established for the consideration of British authors. Longfellow was the chief poet, but Whittier, Lowell, and Holmes all qualified (leaving out their political poems, of course), and Poe was the one "original genius" among them. Ironically, Hayne, at the age of twenty-four, was presented with an opportunity to laud and defend Poe at a gathering of literati in 1854 in Boston. There he maintained that Poe was the "most original genius in all American literature," a view he modified only slightly in 1879 when he asserted: "With the solitary exception of *Nathaniel Hawthorne*, [Poe] was the greatest *Genius* America has yet produced; and in *massive profundity of intellect,* and vivid powers of analysis, he excelled Hawthorne."

Hawthorne, of course, was the major American novelist, but Hayne also considered Cooper and Simms important (Melville he seldom men-

tioned and Poe he viewed mainly as a writer of tales, though he admired *The Narrative of Arthur Gordon Pym*). The fiction of James and Howells he disliked for a lack of "story" and inordinate interest in character analysis. His views of American fiction are characteristically expressed in an essay in three parts he wrote for the *Southern Bivouac* in 1885. In the second of these installments Hayne favorably reviewed Simms's literary career and work and, in so doing, paid his respects to "Aesthetic Realism" as propounded and practiced by James and Howells. Such realism, according to Hayne, dispensed with story, plot, and objective characterization and, indeed, concentrated on style. Howells, he remarked, had already condescended to Scott, and James and Howells both would characterize Cooper and Simms as "uncivilized antiques." In 1886 he pointed out that Howells, in particular, had also "snubbed" Thackeray and Dickens. To these writers, if Hayne had read

James's "The Art of Fiction" in 1884, he could have added the name of Anthony Trollope, a writer whose novels he had reviewed and praised since the 1850s. At any rate, he concluded that the "school of fiction" to which James and Howells belonged—the "James school," he called it—"makes me sick at my moral & mental stomach."

Hayne, then, was a mid-nineteenth-century romantic who accepted, in general, the main tenets of the Anglo-American literary tradition with regard to nature, language, and technique. He opposed forthrightly certain elements of realism—its lack of story and its emphasis on character analysis and style. On 29 May 1882 he wrote a friend, Charles W. Hubner: "The older I grow, the more truly I yearn to come near, and to move the great Heart of Humanity, [and] to elevate, comfort, and console the lives of my fellow-creatures. To illustrate the *Beautiful*, to sing of the *ideal* in its loftiest phrases—these are aims worthy of *any* Poet; but to bind the broken heart, and to stimulate the despondent spirit, and even to celebrate the triumphs of homely toil . . . are nobler achievements still." He assimilated these views in a series of poems he wrote for *Home and Farm* from 1882 to 1885, including "In the Wheat Field," "The Genius of Midsummer Lands," "Midsummer. (On the Farm)," and "Harvest Time," all of which demonstrate the poet's sincere effort to deal with the rural world more closely and to appeal more directly to the "great Heart of Humanity." Believing, too, that the general public needed to be more aware of the importance of literature, Hayne had sought throughout his career to introduce it to the best books and standards in his criticism and in his own work. He did not always succeed, but in six books of poems and in dozens of essays, reviews, and editorial columns he strove to express his standards and to induce public awareness and interest. Throughout the country at large he was known as a poet and not as a critic, for his criticism was published mainly in southern periodicals, but as an unofficial literary spokesman for his region and his art, he was the most influential southern critic of the 1870s and 1880s.

Letters:

A Collection of Hayne Letters, edited by Daniel Morley McKeithan (Austin: University of Texas Press, 1944);

The Correspondence of Bayard Taylor and Paul Hamilton Hayne, edited by Charles Duffy (Baton

Hayne's study at "Copse Hill"

Rouge: Louisiana State University Press, 1945);

Selected Letters: John Garland James to Paul Hamilton Hayne and Mary Middleton Michel Hayne, edited by McKeithan (Austin: University of Texas Press, 1946);

"A Southern Genteelist: Letters by Paul Hamilton Hayne to Julia C. R. Dorr," edited by Duffy, *South Carolina Historical and Genealogical Magazine*, 52 (April 1951): 65-73; 52 (July 1951): 154-165; 52 (October 1951): 207-217; 53 (January 1952): 19-30;

A Man of Letters in the Nineteenth-Century South: Selected Letters of Paul Hamilton Hayne, edited by Rayburn S. Moore (Baton Rouge: Louisiana State University Press, 1982).

Bibliography:

Louis D. Rubin, Jr., ed., *A Bibliographical Guide to the Study of Southern Literature* (Baton Rouge: Louisiana State University Press, 1969); updated annually in spring number, *Mississippi Quarterly*.

References:

Charles Anderson, "Charles Gayarré and Paul Hayne: The Last Literary Cavaliers," *American Studies in Honor of William Kenneth Boyd,* edited by David K. Jackson (Durham: Duke University Press, 1940);

Jack DeBellis, ed., *Sidney Lanier, Henry Timrod, and Paul Hamilton Hayne: A Reference Guide* (Boston: G. K. Hall, 1978);

Max L. Griffin, "Whittier and Hayne: A Record of Friendship," *American Literature,* 19 (March 1947): 41-58;

Jay B. Hubbell, *The South in American Literature, 1607-1900* (Durham: Duke University Press, 1954);

Hubbell, ed., *The Last Years of Henry Timrod* (Durham: Duke University Press, 1941);

Ludwig Lewisohn, "Paul Hamilton Hayne," "The Book We Have Made," *Sunday News* (Charleston, S. C.), 20 September 1903, p. 20;

Daniel McKeithan, "A Correspondence Journal of Paul Hamilton Hayne," *Georgia Historical Quarterly,* 26 (September-December 1942): 249-272;

McKeithan, "Paul Hamilton Hayne and *The Southern Bivouac,*" *Studies in English,* 17 (1937): 112-123;

Rayburn S. Moore, " 'The Absurdest of Critics': Hayne on Howells," *Southern Literary Journal,* 12 (Fall 1979): 70-78;

Moore, " 'A Great Poet and Original Genius': Hayne Champions Poe," *Southern Literary Journal,* 16 (Fall 1983): 105-112;

Moore, "Hayne the Poet: A New Look," *South Carolina Review,* 2 (November 1969): 4-13;

Moore, " 'The Literary World Gone Mad': Hayne on Whitman," *Southern Literary Journal,* 10 (Fall 1977): 75-83;

Moore, "The Old South and the New: Paul Hamilton Hayne and Maurice Thompson," *Southern Literary Journal,* 5 (Fall 1972): 108-122;

Moore, *Paul Hamilton Hayne* (New York: Twayne, 1972);

Moore, "Paul Hamilton Hayne," *Georgia Review,* 22 (Spring 1968): 106-124;

Moore, "Paul Hamilton Hayne and Andrew Adgate Lipscomb: 'Sweet Converse' Between Poet and Preacher," *Georgia Historical Quarterly,* 66 (Spring 1982): 53-68;

Moore, "Paul Hamilton Hayne and Northern Magazines, 1866-1886," in *Essays Mostly on Periodical Publishing in America: A Collection in Honor of Clarence Gohdes,* edited by James Woodress and others (Durham: Duke University Press, 1973): pp. 134-147;

Edd W. Parks, *Ante-Bellum Southern Literary Critics* (Athens: University of Georgia Press, 1962);

Parks, *Henry Timrod* (New York: Twayne, 1964);

Parks, ed., *Southern Poets* (New York: American Book Co., 1936);

William Gilmore Simms, *The Letters of William Gilmore Simms,* 6 volumes, edited by Mary C. Simms Oliphant and others (Columbia: University of South Carolina Press, 1952-1956, 1982).

Papers:

The Paul Hamilton Hayne Papers, housed at the William R. Perkins Library at Duke University, is the chief collection of Hayne's manuscripts, journals, letters, clippings, and memorabilia, including the unpublished manuscript of his uncollected verse published after 1882, "Last Poems of Paul Hamilton Hayne," edited by Hayne's wife and son.

Thomas Wentworth Higginson

(23 December 1823-9 May 1911)

James W. Tuttleton
New York University

See also the Higginson entry in *DLB 1, The American Renaissance in New England.*

BOOKS: *Out-door Papers* (Boston: Ticknor & Fields, 1863);

Malbone: An Oldport Romance (Boston: Fields, Osgood/London: Macmillan, 1869);

Army Life in a Black Regiment (Boston: Fields, Osgood, 1870; revised and enlarged, Boston & New York: Houghton, Mifflin, 1890);

Atlantic Essays (Boston: Osgood, 1871; London: Low, Marston, Low & Searle, 1872);

Oldport Days (Boston: Osgood, 1873);

English Statesmen (New York: Putnam's, 1875);

Young Folk's History of the United States (Boston: Lee & Shepard/New York: Dillingham, 1875);

A Book of American Explorers (Boston: Lee & Shepard, 1877);

Short Studies of American Authors (Boston: Lee & Shepard/New York: Dillingham, 1880);

Common Sense About Women (Boston: Lee & Shepard/London: Sonnenschien, 1882);

Margaret Fuller Ossoli (Boston & New York: Houghton, Mifflin, 1884);

A Larger History of the United States to the Close of President Jackson's Administration (New York: Harper, 1885);

Hints on Writing and Speech-making (Boston: Lee & Shepard/New York: Dillingham, 1887);

The Monarch of Dreams (Boston: Lee & Shepard, 1887);

Women and Men (New York: Harper, 1888);

The Afternoon Landscape: Poems and Translations (New York & London: Longmans, Green, 1889);

Travellers and Outlaws (Boston: Lee & Shepard/ New York: Dillingham, 1889);

Life of Francis Higginson, First Minister in the Massachusetts Bay Colony, and Author of "New England's Plantation" (New York: Dodd, Mead, 1891);

Concerning All of Us (New York: Harper, 1892);

The New World and the New Book (Boston: Lee & Shepard, 1892);

Such As They Are: Poems, by Higginson and Mary Thacher Higginson (Boston: Roberts, 1893);

English History for American Readers, by Higginson and Edward Channing (New York: Longmans, Green, 1893); republished as *English History for Americans* (New York: Longmans,

Green, 1894; revised and enlarged, New York: Longmans, Green, 1902);

Book and Heart: Essays on Literature and Life (New York: Harper, 1897);

The Procession of Flowers and Kindred Papers (New York: Longmans, Green, 1897);

Cheerful Yesterdays (Boston & New York: Houghton, Mifflin, 1898; London: Gay & Bird, 1898);

Contemporaries (Boston & New York: Houghton, Mifflin, 1899);

Old Cambridge (New York & London: Macmillan, 1899);

The Writings of Thomas Wentworth Higginson, 7 volumes (Boston: Houghton, Mifflin, 1900)–includes *Cheerful Yesterdays, Contemporaries, Army Life in a Black Regiment, Women and the Alphabet, Studies in Romance, Outdoor Studies: and Poems,* and *Studies in History and Letters;*

Henry Wadsworth Longfellow (Boston & New York: Houghton, Mifflin, 1902);

John Greenleaf Whittier (New York: Macmillan, 1902); republished as *John Greenleaf Whittier. His Personal Qualities* (New York: Macmillan, 1924);

A Reader's History of American Literature, by Higginson and Henry W. Boynton (Boston, New York & Chicago: Houghton, Mifflin, 1903);

History of the United States from 986 to 1905, by Higginson and William MacDonald (New York: Harper, 1905);

Part of a Man's Life (Boston & New York: Houghton, Mifflin, 1905; London: Constable, 1905);

Life and Times of Stephen Higginson, Member of the Continental Congress (1783) and Author of the "Laco" Letters, Relating to John Hancock (Boston & New York: Houghton, Mifflin, 1907);

Things Worth While (New York: Heubsch, 1908);

Carlyle's Laugh, and Other Surprises (Boston & New York: Houghton Mifflin, 1909);

Descendants of the Reverend Francis Higginson, First "Teacher" in the Massachusetts Bay Colony of Salem, Massachusetts and Author of "New England's Plantation" (1630) (Boston: Privately printed, 1910).

OTHER: *Thalatta: A Book for the Seaside,* edited by Higginson and Samuel Longfellow (Boston: Ticknor, Reed & Fields, 1853);

The Works of Epictetus, translated by Higginson (Boston: Little, Brown, 1865);

Higginson as a senior at Harvard Divinity School, 1846

Harvard Memorial Biographies, edited by Higginson (Cambridge, Mass.: Sever & Francis, 1866);

Poems by Emily Dickinson, edited by Higginson and Mabel Loomis Todd (Boston: Roberts Brothers, 1890);

Poems by Emily Dickinson, second series, edited by Higginson and Todd (Boston: Roberts Brothers, 1891);

Massachusetts in the Army and Navy during the War of 1895-96, 2 volumes, edited by Higginson (Boston: Wright & Potter [State Printers], 1895-1896).

Thomas Wentworth Higginson was an extraordinarily versatile and energetic cultural critic and man of letters in nineteenth-century America. According to Henry James, he reflected almost everything that was in the New England air during his long and frequently tempestuous lifetime. A transcendentalist inspired by Ralph Waldo Emerson and Theodore Parker, Higginson wrote extensively on a wide range of cultural issues including literature and criticism, civil rights, women's liberation, the Civil War, temperance, labor reform, and international politics. Aside from *Army Life in a Black Regiment* (1870), *Common Sense About Women* (1882), and *Cheerful Yesterdays* (1898), which deserve to be better known than they are, Higginson is chiefly remembered for a substantial body of literary criticism that covered the whole span of American writing, from the colonial period to the turn-of-the-century fiction of Edith Wharton.

Born on 23 December 1823 on "Professor's Row" in Cambridge, Massachusetts, to Stephen Higginson and Louisa Storrow Higginson, Thomas Wentworth Higginson matriculated at Harvard when he was thirteen, was converted to the transcendental spiritualism that swept the college, and went on to become an ardent reformer passionately devoted to three lifelong goals—the pursuit of personal liberty, religious freedom, and equality of the sexes. After study at the Harvard Divinity School, he served as a non-denominational minister in Newburyport and Worcester, preaching an undogmatic ethical Christianity founded on a belief in the essential identity of all religions.

As a political activist and radical abolitionist, the Reverend Mr. Higginson stunned Boston by spearheading an assault on the courthouse in 1854 to free Anthony Burns, a fugitive slave. As a member of the "Secret Six" who conspired with John Brown in his effort to smuggle escaped slaves into Canada, Higginson also "rode shotgun" with Free Soil emigrants to Kansas during the "border wars." With the outbreak of the Civil War he was given the command of the First South Carolina Volunteers, the first regiment of freed slaves in the Union Army. His unit liberated hundreds of slaves on the upriver plantations and successfully invaded and occupied Jacksonville, Florida. Wounded in combat and discharged a hero, Colonel Higginson retired to Newport and Boston, where he attained national fame as a spokesman for feminism, labor reform, black rights, temperance, and anti-imperialism. After the Civil War, he also enjoyed a vast reading public and large lecture audiences, thanks to his graceful, passionate, and polemical speeches, essays, and books on American life and letters.

Higginson's criticism, including his three full-length critical biographies, tends toward extravagant praise and is informed by a sincere belief that a well-formed style is the first necessity of all good literature. But in practice Higginson was a didactic critic in the Genteel Tradition who invaria-

Higginson with his daughter Margaret in an 1885 studio photograph

bly judged writing in terms of his political liberalism and his transcendental spiritual idealism. These attitudes are aptly summarized in "Literature As an Art" (1867), "Youth and the Literary Life" (1892), and "Literature As a Pursuit" (1905).

Citing Emerson and Nathaniel Hawthorne as the central figures in American literature, he called for an art that invoked the Declaration of Independence as the touchstone of values for American literature. Since this document affirms the essential dignity and value of the individual, it was, for Higginson, the basis of all democratic art. Arguing against an undue reverence for European literature, he claimed in "A Cosmopolitan Standard" that internationalism in art usually expresses a deference to European social values. More than any other writer of his time he carried forward the torch lit by Emerson in "The American Scholar" (1837) by proposing that originality in American literature would come from the perspective provided by the newly created egalitarian social order and by an attentive use of the native American materials at hand. Given this

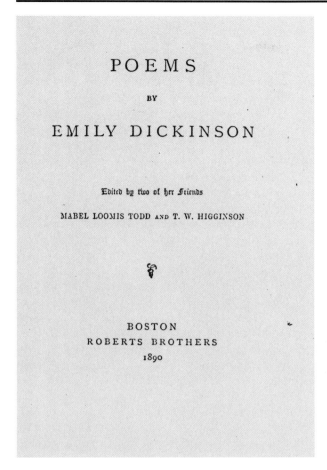

POEMS

BY

EMILY DICKINSON

Edited by two of her Friends

MABEL LOOMIS TODD and T. W. HIGGINSON

BOSTON
ROBERTS BROTHERS
1890

*Title page for the first edition of Emily Dickinson's poems
edited by Higginson and Mabel Loomis Todd*

perspective, Higginson condemned James's biography *Hawthorne* (1879) for describing the American scene as so culturally impoverished that it failed to sustain the American artist. For Higginson, Hawthorne's magisterial fiction, exalted as it was by his spiritual idealism, was the greatest art yet produced in America.

Short Studies of American Authors (1880), *Women and Men* (1888), *Book and Heart: Essays on Literature and Life* (1897), *Contemporaries* (1899), and *A Reader's History of American Literature* (1903) offer a wide range of critical utterances typical of Higginson's lifelong practice of genteel literary criticism. As a religious liberal Higginson argued that the puritan writers were fatally compromised by religious prejudice and that their writing suffered from an indifference to the great Elizabethan models. For Higginson American literature virtually began with Emerson, whom he called the controlling influence, if not the creator, of modern American thought. From Em-

erson arose what was distinctively American and truly excellent in the national literature. Of Emerson's contemporaries, Higginson thought Amos Bronson Alcott to be something of an innocent charlatan, but he praised the Orphic seer for his spiritual idealism. Higginson rejected the view that Henry David Thoreau was merely a follower of Emerson, claiming Thoreau to have had an admirable *lumen siccum,* or dry light, beyond all the men of his day. If Higginson found Oliver Wendell Holmes's work marked by mere fineness rather than depth of feeling, he regarded James Russell Lowell's "Commemoration Ode" (1865) to be the finest single poem yet produced in America. Given his conventional views about poetic form and his high-minded moralism, it is not surprising that Higginson found Walt Whitman's *Leaves of Grass* (1855) to be full of malodorous sexual themes. Calling Whitman a latter-day Ossian, he believed that the poet's experimental revolt against the tyranny of form would not secure him immortality.

Although the regionalist writers after the Civil War used native American materials and celebrated the common man, Higginson was tepid in his criticism of local-color fiction, essentially because it was insufficiently idealistic and only indirectly moral. He called Mark Twain's *The Adventures of Huckleberry Finn* (1884) a distinct step forward in American literature, but he did not find in it the moral depth and social power which later generations have praised. In his early criticism Higginson found Henry James to be prolix, hurried in style, and lacking in the characterization of manly men. Especially repugnant to Higginson was James's insufficient appreciation of the virtue of republicanism, namely, that it develops authentic individuality to the same degree that it diminishes social conventions. But late in his career Higginson was obliged to admit that there were no stories in modern literature quite as good as James's best. Ultimately more pleasing to him, though, was the fiction of William Dean Howells, whose moral delicacy, vivid local color, and stalwart republicanism were enthusiastically acclaimed.

Although Higginson lamented the absence of spiritual idealism in the emergent realism and naturalism of the post-Civil War period, it would be a mistake to imagine that he dismissed the naturalists completely. While he deplored the naturalistic "worship" of Zola, he did praise Frank Norris's use of western settings. And although Stephen Crane's *The Red Badge of Courage* (1895)

Higginson and Samuel Clemens in Dublin, New Hampshire, 1905

dealt ambiguously with Union Army heroism, Higginson found it a work of genius comparable to Tolstoy's best war fiction. Even Edith Wharton's *The House of Mirth* (1905), with its quasi-naturalistic portraits of the social forces that destroy its heroine, Lily Bart, impressed him highly; and in 1905 he surprisingly advanced Wharton to the head of all American novelists, save Hawthorne alone.

Higginson is invariably interesting in his brief critical sketches of those important contemporaries who were his friends or acquaintances, especially Emerson, Thoreau, Hawthorne, Wendell Phillips, William Lloyd Garrison, Bronson Alcott, Holmes, and Lowell. Taken together, his scattered biographical essays and reminiscences, interspersed with critical comment, re-create the Boston-Cambridge-Concord area that was, between 1830 and 1880, the center of American literary life. To these sketches, however, must be added his three full-length biographies: *Margaret Fuller Ossoli* (1884), *Henry Wadsworth Longfellow* (1902), and *John Greenleaf Whittier* (1902). The

best of these biographies is the first, which rescues Margaret Fuller from the common charge that she was a dreamy transcendentalist and emphasizes her as a practical reformer who, despite her overblown rhetorical style, was the most learned American woman of her day. Less satisfactory is Higginson's life of Longfellow, which overemphasizes his Americanness at the expense of his evident advocacy of a cosmopolitan literary culture. Whittier, of course, Higginson found to be the admirable poet of the common man, a writer inspired to a lofty idealism by the great moral crusade of abolitionism, but he lamented Whittier's imperfect rhythms, dubious grammar, and garrulous tendency to the overlong poem laden with a superfluous moral.

Higginson is perhaps most memorable as the "Preceptor" of Emily Dickinson. Responding to his "Letter to a Young Contributor" in the *Atlantic Monthly* in 1862, she sent him some of her poems, asking whether they were alive. He responded in a letter, now lost, recommending, it would seem, revisions that she felt to be "surgery." Even so, she begged him to be her preceptor or literary adviser—a role that he knew he could not play, but tried to, helplessly, until her death in 1886. Some of Dickinson's most ardent admirers have claimed that Higginson's epistolary criticism thwarted her genius and led her to renounce publication. Far from a villain in the drama of her life, Higginson encouraged her, corresponded with her, even visited her twice in Amherst; and, after her death, he edited (with Mabel Loomis Todd) two volumes of her poems, thereby bringing her work to an admiring public. If she would not permit her work to be published in her lifetime, it was because this poet of brilliant gifts was a deeply eccentric woman.

In summary, Higginson's conservative preference for conventional techniques in English poetry, his spiritual idealism, his tendency to the eulogium, and his demand for high moral rectitude in literature inevitably mark him as an exponent of the genteel tradition in nineteenth-century American literary criticism. Yet his fiery abolitionism, his radical views on social democracy, his liberal view of labor issues, and his campaign on behalf of women's rights all distinguish him from other genteel critics like Hamilton Wright Mabie, E. C. Stedman, and Thomas Bailey Aldrich. No better sense of this charming writer can be found than that in his neglected *Cheerful Yesterdays* (1898), a rich treasury of interpretive personal reminiscence, history, and anecdote. Like *Army Life in a Black Regiment*, it is a small masterpiece of autobiographical and literary history.

Letters:

Letters and Journals of Thomas Wentworth Higginson, 1846-1906, edited by Mary Thacher Higginson (Boston & New York, 1921).

Bibliography:

Winifred Mather, *A Bibliography of Thomas Wentworth Higginson* (Cambridge, Mass.: Privately printed [Cambridge Public Library], 1906).

Biography:

Th. Bentzon (Marie Thérèse [de Solms] Blanc), *A Typical American: Thomas Wentworth Higginson*, translated by E. M. Waller (London: Howard Bell, 1902);

Mary Thacher Higginson, *Thomas Wentworth Higginson: The Story of His Life* (Boston: Houghton Mifflin, 1914);

Anna Mary Wells, *Dear Preceptor: The Life and Times of Thomas Wentworth Higginson* (Boston: Houghton Mifflin, 1963);

Howard N. Meyer, *Colonel of the Black Regiment: The Life of Thomas Wentworth Higginson* (New York: Norton, 1967);

Tilden G. Edelstein, *Strange Enthusiasm: A Life of Thomas Wentworth Higginson* (New Haven: Yale University Press, 1968).

References:

John T. Bethell, "The Magnificent Activist," *Harvard Alumni Bulletin*, 70 (13 April 1968): 12-18;

Van Wyck Brooks, *New England: Indian Summer, 1865-1915* (New York: Dutton, 1940);

Edward Channing, *Thomas Wentworth Higginson* (Boston: Proceedings of the Massachusetts Historical Society, 1914);

Octavius Brooks Frothingham, *Transcendentalism in New England* (New York: Putnam's, 1876);

Higginson Journal, edited by Frederick L. Morey (1971-);

William R. Hutchinson, *The Transcendentalist Ministers: Church Reform in New England* (New Haven: Yale University Press, 1959);

Howard Mumford Jones, "Introduction," in *Army Life in a Black Regiment*, by T. W. Higginson (East Lansing: Michigan State University Press, 1960);

E. L. McCormick, "Thomas Wentworth Higginson, Poetry Critic for the *Nation*, 1877-1903," *Serif*, 2 (1965): 14-19;

Howard N. Meyer, "Thomas Wentworth Higginson," in *The Transcendentalists: A Review of Research and Criticism*, edited by Joel Myerson (New York: Modern Language Association, 1984), pp. 195-203;

James W. Tuttleton, *Thomas Wentworth Higginson* (Boston: Twayne, 1978).

Papers:

The most significant collections of Higginson materials are located in the manuscript divisions of the Houghton Library of Harvard University, the Boston Public Library, the Duke University Library, Yale University Library, the Huntington Library, the University of Virginia Library, the Kansas State Historical Society, and the Harvard University Archives. Other important holdings may be found in the manuscript collections of the Massachusetts Historical Society, the American Antiquarian Society, the Plymouth Library of the Pilgrim Society, the Essex Institute (Salem, Massachusetts), Columbia University, Worcester Historical Society, Smith College, and Cornell University.

William Dean Howells

(1 March 1837-11 May 1920)

Gloria Martin
Pacific Lutheran University

See also the Howells entry in *DLB 12, American Realists and Naturalists.*

SELECTED BOOKS: *Poems of Two Friends,* by Howells and John J. Piatt (Columbus: Follett, Foster, 1860);

Lives and Speeches of Abraham Lincoln and Hannibal Hamlin, life of Lincoln by Howells and life of Hamlin by J. L. Hayes (Columbus: Follett, Foster, 1860);

Venetian Life (London: Trübner, 1866; New York: Hurd & Houghton, 1866; expanded, New York: Hurd & Houghton, 1867; London: Trübner, 1867; expanded again, Boston: Osgood, 1872; revised and expanded again, Boston & New York: Houghton, Mifflin, 1907; London: Constable, 1907);

Italian Journeys (New York: Hurd & Houghton, 1867; London: Low, 1868; enlarged, Boston: Osgood, 1872; revised, London: Heinemann, 1901; Boston & New York: Houghton, Mifflin, 1901);

No Love Lost, A Romance of Travel (New York: Putnam's, 1869);

Suburban Sketches (New York: Hurd & Houghton, 1871; London: Low, 1871; enlarged, Boston: Osgood, 1872);

Their Wedding Journey (Boston: Osgood, 1872; Edinburgh: Douglas, 1882);

A Chance Acquaintance (Boston: Osgood, 1873; Edinburgh: Douglas, 1882);

Poems (Boston: Osgood, 1873; enlarged, Boston: Ticknor, 1886);

A Foregone Conclusion (Boston: Osgood, 1874; London: Low, 1874);

Sketch of the Life and Character of Rutherford B. Hayes . . . also a Biographical Sketch of William A. Wheeler (New York: Hurd & Houghton/ Boston: Houghton, 1876);

The Parlor Car. Farce (Boston: Osgood, 1876);

Out of the Question. A Comedy (Boston: Osgood, 1877; Edinburgh: Douglas, 1882);

A Counterfeit Presentment. Comedy (Boston: Osgood, 1877);

William Dean Howells

The Lady of the Aroostook (Boston: Houghton, Osgood, 1879; Edinburgh: Douglas, 1882);

The Undiscovered Country (Boston: Houghton, Mifflin, 1880; London: Low, 1880);

A Fearful Responsibility and Other Stories (Boston: Osgood, 1881); republished as *A Fearful Responsibility and "Tonelli's Marriage"* (Edinburgh: Douglas, 1882);

Dr. Breen's Practice, A Novel (Boston: Osgood, 1881; London: Trübner, 1881);

A Modern Instance, A Novel (1 volume, Boston: Osgood, 1882; 2 volumes, Edinburgh: Douglas, 1882);

The Sleeping Car, A Farce (Boston: Osgood, 1883);

A Woman's Reason, A Novel (Boston: Osgood, 1883; Edinburgh: Douglas, 1883);

A Little Girl Among the Old Masters (Boston: Osgood, 1884);

The Register, Farce (Boston: Osgood, 1884);

Three Villages (Boston: Osgood, 1884);

The Elevator, Farce (Boston: Osgood, 1885);

The Rise of Silas Lapham (1 volume, Boston: Ticknor, 1885; 2 volumes, Edinburgh: Douglas, 1894);

Tuscan Cities (Boston: Ticknor, 1886; Edinburgh: Douglas, 1886);

The Garroters, Farce (New York: Harper, 1886; Edinburgh: Douglas, 1887);

Indian Summer (Boston: Ticknor, 1886; Edinburgh: Douglas, 1886);

The Minister's Charge, or, The Apprenticeship of Lemuel Barker (Edinburgh: Douglas, 1886; Boston: Ticknor, 1887);

Modern Italian Poets, Essays and Versions (New York: Harper, 1887; Edinburgh: Douglas, 1887);

April Hopes, A Novel (Edinburgh: Douglas, 1887; New York: Harper, 1888);

A Sea-Change, or Love's Stowaway: A Lyricated Farce in Two Acts and an Epilogue (Boston: Ticknor, 1888; London: Trübner, 1888);

Annie Kilburn, A Novel (Edinburgh: Douglas, 1888; New York: Harper, 1889);

The Mouse-Trap and Other Farces (New York: Harper, 1889; Edinburgh: Douglas, 1897);

A Hazard of New Fortunes (2 volumes, Edinburgh: Douglas, 1889; 1 volume, New York: Harper, 1890);

The Shadow of a Dream, A Novel (Edinburgh: Douglas, 1890; New York: Harper, 1890);

A Boy's Town Described for "Harper's Young People" (New York: Harper, 1890);

Criticism and Fiction (New York: Harper, 1891; London: Osgood, McIlvaine, 1891);

The Albany Depot, Farce (New York: Harper, 1891; Edinburgh: Douglas, 1897);

An Imperative Duty, A Novel (New York: Harper, 1891; Edinburgh: Douglas, 1891);

Mercy, A Novel (Edinburgh: Douglas, 1892); republished as *The Quality of Mercy* (New York: Harper, 1892);

A Letter of Introduction, Farce (New York: Harper, 1892; Edinburgh: Douglas, 1897);

A Little Swiss Sojourn (New York: Harper, 1892);

Christmas Every Day and Other Stories Told for Children (New York: Harper, 1893);

The World of Chance, A Novel (Edinburgh: Douglas, 1893; New York: Harper, 1893);

The Unexpected Guests, A Farce (New York: Harper, 1893; Edinburgh: Douglas, 1897);

My Year in a Log Cabin (New York: Harper, 1893);

Evening Dress, Farce (New York: Harper, 1893; Edinburgh: Douglas, 1893);

The Coast of Bohemia, A Novel (New York: Harper, 1893; New York & London: Harper, 1899);

A Traveler from Altruria, Romance (New York: Harper, 1894; Edinburgh: Douglas, 1894);

My Literary Passions (New York: Harper, 1895);

Stops of Various Quills (New York: Harper, 1895);

The Day of Their Wedding, A Novel (New York: Harper, 1896); republished in *Idyls in Drab* (Edinburgh: Douglas, 1896);

A Parting and a Meeting, Story (New York: Harper, 1896); republished in *Idyls in Drab*;

Impressions and Experiences (New York: Harper, 1896; Edinburgh: Douglas, 1896);

A Previous Engagement, Comedy (New York: Harper, 1897);

The Landlord at Lion's Head (Edinburgh: Douglas, 1897; New York: Harper, 1897);

An Open-Eyed Conspiracy, An Idyl of Saratoga (New York & London: Harper, 1897; Edinburgh: Douglas, 1897);

Stories of Ohio (New York, Cincinnati & Chicago: American Book Company, 1897);

The Story of a Play, A Novel (New York & London: Harper, 1898);

Ragged Lady, A Novel (New York & London: Harper, 1899);

Their Silver Wedding Journey, 2 volumes (New York & London: Harper, 1899);

Bride Roses, A Scene (Boston & New York: Houghton, Mifflin, 1900);

Room Forty-Five, A Farce (Boston & New York: Houghton, Mifflin, 1900);

An Indian Giver, A Comedy (Boston & New York: Houghton, Mifflin, 1900);

The Smoking Car, A Farce (Boston & New York: Houghton, Mifflin, 1900);

Literary Friends and Acquaintance, A Personal Retrospect of American Authorship (New York & London: Harper, 1900);

A Pair of Patient Lovers (New York & London: Harper, 1901);

Heroines of Fiction, 2 volumes (New York & London: Harper, 1901);

The Kentons, A Novel (New York & London: Harper, 1902);

The Flight of Pony Baker, A Boy's Town Story (New York & London: Harper, 1902);

Mary Dean and William Cooper Howells (the Rutherford B. Hayes Library)

Literature and Life (New York & London: Harper, 1902);

Questionable Shapes (New York & London: Harper, 1903);

Letters Home (New York & London: Harper, 1903);

The Son of Royal Langbrith, A Novel (New York & London: Harper, 1904);

Miss Bellard's Inspiration, A Novel (New York & London: Harper, 1905);

London Films (New York & London: Harper, 1905);

Certain Delightful English Towns With Glimpses of the Pleasant Country Between (New York & London: Harper, 1906);

Through the Eye of the Needle, A Romance (New York & London: Harper, 1907);

Between the Dark and the Daylight, Romances (New York: Harper, 1907; London: Harper, 1912);

Fennel and Rue, A Novel (New York & London: Harper, 1908);

Roman Holidays and Others (New York & London: Harper, 1908);

The Mother and the Father, Dramatic Passages (New York & London: Harper, 1909);

Seven English Cities (New York & London: Harper, 1909);

My Mark Twain, Reminiscences and Criticisms (New York & London: Harper, 1910);

Imaginary Interviews (New York & London: Harper, 1910);

Parting Friends, A Farce (New York & London: Harper, 1911);

New Leaf Mills, A Chronicle (New York & London: Harper, 1913);

Familiar Spanish Travels (New York & London: Harper, 1913);

The Seen and Unseen at Stratford-On-Avon, A Fantasy (New York & London: Harper, 1914);

The Daughter of the Storage and Other Things in Prose and Verse (New York & London: Harper, 1916);

The Leatherwood God (New York: Century, 1916; London: Jenkins, 1917);

Years of My Youth (New York & London: Harper, 1916);

The Vacation of the Kelwyns, An Idyl of the Middle Eighteen-Seventies (New York & London: Harper, 1920);

Mrs. Farrell, A Novel (New York & London: Harper, 1921);

Prefaces to Contemporaries (1882-1920), edited by George Arms, William M. Gibson, and Frederic C. Marston, Jr. (Gainesville, Fla.: Scholars' Facsimiles & Reprints, 1957);

Criticism and Fiction and Other Essays, edited by Clara Marburg Kirk and Rudolf Kirk (New York: New York University Press, 1959);

The Complete Plays of W. D. Howells, edited by Walter J. Meserve (New York: New York University Press, 1960);

W. D. Howells as Critic, edited by Edwin H. Cady (London & Boston: Routledge, 1973);

Editor's Study: A Comprehensive Edition of W. D. Howells' Column (Troy, N.Y.: Whitson Publishing Co., 1983).

Collection: *A Selected Edition of W. D. Howells*, edited by Edwin H. Cady, Ronald Gottesman, Don L. Cook, and David Nordloh, 20 volumes (Bloomington: Indiana University Press, 1968-   ).

OTHER: "Novel-Writing and Novel-Reading, an Impersonal Explanation," in *Howells and James: A Double Billing*, edited by William M. Gibson and Leon Edel (New York: New York Public Library, 1958).

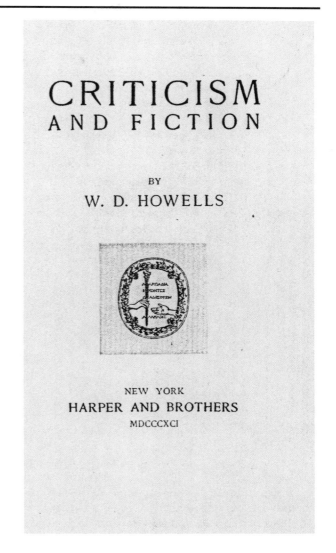

CRITICISM
AND FICTION

BY

W. D. HOWELLS

NEW YORK
HARPER AND BROTHERS
MDCCCXCI

Title page for Howells's 1891 book in which he collected several of his "Editor's Study" columns originally published in Harper's *magazine*

William Dean Howells was known from the 1880s to his death in 1920 as the preeminent literary realist in America. Though Howells was a part of the international realism movement, his was essentially an American literary realism whose foundation was democratic, whose frame of reference was political, and whose philosophical grounding was pragmatic. His criticism was characterized by an Emersonian earnestness and a tone of rebellion. Critics have provided an appropriate metaphor for Howells's crusade and spirit when they describe him as heading the most serious campaign of the "realism war." An insurgent who learned early to work within the establishment, he later became the establishment itself, though he was never to escape the hostility of his opponents.

Most of the very basic principles that led Howells to realism changed little from the 1880s to his death in 1920. Howells's theory was shaped by his response to the books he read and by those he reviewed in such prominent American journals as *Harper's Monthly*, the *North American Review*, and *Harper's Weekly*, where his regular columns offered him the opportunity to air his own views more fully than he had in the 1870s as editor and reviewer for the *Atlantic Monthly*. Over the years he refined and modified his beliefs, especially those concerned with American society and its relation to art, but most of Howells's lifelong literary criteria can be found in his "Editor's Study" columns in *Harper's* (1886-1892), some of which Howells collected in a volume titled *Criticism and Fiction* (1891).

Since Howells developed a theory built on individual example rather than on a logically struc-

Howells in Columbus, Ohio, circa 1860

tured argument, his definitions of the term "literary realism" are nowhere succinctly synthesized. However, a reading of Howells's "Editor's Study" columns and of his later criticism can provide a useful, if occasionally contradictory, definition.

Howells believed that realism was not new to his age; he found the "realistic treatment of material" in the literature of all centuries. Jane Austen, for example, was a realist in her time. Her novels, Howells wrote in *Criticism and Fiction,* "were beautiful, because she and they were honest, and dealt with nature nearly a hundred years ago as realism deals with it to-day. Realism is nothing more and nothing less than the truthful treatment of material, and Jane Austen was the first and the last of the English novelists to treat material with entire truthfulness."

Howells contended, however, that the nineteenth century was the first age in which a school of writers made a concerted, self-conscious effort to write in a realistic mode. The romantic school, he wrote, had labored to overturn worn-out conventions, but it had "exhausted itself " in the ef-

fort, and "it remained for realism to assert that fidelity to experience and probability of motive are essential conditions of great imaginative literature." By Howells's time, realists were making a concentrated effort to emphasize character rather than plot; probability rather than romantic possibility; the present rather than the past; the commonplace rather than the ideal; the ordinary citizen rather than the heroic individual; and objectivity rather than authorial manipulation. These features, for Howells, defined realism.

The realist should depict commonplace situations and use the language of everyday speech. Howells preached Emerson's dictum—which he believed both democratic and realistic—to paint domestic, unidealized pictures of everyday life. "It is only the extraordinary person," wrote Howells in *Criticism and Fiction,* "who can say, with Emerson: 'I ask not for the great, the remote, the romantic. . . . I embrace the common; I sit at the feet of the familiar and the low.' "

The realist also strove for verisimilitude. Though great literature was "deeper and finer" than simple "local color well ascertained," one of the realist's tasks was to achieve an illusion of reality. Part of that illusion was created by the appearance of objectivity, the illusion that the writer was not manipulating or commenting on events.

Howells's repeated insistence on the appearance of objectivity in fiction seems narrow to a modern reader. One is uneasy when one reads in *Criticism and Fiction* that although Anthony Trollope had "simple honesty and instinctive truth," his weakness was that he sometimes copied "the caricaturist Thackeray" and stood about "in his scene, talking it over with his hands in his pockets, interrupting the action, and spoiling the illusion in which alone the truth of art resides." But it is clear elsewhere that for Howells the truth of art certainly did not reside alone in the appearance of objectivity. Victor Hugo and Charles Dickens, while often guilty in Howells's view of such indiscretions, both appear as "great men" in his brief list of significant authors in his 1899 lecture published in 1958 as "Novel-Writing and Novel-Reading, an Impersonal Explanation." It is also important to note that Howells's insistence on the look of objectivity did not limit the writer's choice of form.

Howells described the three primary forms of the novel in his lecture as the "autobiographical," in which the narrator tells the reader only of events and motivations that he or she could know; the "biographical," in which a central fig-

William Dean and Elinor Mead Howells in Venice shortly after their marriage (the Rutherford B. Hayes Library)

ure reports events and emotions; and the "historical," the "great form," in which events are treated as "real history" reported by a narrator as if from research into original documents. Since the author of the historical form may enter into the minds of the characters, quote dialogue, and report intimate feelings and thoughts, this form allows "a thousand contradictions, improbabilities," and yet paradoxically, "nothing in fiction is more impressive, more convincing of its truth." The appearance of objectivity for Howells was not dependent on the "outward shape" of the novel; he never claimed that realistic fiction was a slice of life. "After all," he wrote, however sincerely the writer toils to paint life truly, he or she "will have only an *effect* of life." Howells compared the effect of a novel to that of a cyclorama in which "up to a certain point there is real ground and real grass," and then the effect "is carried indivisibly on to the canvas" by the painter. A writer can imitate only what she or he has known of life and if "skillful and very patient" can "*hide the*

joint" between the real and the painted grass. The author will not meet the ideal of perfect realism but can avoid "copying the effect of some other's effort to represent real ground and real grass."

Though Howells understood that the artist could probably never fully "hide the joint," he repeatedly called upon realists to maintain the appearance of objectivity because he hoped to make fiction a more serious, streamlined, and respectable art; he viewed contemporary fiction writers and critics as part of a modern scientific and pragmatic movement, one particularly suited to nineteenth-century America. Howells's discussions of the writer's rendering of "truth" were clothed in the language of contemporary philosophical and scientific inquiry. He clearly modeled his criticism on the process of scientific investigation. The realist, he wrote in *Criticism and Fiction*, is "careful of every fact, and feels himself bound to express or to indicate its meaning at the risk of over-moralizing. In life he finds nothing insignificant; all tells for destiny and character. . . . He cannot look upon human life and declare this thing or that thing unworthy of notice, any more than the scientist can declare a fact of the material world beneath the dignity of his inquiry."

The task of author and critic, Howells believed, was to discover truth, but truth was not static. Howells viewed the nature of truth as evolutionary and progressive, allowing that the older critics "perhaps caught the truth of their day," but their "routine life has been alien to any other truth." That is, all writers, however discerning, are in some ways limited by the beliefs of their time and society. The modern critic's task, Howells wrote in *Criticism and Fiction*, is no longer "to display himself" but rather to approach literature scientifically, "to place a book in such a light that a reader shall know its class, its function, its character." The critic must "classify and analyze the fruits of the human mind very much as the naturalist classifies the objects of his study, rather than . . . praise or blame them." The critic is in the business of "observing, recording, and comparing" as well as "analyzing the material" and synthesizing its impressions. Howells proposed not authority and personal taste but instead a taxonomy of fiction based on this description and classification.

Howells avoided the dangers of subjectivity in such a description of fiction by placing it in a necessary social context. He shared the belief of the American philosopher and pragmatist Char-

The Howells family, circa 1875 (Howells Collection, Houghton Library, Harvard University)

les Peirce in the importance of a community of investigators. The new critic using the scientific method, Howells wrote, will have to know something of the laws and "generic history" of a larger mind beyond his own. Howells stressed the importance of synthesizing the collective judgments of critics and saw a similar consensus emerging from American writers all over the United States who were writing truthfully about their own experiences and locales and collectively producing the "great American novel." Howells was only partially jesting when he wrote in an 1891 "Editor's Study" column that all of America will not be portrayed in a literary work "till the great American novel is conceived in an encyclopedical form, with a force of novelists apportioned upon the basis of Congressional representation, and working under one editorial direction." Howells's view of the artist's method is captured in Peirce's description of scientific investigation in "How to Make Our Ideas Clear," in which individuals at first perhaps obtain different results but perfect their methods and processes and move "steadily

together toward a destined center." Howells hoped that a similar process would bring writers to a consensus, a collective truth, in literature. Although Howells's criticism offers few theoretical definitions of truth, instead suggesting a guarded optimism that the sincere efforts of talented, tough-minded realists will lead to truth or reality, he seems to have believed with Peirce that "the opinion which is fated to be ultimately agreed to by all who investigate is what we mean by the truth, and the object represented in this opinion is the real."

Howells did not deny that realistic writers were inevitably somewhat biased and subjective as observers, but he believed that the community of readers would come closer to truth than they might have come had they not shared the fictional investigation with the author; furthermore, the reader would be encouraged to seek further evidence in the world itself and view that world differently once the veil of the picturesque and sentimental had been removed. Howells admitted that as a young writer he wore "English glasses," which he had to remove in order to "look at American life with my own American eyes." Howells never pretended that an artist does not select or that the literary work does not reflect the mind of the author. "An artist's individual stamp is upon his work," Howells wrote in "Novel-Writing and Novel-Reading." "For the novelist there is no replica. . . . All Mr. James's books are like Mr. James; all Tourguenieff's books are like Tourguenieff." But Howells had faith in the efficacy of a work created by the imaginative process of the individual inquiring mind to contribute to the formation of that "opinion" that is "the real."

Scientific method, observation, and understanding were related in Howells's theory. Understanding for Howells was an active process. His strident rebellion against traditional literary conventions reflected his faith in rigorous observation and inquiry. Both artist and reader are often the victims of conventional artistic representations, Howells said early in *Criticism and Fiction*. Readers feel at home, for example, in the "familiar environment" of a sentimental novel. "They know what they are reading; the fact that it is hash many times warmed over reassures them." Purveyors of the old conventions, Howells believed, would say to the artist, "I see that you are looking at a grasshopper there which you have found in the grass, and I suppose you intend to describe it. Now don't waste your time and sin against culture in that way. I've got a grasshop-

Howells in the library of his Fifty-ninth Street house, New York

per here, which has been evolved at considerable pains and expense out of the grasshopper in general; in fact, it's a type. It's made up of wire and card-board, very prettily painted in a conventional tint, and it's perfectly indestructible. It isn't very much like a real grasshopper, but it's a great deal nicer, and it's served to represent the notion of a grasshopper ever since man emerged from barbarism."

Because most books portray only this ideal grasshopper, insisted Howells, readers are not prepared to recognize as true the fresh grasshopper presented by the artist observing it firsthand. The assumption for Howells, of course, was that it is possible to depict a grasshopper in a truer way. Many modern critics would instead say that to depict a new grasshopper is simply to shift to a new convention; the relationship between the new description and the actual grasshopper does not represent a closer relationship between object and description. That is, they would claim that Howells was confusing absolute truth with modes

of representation, which are merely relative. Certainly his columns abounded with praise of books that created an illusion of reality and that eschewed romantic conventions, and he often described such books as "truthful." But Howells also had a strong sense of political and literary history, recognizing that literary realism incorporated as well as rejected the art that went before it; he saw his own mode as temporal and relative.

Very early in his battle for realism, Howells presented an accurate perspective on his own movement's relation to the past. Realism, he wrote in *Criticism and Fiction,* "is no new thing in the history of literature; whatever is established is sacred with those who do not think. At the beginning of the century, when romance was making the same fight against effete classicism which realism is making to-day against effete romanticism, the Italian poet Monti declared that 'the romantic was the cold grave of the Beautiful,' just as the realistic is now supposed to be. The romantic of that day and the real of this are in a certain degree the same. Romanticism then sought, as realism seeks now, to widen the bounds of sympathy, to level every barrier against aesthetic freedom, to escape from the paralysis of tradition."

Howells recognized that the goal of realism was to challenge conventions that had grown thin and stale. At the same time, Howells did see progress in literary history, especially in America and Russia. He believed that the realistic method, in the hands of talented writers, would produce truer, more moral books. The key to morality in art for Howells was fidelity to human behavior and to what he called "the God-given complexity of motive which we find in all the human beings we know."

Howells posited a moral universe, for he believed that if the artist were able to see the "meaning of things" and could convey it to others, the work would be beautiful–moral. The artist "feels this effect" and imparts it. Howells asserted that the reality and meaning in literature are products of the artist's mind, but his underlying premise was that the literature is complete when the mind of the reader meets the mind of the artist and the result is the discovery of meaning. According to Howells, "there is no joy in art except this perception of the meaning of things and communication."

The truth discovered in a literary work is perhaps a relative truth, but it represents the highest social values, the most humane spirit, and the most refined artistry. Howells suggested that only

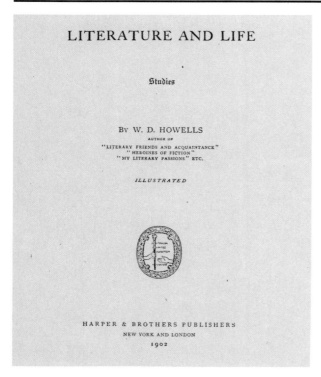

LITERATURE AND LIFE

Studies

By W. D. HOWELLS
AUTHOR OF
"LITERARY FRIENDS AND ACQUAINTANCE"
"HEROINES OF FICTION"
"MY LITERARY PASSIONS" ETC.

ILLUSTRATED

HARPER & BROTHERS PUBLISHERS
NEW YORK AND LONDON
1902

Title page for Howells's 1902 collection of literary essays

the documentation of true feeling, shaped by the mind of the gifted, serious artist, creates that harmony in the work that Howells called truth and morality. "Morality penetrates all things, it is the soul of all things," Howells wrote in an 1886 "Editor's Study," and the test of any work of literature is whether or not it is "true to the motives, the impulses, the principles that shape the life of actual men and women."

In spite of doubts about the existence of absolute truths, Howells seems to have shared with his friend, the philosopher and psychologist William James, the working premise that wherever living "minds exist, with judgments of good and ill, and demands upon one another, there is an ethical world in its essential features." Howells believed that, in a subtle way, literature could reveal an order in the world, a morality. His convictions about the existence of such an order were more convincing in his criticism than in his fiction. According to his critical theories, art could reveal order, provide "probability of motive." In his fiction, on the other hand, improbability permeated the pragmatist's world of risk and chance.

Doubt, of course, was an ingredient of Howells's pragmatic realism. The value of scientific inquiry was that it defined the nature of un-

certainties. "Better than science," wrote Howells in an 1890 "Editor's Study" column, "seems the scientific spirit" that "denies nothing in wishing to prove all things; which neither grovels nor persecutes, and seeks only the truth." The errors of science, Howells believed, "teach wisdom" because they "'carve out free space for every human doubt that the whole mind may orb about' in the untrammeled search for truth." And "no one need abandon any belief that truly comforts or shelters him. Some dogmas indeed we must hold passively, till science has ceased to change her mind, and declares finally and forever that the world is round and moves."

Doubt, then, is compatible with belief. In an 1891 "Editor's Study" column, Howells agreed with–judged "admirable"–William James's premise in *The Principles of Psychology* (1890) that we view any given fact from a different angle each time we observe it; as a consequence we find absolutes difficult to hold on to, and if that is the case, "the import of common duties and common goods" becomes more significant. The end of art, for Howells, was the common good. When the artist portrayed scenes that were true to human nature, the mass of readers, Howells believed, would be moved. If fiction could "cease to lie about life" and "portray men and women as they are, actuated by the motives and the passions in the measure we all know," then literature would "find a response in all readers." The author must not pander to the popular taste yet must speak to the man and woman on the street.

The question of whether fidelity to human nature, probability of human motive, is a criterion for first-rate fiction remains alive in twentieth-century criticism. Many critics and teachers judge literary value by whether a literary work represents what is known of human motive and behavior. When Howells says that he takes the novel "to be the sincere and conscientious endeavor to picture life just as it is, to deal with character as we witness it in living people, and to record the incidents that grow out of character," the modern reader may find the definition limited but not outmoded, because as readers they bring knowledge of human nature to art. Howells's models clearly work best for the novel of domestic drama, and he acknowledged this, believing that realism's tenets did not apply to all literature and recognizing distinctions between literary forms. In "Novel-Writing and Novel-Reading," Howells drew significant distinctions between two literary forms, the romance and the novel. Romances like

Howells, Samuel Clemens, George Harvey (president of Harper's*), Henry Mills Alden (editor of* Harper's *magazine), David Munro (editor of* North American Review*), and M. W. Hazeltine (former literary editor of the* New York Sun*) at a farewell luncheon given for Howells before his departure for Italy in 1908 (Mark Twain Memorial)*

Hawthorne's *The Scarlet Letter* (1850) and *The Marble Faun* (1860), Mary Shelley's *Frankenstein* (1818), and Robert Louis Stevenson's *The Strange Case of Dr. Jekyll and Mr. Hyde* (1886) "are not to be judged by the rules of criticism that apply to the novel." They "partake of the nature of poems" and frankly place themselves outside of familiar experience and circumstance." Such judgments suggest again that Howells's theory of art was not so limited as some of his individual critical statements might suggest. But literature that pictured "life just as it is" was clearly, for Howells, the highest art form, and he delighted in works that reflected his own moral beliefs.

When Howells spoke of the deepest truths of realistic fiction, he was clearly speaking about moral values. The subject matter of realism, its interest in the plight of the common man and woman, led to social awareness and often an implied criticism of society. When Howells asserted in *Criticism and Fiction* that the writer must "forbear to preach pride and revenge" and "egotism

and prejudice, but frankly own these for what they are...," he summarized in brief his democratic moral values. As he grew into middle age, Howells's concern about human tolerance and complicity increased. Justice, egalitarianism, and humanitarianism were the themes worthy of serious literature. Howells noted at the end of *Criticism and Fiction* that until his day, "the humanitarian impulse has never so generally characterized all fiction." Toward the end of his career, Howells's optimism about this progress diminished, but he continued to praise sympathy and compassion in literature.

It can be argued that Howells's focus on the ethical suggests that literary realism concealed an undermining didacticism, that it offered prescription and instruction rather than art. However, Howells did not deny that the new subject matter of the literary realists often suggested social criticism or that it tempted writers to moralize. But Howells's definition of literary realism asserted that the artist must not moralize. As Howells wrote of Juan Valera in *Criticism and Fiction,* "I heartily agree with him that it is 'in very bad taste, always impertinent and often pedantic, to attempt to prove theses by writing stories.' " Realistic fiction should offer truth but avoid didacticism. The reader of Valera's *Pepita Jimenez* (1874) will do "a great deal of serious thinking on a very serious subject," Howells pointed out, "which is none the less serious because it is couched in terms of delicate irony." In great works of art, "the finest effect of the 'beautiful' will be ethical and not aesthetic merely."

Realists did not always succeed in teaching without moralizing. In theory, however, the conflict was partially resolved in Howells's description of his pragmatic method of composition. He believed that the writer's ability to set things in proper perspective did not depend on access to an absolute truth. Howells conceded that the artist had a special insight into truth, but, for Howells, a novel was not the working out of a preestablished thesis. Harriet Beecher Stowe's *Uncle Tom's Cabin* (1852), for example, was ethically admirable—had a worthy thesis—but in Howells's view was not art. The "pleasure and instruction" of art, Howells wrote in *Criticism and Fiction,* "will follow from such measure of truth as the author has in him to such measure of truth as the reader has in him. . . . If it is a work of art, it promptly takes itself out of the order of polemics or of ethics, and primarily consents to be nothing if not aesthetical." Much of an artist's work is "unintentional and involuntary," he explained in "Novel-Writing and Novel-Reading." "For instance, each novel has a law of its own, which it seems to create for itself. Almost from the beginning it has its peculiar temperament and quality, and if you happen to be writing that novel you feel that you must respect its law. You, who are master of the whole affair, cannot violate its law without taking its life. . . . [The imaginative process] is scarcely more subject to the author's will than the reader's; . . . the mind fathers creatures which are apparently as self-regulated as any other offspring. They are the children of a given mind; they bear a likeness to it; they are qualified by it; but they seem to have their own life and their own being apart from it."

However clever the technique of a literary work, Howells could not value it if its picture of life had been distorted for the sake of art or dogma. In "Novel-Writing and Novel-Reading," he described how in his own imaginative process, amid false starts, he kept "trying to hark back to

Howells with his longtime friend Samuel Clemens in 1909

the truth as I knew it, and start afresh. A hundred times in the course of a story I have to retrace my steps, and efface them. Often the whole process is a series of arduous experiments, trying it this way, trying it that; testing it by my knowledge of myself and my acquaintance with others; asking if it would be true of me, or true of my friend or my enemy; and not possibly resting content with anything I thought gracious or pleasing in my performance till I have got the setting of truth for it. This sort of scrutiny goes on perpetually in the novelist's mind. His story is never out of it."

It is indeed possible, according to Howells, for a writer with specific social and moral values to write literature that does not preach. First-rate fiction will not be reduced to propaganda because, whatever the writer's moral and social theories, the imaginative process transcends dogma. It is a rational but organic process. Patient scrutiny of detail is the "soil" that realistic fiction "must grow out of; without that, and the slow, careful thinking which supplies it, the effect is a sickly and spindling growth." Howells's realism is not socialist because for the socialist or Marxist, the chief end is to describe a preestablished, inevitable future. Howells's pragmatism disallowed absolutes.

For Howells literature had truth value, but he believed that "reality is bound to no thesis. You cannot say where it begins or where it leaves off; and it will not allow you to say precisely what its meaning or argument is." Ibsen's plays, he argued in a November 1902 *North American Review* article which focused on the works of Emile Zola, are "perfect pieces of realism." They "have all or each a thesis, but do not hold themselves bound to prove it, or even fully to state it; after these, for reality, come the novels of Tolstoy, which are of a direction so profound because so patient of aberration and exception." The careful, inquiring realist strives to be true to probable human motivation and behavior but also considers the "aberration and exception." This is why realistic writers, more than others, must have life experience as well as insight. The more they know of life, the better they are able to judge the veracity of their own imagined scenarios.

It is difficult to see a consistency between Howells's belief that the best literature should depict the probable and the commonplace and his appreciation of the great realists of his day who instead often portrayed the aberrant and exceptional rather than the ordinary. His focus on probability also would seem to imply a literary philosophy that inadequately accounts for writers such as Tolstoy and Hardy who created unique imagined worlds. It is difficult to explain Howells's uncanny record of hailing those artists who, even though rejected by many of their contemporaries, today are recognized as masters. William M. Gibson describes Howells as "clairvoyant." Howells defended Hardy, who had a popular readership in America but who was attacked by American critics; Tolstoy, who was untranslated when Howells introduced him to American readers; and Zola, who was decried in the American and British press as a monster.

Howells never developed a full-blown theory about the value of such unique but fully imagined fictional worlds as these writers created. However, he occasionally discussed the question in relation to individual works. In his 1895 *Harper's Weekly* review of *Jude the Obscure*, he clearly praised Hardy's genius and defended the world

Hardy created. Howells confessed that though "the common experience" and "the common knowledge of life" contradict Hardy's portrayal of sex and marriage, Hardy's world is true. While "commonly, the boy of Jude's strong aspiration" succeeds "in some measure" and "a girl like Sue flutters through the anguish of her harassed and doubting youth and settles into acquiescence with the ordinary life of woman," the "author makes me believe that all he says to the contrary inevitably happened." Howells recognized the truth and genius of Hardy's work in spite of the tenets of his theory of realism that would seem to contradict this judgment. *Jude the Obscure* is hardly a portrait of the commonplace painted in the light of common day, but Howells accepted Hardy's truth, admitting that although the dark events of Hardy's novel, "like Sue's willful self-surrender to Philotson," make the reader "shiver with horror and grovel with shame," "we know that they are deeply founded in the condition, if not in the nature of humanity." Howells's review described in patient detail the effect that Hardy's work had on him and encouraged the reader to be equally receptive.

Howells's argument for fidelity to probability also invites questions about reader responsibility. If a work seems false, the fault lies perhaps in the reader's narrow experience. Some critics argue that the author's task is to have convinced readers to believe a character's behavior, regardless of their own experience. Howells touched upon this question when, in his November 1902 defense of Zola in the *North American Review*, he insisted that "a whole world seems to stir in each of his books; and, though it is a world altogether bent for the time being upon one thing, as the actual world never is, every individual in it seems alive and true to the fact." Howells questioned the relevance of reader experience when he challenged one of Zola's critics, M. Brunetiere, for complaining that "Zola's characters are not true to the French fact; that peasants, working-men, citizens, soldiers are not French, . . . but this is merely M. Brunetiere's word against Zola's word. . . . Word for word, I should take Zola's word as to the fact, not because I have the means of affirming him more reliable, but because I have rarely known the observant instinct of poets to fail, and because I believe that the reader will find in himself sufficient witness to the veracity of Zola's characterizations."

Howells implied that not resemblance alone but also the energy of an author's animating imagi-

Howells at work

nation sparks a response in the perceptive reader. That transmitted understanding constitutes truth. It was in characterizations, Howells wrote, that "the reality of Zola, unreal or ideal in his larger form, his epicality, vitally resided. His people live in the memory as entirely as any people who have ever lived; and, however devastating one's experience of them may be, it leaves no doubt of their having been." And in 1886 he wrote of Dostoyevski's *Crime and Punishment* (1866) that its "truth is a very old one, but what makes this book so wonderful is the power with which it is set forth." Masters like Dostoyevski and Zola keep faith with the reader, it would seem, by vitally putting into words a truth that is perhaps as yet unarticulated elsewhere but at a deep level commonly felt.

Though Howells was able to find Hardy's and Zola's characterizations "true," he never established a final definition of "truth," though his judgment was always connected to life, experience, and the real world. He suggested that when readers are offered a text which calls upon an imaginative and intuitive response, they instinc-

tively adapt and rearrange what they know of the world. A great author asks them to see anew but does not require that they divorce themselves from all that they know of the world. "It is a well ascertained fact concerning the imagination," wrote Howells in "Novel-Writing and Novel-Reading," "that it can work only with the stuff of experience. It can absolutely create nothing; it can only compose."

Howells certainly saw the limitations of the term "realism" in reference to the great literary masters. In an 1886 "Editor's Study," he wrote of Turgenev, Tolstoy, and Dostoyevski that "they are all so very much more than realists that this name, never satisfactory in regard to any school of writers, seems altogether insufficient for them. They are realists in ascertaining an entire probability of motive and situation in their work; but with them this is only the beginning; they go so far beyond it in purpose and effect that one must cast about for some other word if one would try to define them. Perhaps humanist would be the best phrase. . . ." For Howells the "humanist" possessed "a profound sense of that individual responsibility from which the common responsibility can free no one." The mind of the great writer was finally a moral mind.

The realist's choice of which experience to cherish and portray was shaped by his or her moral world view. The experience that Howells treasured, of course, was not that of the elite. He was a democrat interested in economic and political equality and in popular culture and the reading habits of the masses. Serious literature, he believed, should not be watered down, though it should be accessible to all readers. "I hope the time is coming," he wrote in *Criticism and Fiction*, "when not only the artist, but the common, average man, who always 'has the standard of the arts in his power,' will have the courage to apply it, and will reject the ideal grasshopper wherever he finds it, in science, in literature, in art. . . ." Howells set out to demystify yet dignify the process of artistic creation and to reconnect art to everyday life. "It is the conception of literature as something apart from life, superficially aloof, which makes it really unimportant to the great mass of mankind, without a message or a meaning for them," he wrote. "We may fold ourselves in our scholars' gowns, and close the doors of our studies, and affect to despise this rude voice but we cannot shut it out. It comes to us from wherever men are at work, from wherever they are truly living, and accuses us of unfaithfulness, of triviality, of mere stage-play."

Isolation or alienation was devastating for the literary realist because it cut the writer off from the mainstream of public opinion which underpinned the realist's art. A writer could be temporarily out of step with, ahead of, the mass of readers and could criticize society, but the writer's function was finally a social one in which communication with readers was essential.

Howells observed in "The Man of Letters as a Man of Business" (collected in *Literature and Life,* 1902) that in America, "in the social world, as well as in the business world, the artist is anomalous, in the actual conditions, and he is perhaps a little ridiculous." His observation anticipated that of the influential American philosopher and teacher John Dewey, who would later describe the artist of his day as "less integrated than formerly in the normal flow of social services." Howells had earlier perceived that what Dewey was to call "a peculiar esthetic 'individualism' " encouraged the public to dismiss art as "independent and esoteric." Throughout his career, the democratic Howells battled esoteric views of art both

in fiction and criticism. The young author, he complained, "is approached in the spirit of the wretched pedantry into which learning, much or little, always decays when it withdraws itself and stands apart from experience in an attitude of imagined superiority. . . ." Howells's criticism and fiction opposed effetism, on the one hand, and superficiality and sensationalism, on the other.

Howells's criticism, like much of his fiction, is still good reading, and Howells is important historically as the chief spokesman for the literary realism that shaped taste in his day and influenced generations of writers to come. His personal encouragement of scores of writers, among them Stephen Crane, Hamlin Garland, Bret Harte, Edgar Lee Masters, Edith Wharton, Henry James, Mark Twain, Vachel Lindsay, Edwin Arlington Robinson, Charles Chestnut, and Robert Frost, was a legacy to American literature. As Van Wyck Brooks described him, Howells was "the one American writer who was aware of all the others." Even his critic H. L. Mencken recognized his "eager curiosity, his gusto in novelty." Howells introduced a provincial readership to unread native authors and to international writers like Turgenev, Stendhal, Balzac, Zola, Dostoyevski, Galdós, Verga, Valdés, Björnson, Ibsen, and Tolstoy.

Howells was a champion of gifted women writers and an advocate of woman's suffrage and equality. A review of the names of the women artists whom Howells reviewed and praised in his columns provides a checklist of those writers who were rediscovered and reprinted in the 1970s and 1980s. He and Thomas Wentworth Higginson spoke as solitary voices in praising the newfound poetry of Emily Dickinson in 1891, and Howells's review was by far the more positive and perceptive.

Howells's political positions also mirrored the democratic virtues and the integrity he championed in literature. Alone among American writers, Howells supported eight Chicago anarchists whom he believed unjustly imprisoned in 1886 for their political opinions. Though he feared the loss of his position at Harper's, Howells publicly condemned the court decision to convict the men and to execute seven of them and received a violently hostile public response. His literary and political values also led him to support the founding of the National Association for the Advancement of Colored People, call for serious literature from the black community, and insist that the time had come for the New York Jewish writers to make significant contributions to American

Howells, with his grandsons William White Howells and John Noyes Mead Howells, on his eightieth birthday

literature. At the end of his life, Howells's rejection of the insistently masculine tone in literature that he labeled "rugged masculinity" provoked a hostility against him much like the outrage that his pugnacious defenses of realism and American artists had elicited from an earlier generation.

Howells's nature was to look forward rather than back, to welcome innovation. Realism, he believed, was the finest art form, but he was willing to imagine a literary progress beyond realism. "Fiction is now a finer art than it has ever been hitherto, and more nearly meets the requirements of the infallible standard," he observed in *Criticism and Fiction*, "but I am by no means certain that it will be the ultimate literary form, or will remain as important as we believe it destined to become. On the contrary, it is quite imaginable that when the great mass of readers, now sunk in the foolish joys of mere fable, shall be lifted to an interest in the meaning of things through the faithful portrayal of life in fiction, then fiction the most faithful may be superseded by a still more faithful form of contemporaneous history." Until his

death in 1920, Howells remained a compassionate, intelligent, and bold voice.

Letters:

Life in Letters of William Dean Howells, edited by Mildred Howells, 2 volumes (Garden City: Doran, 1928; London: Heinemann, 1929);

The Correspondence of Samuel L. Clemens and William D. Howells, 1872-1910, edited by Henry Nash Smith and William M. Gibson, 2 volumes (Cambridge: Harvard University Press, 1960);

Selected Letters, 1852-1872, edited by George Arms and others (Boston: Twayne, 1979);

Selected Letters, 1873-1881, edited by Arms and Christoph K. Lohmann (Boston: Twayne, 1979);

Selected Letters, 1873-1891, edited by Robert C. Leitz III (Boston: Twayne, 1980);

Selected Letters, 1892-1901, edited by Thomas Wortham (Boston: Twayne, 1981);

Selected Letters, 1902-1911, edited by William C. Fischer and Lohmann (Boston: Twayne, 1983);

Selected Letters, 1912-1920, edited by Gibson and Lohmann (Boston: Twayne, 1983).

Interviews:

Ulrich Halfmann, ed., *Interviews with William Dean Howells* (Arlington, Tex.: American Literary Realism, 1974).

Bibliographies:

George Arms and William M. Gibson, *A Bibliography of William Dean Howells* (New York: New York Public Library, 1948; revised edition, New York: Arno Press, 1971);

James Woodress and Stanley P. Anderson, "A Bibliography of Writing about William Dean Howells," *American Literary Realism,* Special Number (1969): 1-139;

Vito J. Brenni, *William Dean Howells: A Bibliography* (Metuchen, N.J.: Scarecrow, 1973);

Clayton L. Eichelberger, *Published Comment on William Dean Howells through 1920: A Research Bibliography* (Boston: G. K. Hall, 1976).

Biographies:

Edwin H. Cady, *The Road to Realism: the Early Years, 1837-1885, of William Dean Howells* (Syracuse: Syracuse University Press, 1956);

Cady, *The Realist at War: the Mature Years, 1885-1920, of William Dean Howells* (Syracuse: Syracuse University Press, 1958);

Van Wyck Brooks, *Howells: His Life and World* (New York: Dutton, 1959);

Edward S. Wagenknecht, *William Dean Howells: The Friendly Eye* (New York: Oxford University Press, 1969);

Kenneth S. Lynn, *William Dean Howells: An American Life* (New York: Harcourt Brace Jovanovich, 1971).

References:

George N. Bennett, *The Realism of William Dean Howells: 1889-1920* (Nashville: Vanderbilt University Press, 1973);

Bennett, *William Dean Howells: The Development of a Novelist* (Norman: University of Oklahoma Press, 1959);

Edwin H. Cady, "The Howells Nobody Knows," *In The Light of Common Day, Realism in American Fiction* (Bloomington: Indiana University Press, 1971);

Cady and Norma W. Cady, *Critical Essays on William Dean Howells* (Boston: G. K. Hall, 1983);

Cady and David L. Frazier, eds., *The War of the Critics over William Dean Howells* (Evanston, Ill.: Row, Peterson, 1962);

George C. Carrington, Jr., *The Immense Complex Drama: The World and Art of the Howells Novel* (Columbus: Ohio State University Press, 1966);

Everett Carter, *Howells and the Age of Realism* (Philadelphia: Lippincott, 1954);

Delmar G. Cooke, *William Dean Howells* (New York: Dutton, 1922);

John W. Crowley, *The Black Heart's Truth, The Early Career of W. D. Howells* (Chapel Hill: University of North Carolina Press, 1985);

James L. Dean, *Howells' Travels Toward Art* (Albuquerque: University of New Mexico Press, 1970);

Kenneth E. Eble, ed., *Howells: A Century of Criticism* (Dallas: Southern Methodist University Press, 1962);

Eble, *William Dean Howells,* second edition (Bloomington: Twayne, 1982);

Oscar Firkins, *William Dean Howells* (Cambridge: Harvard University Press, 1924);

Olov W. Fryckstedt, *In Quest of America: A Study of Howells's Early Development as a Novelist* (Cambridge: Harvard University Press, 1958);

William M. Gibson, *Theodore Roosevelt Among the Humorists: W. D. Howells, Mark Twain, and Mr. Dooley* (Knoxville: University of Tennessee Press, 1980);

Gibson, *William D. Howells* (Minneapolis: University of Minnesota Press, 1967);

Robert L. Hough, *The Quiet Rebel: William Dean Howells as Social Commentator* (Lincoln: University of Nebraska Press, 1959);

Clara M. Kirk, *W. D. Howells: Traveler from Altruria, 1889-1894* (New Brunswick: Rutgers University Press, 1962);

Kirk, *W. D. Howells and Art in His Time* (New Brunswick: Rutgers University Press, 1965);

Kirk and Rudolf Kirk, *William Dean Howells* (New York: Twayne, 1962);

Leonard Lutwack, "William Dean Howells and the 'Editor's Study,' " *American Literature,* 24 (March 1952): 195-207;

William McMurray, *The Literary Realism of William Dean Howells* (Carbondale: Southern Illinois University Press, 1967);

Elizabeth S. Prioleau, *The Circle of Eros: Sexuality in the Work of William Dean Howells* (Durham, N.C.: Duke University Press, 1983);

Kermit Vanderbilt, *The Achievement of William Dean Howells* (Princeton: Princeton University Press, 1968);

Max Westbrook, "The Critical Implications of Howells' Realism," *Texas Studies in English,* 36 (1957): 71-79;

James Woodress, "The Dean's Comeback: Four Decades of Howells Scholarship," *Texas Studies in Literature and Language,* 2 (Spring 1960): 115-123.

Papers:

The largest collection of William Dean Howells's papers is at Harvard University, which has over 7,000 letters to and from Howells plus manuscripts and journals. The Huntington Library, the Library of Congress, Yale and Columbia Universities, and the Rutherford B. Hayes Library in Freemont, Ohio, also hold collections.

Henry Norman Hudson

(28 January 1814-16 January 1886)

Stephen A. Black
Simon Fraser University

BOOKS: *Lectures on Shakespeare,* 2 volumes (New York: Baker & Scribner, 1848);

Old Wine in New Bottles A Sermon Preached at Boston, at Lowell, and at New York (Boston: C. Stimpson, 1850); republished as *Old Wine in Old Bottles, A Sermon at the Church of the Advent, Boston* (Boston, 1850);

A Word for Trinity Church (New York: E. P. Allen, 1857);

Christian Patriotism, A Sermon Preached in St. Clement's Church, New York City, Friday, January 4th, 1861 (New York: F. D. Harriman, 1861);

A Chaplain's Campaign with General Butler (New York: Printed for the author, 1865); republished, with appendix, as *General Butler's Campaign on the Hudson* (Boston: Cushing, 1883);

Shakespeare: His Life, Art, and Characters, With an Historical Sketch of the Origin and Growth of the Drama in England (Boston: Ginn, 1872; revised, 2 volumes, Boston: Ginn & Heath, 1882);

Sermons (Boston: Ginn, 1874);

English in Schools, A Series of Essays (Boston: Ginn & Heath, 1881);

Webster Centennial, A Discourse Delivered on the Hundredth Anniversary of the Birth of Daniel Webster, January 18, 1882 (Boston: Ginn & Heath, 1882);

Essays on Education, English Studies, and Shakespeare

Henry Hudson

(Boston: Ginn & Heath, 1882); enlarged as *Essays on English Studies* (Boston & New York: Ginn, 1906);

Studies in Wordsworth, Culture and Acquirement, Ethics of Tragedy and Other Papers (Boston: Little, Brown, 1884);

Rolfe versus Hudson (Cambridge, Mass.: 21 February 1884); controversy.

OTHER: *The Works of Shakespeare*, 11 volumes, edited by Hudson (Boston & Cambridge: J. Munroe & Co., 1851-1858);

Text-book of Poetry; from Wordsworth, Coleridge, Burns, Beattie, Goldsmith, and Thomson, edited, with introductions and explanatory notes, by Hudson (Boston: Ginn, 1875);

Text-book of Prose; from Burke, Webster, and Bacon, edited, with introductions and explanatory notes, by Hudson (Boston: Ginn, 1876);

Plays of Shakespeare, Selected and Prepared for Use in Schools, Clubs, Classes, and Families, expurgated and edited, with introductions and explanatory notes, by Hudson (Boston: Ginn, 1876);

Classical English Reader, Selections from Standard Authors, edited, with explanatory and critical footnotes, by Hudson (Boston: Ginn & Heath, 1878);

Shakespeare's Julius Caesar, expurgated and edited, with an introduction and notes, by Hudson (Boston: Ginn & Heath, 1879);

Shakespeare's The Tempest, expurgated and edited, with an introduction and notes, by Hudson (Boston: Ginn & Heath, 1879);

Shakespeare's Tragedy of King Lear, expurgated and edited, with an introduction and notes, by Hudson (Boston: Ginn & Heath, 1879);

The Complete Works of William Shakespeare, Harvard Edition, 20 volumes, edited, with introductions and notes, by Hudson (Boston: Ginn & Heath, 1880-1881);

Shakespeare's As You Like It, expurgated and edited, with an introduction and notes, by Hudson (Boston: Ginn & Heath, 1880);

Shakespeare's King Henry the Fifth, expurgated and edited, with an introduction and notes, by Hudson (Boston: Ginn & Heath, 1880);

Shakespeare's Henry Fourth, Part First, expurgated and edited, with an introduction and notes, by Hudson (Boston: Ginn & Heath, 1880);

Shakespeare's Henry Fourth, Part Second, expurgated and edited, with an introduction and notes, by Hudson (Boston: Ginn & Heath, 1880);

Shakespeare's History of King John, expurgated and edited, with an introduction and notes, by Hudson (Boston: Ginn & Heath, 1880);

Shakespeare's King Henry the Eighth, expurgated and edited, with an introduction and notes, by Hudson (Boston: Ginn & Heath, 1880);

Shakespeare's King Richard the Third, expurgated and edited, with an introduction and notes, by Hudson (Boston: Ginn & Heath, 1880);

Shakespeare's A Midsummer Night's Dream, expurgated and edited, with an introduction and notes, by Hudson (Boston: Ginn & Heath, 1880);

Shakespeare's Much Ado About Nothing, expurgated and edited, with an introduction and notes, by Hudson (Boston: Ginn & Heath, 1880);

Shakespeare's Tragedy of Macbeth, expurgated and edited, with an introduction and notes, by Hudson (Boston: Ginn & Heath, 1880);

Shakespeare's Twelfth Night, or, What You Will, expurgated and edited, with an introduction and notes, by Hudson (Boston: Ginn & Heath, 1880);

Shakespeare's The Winter's Tale, expurgated and edited, with an introduction and notes, by Hudson (Boston: Ginn & Heath, 1880);

Shakespeare's Antony and Cleopatra, expurgated and edited, with an introduction and notes, by Hudson (Boston: Ginn & Heath, 1881);

Shakespeare's Tragedy of Cymbeline, expurgated and edited, with an introduction and notes, by Hudson (Boston: Ginn & Heath, 1881);

Shakespeare's Othello the Moor of Venice, expurgated and edited, with an introduction and notes, by Hudson (Boston: Ginn & Heath, 1881);

Shakespeare's Romeo and Juliet, expurgated and edited, with an introduction and notes, by Hudson (Boston: Ginn & Heath, 1881);

Shakespeare's Tragedy of Coriolanus, expurgated and edited, with an introduction and notes, by Hudson (Boston: Ginn & Heath, 1881);

Shakespeare's King Richard the Second, expurgated and edited, with an introduction and notes, by Hudson (Boston: Ginn & Heath, 1884);

Shakespeare's Merchant of Venice, expurgated and edited, with an introduction and notes, by Hudson (Boston: Ginn & Heath, 1884);

Shakespeare's Tragedy of Hamlet, expurgated and edited, with an introduction and notes, by Hudson (Boston: Ginn & Heath, 1884).

PERIODICAL PUBLICATIONS: "Education," *United States Magazine & Democratic Review*,

LECTURES

ON

SHAKSPEARE.

BY

H. N. HUDSON.

IN TWO VOLUMES.

VOL. I.

NEW YORK:
BAKER AND SCRIBNER,
36 PARK ROW AND 145 NASSAU STREET.
1848.

Title page for the first volume of Hudson's early lectures on Shakespeare

16 (May 1845): 468-482; 17 (July 1845): 40-50;

"Thoughts on Reading," *American Review*, 1 (May 1845): 483-496;

"Festus," *American Review*, 5 (January & February 1847): 43-61, 123-143;

"Religious Union of Associationists," *American Review*, 5 (May 1847): 492-503;

"Macaulay's Essays," *American Whig Review*, 9 (May 1849): 499-512;

"Furness's Shakespeare," *North American Review*, 117 (January 1874): 475-483;

"An Outline History of the American Carlyle," *Boston Sunday Herald*, 3 October 1880;

"Tragedy," *Shakespeariana*, 1 (January 1884): 78-81.

Henry Norman Hudson reached prominence in the second half of the nineteenth century as a popular lecturer on Shakespeare, as an editor and critic of the plays, and as professor of Shakespeare at Boston University. Contemporary Shakespeare scholar S. Schoenbaum calls him one "of the two most notable nineteenth-century American authorities" on the playwright's life and art. Although Schoenbaum praises Hudson as one praises a trickle in the desert, Alfred van R. Westfall recalls H. H. Furness's 1929 assessment of Hudson as "our greatest aesthetic critic." Most commentators, like Furness, place Hudson in the school of "aesthetic" critics.

Hudson's Shakespearean editions do not pass twentieth-century examination; and his critical theorizing conveys more enthusiasm than philosophical substance. In explanatory notes, in theorizing, and in practical criticism, Hudson borrows ideas from Coleridge, Lamb, Hazlitt, and the German romantics, and his reviewers justly criticize his frequent failure to acknowledge scholarly debts. The *Lectures on Shakespeare* (1848) often exhibit the inhibiting effect of an exceptional innocence in Hudson's attitude not only toward scholarship but also toward women and marriage, politics and religion.

Despite these faults and others, Hudson remains a critic worth reading. Jane Sherzer describes his early prose style as "high-flown, witty, sarcastic, brilliant, exceedingly addicted to the antithetical balanced structure, on the whole pleasing and popular." Westfall, Sherzer, Augustus Ralli, and R. K. Root (in his *Dictionary of American Biography* entry) speak respectfully of Hudson's genuinely literary sensibility, especially his character studies which employ what psychoanalysts call "psychological-mindedness," the power of empathy, and the power accurately to observe oneself while empathizing, and while in the act of thinking and feeling.

Hudson was born on 28 January 1814 near Cornwall, Vermont. When he was eighteen years old he was apprenticed to a carriage maker. Four years later, in 1836, he entered Middlebury College. From 1840 to 1844 he taught school in Vermont, Kentucky, and, finally, Alabama, where he began giving public lectures on Shakespeare. The lectures brought success in Huntsville, Mobile, Cincinnati, and Boston, where he settled. Emerson arranged for Hudson to speak on *Macbeth* at the Concord Lyceum on 1 January 1845. The lectures brought Hudson to the attention not only of Emerson but also Poe (who mocked the lecturer's Yankee diction and farm-boy gestures in his *Broadway Journal*), Whitman, the

Duyckinck brothers, George W. Peck, E. P. Whipple, and other literati.

In several long essays published between 1845 and 1849 Hudson aligns himself with the Whig aristocrats and declares war against Democrats and any others he takes for opponents of taste and tradition. "Thoughts on Reading," published in the *American Review* in May 1845, romantically ponders talent and genius, a topic he probably encountered in chapter eleven of the *Biographia Literaria*. Otherwise the essays are most notable for the heat and intricacy of invective Hudson marshals against Boston reformers, liberals, and transcendentalists, especially W. H. Channing and his Fourierist friends. Following John Stafford, John W. Rathbun describes the "religious and political bias" emerging from these essays as "that of a High Church Anglican and aristocratic Whig."

Stafford sees Hudson's advocacy of Shakespeare as a reflection of political conservatism and links Hudson to the opponents of "Young America." However, the notion that Hudson's politics precede or determine his literary values overlooks the importance Hudson places upon aesthetics as well as his unmistakably personal and authentic passion for Shakespeare. With Hudson, aesthetics precede politics. Aesthetics lead him to exalt the traditions that give rise to genius, to value discriminating taste, and to oppose whoever denies the preeminence of taste. Taste, he maintains, cannot fail to lead anyone who cultivates it to idolize Shakespeare as he does.

Although Westfall claims that "in his early years" Hudson cannot "deal with a critical question," he might more accurately say that Hudson in those years can seldom clearly *formulate* a critical question. On the other hand, when someone establishes the problem, Hudson shows marked deductive abilities. The following description of the moral problem posed by the witches in Hudson's favorite tragedy, *Macbeth*, supports Westfall's assertion that Hudson's most effective critical writings are responses to statements by writers like Coleridge, Schlegel, or Hazlitt.

Hudson begins with an unacknowledged borrowing from Coleridge, a description of the antecedents in Norse mythology of the witches. But the rest of the discussion owes to Coleridge only an undeveloped statement of the problem. Do the sisters "create the evil heart or only untie the evil hands?" Hudson asks, and he finds a logically parsimonious answer, that their power "extends only to the inspiring of confidence in what

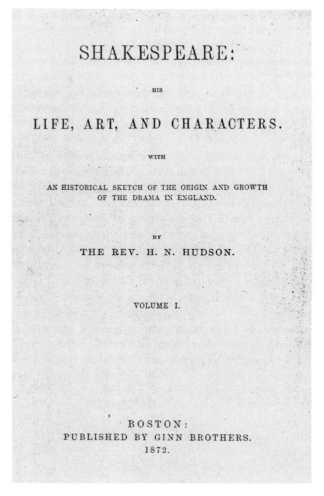

SHAKESPEARE:

HIS

LIFE, ART, AND CHARACTERS.

WITH

AN HISTORICAL SKETCH OF THE ORIGIN AND GROWTH
OF THE DRAMA IN ENGLAND.

BY

THE REV. H. N. HUDSON.

VOLUME I.

BOSTON:
PUBLISHED BY GINN BROTHERS.
1872.

Title page for Hudson's major critical achievement

they predict," a confidence felt as strongly by Banquo as by Macbeth. "They furnish the motives, not the principles of action," Hudson infers.

In the 1840s Hudson underwent a conversion, in Boston, from the Congregationalism of his youth to the Protestant Episcopal Church. After moving to New York he was ordained a priest, in 1849, in Trinity Church. On 18 December 1852 he married Emily Sarah Bright and until 1858 earned a living for his new family by editing the *Churchman* and the *American Church Monthly*. From 1858 to 1860 he served as rector to the Episcopal Church of Litchfield, Connecticut. In 1860 and 1861 he resumed his career as a traveling lecturer on Shakespeare.

In 1850 Hudson had begun to prepare Shakespearean texts for an eleven-volume set which he completed in 1858. Evert A. and George Duyckinck, in the 1854 edition of their *Cyclopædia of American Literature*, praised it as "a thorough revision and restoration of the text according to the ancient copies," together with careful notes and introductions. Other contemporary and later scholars have been less kind to the edition. J. O. Halliwell complained that Hudson pirated material from Halliwell's own edition in progress, and Sherzer, surveying the situation half a century later, corroborated the complaint. Hudson's naïveté may be seen in his claim that the edition was the first in America based on the Chiswick edition; Sherzer found that fifteen versions of the Chiswick edition had been printed in America by 1850.

In 1862 the forty-eight-year-old Hudson volunteered for the military, serving as chaplain with the First New York Volunteer Engineers. After witnessing a strategic blunder that cost many lives, he wrote a published letter critical of his commanding officer, Gen. B. F. Butler. Butler retaliated by imprisoning the chaplain for several weeks without bringing charges, for which General Grant reprimanded Butler. In February 1865 Hudson printed an account that charged Butler with illegal and impulsive behavior; Butler answered, in turn, with a pamphlet of his own. Hudson's account of the matter, somewhat heavy-handed and self-righteous in tone, probably won the campaign on debating points but both parties were still firing two decades later. It was not the last controversy of Hudson's life.

After his release from service Hudson settled in Cambridge, Massachusetts, where he resumed writing and lecturing about Shakespeare at Boston University and teaching English literature at the Boston School of Oratory. In addition to "The Harvard Shakespeare" editions, Hudson published several anthologies of English writers and expurgated Shakespeare "for use in schools and families." He published collections of his own sermons and essays and a monograph on Wordsworth, whom he admired almost as unreservedly as he did Shakespeare.

Perhaps the experience of the war contributed to the maturity found in Hudson's later Shakespeare criticism. *Shakespeare: His Life, Art, and Characters* (1872) was to be Hudson's major critical achievement. The two-volume work went through at least fourteen editions and printings between 1872 and 1912 and was reprinted again in 1973. The commentaries showed greater depth and profundity of judgment, and more consistency, than the lectures published in 1848. The reviewer for the *Shakespeare Jahrbuch,* while discounting Hudson's attempt at biography, the

sketch of pre-Shakespearean drama, and the efforts at theorizing, praised the book as a whole because of the excellence of many of the character studies.

The analyses of characters, scenes, and the effects Shakespeare creates in his audiences often seem sound and original a century after the writing. Describing Othello, Hudson's disapproval of Iago coexists with empathy. He sees the Moor simultaneously through his own sensibility and through Iago's. In so doing he reveals the complexities and depths of both characters as well as their relation with each other and does it all with sensitivity and subtlety.

"Othello's mind," Hudson argues, is suffused with "high principle and earnest feeling; which gives a certain elevated and imaginative turn to his speech." The Moor's rhetoric and demeanor provoke envy and hate in Iago, who cannot distinguish Othello's high style from "bombast and evasion." Knowing that Othello will never stoop to explain or defend himself, nor seem to solicit the approval of others, provides Iago the opportunity to act even as it arouses his envy. Othello's certainty of his own rectitude ensures his own success and establishes his place in the world. Furthermore, Othello's "solid virtue" makes him appear invulnerable to "The shot of accident [or] dart of chance," an appearance that challenges Iago to try his best to "pierce" virtue's armor. Othello's rhetoric and the sense of honor it implies do not permit the Moor to defend himself and make him vulnerable to deviousness. His "conscience of rectitude," which does not permit him to imagine deceit or envy, and the hauteur, which prevents him from imagining that his ensign might be clever enough to outwit him, further incite Iago's hatred. Hudson's empathy enables him to intuit, as if with direct knowledge, Iago's attraction to the Moor and the ambivalent hatred inspired by Othello's rhetorical aloofness.

Empathizing with Iago taxes Hudson less than certain other problems he encounters throughout Shakespeare's plays. He has little grasp of Hamlet, the character, or *Hamlet,* the play. The domestic or feminine consistently evokes irrationality, as when he describes as fact the bliss he imagines of Shakespeare's marriage. Challenging the views of Coleridge and Hallam, who find the play *Measure for Measure* "hateful" and the character Isabella "unamiable," Hudson asserts that the lady is the finest and noblest, the most perfect of Shakespeare's women. But Hud-

STUDIES

IN

WORDSWORTH

CULTURE AND ACQUIREMENT
ETHICS OF TRAGEDY
AND OTHER PAPERS

BY

HENRY N. HUDSON

BOSTON
LITTLE, BROWN, AND COMPANY
1884

Title page for Hudson's most significant work outside the field of Shakespearean criticism

son often succeeds with the history plays. J. Dover Wilson credits Hudson with anticipating major points of his own conclusions about Prince Hal and Falstaff.

Hudson's chief non-Shakespearean critical venture is his monograph on Wordsworth in which he sketches the poet's life, studies the reviewers and critics, and elaborates the poetic principles. To Hudson, Wordsworth's firm control of passions does not make the poems passionless but the opposite. Passion enfolded in intellect is expressed as a music almost "too deep and sweet for [superficial readers] to hear." *Studies in Wordsworth, Culture and Acquirement, Ethics of Tragedy and Other Papers* (1884) shows Hudson reversing his former antipathy toward the modern. Writing about Wordsworth's originality Hudson sounds distinctly Emersonian: "Wordsworth's originality came, like Shakespeare's, from taking nothing at second hand; from looking at things with his own eyes, not with other men's, or 'through the spectacles of books'; from living and talking with Nature face to face, drawing his thoughts directly from her lips." Here, near the end of his life, Hud-

son endorses a chief tenet of his old opponents, the "Young Americans."

A decade earlier, Evert Duyckinck, in the 1875 edition of the *Cyclopædia of American Literature,* implicitly testified to Hudson's prominence in American letters when he devoted almost six columns to his old friend's life and work. A contemporary portrait shows Hudson to have been of impressive, rather severe appearance. An anonymous longtime friend, writing an obituary for the journal *Education,* describes Hudson's "intense individuality that made him at times appear harsh. His whole power seemed concentrated in whatever he undertook. He would not yield a hair to the customs of society. . . . To the outside world he was very stern and uncompromising, but to his personal friends he was as simple as a child." In 1927 Middlebury College, his alma mater, erected a bronze tablet in the name of Henry Norman Hudson.

References:

A. J. George, "Introduction," in *Essays on English Studies by Henry N. Hudson, L.L.D.* (Boston & New York: Ginn, 1906);

"Henry Norman Hudson," *Boston Transcript* (18 January 1886);

"Henry Norman Hudson," *Education* (March 1886): 448-450;

"Mr. Hudson's Lectures on Shakespeare," *United States Magazine & Democratic Review,* 16 (April 1845): 412-413;

N. N., "Shakespeare: His Life, Art, and Characters," review in *Shakespeare Jahrbuch,* 8 (1873): 357-360;

George W. Peck, "Hudson's Lectures on Shakespeare," *American Whig Review,* 8, new series 1 (July 1848): 39-53;

[Edgar Allan Poe], "Editorial Miscellany," *Broadway Journal,* 2 (13 December 1845);

Poe, "The Magazines," *Broadway Journal,* 1 (10 May 1845);

Poe, "Mr. Hudson, the New Lecturer on Shakespeare," *Broadway Journal,* 1 (5 April 1845);

Augustus Ralli, *A History of Shakespearian Criticism* (Oxford: Oxford University Press, 1932);

John W. Rathbun, *American Literary Criticism, 1800-1860,* volume 1 (Boston: Twayne, 1979);

S. Schoenbaum, *Shakespeare's Lives* (Oxford & New York: Clarendon Press & Oxford University Press, 1970);

Jane Sherzer, "American Editions of Shakespeare," *PMLA,* 22 (1907): 633-697;

John Stafford, "Henry Norman Hudson and the Whig Use of Shakespeare," *PMLA*, 66 (1951): 649-661;

Alfred van R. Westfall, *American Shakespearean Criticism, 1607-1865* (New York: Wilson, 1939);

E. P. Whipple, "Verplanck and Hudson: Shakespeare's Plays," *North American Review*, 67 (July 1848);

Charles B. Wright, *The Place in Letters of Henry Norman Hudson* (Middlebury, Vt.: Middlebury College, 1915).

Sidney Lanier

(3 February 1842-7 September 1881)

Jack De Bellis
Lehigh University

BOOKS: *Tiger-Lilies, A Novel* (New York: Hurd & Houghton, 1867);

Florida: Its Scenery, Climate, and History. With an Account of Charleston, Savannah, Augusta, and Aiken; A Chapter for Consumptives; Various Papers on Fruit-Culture; and a Complete Handbook and Guide (Philadelphia: Lippincott, 1876);

Poems (Philadelphia: Lippincott, 1877);

The Boy's Froissart, Being Sir John Froissart's Chronicles, Edited for Boys (New York: Scribners, 1879);

The Science of English Verse (New York: Scribners, 1880);

The Boy's King Arthur, Being Sir Thomas Malory's History of King Arthur and His Knights of the Round Table, Edited for Boys (New York: Scribners, 1880);

The Boy's Mabinogion, Being the Earliest Welsh Tales of King Arthur in the Famous Red Book of Horgest, Edited for Boys (New York: Scribners, 1881);

The Boy's Percy, Being Old Ballads of War, Adventure, and Love from Bishop Thomas Percy's Reliques of Ancient English Poetry, Edited for Boys (New York: Scribners, 1882);

The English Novel And the Principle of Its Development (New York: Scribners, 1883); revised and republished as *The English Novel: A Study in the Development of Personality* (New York: Scribners, 1897);

Poems of Sidney Lanier Edited by His Wife (New York: Scribners, 1884; revised and enlarged, New York: Scribners, 1891; revised and enlarged, New York: Scribners, 1916);

Sidney Lanier (Charles D. Lanier Collection, Milton S. Eisenhower Library, Johns Hopkins University)

Music and Poetry, Essays Upon Some Aspects and Inter-Relations of the Two Arts (New York: Scribners, 1898);

Retrospects and Prospects, Descriptive and Historical Essays (New York: Scribners, 1899);

Bob, The Story of Our Mocking-Bird (New York: Scribners, 1899);

Shakspere and His Forerunners, Studies in Elizabethan Poetry and Its Development from Early English (New York: Scribners, 1902);

Hymns of the Marshes (New York: Scribners, 1907);

Poem Outlines (New York: Scribners, 1908).

Collection: *Centennial Edition of the Works of Sidney Lanier,* 10 volumes: volume 1, edited by Charles R. Anderson; volume 2, edited by Paull Franklin Baum; volume 3, edited by Kemp Malone; volume 4, edited by Malone and Clarence Gohdes; volume 5, edited by Garland Greever with the assistance of Cecil Abernethy; volume 6, edited by Philip Graham; volume 7, edited by Aubrey H. Starke and Anderson; volumes 8-10, edited by Anderson (Baltimore: Johns Hopkins Press, 1945).

Sidney Clopton Lanier has been acknowledged as being one of the finest poets produced by the South in the nineteenth century. Though critics differ about his importance to twentieth-century poetry, it is generally accepted that he stands with Walt Whitman, Emily Dickinson, the New England poets, and Herman Melville as a major contributor to the making of American poetry of the last century. Apart from this, he has a minor reputation for his controversial critical theory, which sought to unite poetry and music, and for his studies of Shakespeare, the "forerunners" of Shakespeare, and George Eliot. The considerable number of anthologies which include his poetry testify to his established place in the history of American romanticism. His criticism casts some interesting light on his development as a poet, and the poetry helps to explain his purpose in exploring his scholarly interests.

Few lives present outlines more mythic than that of Sidney Lanier. He was born 3 February 1842 in Macon, Georgia, to Robert Sampson Lanier, a lawyer, and Mary Jane Anderson Lanier. Nurtured in a family steeped in Southern traditions of music and literature, Lanier read widely in his parents' library before entering Oglethorpe College in 1857, and there he distinguished himself in debating societies like the Thalian Club, read avidly, and showed precocious talent with the flute. Deeply impressed with his philosophy professor, James Woodrow, he decided to pursue a Ph.D. at Heidelberg University, but the Civil

War directed him instead to the Macon Volunteers, which he joined in 1860 with his brother Clifford. His life encompasses revered images of the ante- and post-bellum periods–moonlight rides from his bivouac to serenade a local beauty in her castle, gallant service on a blockade runner, national exposure as a major contributor to the 1876 Centennial, installation as a lecturer at Johns Hopkins, publisher of poetry of startling originality while fighting off prison-contracted tuberculosis–such images limn a virtually archetypal American writer not only rising from poverty to prominence, but seeking in his own life the natural symbols which incorporate a truth of the American experience.

Although Lanier was not a professional scholar, he strove to explain what seemed to him the musical foundations of poetry in his critical study, *The Science of English Verse* (1880). This book, which was in part an attempt to apply his theory to his own poetry, remains his main contribution to the history of criticism. His lectures, primarily undertaken to provide Lanier a university post he had dreamed of since prewar days, formed the basis of essays exploring the moral direction of English literature. He had very little to say about contemporary writers. However, his own attempt to discover his methods while involved in a serious program of moral reeducation of his age yields provoking evidence of his original abilities. His volumes on metrics and Shakespeare were directly related to his own explorations of the musicality of his verse, especially in the rhythms of his alternating long and short lines in his marsh poems.

The story of Lanier's interest in criticism and scholarship begins with his attempt to explain his own poetic interests when he began to write poetry shortly before the war. He was delighted to discover in writing his first poem that, as he told his father, he could write "Composite metre!" He proudly announced to a friend his realization that he could fashion subtle and covert meanings, for beyond his literal meaning is "another secondary idea." Such subtlety was not encouraged by his father, who urged him to write heroic couplets, an outmoded form. Nor did his admiring friends or his instructors at Oglethorpe College (dedicated to the "heart") stimulate his literary and critical abilities.

Yet Oglethorpe provided Lanier a place where he might debate leading issues of the day, and one such debate led him to argue that the conflict between North and South was the result of

Carrie Lignon, Lanier, Wilhelmina Clopton, and Clifford Lanier on Lookout Mountain near Chattanooga, Tennessee, 1866

the North's "unharmonious education," which misled it to overvalue intellect at the expense of feeling. Declaring that *"the initial step of every plan and every action is an emotion,"* primacy of feeling was the groundwork for his own poems and his criticism. As an amateur flutist he recognized that music and the music underlying poetry provoked emotions most successfully. His first works are instructive in that they show his attempt to clarify to himself the place of music, poetry, feeling, and moral action.

In his only work of fiction, *Tiger-Lilies* (1867), Lanier probed these interrelationships. After the hero, Philip Sterling, has performed on the flute, "the instrument of the future," his sister explains the meaning of his piece: "Music means harmony, harmony means love, and love means—God!" (Later Lanier would end a crucial poem, "The Symphony," with "Music is Love in search of a word.") Sterling's foil, John Cranston, plays upon a Satanic violin, so it is not surprising that he brings havoc upon the pleasant Sterling household and uses his position as a Yankee officer to perpetrate disorder during the Civil War. The link in Lanier's mind between music, feeling, and poetry was to lead him eventually to construe a "science" of English verse, an attempt to discover similarities between the laws of musical rhythm and harmony.

Quite early Lanier recognized that his aesthetic might well lead to problems in composition—either didacticism or diffuseness. Yet he admits that he often noticed a "tendency to the diffuse style" created by a "multitude of words to heighten the pat-ness of the image, and so making of it rather a *conceit* than a metaphor." Instead of controlling this tendency, however, Lanier learned to exploit it for the sake of his musicality of verse, which he believed would subtly educate the feelings of his audience.

His first attempt to apply his aesthetic to his poetry, in "The Jacquerie" (1868-1874), suffered from didacticism, though the chivalric situation and language at least restrained Lanier's diffuseness of imagery. "Corn" (1874), the most effective of Lanier's vocative poems, developed from the dialect poems of the early 1870s and sought to arouse the reader's awareness to the plight of the Southern farmer. Lanier controlled the vocative voice by blending suggestive symbolism of the "corn-captain" to diffuse nature imagery, underscored by rhythmic effects. In this persona of "corn-captain" Lanier employed the prototype of his "catholic man" who would speak for transcendental wholeness in the marsh poems a few years later. The writing of the poem coincided with Lanier's pronouncement that his artistic ability was "purely musical," his verse "a mere tangent."

Lanier had written dozens of pieces for flute (one of which a critic likened in style to Berlioz), and his virtuosity was acclaimed by such serious musicians as Leopold Damrosh, a friend of Richard Wagner. Such praise helped him secure positions with the Peabody Orchestra and the New York Philharmonic. Lanier's theory of poetry assumed that the most musical was also the most emotionally powerful, and since he wished to reeducate the emotions of his audience, his poetry should exploit its music. His poem "The Symphony" gave speaking parts to the instruments of the orchestra, deriving ingenious musical effects through his manipulations of alliteration, assonance, rhyme, and meter.

The poem provides each of his "instruments" with a special tone color created by rhythm and sound devices. In the violin segment,

for example, he uses tetrameter triplets with frequent anapestic substitution and little end-stopping, but within the "surging strings" is a counter-element composed of couplets and internal rhymes. He provides a "string sonority" by employing sounds derived from phonetic relations of liquids (r and l) and the "d-t" groups of sounds derived from the "N" family. Such sounds are also employed coliteration, and acrostic and concealed alliteration. For example, he links words together which contain sounds related to his key word, *Trade*. The violins want Trade dead, for "The Time needs heart—'tis tired of head." He changes his musical devices to fit the special voices of the flute, clarinet, French horn, and bassoon. The last voice, that of the bassoon, utters Lanier's most famous line, implicit in every line in the poem, "Music is Love in search of a word."

Subsequently, Lanier needed to curb his overzealous attempt to subordinate everything to music; otherwise this effort would create a mannerism from what had been a brilliant inspiration. "The Symphony," therefore, inevitably developed from Lanier's slowly formulating conception of his poetry. He had also commented on the rhythm and meter of his fellow poets John Bannister Tabb, Henry Timrod, Paul Hamilton Hayne, and Bayard Taylor, writing that Timrod never had time to learn "the mere craft of the poet—the technique of verse" and praising Hayne's sense of rhythm as an unbroken perfect "flower of melody." Hayne rejected Lanier's view of Timrod. Additionally, Taylor thought Lanier misapplied the "laws of Music" to poetry in suggesting that Taylor recast a poem so that it ended "on a tonic." Yet Lanier pursued his conviction that music and poetry were inextricably linked.

"The Symphony" drew the attention of Bayard Taylor, who arranged for the Philadelphia Centennial Commission to offer Lanier the chance to write the cantata for the Centennial's opening ceremonies. Taking Taylor's advice, Lanier recorded the "general" and not "individual ideas of the nation," forcing his poetry into greater diffuseness. In doing so he lost his linkage of musicality to imagery. When the poem was inadvertently published before its performance with Dudley Buck's music, it raised such a furor that Lanier and Taylor each wrote a lengthy defense of it. Unfortunately, performance with the music proved the cantata difficult to sing. Lanier, fashioner of an original musical poetry, found it almost impossible to write poetry

Early draft from the manuscript for Tiger-Lilies, *Lanier's only novel (Clifford A. Lanier Collection, Milton S. Eisenhower Library, Johns Hopkins University)*

Mary Day, whom Lanier married in 1867 (Charles D. La-
nier Collection, Milton S. Eisenhower Library, Johns
Hopkins University)

to musical accompaniment. It is also ironic that
Taylor pronounced Lanier "the representative of
the South in American song" at exactly the time
that Lanier sought to cut regional ties to the
"tobacco-sodden bosh" of Southern literary
editors.

The "Cantata" won him the commission to
write "The Psalm of the West," which repeats
many of the effects of "The Symphony," though
with less pertinent match between the conventional subject matter (such as the voyage of
Columbus) and the music. To Lanier, such poetry as "The Psalm of the West" was the start of a
new poetry of freedom, more like music, "etherealized" by loosening its binding limits. This idea—
first encountered at Oglethorpe—became a
guiding thought for him in his critical writing as
well as in his later poetry. Such etherealization
again takes place in Lanier's "The Song of the
Chattahoochee," for the musicality of the poem,
which represents the river, removes the river
from its natural bonds and enables us to feel its al-

legorical significance. In nature Lanier had returned to his true subject, and in exploring the
marshes of Glynn County he wrote his greatest
work, *Hymns of the Marshes* (1907).

After marshaling his reactions to the "salt-
sea spray" of Whitman's poetry, Lanier, in "The
Marshes of Glynn" and subsequent poems, such
as "Sunrise," took a deeper plunge into the musicality of verse. With an extraordinary assemblage
of suggestive details and rich connotation, he
blended a sonorous verse unmatched in anything
else he ever wrote, distributing a rich variety of
sounds fused to dominant sonorities and sweeping lines which imitated the flow of the streams
in the marshes. This long preparation made possible the writing of his first formal criticism, *The Sci-*
ence of English Verse. During 1878 Lanier offered
his ideas on the musicality of poetry as a lecture series at Peabody Institute. His love of his subject
led him to extravagant claims. For example, in selecting the word *science*, Lanier led readers to believe he wished to formulate ultimate laws of
poetic construction. Actually, he demonstrates
only how some poetry had achieved its effects.
Probably he meant versification for "verse" as
well, for he offers no comment on many aspects
of verse unrelated to versification. To him
"verse" meant the relations of sounds in poetry;
all that distinguishes music from poetry, for Lanier, is the tone color of vowels and consonants
compared to that of flutes and strings.

Lanier boldly insists that the laws governing
poetry and music are the same and analyzes each
according to rhythm, tune, and tone color and advances the bold idea that music and speech share
these elements. Even variations are shared. For example, if music shifts the accent away from the
basic music rhythm, it creates special interest by
such variation from the pattern. Poetry can do
the same by using the stress of a word to counter
the rhythm of a line. Lanier thought such variation would "free" poetic verse from bondage to established meters; he seemed to suggest that
cadenced prose might represent the verse of the
future, though he rejected the idea that "prose poetry" would be created because the regularity of
rhythm would not permit this.

The Science of English Verse has won the admiration of poets and critics alike. Karl Shapiro has
defended it, as "the most famous and influential
in the field of temporal prosody . . . in no sense
dated" and "one of the best expositions of its theory in the literature of metrics." In *Time and*
Stress in English Verse, With Special Reference to

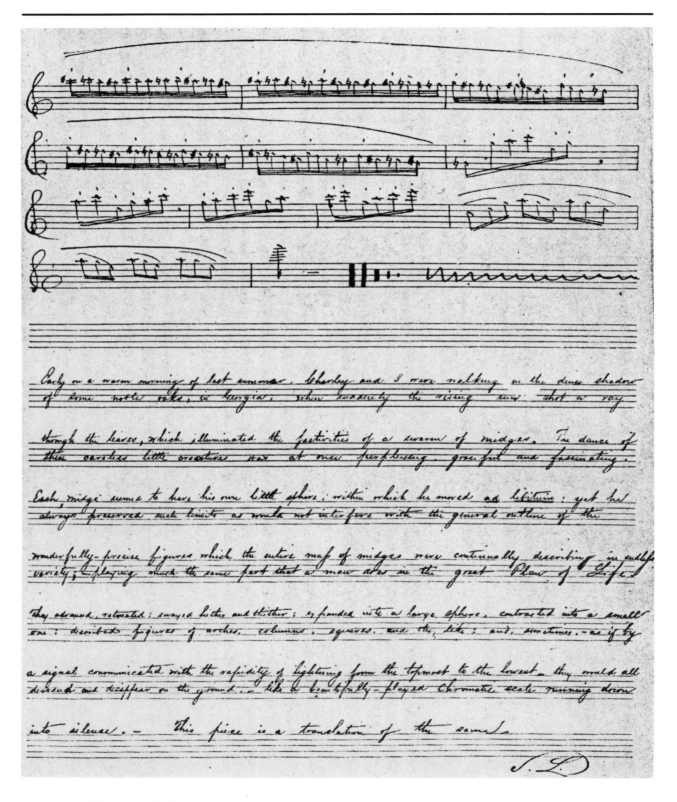

Second page of the manuscript for Lanier's "Danse des Moucherons" (Midge Dance), a composition for flute and piano written in December 1873 (courtesy of Mr. Henry W. Lanier)

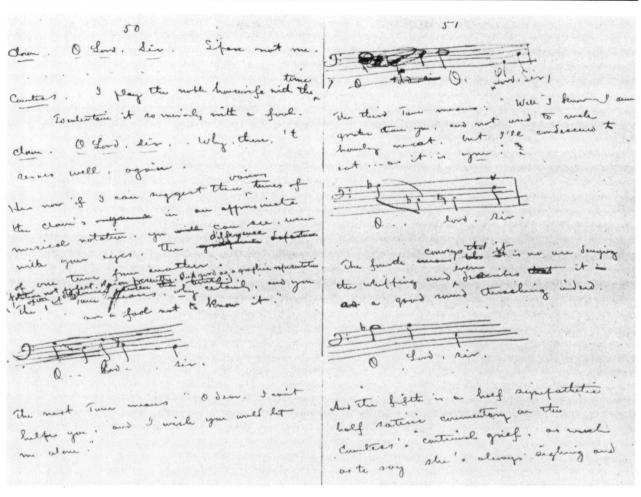

Pages from the manuscript for "English Verse," Lanier's second lecture delivered at Johns Hopkins University in 1879 (Charles D. Lanier Collection, Milton S. Eisenhower Library, Johns Hopkins University)

Lanier's Theory of Rhythm, Joseph Hendren has found that Lanier's reluctance to expel devices of traditional scansion from his scheme forms his only fault. Since he wanted to demonstrate how rhythm in poetry depends on the temporal relation of accents, a different stress notion should have been used, one employing musical notation. The clustering of sounds in monosyllables forces some to longer duration of expression than others ("it is" versus "was grouped"). With such variation in quantitative difference Lanier would mislead if he said these words had the same foot length. Modern laboratory studies in linguistics have shown that identifications of duration are subjective; still, musical notation would more closely indicate rhythm that the stress-system.

Lanier lists several rhythms of English verse according to the ear's intuitive grouping of sounds. Primary rhythm is the ticking of a clock without imposed pattern. Secondary rhythm is the pattern of clock ticks. If the second sound of a syllable is twice, thrice, or four times the previous one, then duple, triple, or quadruple time is constructed, just as it is in music. Lanier's other kinds of rhythms are not as useful, and he fails in this work to explore alliteration or assonance. Nevertheless, his demonstration that poetry can be scanned differently helped to make the musical study of verse a permanent part of English prosody.

Paul Fussell, Jr., has directed attention to a basic problem in Lanier's approach: the addition of musical notation implies too much identity of music and poetry. Yet disputes among Lanier critics about the "meter" of "The Marshes of Glynn" would clearly be reduced by recourse to Lanier's notation. Hendren addresses this aspect of Lanier's theory in frankly seeking to "rescue" *The*

Science of English Verse from "discredit and neglect." He underlines the importance of Lanier's description of the duration of sounds by showing that two dactylic lines may take different times to speak, one in duple, another in triple time. He corrects Lanier's mistake of thinking a foot is a "definable entity" and notes the contradiction of Lanier's method of constructing a musical theory within the traditional use of the barred foot which his theory itself opposed. However, Hendren emphatically concludes that "the consensus of modern poetry" is solidly behind Lanier's assertion that rhythm depends on measured time and that the very lines are divisible into sensibly equal time periods which are subdivided into beats by syllable configuration. Hendren has nothing to say of Lanier's moral view of the relation of rhythm to feeling, but Lanier found this concept integral to his plan to educate the feelings. In a peroration he proclaims, "The father of metre is rhythm, and the father of rhythm is God."

Lanier addressed *The Science of English Verse* to his fellow poets, and it surely appealed to them far more than his Shakespeare lectures. The Shakespeare lectures were public ones and thus gave Lanier a forum for his personal feelings about literature and morality. Included in a lecture series on the development of English literature at the Peabody Institute and Johns Hopkins University, the lectures on fiction were published posthumously under the title *The English Novel And the Principle of Its Development* (1883). The Shakespeare essays were later collected with essays on Tudor and Elizabethan literature as *Shakspere and His Forerunners, Studies in Elizabethan Poetry and Its Development from Early English* (1902). (Lanier's adoption of the Stratford spelling rather than "Shakespeare" of the London documents may show he preferred the *man* to the *playwright*.) Essays elsewhere discuss the development of the sonnet. Lanier uses a moral approach: literature is intended to stimulate the reader to feel rightly, think rightly, and finally act rightly.

In his criticism of Shakespeare Lanier notes paradoxes in the sonnets. His view of Shakespeare's work as divided into "Bright," "Dark," and "Heavenly" periods is a commonplace observation (though Arthur Eastman calls it "graceful"), but his perception–that each period is characterized by a different sort of poetry–required care in recognizing the specific qualities of the poetry. Like *The Science of English Verse,* these lectures were written to explore an area of technical and moral interest. Shakespeare, to Lanier, was the synthesis of artistic originality and moral growth, the logical outcome of the history of English literature. Lanier supports this insight with illustrations from the sonnets and the plays. The essays establishing Shakespeare in the tradition of *Beowulf* (which reveals the ancient savagery of nature that has since etherealized in Shakespeare) and Chaucer (whose humane bawdiness found a richer expression in the lovers in some of Shakespeare's comedies) show the careful work of a passionate amateur. His care in translating Old English poetry, like his attention to detail in the neglected work of Thomas Wyatt, John Lyly, and others, reveals the devotion of a serious scholar. About 1875, when Lanier conceived his Shakespeare lectures, he gained the enthusiastic support of Horace Howard Furness, who had just begun his Shakespeare New Variorum series.

Developing the theories of Frederick Fleay and Edward Dowden, Lanier embellishes their arguments. Thus Fleay (following Frederick James Furnivall) supplies a statistical method which shows that Shakespeare's development can be seen in "the Rime test, the Run-on and End-stopped line test, the Weak-ending test, and Double-ending test and the Rhythmic Accent test." Lanier construes this to mean that Shakespeare's life was "morally musical." In every case Shakespeare moved toward greater freedom, so the tests prove him to have developed along Lanier's own lines. The "scientific" aspect of such study appealed to Lanier as much as the formulation of a "science" of English verse. From Dowden he derives the idea that Shakespeare's plays developed from innocent relations of man to nature (*A Midsummer Night's Dream*), to dark relations of man to man (*Hamlet*), to the heavenly relation of man to God (*The Tempest*). As a consequence, Lanier, like his fellow commentators, prefers not to analyze the plays beyond assigning labels to those which chart Shakespeare's progress: *Hamlet* represents man's superstitious attitude toward heaven and hell; *Cymbeline,* the importance of forgiveness. Lanier's criticism, of course, follows the sentimental spirit of his time and of Southern chivalry, particularly in its treatment of Shakespeare's heroines. While establishing this theory, Lanier suggests that Shakespeare also presented a philosophy of man's relation to nature: the early plays reveal that man is subject to chance in nature (for example the character Bottom); the middle plays show

THE SCIENCE

OF

ENGLISH VERSE

BY

SIDNEY LANIER

So preye I God that non myswrite the,
Ne the mysmetere for defaute of tonge.
         CHAUCER: *Troylus and Cryseyde.*

If . . . some perfect platform or Prosodia of versifying were . . ratifyed and
sette downe. — WEBBE: *Discourse of Eng. Poetrie.*

A Poet, no industrie can make, if his owne Genius bee not carried unto
it. . . . Yet . . . must the highest flying wit have a *Dedalus* to guide him. —
SIR PHILIP SIDNEY: *Apol. for Poetrie.*

,. . Gif Nature be nocht the cheif worker in this airt, Reulis wilbe bot a
band to Nature . . . ; quhair as, gif Nature be cheif, and bent to it, reulis
will be ane help and staff. . . . — KING JAMES I.: *Reulis and Cautilis, &c.*

Poesie therefore may be an Art in our vulgar, and that verie methodicall
and commendable. — PUTTENHAM (?): *Arte of Eng. Poesie.*

But the best conceptions cannot be, save where science and genius are. —
Trans. from DANTE: *De Vul. Eloq.*

NEW YORK
CHARLES SCRIBNER'S SONS
743 AND 745 BROADWAY
1880

*Title page for Lanier's most important critical work, in which
he attempted to reconcile the principles of poetry and music*

man's inquiry into nature (Hamlet); and the last "Ideal" dramas present man's mastery over nature (Prospero).

There is also his curious assertion that George Eliot is superior to Shakespeare, which he made in his lectures on the English novel given in 1881 and published posthumously in 1897 in the revised edition of *The English Novel,* subtitled "A Study in the Development of Personality." In these Peabody Institute lectures Lanier, as usual, had a very ambitious plan founded on his insight that literature since the Greeks reflected increased concern with personality, or what "the evolutionist" might call "Spontaneous Variation peculiar to the human species." (Lanier's scientific term reflected his recent purchase of *On the Origin of Species.*) This evolution of the human spirit resulted in growth of personality "toward the Unknown, toward fellowman, and toward nature," unified by "the conception of Love as the organic idea of moral order."

Lanier advocates a new understanding of the form of the novel, for it blends science and poetry as well as an etherealization of language, since prose (as he said in the Shakespeare lectures) is a freer form than poetry. (He notes once again that Whitman's art is wrong because it mistakenly declares that freedom from forms represents the modern direction.) Development from drama to novel was the inevitable result of "the more complex relations between modern personalities." If the drama was a "powerful sermon," the very inception of the novel originated in didacticism and ascended, despite Zola's Naturalism, to the purified morality of George Eliot. Eliot's superiority to Shakespeare resulted from the modern habit of "looking all phenomena in the face," including what Carlyle called "the mystery of *I*" explored by Eliot in "the mystery of love."

All human history, Lanier asserts, reveals mankind's progress "to secure perfect freedom" in which love can develop. More closely linked to Jesus than Shakespeare, Eliot continuously concentrates on forgiveness. And since the novelist can claim "holy" omniscience and a dramatist cannot, Lanier argues, Eliot in a sense can become God. This raises the novel "to the very highest and holiest plane of creative effort." More, the novelist "proposes . . . to bring about the revelations of Judgment Day long before the trumpet has sounded." Apparently Eliot had dimly divined "the overflowing charitable instincts of society" in establishing her work. (Lanier had come a long way since he detected the failure of charity in "The Symphony" to be the leitmotiv of his age.) Finally, Lanier concludes, "moral beauty" must triumph over artistic beauty since time's judgments are "inexorably moral."

In this highly ambitious course of lectures from Aeschylus to Eliot, Lanier frequently digresses to Chaucer and Shakespeare when discussing Eliot in order to examine her greatness and the direction of history. History, Lanier urges, has moved toward increasing depth in "personality," but "personality" to Lanier in fact means "morality." His systematic study of Eliot's work to 1880 asks his audience to respond to the moral power of the novelist and the moral purpose of history. For Lanier, history has etherealized since the Renaissance—upward toward music while lifting science and nature; and the nineteenth century has developed the exploration of personality through the art of the novel. But Lanier carefully distinguishes the "draggled, muddy, miserable" feeling of the eighteenth-century novelists (which he "would blot . . . from the face of the earth") from the moral purpose of Dickens and Eliot. He further distinguishes between the satiric approach of Dickens, which tends to emphasize man's vice, and the approach of Eliot, whose subject is love and repentance. Unlike the naturalists, Lanier argues, Eliot creates lovable characters "with all the advantages of completeness derivable from microscopic analysis, scientific precision and moral intent." Lanier argues that, while the naturalistic novel of Zola is unscientific, a physical impossibility, and "artistic absurdity," Eliot's *Daniel Deronda* (1874-1876) gives characters who are "embodiements in flesh and blood of the scientific relations between all her facts."

Lanier's method in each lecture relies upon the power of his generalizations. He never directly analyzes the novels; instead, he pairs passages from Eliot with passages from Shakespeare and others—crossing genres to compare her novels with drama and poetry—in order to elucidate themes. Consequently, he never approaches the works from the point of view of their artistry as novels (though he affirms that they are works of art), nor does he give a comprehensive view of the elements of each of her works. Instead he selects lengthy passages as illustrations or touchstones which reveal her adherence to his generalizations about the development of western culture and literature. *Daniel Deronda* is thus "the most uplifting of modern books" for its solid characters, subtle yet analytical art, and perfect treatment of local color. But most importantly, she surpasses even Shakespeare in this novel in her treatment of the theme of repentance—a theme so powerful in its "direct presentation of goodness" that everyone is uncomfortable in reading it. But time will declare the novel a masterpiece since "the judgments of time are inexorably moral." Finally he supplies a brief biography of Eliot which brings him to compare her favorably to Christ, for she kept His two commandments perfectly.

Curiously, no Eliot specialists have noted even the existence of Lanier's provoking thoughts. Early reviews of his book, however, observed his similarity to the French critic Hippolyte Adolphe Taine in his philosophical insight into fiction, and *Harper's Monthly* called it the best recent fiction criticism for its illustration of the simultaneous and synthetic development of music, science, personality, and the novel (though other critics wished that Lanier had had time to revise and support his ideas more solidly). Three decades ago Floyd Stovall considered *The English Novel* to represent "The twilight of transcendental thought in criticism." Yet even these unfinished lectures show the need for a corrective to isolating textual analysis which seems to dissect the literary work only to murder it by leaving it self-contained and outside the historical and social forces that brought it into being.

Since Lanier's criticism continuously reflects his personal assessment of his own work, he undoubtedly refracted his own hope for literary immortality in his comments on the science of English verse and the genius of Shakespeare and George Eliot. Lanier's intensely moral criticism urges the reader to respond from the same standpoint that he had advocated as a student in 1859, that right feeling can lead to right moral action. His criticism concludes that the course of evolution in human affairs is better directed by fiction than by poetry. The reader may wonder if he might have returned to the novel had he lived longer. Clearly, his literary criticism must be understood as a Siamese twin to his creative development. Lanier's criticism may strike us today as subjective, impressionistic, and insufficiently documented in analytical argument. But no one could fault him for moral earnestness. He died 7 September 1881, age thirty-nine, of the tuberculosis he had contracted in a Union prison camp.

Letters:

Letters of Sidney Lanier, Selections from His Correspondence, 1866-1881, edited by Henry W. Lanier (New York: Scribners, 1899);

Some Reminiscences and Early Letters of Sidney Lanier, by George Herbert Clarke (Macon, Ga.: Burke, 1907);

Letters of Sidney Lanier to Col. John G. James, edited by Margaret Lee Wiley (Austin: The University of Texas Press, 1942).

Bibliography:

Jack De Bellis, *Sidney Lanier, Henry Timrod and Paul Hamilton Hayne: A Reference Guide* (Boston: G. K. Hall, 1978).

Biographies:

Edwin Mims, *Sidney Lanier* (Boston: Gordon, 1905);

Aubrey H. Starke, *Sidney Lanier: A Biographical and Critical Study* (Chapel Hill: University of North Carolina Press, 1933).

References:

Darrell Abel, "Sidney Lanier," in his *American Literature* (Woodbury, N.Y.: Barron's Educational Series, 1963), II: 498-517;

Charles R. Anderson, "Introduction," in *Centennial Edition of the Works of Sidney Lanier,* volume 1, edited by Anderson (Baltimore: Johns Hopkins Press, 1945), pp. xxi-xc;

Anderson, "Introduction," in *Centennial Edition of the Works of Sidney Lanier,* volume 7, edited by Anderson and Aubrey H. Starke (Baltimore: Johns Hopkins Press, 1945), pp. vii-lxiii;

Anderson, "Introduction," in *Sidney Lanier: Poems and Letters,* edited by Anderson (Baltimore: Johns Hopkins Press, 1969), pp. 1-15;

Paull F. Baum, "Introduction," in *Centennial Edition of the Works of Sidney Lanier,* volume 2, edited by Baum (Baltimore: Johns Hopkins Press, 1945), pp. vii-xlviii;

Jack De Bellis, *Sidney Lanier* (New York: Twayne, 1972);

Clarence Gohdes, "Introduction," in *Centennial Edition of the Works of Sidney Lanier,* volume 4, edited by Gohdes and Kemp Malone (Baltimore: Johns Hopkins Press, 1945), pp. vii-xi;

Philip Graham, "Introduction," in *Centennial Edition of the Works of Sidney Lanier,* volume 6, edited by Graham (Baltimore: Johns Hopkins Press, 1945), pp. 7-25;

Garland Greever, "Introduction," in *Centennial Edition of the Works of Sidney Lanier,* volume 5, edited by Greever and Cecil Abernethy (Baltimore: Johns Hopkins Press, 1945), pp. vii-lx;

Joseph Hendren, *Time and Stress in English Verse, With Special Reference to Lanier's Theory of Rhythm, Rice Institute Pamphlets,* 46 (July 1959): v-vii, 1-72;

Kemp Malone, "Introduction," in *Centennial Edition of the Works of Sidney Lanier,* volume 3, edited by Malone (Baltimore: Johns Hopkins Press, 1945), pp. vii-xxiv;

Malone, "Introduction," in *Centennial Edition of the Works of Sidney Lanier,* volume 4, edited by Malone and Gohdes (Baltimore: Johns Hopkins Press, 1945), pp. 255-257;

Roy Harvey Pearce, *The Continuity of American Poetry* (Princeton: Princeton University Press, 1961);

John Crowe Ransom, "Hearts and Heads," *American Review,* 2 (March 1934): 554-571;

Robert Ross, "The Marshes of Glynn: Study in Symbolic Obscurity," *American Literature,* 32 (January 1961): 403-416;

Thomas Daniel Young, "Lanier and Shakespeare," in *Shakespeare and Southern Writers: A Study in Influence,* edited by Philip Kolin (University: University Press of Mississippi, 1985), pp. 49-61.

Papers:

The Lanier Room at Johns Hopkins University houses a vast collection of letters, notebooks, journals, books, and memorabilia. Other important collections may be found at Cornell and Duke universities.

James Russell Lowell

(22 February 1819-12 August 1891)

Dennis Berthold
Texas A&M University

See also the Lowell entries in *DLB 1, The American Renaissance in New England,* and *DLB 11, American Humorists, 1800-1950,* Part 1.

BOOKS: *Class Poem* (Cambridge, Mass.: Metcalf, Torry & Ballou, 1838);

A Year's Life and Other Poems (Boston: Little & Brown, 1841);

Poems (Cambridge, Mass.: Owen, 1844; London: Mudie, 1844);

Conversations on Some of the Old Poets (Cambridge, Mass.: Owen, 1845; London: Clarke, 1845);

Poems. Second Series (Cambridge, Mass.: Nichols/ Boston: Mussey, 1848; London: Wiley, 1848);

A Fable for Critics (New York: Putnam's, 1848; London: Chapman, 1848);

The Biglow Papers (Cambridge, Mass.: Nichols/ New York: Putnam's, 1848; London: Chapman, 1849);

The Vision of Sir Launfal (Cambridge, Mass.: Nichols, 1848; London: Sampson & Low, 1876);

Poems, 2 volumes (Boston: Ticknor, Reed & Fields, 1849; London: Routledge, 1851-1852);

The Biglow Papers. Second Series (3 parts, London: Trubner, 1862; Boston: Ticknor & Fields, 1867);

Fireside Travels (Boston: Ticknor & Fields, 1864; London: Macmillan, 1864);

Ode Recited at the Commemoration of the Living and Dead Soldiers of Harvard University, July 21, 1865 (Cambridge, Mass.: Privately printed, 1865);

Under the Willows and Other Poems (Boston: Fields, Osgood, 1869);

The Cathedral (Boston: Fields, Osgood, 1870);

Among My Books (Boston: Fields, Osgood, 1870; London: Macmillan, 1870);

My Study Windows (Boston: Osgood, 1871; London: Sampson, Low, 1871);

James Russell Lowell (Harvard University Archives)

Among My Books. Second Series (Boston: Osgood, 1876; London: Sampson, Low, 1876);

Three Memorial Poems (Boston: Osgood, 1877);

Democracy and Other Addresses (Boston & New York: Houghton, Mifflin, 1887; London: Macmillan, 1887);

Heartsease and Rue (Boston & New York: Houghton, Mifflin, 1888; London: Macmillan, 1888);

Political Essays (Boston & New York: Houghton, Mifflin, 1888; London: Macmillan, 1888);

Latest Literary Essays and Addresses, edited by Charles Eliot Norton (Boston & New York:

Houghton, Mifflin, 1892; London: Macmillan, 1892);

The Old English Dramatists, edited by Norton (Boston & New York: Houghton, Mifflin, 1892; London: Macmillan, 1892);

Last Poems, edited by Norton (Boston & New York: Houghton, Mifflin, 1895);

Lectures on English Poets, edited by S. A. Jones (Cleveland: Rowfant Club, 1897);

Impressions of Spain, compiled by Joseph B. Gilder (Boston & New York: Houghton, Mifflin, 1899);

The Anti-Slavery Papers of James Russell Lowell, 2 volumes (Boston & New York: Houghton, Mifflin, 1902);

Early Prose Writings (London & New York: Lane, 1902);

Uncollected Poems, edited by Thelma M. Smith (Philadelphia: University of Pennsylvania Press, 1950).

Editions and Collections: *The Writings of James Russell Lowell,* Riverside Edition, 10 volumes (Boston & New York: Houghton, Mifflin, 1890);

The Complete Poetical Works, Cambridge Edition, edited by Horace Elisha Scudder (Boston & New York: Houghton, Mifflin, 1897);

The Complete Writings of James Russell Lowell, Elmwood Edition, edited by Charles Eliot Norton, 16 volumes (Boston: Houghton, Mifflin, 1904);

The Function of the Poet and Other Essays, edited by Albert Mordell (Boston & New York: Houghton Mifflin, 1920);

James Russell Lowell: Representative Selections, edited by Harry Hayden Clark and Norman Foerster (New York: American Book Company, 1947);

Lowell: Essays, Poems and Letters, edited by William Smith Clark II (New York: Odyssey, 1948);

Literary Criticism of James Russell Lowell, Regents Critics series, edited by Herbert F. Smith (Lincoln: University of Nebraska Press, 1969);

The Biglow Papers [First Series]: *A Critical Edition,* edited by Thomas Wortham (De Kalb: Northern Illinois University Press, 1977).

OTHER: *The Poetical Works of John Keats,* edited by Lowell (Boston: Little, Brown/New York: Evans & Dickerson/Philadelphia: Lippincott, Grambo, 1854);

The Poetical Works of John Dryden, 5 volumes, edited by Lowell (Boston: Little, Brown, 1854);

The Poetical Works of William Wordsworth, 7 volumes, edited by Lowell (Boston: Little, Brown/New York: Evans & Dickerson/Philadelphia: Lippincott, Grambo, 1854);

The Poetical Works of Percy Bysshe Shelley, edited by Mary Shelley, with a memoir by Lowell (Boston: Little, Brown/New York: Dickerson/Philadelphia: Lippincott, Grambo, 1855);

The Poetical Works of Dr. John Donne, With a Memoir, edited by Lowell (Boston: Little, Brown/New York: Dickerson/Philadelphia: Lippincott, 1855);

The Poetical Works of Andrew Marvell, With a Memoir of the Author, edited by Lowell (Boston: Little, Brown, 1857);

Isaak Walton, *The Complete Angler, or the Contemplative Man's Recreation, of Izaak Walton and Charles Cotton,* 2 volumes, introduction by Lowell (Boston: Little, Brown, 1889).

Despite controversies about the significance of his critical writings, James Russell Lowell stands alongside Edgar Allan Poe as one of the two most important literary critics America produced before 1850. Unlike Poe, however, Lowell became in his own time an influential arbiter of literary taste and value, a popular spokesman for genteel American culture, and a widely read and internationally respected man of letters. In 1878 Edward Fitzgerald, the author of *The Rubaiyat of Omar Khayyam,* declared Lowell "altogether the best critic we have; something of what Ste. Beuve is in French," and even today the largest professional organization of literary scholars and critics, the Modern Language Association, annually awards the outstanding book by one of its members the James Russell Lowell Prize. During his life Lowell published four collections of critical essays, and after his death admirers gathered his fugitive pieces in another half-dozen volumes. In this century his reputation as a critic brought forth staunch defenders such as Norman Foerster and the New Humanists and equally determined detractors such as Joseph J. Reilly, Richmond Croom Beatty, and Leon Howard. Whether being praised or damned, then, Lowell's literary criticism has provoked as much or more discussion than his poetry and provided the foundation for his reputation as America's first man of letters. Nevertheless, his criticism is hardly read today, certainly less than Poe's. Most scholars consider it too impressionistic, unsystematic, and subjective to be taken seriously, even while admitting its considerable historical interest. Read

Lowell in 1844, at about the time of his engagement to Maria White. Lowell and White were married 26 December 1844.

sympathetically, his best essays retain the power to move and enlighten; read analytically, they exhibit the faults not just of the man, but also, as he would say himself, the age as well.

Born on 22 February 1819 to Charles Russell and Harriet Spence Lowell into the Brahmin culture of Cambridge and Boston, Lowell was keenly aware that his generation of Americans had a peculiar calling to claim international distinction for the new republic's heretofore provincial efforts in literature. Looking back on these early years of his education, he recalled that Americans had Jonathan Edwards's sermons, Joel Barlow's *Hasty Pudding*, Timothy Dwight's *Conquest of Canaan*, Philip Freneau's nature lyrics, and John Trumbull's burlesque epic, *M'Fingal*: "But of true literature we had next to nothing. Of what we had, [Evert] Duyckinck's *Cyclopædia of American Literature* gives us an almost too satisfactory notion. Of what we had not, there was none to tell us, for there were no critics." As an undergraduate at Harvard, Lowell first engaged this

problem by becoming a poet—he wrote (but was not allowed to recite) the class poem for 1838 and published his first book, *A Year's Life and Other Poems,* in 1841. But he was no more single-mindedly a poet than he was a lawyer (he took a law degree at Harvard in 1840 but only practiced a few years). He had dipped into criticism with brief essays on reviewing and theme writing in *Harvardiana,* the class magazine he edited in 1837-1838; and when *A Year's Life and Other Poems* met with a lukewarm reception, he enthusiastically began the *Pioneer,* a periodical designed to offer the best in original criticism, fiction, book reviews, and poetry. After publishing a second volume of poetry in 1844, he produced a critical dialogue on early English writers and dramatists, *Conversations on Some of the Old Poets* (1845). In 1848 he combined his two loves in his most durable creation, *A Fable for Critics,* a versified commentary on the leading lights of American letters, a virtual *Cyclopædia of American Literature* in anapests.

While Lowell enjoyed increasing success as a poet and became ever more involved in politics, especially abolitionism, his tendencies toward criticism and scholarship asserted themselves in the mid 1850s. He edited six volumes of poetry, delivered a successful series of lectures before the Lowell Institute in Boston, and in 1855 was appointed Professor of Modern Languages at Harvard, a position that necessarily encouraged his scholarly tendencies. Many of his most important critical essays originated as classroom lectures—a fact to remember when condemning their discursiveness—and Lowell himself later apologized for the "more rhetorical tone" oral delivery left upon his prose. The professorship, combined with editorships of the *Atlantic Monthly* and the *North American Review* from 1857-1872, made Lowell's middle years the most productive period for his critical efforts. This era culminated with two major works of criticism, *Among My Books* (1870) and *My Study Windows* (1871), followed in 1876 with the lesser but still important collection, *Among My Books. Second Series.* In 1877 Lowell was appointed minister to Spain followed in 1880 with appointment as minister to England. As a representative of New England's Brahmin culture, he was sought after as a speaker who could elevate the tone of the most distinguished occasions. He spoke at the unveiling of busts of Henry Fielding, Thomas Gray, and Samuel Coleridge (the latter in Westminster Abbey); addressed the London Browning Society, the Royal Academy, the Wordsworth Society (of which he was president), and read his "Notes on Don Quixote" at the Working Men's College. Later collected in three volumes, many of these miscellaneous pieces offer evidence of Lowell's continuing commitment to literary criticism, even when his official duties called him from the library to the podium. When his second wife, Francis Dunlap, died in 1885 (his first wife, Maria White, died in 1853), he retired from the diplomatic service to spend the final years of his life traveling to England and presiding over his large and active family at Elmwood, the family estate in Cambridge, where he died quietly in 1891.

As editor, professor, and public lecturer, Lowell wrote major essays on thirty authors from Dante to Thoreau and reviewed scores of books ranging from Plutarch's *Morals* to Henry James's *Transatlantic Sketches*. Even his slightest critical notice revealed his vast learning, as he freely alluded to Homer, Greek drama, Roman poetry, German critical theory, and English literature from Chaucer to Trollope. Yet he had no overriding theory of criticism and believed his role was to record his "impressions, which may be valuable or not, according to the greater or less ductility of the senses on which they are made." As a result, his criticism is riddled with inconsistencies and contradictions that defy any attempts to systematize it. He sometimes argued for, sometimes against, such major issues as literary nationalism, moral aestheticism, and historicism. He detested provincialism, realism, and much romanticism; yet he wrote poems in New England dialect, published Rebecca Harding Davis in the *Atlantic Monthly,* and praised the poetry of Keats. Even his methodology was inconsistent. In his 1864 review of Thackeray, he condemned "comparative criticism . . . which brings forward the merit of one man as if it depreciated the merit of another" and then went on to weigh Thackeray against Dickens. He customarily "ranked" poets and judged them against his list of "Five Indispensable Authors," Homer, Dante, Cervantes, Goethe, and Shakespeare (sometimes he substituted Virgil for Homer). He could condemn the abject James Gates Percival for not being Homer as readily as he could praise Shakespeare for rising above the narrow forms of Greek drama. And he oscillated happily between the topical and the universal, sometimes in the same paragraph. Maddeningly contradictory as this approach is, it does underscore Lowell's "cosmopolitanism," his distillation of ideas as distant as Plato's and Goethe's into a flexible, wide-ranging criticism that, as he

Crayon portrait of Maria White by Samuel W. Rowse (Harvard University)

said, had "as many entrances for unbidden guests as was fabled of the Arabian Prince's tent." To appreciate Lowell's criticism fully requires as much tolerance and sympathy as he put into it.

Two complementary polestars of Lowell's thought recur in every context: Platonism and organicism. The first stands for the principle of ideality in literature, the firm belief that art should represent universals, not "unessential particulars," the permanent and eternal, not the ephemeral and transitory. In "The Imagination," an unfinished essay rooted in the 1855 lecture "Definitions," Lowell wrote, "Art always Platonizes: it results from a certain finer instinct for form, order, proportion, a certain keener sense of the rhythm there is in the eternal flow of the world about us, and its products take shape around some idea preexistent in the mind, are quickened into life by it, and strive always (cramped and hampered as they are by the limitations and conditions of human nature, of individual temperament, and outward circumstances) toward ideal perfection–toward what Michelangelo called 'ideal form, the universal mold.' "

Organicism, the second principle, brought Lowell back to earth. Drawing on Herder, Schiller, Goethe, and Coleridge, Lowell subordinated the individual writer's imagination to this larger principle of natural form. In the same essay, he condemned the poet who "substitutes his own *impression* of the thing for the thing itself," who "forces his own consciousness upon it." If habitually practiced, this leads to the "disease" of sentimentalism, rendering the imagination no more than "dyspepsia, liver-complaint–what you will." But as the true handmaid of art, the imagination "has two duties laid upon her: one as the *plastic* or *shaping* faculty, which gives form and proportion, and reduces the several parts of any work to an organic unity foreordained in that idea which is its germ of life; and the other as the realizing energy of thought which conceives clearly all the parts, not only in relation to the whole but each in its several integrity and coherence."

Combined with Lowell's vast learning, these two fundamental principles produced essays that blended the practical and the theoretical, the universal and the particular, in an unsystematic but challenging mix of historical, aesthetic, and appreciative criticism. Although he had his blind spots and prejudices, he admired writers as different as Fielding, Emerson, Donne, and Milton and usually stressed the positive aspects of the works before him. He stated his governing principle of criticism best in a manuscript fragment called "Criticism and Culture" which was later collected in *Literary Criticism of James Russell Lowell* (1969): "The object of all criticism is not to criticize, but to understand. More than this. As you will find it more wholesome in life, and more salutary to your own character to study the virtues than the defects of your friends, so in literature it seems to me wiser to look for an author's strong points than his weak ones, and to consider that every man, as the French say, is liable to have the defects of his qualities. Above all, criticism is useful in inducing a judicial habit of mind, and teaching us to keep our intellectual tempers." While such broad humanistic aims may encourage diffuseness and inconsistency, they also teach the willing reader much about literature, history, and taste.

Some of the inconsistencies first appear in the *Pioneer,* the periodical Lowell began with Rob-

ert Carter in 1842. The title implicitly dedicated the magazine to the cause of American literature, and the prospectus promised readers "articles chiefly from American Authors of the highest reputation." Although only three issues were printed (January, February, and March 1843), the magazine quickly established a solid reputation by publishing such popular American writers as Poe, Hawthorne, Whittier, John Neal, and W. W. Story. Behind these nationalistic choices, however, lay a theory that seemed to contradict the practice. In the first number, Lowell argued that criticism should be governed "by the eternal and unchanging laws of beauty which are part of the soul's divine nature." Mere literary chauvinism crumbled before such an august standard: "We are the farthest from wishing to see what many so ardently pray for–namely, a *National* literature; for the same mighty lyre of the human heart answers the touch of the master in all ages and in every clime, and any literature, as far as it is national, is diseased, inasmuch as it appeals to some climatic peculiarity, rather than to the universal nature." Making a fine and important distinction, Lowell explained that the *Pioneer* stood for "a *natural* literature. One green leaf, though of the veriest weed, is worth all the crape and wire flowers of the daintiest Paris milliners." For Lowell, American literature would be best served by following the timeless principles of idealism and organicism, two great aesthetic doctrines that promoted originality, truth, and beauty: "We want a manly, straightforward, *true* literature, a criticism which shall give more grace to beauty, and more depth to truth, by lovingly embracing them wherever they may lie hidden, and a creed whose truth and nobleness shall be ensured, by its being a freedom from all creeds."

In this spirit of enthusiastic and high-minded eclecticism, Lowell contributed to the *Pioneer* nearly two dozen poems and book reviews and a long critical essay on Thomas Middleton. The reviews admirably avoided the puffery common to literary journalism of the day, while the essay demonstrated the truth of Shelley's dictum that great literature of any age is universal. Unfortunately, these early excursions into critical theory and practice were cut short when Lowell contracted an eye disease and was unable to work on the second and third issues. Carter failed to maintain printing deadlines, and the *Pioneer* went into premature and undeserved bankruptcy. Poe, among others, recognized the loss to letters when he termed it "a most severe blow to the good

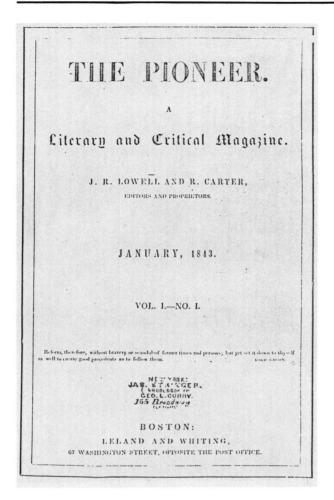

THE PIONEER.

A

Literary and Critical Magazine.

J. R. LOWELL AND R. CARTER,
EDITORS AND PROPRIETORS.

JANUARY, 1843.

VOL. I.—NO. I.

Reform, therefore, without bravery or scandal of former times and persons; but yet set it down to thyself as well to create good precedents as to follow them.   LORD BACON.

NEW YORK:
JAS. STACGER,
WHOLESALE
GEO. L. CURRY.
165 Broadway

BOSTON:
LELAND AND WHITING,
67 WASHINGTON STREET, OPPOSITE THE POST OFFICE.

Title page for the first issue of the journal Lowell edited with Robert Carter. In the prospectus the editors promised readers "articles chiefly from American Authors of the highest reputation."

cause–the cause of a Pure Taste."

Lowell had better luck with his first attempt at book-length criticism, *Conversations on Some of the Old Poets* (1845). With sections focusing on Chaucer, George Chapman, John Ford, and "The Old Dramatists" Philip Massinger and John Webster, this volume capitalized on the reading public's renewed interest in Elizabethan drama. These "conversations" between two young men, Philip and John, may represent two sides of Lowell's own personality, the idealistic liberal versus the more judicious conservative. The form allowed Lowell freedom to express his opinions upon the antislavery movement, the church, and public manners, as well as a wide range of literary topics. He casually mentions over eighty English and American writers and offers some judgment, however slight, upon each one. Some

of these terse comments foreshadow the opinions of a lifetime: Pope is too mechanical to be a true poet, Gray demonstrates "originality" and "grace," Dryden has a "sturdy English spirit," and Goldsmith is "delightful." Burns, Coleridge, and Keats are admirable, while Wordsworth, Shelley, and Tennyson are nearly as much so. Unfortunately, Lowell praised his countrymen N. P. Willis, Cornelius Mathews, and T. W. Parsons in similar terms in a display of uncritical enthusiasm he always had difficulty restraining.

Conversations on Some of the Old Poets nurtured Lowell's infant critical method and confirmed him in his impressionism and eclecticism. Conscious of his youth (he was only twenty-four), he added an apologetic preface defending his subjective and formless ramblings: "An author's opinions should be submitted to no arbitration but that of solitude and his own conscience," he wrote, for "an author's object in writing criticisms is not only to bring to light the beauties of the works he is considering, but also to express his own opinions upon those and other matters." Because rules are as impossible to establish for criticism as they are for poetry, and taste is arbitrary, the only safe critical method is "to point out what parts of a poem please" and let the rest go. Since posterity will reverse judgment in almost every case, it is better to be censured for kindness than severity.

The book sold surprisingly well, better than the two preceding volumes of poetry together. The first edition of 1,000 copies earned Lowell $100, and the second edition of an equal number paid him a royalty of ten cents per copy printed. An English edition appeared in 1845 and Lowell wrote his friend Charles F. Briggs that his publisher owed him $300 in royalties. Although much of the book's success was due to Lowell's outspoken comments on the church and abolitionism, reviewers placed the volume alongside the works of Coleridge, Charles Lamb, Thomas de Quincey, and William Hazlitt as a guide to the beauties of Elizabethan drama, the first critical book by an American to earn such praise.

Throughout the 1840s Lowell became increasingly involved in politics, taking up the cause of abolition and composing one of his most durable works, *The Biglow Papers* (1848), a verse satire against the Mexican War. In the same year he composed his critical tour de force, *A Fable for Critics*, a 1,800-line poem in jog-trot anapests that is certainly his most memorable and widely known contribution to criticism. The poem com-

John Holmes, Estes Howe, Robert Carter, and Lowell at their Whist Club

bines. satire, humor, and literary caricature with commonsense assessments of literary value in its parade of twenty-six American literati from all groups in the literary spectrum. The Boston Brahmins–Oliver Wendell Holmes, Longfellow, Whittier, and Richard Henry Dana, Sr.–receive the most sympathetic treatment. Except for the flattering portrait of Lowell's personal friend Emerson, the transcendentalists are sketched in harsher colors: Orestes Brownson, Theodore Parker, Bronson Alcott, Sylvester Judd, Margaret Fuller, and briefly, Thoreau. The New York Knickerbockers are represented by Cooper, Irving, Fitz-Greene Halleck, and Bryant; and the "Young America" group, also centered in New York, are represented by Cornelius Mathews, N. P. Willis, Charles F. Briggs, and Evert Augustus Duyckinck. In addition, Lowell included sallies at less-easily categorized writers such as Hawthorne, Poe, Lydia Maria Child, and a few

minor reviewers and critics, including himself.

Although literary historians agree with most of the assessments in *A Fable for Critics,* Lowell clearly devoted excessive praise to his good personal friend Lydia Maria Child while erring in the opposite direction with an unstintingly negative attack on Margaret Fuller. Two years earlier Fuller had reviewed Lowell's 1844 volume of poems and written that "his verse is stereotyped, his thought sounds no depth." Lowell retaliated with lines he later wished he had omitted, a caricature of one "Miranda" who

will take an old notion, and make it her own,
By saying it o'er in her Sibylline tone . . .
There is one thing she owns in her own single right,
It is native and genuine–namely, her spite;
Though, when acting as censor, she privately blows
A censer of vanity 'neath her own nose.

In most other portraits Lowell balanced praise with attack and maintained a healthy good humor. For example, his lines on Poe angered their target but pose a reasonably balanced assessment of his fellow poet-critic:

> There comes Poe, with his raven, like Barnaby
>   Rudge,
> Three fifths of him genius and two fifths sheer
>   fudge,
> Who talks like a book of iambs and pentameters,
> In a way to make people of common sense damn
>   metres,
> Who has written some things quite the best of their
>   kind,
> But the heart somehow seems all squeezed out by
>   the mind.

And his lines on the largely forgotten poet and novelist John Neal, a writer known for his fiery and bombastic prose, suggest Lowell's own critical principles of decorum, balance, and harmony:

> Ah, men do not know how much strength is in poise,
> That he goes the farthest who goes far enough,
> And that all beyond that is just bother and stuff.
> No vain man matures, he makes too much new
>   wood;
> His blooms are too thick for the fruit to be good;
> 'T is the modest man ripens, 't is he that achieves,
> Just what's needed of sunshine and shade he
>   receives;
> Grapes, to mellow, require the cool dark of their
>   leaves;
> Neal wants balance; he throws his mind always too
>   far,
> Whisking out flocks of comets, but never a star.

In temporizing contrast is the gentle critique of Bryant, whose poetry is perhaps *too* poised and mellow:

> There is Bryant, as quiet, as cool, and as dignified,
> As a smooth, silent iceberg, that never is ignified,
> ....
> He's too smooth and too polished to hang any zeal
>   on:
> Unqualified merits, I'll grant, if you choose, he has
>   'em,
> But he lacks the one merit of kindling enthusiasm;
> He'll stir you at all, it is just, on my soul,
> Like being stirred up with the very North Pole.

The portrait of Emerson vividly expresses Lowell's abiding principle of organic form, the standard that allowed him to reconcile the romantic and classical extremes of Neal and Bryant:

> In the worst of his poems are mines of rich matter,
> But thrown in a heap with a crash and a clatter;
> Now it is not one thing nor another alone
> Makes a poem, but rather the general tone,
> The something pervading, uniting the whole,
> The before unconceived, unconceivable soul,
> So that just in removing this trifle or that, you
> Take away, as it were, a chief limb of the statue;
> Roots, wood, bark, and leaves singly perfect may be,
> But, clapt hodge-podge together, they don't make a
>   tree.

A Fable for Critics was a great success. While Poe was angry at being included, others, such as William Gilmore Simms, were outraged at being ignored. The staunch Bostonian Thomas Wentworth Higginson objected to the harshness of the Fuller caricature, but Longfellow and Holmes admired the work's lively humor. The volume quickly sold out three editions of 1,000 copies each and established its author as a sharp-eyed, sometimes acidulous, always wry observer of the literary scene. After its initial notoriety had worn off, the poem took a back seat to *The Biglow Papers* and Lowell's new medieval romance in verse, *The Vision of Sir Launfal,* also published in 1848. But the poem's witty epigrams firmly established Lowell's reputation as a critic.

Lowell's larger purpose during these years was to reconcile the ardent demands of literary nationalism with the broader and more dispassionate standards of aesthetic idealism, an aim that invited contradiction. On the one hand, he echoed Emerson's cry for an American literature: "We are in need of a literary declaration of independence; our literature should no longer be colonial," he wrote in an 1847 review; on the other hand, he chided Americans for their impatience and feared that in their rush for a new culture to match their new nation they would forget their indebtedness to the great works of the past: "We must get rid also of this unhealthy hankering after a National Literature. The best and most enduring literature is that which has no nationality except of the heart,—that which is the same under all languages and under all skies." Only such reminders, Lowell believed, would restrain the vulgarity and barbarism he detected in his countrymen. In an important essay written just after *A Fable for Critics,* "Nationality in Literature," he counseled patience, realizing that Americans by nature will address the practical problems of business and industry before seeking the "unoccupied territories of the intellect." In the

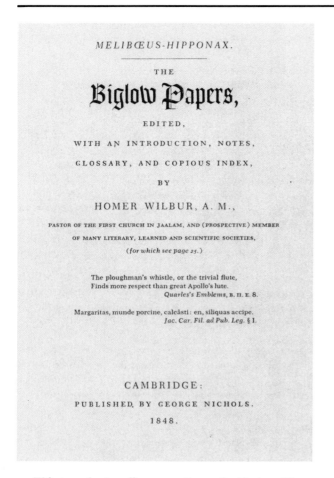

Title page for Lowell's verse satire on the Mexican War

meantime, literature should avoid outworn conventionalities and espouse our political ideals. "Let it give a true reflection of our social, political, and household life.... Let an American author make a living character, even if it be antediluvian, and nationality will take care of itself."

Perhaps as a result of a European trip in 1851-1852, Lowell grew in his respect for tradition, permanence, and stability, and tempered his earlier radicalism with an increased desire for order and unity. These ideals inform the series of lectures on the English poets he gave in the winter of 1855 at the Lowell Institute in Boston. Since 1839 the institute, a vehicle for adult education, had presented such distinguished speakers as Asa Gray on botany, Jared Sparks on American history, Charles Lyell on geology, and Louis Agassiz on creation. Although a cousin sat on the board of trustees, Lowell was chosen for his reputation, not his name. The invitation was first extended in early 1853, giving Lowell nearly two

years to prepare. But the melancholia resulting from the death of his first wife, Maria, in October of 1853, prevented him from working steadily on the twelve hour-long lectures the Institute required. Also, he busied himself during 1854 by preparing editions of Dryden, Donne, and Marvell and introductions on Keats and Wordsworth for Francis J. Child's British Poets series. Although the lectures were due to begin on 9 January 1855, by December Lowell had completed only five.

Lowell's dilatory preparation apparently made no difference. The lectures were enthusiastically received and well attended. Admission was free, and four out of five persons who wanted to attend opening night were turned away. To accommodate these people Lowell repeated his talk the next afternoon to another large crowd. Although attendance dwindled somewhat for the rest of the series, each lecture was dutifully reported in the *Boston Daily Advertiser* and the *Boston Traveller*, ensuring Lowell an audience beyond the lecture hall. The lectures distilled ideas from Lowell's omnivorous reading in Schelling, Gray, Samuel Johnson, Emerson, Coleridge, and perhaps the Scottish "commonsense" philosopher Dugald Stewart. They also set forth Lowell's own critical theories with greater system and clarity than he ever employed again and provided the intellectual and rhetorical framework he used in his mature criticism.

Topics included the early metrical romance, ballads, William Langland, Chaucer, Spenser, Milton, Butler, Pope, poetic diction, and Wordsworth. In most cases, Lowell offered assessments and opinions he never altered. Chaucer was the first great poet to mirror contemporary life objectively; Spenser personified the purest poetic sense and temperament; the early seventeenth century brought energy and originality to the language that were snuffed out by the barrel-organ artificiality of eighteenth-century versification; but Wordsworth restored an even earlier simplicity and directness. In the introductory and concluding lectures, Lowell first espoused his key critical principles of Platonism and organicism. In "Definitions" (collected in *Lectures on English Poets*, 1897) he asserted that "The first great distinction of poetry is *form* or arrangement," yet its source is spirit, as evidenced in Spenser's lines, "For of the soul the body form doth take,/For soul is form and doth the body make." This is the "organic law" we see in nature, as in the symmetrical branches of the pine or the regular rhythms of a songbird's flight. Echoing Coleridge, Lowell maintained that the imagination was superior to both fancy and the understanding; echoing Emerson, he maintained that the "Poet's office, whether we call him Seer, Prophet, Maker, or Namer, is always this–to be the Voice of this lower world" and make audible that "divine instinct" inherent in both man and nature.

The concluding lecture, "The Function of the Poet," is among Lowell's most important critical statements. It not only defends the place of poetry in a scientific and materialistic age but also argues that writers must be judged historically, in the context of their times: "The lives of the great poets teach us that they were the men of their generation who felt most deeply the meaning of the Present." The best writers, of course, will go beyond their era to the universal, for "The poet is he who can best see or best say what is ideal; what belongs to the world of soul and of beauty." The decline of poetic faculties–the capacity for "wonder"–is only temporary because, as Lowell added in a later version of this lecture, "Nature insists above all things upon balance. She contrives to maintain a harmony between the material and spiritual, nor allows the cerebrum an expansion at the cost of the cerebellum." Every age needs its poets to express to itself what is most representative–most "ideal"–in that age. The poet, then, is for Lowell, as he was for Whitman and Emerson, a "Representative Man," a figure both of his time and beyond it.

With these lectures Lowell crossed the threshold into a full-time career as a critic and scholar. Midway through the series, the Corporation of Harvard College suspended its consideration of six candidates for the Smith chair of Modern Languages from which Longfellow was retiring and offered the prestigious post to Lowell. Since he had not even applied for the job, he debated for a short time before accepting it. When he was assured he could spend a year in Europe to prepare himself in German and review his Spanish and French, he accepted gladly. When he returned in the fall of 1856, he only taught half time; but with his second marriage in 1857, he assumed full-time duties to increase his salary from $1,200 to $2,200 per year. The intellectual ambience of Harvard nourished Lowell's growth as a critic and scholar. Although he sometimes resented the drudgery of grading examinations and teaching routine courses in grammar, he thoroughly enjoyed lecturing on German, Italian, and Spanish literature and gained a considerable

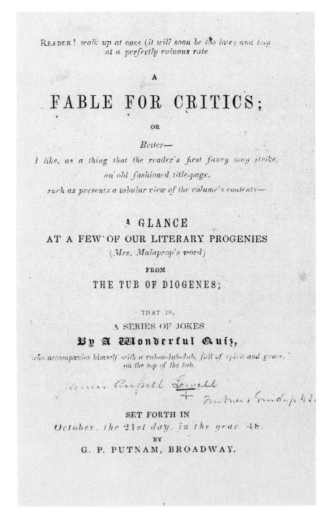

Title page for Lowell's most widely known contribution to criticism, a 1,800-line satiric poem which portrays twenty-six American literati from all groups in the current literary spectrum

reputation for his informal, rambling, yet demanding fireside talks with small groups of students in his home.

In addition to his academic position, Lowell served as editor of two leading periodicals, the *Atlantic Monthly* (1857-1861) and the *North American Review* (1863-1872). As a cofounder and first editor of the *Atlantic Monthly*, he consolidated his claims to literary distinction and, with a salary of $3,000 per year, attained his first real measure of financial security. He wrote numerous book reviews and corresponded (sometimes unhappily) with the most important writers of his time. He published and reviewed the work of established writers such as Hawthorne, Emerson, Holmes, and Whittier, and of such new writers as William

Dean Howells and Bret Harte. But he disliked Whitman's poetry, overlooked Melville, and got into a spat with Thoreau about some editorial deletions that permanently poisoned their relationship. Under his leadership the new magazine's first issue sold 20,000 copies and within two years had a respectable circulation of 30,000, some of it due to Lowell's controversial essays attacking Northern compromise with the South. When Ticknor and Fields purchased the *Atlantic Monthly* Lowell resigned, and two years later, in 1863, he became coeditor of the *North American Review* with his old friend Charles Eliot Norton. Unlike the *Atlantic Monthly,* the *North American Review* was a proud old conservative literary journal whose quality and influence had declined considerably since Lowell first wrote for it in 1847. Although he was unable to recapture its former glory as the leading arbiter of New England values, he wrote several provocative political essays that won the magazine new respect. Most important, his literary criticism flourished there. He reviewed books by a wide range of authors, from Longfellow, Holmes, Whittier, Howells, and Francis Parkman, to Thackeray, Tennyson, and the newcomer E. C. Stedman. Of the twenty-four critical essays he eventually collected, sixteen first appeared in the *North American Review,* including such central pieces as "Shakespeare Once More," "Rousseau and the Sentimentalists," "Pope," "Spenser," "Dante," and "The Life and Letters of James Gates Percival." Almost all of Lowell's significant criticism, in fact, bears the stamp of the genteel tradition represented by the *North American Review.*

In 1870 Lowell collected six of his best *North American Review* essays in his first major work of criticism, *Among My Books.* Four essays deal with writers—Shakespeare, Dryden, Lessing, and Rousseau—and two with New England history—"Witchcraft" and "New England Two Centuries Ago." The literary essays follow the familiar pattern of the classroom lecture: a general overview of the period; a biography interspersed with favorite quotations; a few explications of longer passages; and a concluding, usually favorable estimation of the writer's "place" in literature. The method mixes information with interpretation and some notable but all too rare epigrammatic insights. For the most part, Lowell traverses familiar territory, rather tediously giving background without integrating it into his personal opinion of the writer. He stays on safe ground, characteristically temporizes, and offers few un-

predictable interpretations. In their very looseness and familiarity, however, these essays achieve Lowell's primary aim: to avoid dogmatic labeling and categorizing in order to demonstrate how an author attained his reputation, not to question it. Lowell's model is Charles Lamb, whom he praises for having so few critical dicta, and his program follows Goethe's maxim, which he quotes appreciatively in the piece on Shakespeare: "there is a destructive criticism and a productive. The former is very easy; for one has only to set up in his mind any standard, any model, however narrow, and then boldly assert that the work under review does not match with it, and therefore is good for nothing,—the matter is settled, and one must at once deny its claim. Productive criticism is a great deal more difficult; it asks, What did the author propose to himself ? Is what he proposes reasonable and comprehensible? and how far has he succeeded in carrying it out?" Such questioning produces impressionistic essays, yet it is an impressionism informed by great sympathy and learning and a firm command of a writer's entire canon. The focus is always on the author, his times, and his works, in what might be termed an organic or genetic approach buttressed by a firm command of literary history.

Lowell follows this program best in "Shakespeare Once More." Shakespeare, Lowell observes, has often been condemned for not following the "rules"; yet every generation reads him in its own way, suggesting that here was a genius that went beyond the rules. Criticism, to appreciate and understand such a writer, must take a similarly tolerant view, avoiding such meaningless labels as "Greek" and "Gothic" and instead viewing the plays for what they are. For while the Greeks have left their stamp upon aesthetics, "the true poetic imagination is of one quality, whether it be ancient or modern, and equally subject to those laws of grace, of proportion, of design, in whose free service, and in that alone, it can become art." Thus we accept Shakespeare as we do nature herself, seeking to understand and enjoy, not judge and compare. As Shakespeare's satire on "dogmatical and categorical aesthetics" in the cloud scene between Polonius and Hamlet shows, "In the fine arts a thing is either good in itself or it is nothing. It neither gains nor loses by having it shown that another good thing was also good in itself, any more than a bad thing profits by comparison with another that is worse. The final judgment of the world is intuitive, and is based, not on proof that a work possesses some

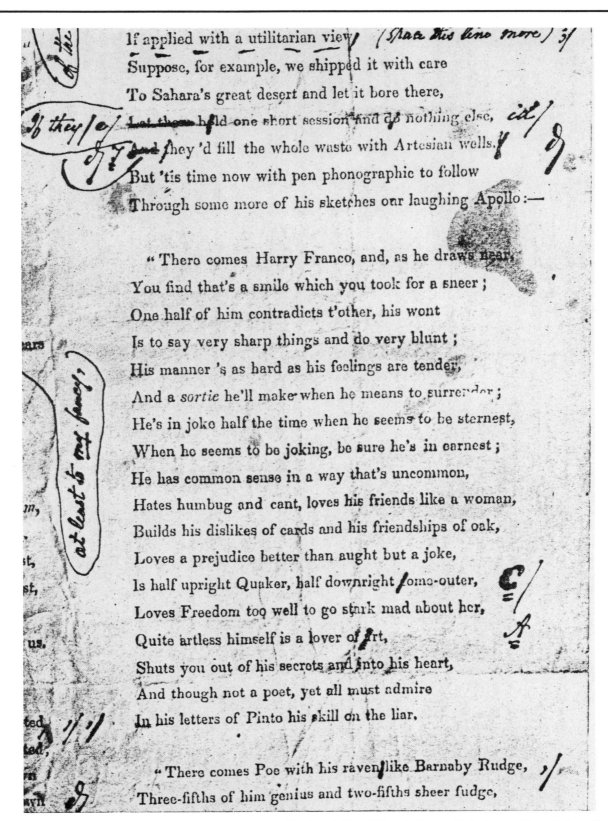

If applied with a utilitarian view

Suppose, for example, we shipped it with care

To Sahara's great desert and let it bore there,

Let them hold one short session and do nothing else,

And they 'd fill the whole waste with Artesian wells.

But 'tis time now with pen phonographic to follow

Through some more of his sketches our laughing Apollo:—

"There comes Harry Franco, and, as he draws near,

You find that's a smile which you took for a sneer ;

One half of him contradicts t'other, his wont

Is to say very sharp things and do very blunt ;

His manner 's as hard as his feelings are tender,

And a *sortie* he'll make when he means to surrender ;

He's in joke half the time when he seems to be sternest,

When he seems to be joking, be sure he's in earnest ;

He has common sense in a way that's uncommon,

Hates humbug and cant, loves his friends like a woman,

Builds his dislikes of cards and his friendships of oak,

Loves a prejudice better than aught but a joke,

Is half upright Quaker, half downright come-outer,

Loves Freedom too well to go stark mad about her,

Quite artless himself is a lover of Art,

Shuts you out of his secrets and into his heart,

And though not a poet, yet all must admire

In his letters of Pinto his skill on the liar.

"There comes Poe with his raven, like Barnaby Rudge,

Three-fifths of him genius and two-fifths sheer fudge,

Proof sheet with Lowell's corrections, of a page from A Fable for Critics (Edward Everett Hale, James Russell Lowell and His Friends, *1899*)

of the qualities of another whose greatness is acknowledged, but on the immediate feeling that it carries to a high point of perfection certain qualities proper to itself."

Meddling editors like Malone and Johnson who correct alleged "corruptions" misunderstand the two great rules of art, both of which Shakespeare follows: first, art must be "*in keeping*" with itself; second, it must satisfy "the superhistoric sense" of "*imaginative truth.*" Thus Shakespeare's anachronisms and "low characters" are merely trivial parts of a grander whole that commands our admiration even when it fails to convince us logically. In an important metaphor, Lowell compares this combination of spontaneity and form, romantic and classic, to artfully launched fireworks: "Our thought is so filled with the rocket's burst of momentary splendor so far above us, that we forget the poor stick, useful and unseen, that made its climbing possible."

Lowell's organicism allows him to appreciate a work regardless of its time period; yet he is also interested in the historical circumstances that give rise to great writers. For instance, he finds that even Shakespeare's mixed Saxon and Norman parentage foreordained him to be a "representative Englishman" who "knew that great poetry, being universal in its appeal to human nature, can make any language classic, and that the men whose appreciation is immortality will mine through any dialect to get at an original soul." Living as he did at a time when the language was rapidly changing, Shakespeare was able to draw on the best of the past and interfuse it with the dynamism of the present. He lived between revolutionary times—the Reformation and the Puritan revolution—and so profited from the ferment of ideas without succumbing to them. "If circumstances could ever make a great national poet, here were all the elements mingled at melting-heat in the alembic, and the lucky moment of projection was clearly come." Shakespeare, who placed art before nationality even while representing his nation better than any other writer, thus becomes one of Lowell's "cosmopolitans," a writer for all times and peoples.

The essay on Dryden shows how Lowell's principles allowed him to sympathize with an author he consigned to the second ranks. Lowell thought Dryden "one of the most unequal, inconsistent, and faulty writers that ever lived." By examining the whole canon of Dryden's works, including letters and prefaces, however, Lowell can appreciate Dryden's thought and character,

Lowell, age 38, in a photograph by Mathew Brady (Library of Congress)

not just his writing. Although individual works may not satisfy, his style gave English prose a colloquial, "familiar dignity" that "freed it from the cloister of pedantry." His prefaces are "a mine of good writing and judicious criticism," particularly in his preference of varied meters: "What a dreary half century would have been saved to English poetry, could Pope have laid these sentences to heart," Lowell observes. For common sense, clarity, and integrity, Dryden has few equals: "amid the rickety sentiment looming big through misty phrase which marks so much of modern literature, to read him is as bracing as a northwest wind. He blows the mind clear."

A slighter essay is "Rousseau and the Sentimentalists," the shortest in the volume. It is less about Rousseau than about his "sentimentalist" imitators, a group of writers Lowell cannot abide. For Lowell, sentimentalism is an "aesthetic view of morals and politics," a "degenerate modern tendency" that originated in Petrarch and has continued in Byron and Coleridge. "In the whole school," he adds, "there is a sickly taint." The real culprit, however, is less sentimentalism than some writers' desires to impose it on others. From this charge Rousseau is free, largely by virtue of his sincerity, originality, and genius. In fact, Rousseau himself was "divinely possessed," and given his personal misfortunes and struggles, worthier of pity than condemnation, unlike his pale imitators Chateaubriand and Lamartine. As an exercise in definition and an example of Lowell's breadth of sympathy, "Rousseau and the Sentimentalists" is a valuable specimen.

The least satisfactory essay in this collection is the digressive piece on the German critic Gotthold Ephraim Lessing. Largely a critique of Adolf Stahr's biography, the essay tediously reviews the facts of Lessing's life and praises his bold departure from critical pedantry. Perhaps unconsciously, Lowell comments most favorably on those qualities he shares with Lessing. He admires Lessing for "apprehending the many-sidedness of truth" even when it results in fragmentary or incomplete work and even finds justification for critical impressionism in Lessing's statement, "I am quite willing that my thoughts should seem to want connection,–nay, even to contradict each other,–if only there are thoughts in which they [my readers] find material for thinking themselves. I wish to do nothing more than scatter the *fermenta cognitionis*." "No writer," comments Lowell, "can leave a more precious legacy to posterity than this."

The two nonliterary essays in the volume, "Witchcraft" and "New England Two Centuries Ago," reveal Lowell as a reasonably objective historical scholar. He sarcastically condemns Puritan intolerance toward Quakers and Indians as a product of "that religion of Fear which casts out Love" and mocks those who make heroes out of ordinary men: "I have little sympathy with declaimers about the Pilgrim Fathers, who look upon them all as men of grand conceptions and superhuman foresight. An entire ship's company of Columbuses is what the world never saw." Yet neither were the Puritans tyrannical monsters. When viewed in the broad context of the international history of witchcraft, the infamous Salem trials were simply one more example of how witchcraft–a phenomenon rooted in nature and myth–can degenerate into a superstition that produces "that misguided energy of faith which justified conscience in making men unrelentingly cruel." But Lowell cautions against smugness. Every age, even the enlightened nineteenth century, is susceptible to that degenerate manifesta-

tion of the universal human imagination we call superstition. Like ourselves, the Puritans "were not in advance of their age, as it is called, for no one who is so can ever work profitably in it; but they were alive to the highest and most earnest thinking of their time."

This volume of criticism was an enormous success, going through over thirty printings in Lowell's lifetime and encouraging its author to follow it up the next year with *My Study Windows,* a miscellany of thirteen generally undistinguished reviews, personal tributes, and familiar essays written over the previous thirteen years. He skimmed the cream off his *North American Review* articles in the first collection; now only thin milk remained. If any principle distinguishes his choices for the two volumes, it is probably Goethe's maxim on destructive and productive criticism. In contrast to *Among My Books,* the literary essays in *My Study Windows* are decidedly negative, at times openly hostile, and in at least one case–that of James Gates Percival, a dramatist once hailed as the "American Shakespeare"–so damagingly contemptuous that they destroyed what little remained of the author's reputation: "Shelley has his gleams of unearthly wildfire, Wordsworth is by fits the most deeply inspired man of his generation; but Percival has no lucid interval. He is pertinaciously and unappeasably dull, –as dull as a comedy of Goethe."

Some of these "destructive" essays satisfy because they show Lowell, like Poe before him, holding to high standards of scholarship unusual for his day. The Harvard professor shines through the "Library of Old Authors," a long review of a fifteen-volume anthology of British literature. Lowell had originally published this essay in 1858, shortly after he edited anthologies himself, and thus felt competent to attack the volumes for poor typography, inaccurate texts, and uninformed introductions. With unsparing precision he pinpoints and corrects factual errors, bad grammar, poor punctuation, inexact glosses, inconsistent spellings, and blundering emendation. These faults culminate in the four volumes edited by a Mr. W. Carew Hazlitt, whose "pretentious charlatanry" Lowell exposed with glee. Hazlitt's only intelligent editorial decision was "the omission of a glossary. It would have been a nursery and seminary of blunder." In this case, "destructive criticism" seems justified, and we can only applaud Lowell's insistence on high standards of textual scholarship.

Letter from Lowell to Thomas Wentworth Higginson discussing opposition of other members to Frederick Douglass's membership in the Town and Country Club (Alderman Library, University of Virginia)

Similarly, the negativism of "Percival," "Swinburne's Tragedies," and "Pope" derives from principles, not personal pique. These essays are practical applications of Lowell's critical ideals, particularly his often conflicting standards of organic form and historical relativism. Percival's great crime was sentimentalism: he overvalued the individual and the mystical at the expense of the social and intellectual. But this error was to be expected given his historical milieu. He was a product of his time, a result of Americans' over-anxious desires for a national literature. In the 1840s, Lowell trenchantly observes, "Percival was only too ready to be invented." In "Swinburne's Tragedies," Lowell's organicism and idealism counterbalance the relativity of historical judgments. He admires the "maidenly reserve" of *Atalanta in Calydon* but elsewhere finds a "pseudo-classicism" that imitates Greek poetry in form but not spirit and thus produces artifice instead of art. For Lowell, "Truth to nature can be reached ideally, never historically; it must be a study from the life, and not from the scholiasts."

In "Pope," a *North American Review* essay expanded from the 1855 lecture, Lowell delicately balances the relative judgments of historicism with the ideal standards of organicism. Lowell personally disliked Pope's poetry for its trivial subjects, narrow intellectual scope, and limited form. He thought the philosophy of *The Essay on Man* "inconsistent" and "absurd" and the invective in the *Dunciad* "even nastier than it is witty. It is filthy even in a filthy age, and Swift himself could not have gone beyond some parts of it. One's mind needs to be sprinkled with some disinfecting fluid after reading it." Blind to the idealizing aim of poetry, Pope was too ready to condemn rather than praise, too quick to see blemishes rather than charms. Despite these reservations, Lowell found much to praise, especially "The Rape of the Lock" with its elegance, satiric force, epigrammatic skill, and tersely accurate observations of society. If Pope failed the test of ideality, he passed the test of historicism. In his devotion to the social, intellectual, and material at the expense of the moral and emotional, "Pope had one of the prime qualities of a great poet in exactly answering the intellectual needs of the age in which he lived, and in reflecting its lineaments. He did in some not inadequate sense hold the mirror up to Nature. . . . It was a mirror in a drawing-room, but it gave back a faithful image of society, powdered and rouged, to be sure, and intent on trifles, yet still as human in

its own way as the heroes of Homer in theirs." Lowell essentially balances the poet as seer against the poet as sayer in a judicious assessment few would dispute: Pope "was the chief founder of an artificial style of writing, which in his hands was living and powerful, because he used it to express artificial modes of thinking and an artificial state of society. Measured by any high standard of imagination, he will be found wanting; tried by any test of wit, he is unrivalled."

The closer Lowell's personal acquaintance with his subjects, the less objective his critiques. This is evident in his two most "destructive" essays, "Carlyle" and "Thoreau." Both pieces first appeared in the *North American Review* and confirm the hostility toward transcendentalism Lowell shared with the journal. While transcendentalism had long been a favorite target, Lowell usually leavened his sarcasm with humor. Here, however, he mixed personal attack with scathing denunciations of style and contemptuous accusations of unoriginality as he attempted to account for each writer's literary "degeneration." "Since 'Sartor Resartus' Mr. Carlyle has done little but repeat himself with increasing emphasis and heightened shrillness. . . . The same phrase comes round and round, only the machine, being a little crankier, rattles more, and the performer is called on for a more visible exertion." Carlyle's repetitious cant borrows so much from his earlier work "that we may at least be sure that he ceased growing a number of years ago, and is a remarkable example of arrested development." While his prose has become "stylistically lawless," striking and picturesque at the expense of sound reasoning, his cynicism "has gone on expanding with unhappy vigor." These faults combined with a penchant for "brute force," the "Hero-cure," and contempt for the common man, utterly disqualify Carlyle as a reliable historian. Lowell briefly temporizes at the end of his essay by calling Carlyle "the profoundest critic and the most dramatic imagination of modern times," "the continuator of Wordsworth's moral teaching." But no final two-page appeal can outweigh the previous forty-five pages of invective, the most unrelieved tirade in Lowell's career.

The essay on Thoreau, written shortly after the young transcendentalist's death, blends attack and insight in what initially promises to be a good-humored, richly punning jab at a movement Lowell flirted with in his youth: "What contemporary . . . will ever forget what was somewhat vaguely called the 'Transcendental Movement' of thirty

Lowell, photographed circa 1865 by W. J. Stillman (Harvard University Archives)

years ago? Apparently set astir by Carlyle's essays on the Signs of the Times, and on History, the final and more immediate impulse seemed to be given by 'Sartor Resartus.' . . . Every possible form of intellectual and physical dyspepsia brought forth its gospel. Bran had its prophets, and the presartorial simplicity of Adam its martyrs, tailored impromptu from the tar-pot by incensed neighbors. . . . No brain but had its private maggot, which must have found pitiably short commons sometimes. Not a few impecunious zealots abjured the use of money (unless earned by other people), professing to live on the internal revenues of the spirit. Some had an assurance of instant millennium so soon as hooks and eyes should be substituted for buttons. Communities were established where everything was to be common but common sense."

Unfortunately, Lowell soon abandons his satiric backward glance for unremitting personal attack. Even more than with Margaret Fuller, Lowell here spares no occasion to belittle his victim. The main charge is unoriginality. Thoreau's

works—all six volumes—are merely "strawberries from his [Emerson's] own garden," with little new that is not merely eccentric. In his solitary egotism, Thoreau hypocritically "thought everything a discovery of his own, from moonlight to the planting of acorns and nuts by squirrels." In truth, "He discovered nothing." What Thoreau believed to be new thought was merely indigestion, ill temper, misanthropy, the narrow provincialism of the self. He is, finally, no better than the shallow imitators Lowell attacked in "Rousseau and the Sentimentalists." Like them, Thoreau worshipped nature instead of man, preferring to "snuff up the stench of the obscene fungus" rather than study the divine organization of "men in communities."

Lowell cannot praise anything in Thoreau without immediately turning it against him. Even Thoreau's main strength as a stylist—sentences "as perfect as anything in the language"—reveals his lack of system, his scattered brilliance that, like individual stars, is unrelated to any larger whole. His high and noble aims of "plain living and high thinking" are but another example of his unoriginality, "a practical sermon on Emerson's text that 'things are in the saddle and ride mankind.' " While some of this vitriol may have overflowed from Lowell's editorial squabble with Thoreau ten years earlier, the tone suggests larger objections. Thoreau simply stands for everything Lowell hates—provincialism, imitativeness, primitivism, sentimentalism, egotism, narrowness, hypocrisy, and a profound disregard for the traditions and conventions of civilized society, traits he had found in Carlyle and even the abject Percival. Unable to temporize and thus build on his perceptions of Thoreau's genuine shortcomings—for instance, his self-consciousness or his lack of warmth—Lowell ends up writing an essay of almost unrelieved disdain, perhaps his most unfair and splenetic portrait of any writer.

In contrast to the fine abusiveness of such "destructive criticism," the appreciative essays in *My Study Windows* are weaker and altogether less interesting. Some of them are personal tributes to friends, such as the essay on "A Great Public Character," by whom Lowell means Josiah Quincy, a former president of Harvard. The piece on Abraham Lincoln rather conventionally praises Lincoln for his common touch, his honesty, and his place as "our representative man." The two nature essays, "My Garden Acquaintance" and "A Good Word for Winter," are poor attempts in a genre crowned by *Walden* and may suggest that Lowell's distaste for Thoreau stemmed in part from professional jealousy. And Lowell's nationalism revived briefly in the political essay "On a Certain Condescension in Foreigners," a defense of American manners motivated by current diplomatic strains between Great Britain and the United States. For all of Lowell's aspirations toward gentility and tradition, he cannot be called an Anglophile, as this essay makes clear. America has its own past and traditions, he insists, and need not rely on England for its culture: "the truth is that we are worth nothing except so far as we have disinfected ourselves of Anglicism."

Only two essays qualify as "productive criticism," a long and unremarkable academic piece on Chaucer and a personal effusion on Emerson. In the first Lowell reviews recent scholarship on Chaucer and celebrates the founding of the Chaucer Society. He summarizes biography, offers opinions on sources and influences, examines Chaucer's good effect on the language, and praises his versification, even including several pages of formal scansion to make his point. Echoing his 1855 lecture, he considers Chaucer most important as a storyteller and vivid describer, and even compares the "breadth of his humanity" to Homer's.

"Emerson, The Lecturer" was inspired by Lowell's attending a series of lectures Emerson gave in Boston in the fall of 1868. The experience stimulated Lowell's nostalgia for his youthful infatuation with transcendentalism and occasioned praise that counterbalances the negativism of "Thoreau" and "Carlyle." At the same time, its starkly contrasting appreciative tone again demonstrates how friendship blunted Lowell's critical judgment. Although the 1868 Boston lectures were among Emerson's most remunerative speaking engagements, his oratorical powers were already waning because of senility. The English critic Leslie Stephen, a friend of Lowell's, attended and found the first lecture rambling and incoherent. Lowell admitted that it was "disjointed" but rationalized this defect into a virtue: "It was as if, after vainly trying to get his paragraphs into sequence and order, he [Emerson] had at last tried the desperate expedient of *shuffling* them. It was chaos come again, but it was a chaos full of shooting-stars, a jumble of creative forces." In the face of originality and genius–and personal friendship–the rocket outweighs the stick. Character excuses all: "We do not go to hear what Emerson says so much as to hear

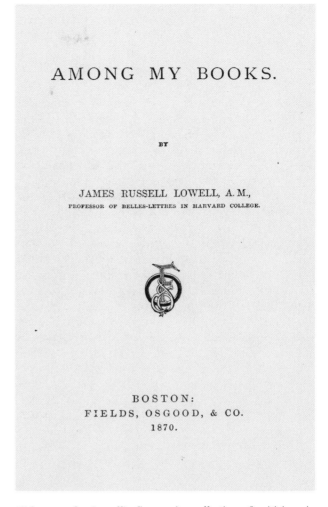

AMONG MY BOOKS.

BY

JAMES RUSSELL LOWELL, A.M.,
PROFESSOR OF BELLES-LETTRES IN HARVARD COLLEGE.

BOSTON:
FIELDS, OSGOOD, & CO.
1870.

Title page for Lowell's first major collection of criticism, in which he included six essays he originally wrote for the North American Review

Emerson." Lowell praises Emerson for combining Yankee practicality with mystical insight and looks upon him "as one of the few men of genius whom our age has produced, and there needs no better proof of it than his masculine faculty of fecundating other minds." In sharp contrast to his attitude in "Thoreau," he nostalgically recalls hearing Emerson speak thirty years before and remembers the experience with warmth and enthusiasm: "Cynics might say what they liked. Did our own imaginations transfigure dry remainder-biscuit into ambrosia? At any rate, he brought us *life*, which, on the whole, is no bad thing. Was it all transcendentalism? magic-lantern pictures on mist? As you will. Those, then, were just what we wanted. But it was not so. The delight and the benefit were that he put us in communication with a larger style of thought, sharpened our wits with a more pungent phrase, gave us ravishing glimpses of an ideal under the dry husk of our New England; made us conscious of the supreme and everlasting originality of whatever bit of soul might be in any of us; freed us, in short, from the stocks of prose in which we had sat so long that we had grown well-nigh contented in our cramps." As he says more pithily, "Emerson awakened us, saved us from the body of this death." Clearly, where Thoreau could do no right, Emerson could do no wrong.

My Study Windows was the most popular book of criticism Lowell ever wrote. It went through at least forty-three printings and several editions in the United States, enjoyed nearly as much success in England, and brought Lowell to the peak of his fame as a critic. But it failed to bring him money. The expenses of maintaining Elmwood had grown beyond his means, and in 1871 he sold off most of its land (about $75,000 worth) and invested the receipts for an annual income of over $4,000. Worn down with fifteen years of continuous teaching, he asked Harvard for a two-year sabbatical which he hoped would rekindle his poetic fires. When the college refused his request, he resigned and undertook an extended tour of Europe from 1872 to 1874. He received honorary degrees from both Oxford and Cambridge but had little success at poetry. When the opportunity came to return to Harvard, he gladly accepted and in the fall of 1874 resumed his teaching post and soon produced his final collection of literary criticism, *Among My Books. Second Series* (1876).

It is difficult to quarrel with Lowell's own frank assessment of this miscellaneous collection: it is "third-rate." Its five essays, some of them over twenty years old, lack both the opinionated piquancy of his waspish "destructive" criticism and the originality and depth of his best "productive" criticism. They continue to exemplify his wide learning and devotion to universal standards and restate more clearly some of his most cherished critical principles.

Three new essays, "Dante," "Spenser," and "Milton," expand *North American Review* articles, most fully in the case of "Dante." Lowell had taught the writings of the great Italian poet for twenty years, written an encyclopedia article on him, and now composed a 170-page study that commands respect if not interest. Although the essay frequently lapses into tedious overquotation and biographical detail, its erudition

and scope usefully clarify Lowell's criteria for literary greatness. Because of a moral power derived from Christianity, Lowell places Dante second only to Shakespeare in the hierarchy of literary value. Dante combined understanding and intuition, head and heart, realism and idealism: "Dante was a mystic with a very practical turn of mind. A Platonist by nature, an Aristotelian by training. . . ." As the first writer to make a poem out of his life, he was the father of modern literature; yet, "Like all great artistic minds, Dante was essentially conservative." Those commentators who read only the *Inferno*–Lowell cites Coleridge and Carlyle–overemphasize Dante's romanticism. Seen whole, Lowell believes, he attains universality because, unlike the pure romanticist, he makes his theme "man, not a man."

"Spenser," less analytical but nearly as prolix as "Dante," praises "the poets' poet" for his elegance, imaginativeness, restful dreaminess, and moral instructiveness. Always the historicist, Lowell reviews at length the English literary scene of the fifteenth and sixteenth centuries in order to judge Spenser not only for "what he was, but what, under the given circumstances, it was possible for him to be." He therefore excuses the allegory in *The Faerie Queene* as the fashion of the age and admires its idealism, formal design, and sparkling fusion of painting and poetry. "No man can read the 'Faery Queen,' " Lowell concludes, "and be anything but the better for it." The least-successful new essay is "Milton," a little-revised, very negative review of David Masson's *The Life of John Milton*. Parading his own considerable editorial knowledge, Lowell the scholar attacks Masson's biography and three-volume edition of the poetry for their historical and biographical minutiae, colloquial and idiomatic style, and misunderstandings of Milton's prosody.

Perhaps in response to the contemporary literary excesses of aestheticism, Lowell addressed himself in these essays to the relationship between aesthetics and morals, a dichotomy he found troublesome and never adequately resolved. In "Dante" he admitted, "with proper limitations, the modern distinction between the Artist and the Moralist. With the one Form is all in all, with the other Tendency. The aim of the one is to delight, of the other to convince. The one is master of his purpose, the other mastered by it." *The Divine Comedy*, by virtue of its organic combination of poetic imagination and religious sentiment, so blends these two qualities that it achieves the rarest height, universality. Lesser

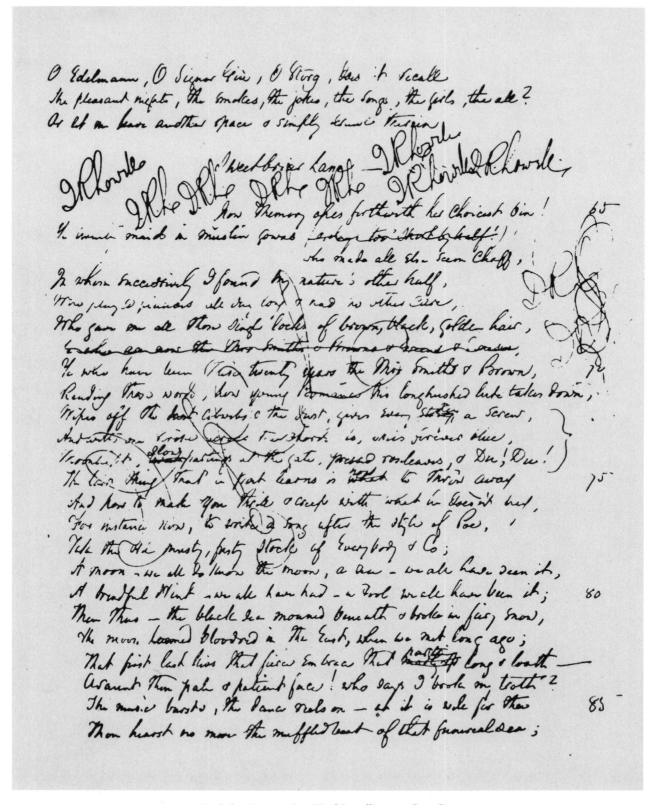

Draft for "Progression F" of Lowell's poem Our Own

works that seek to moralize–say, the poetry of Pope or Swinburne–err at one extreme or the other. Only the very greatest art could fuse beauty and morality without denying the virtues of either.

Such insistence on this double philosophy may explain Lowell's difficulty in appreciating the romantic poets. He filled out his collection by reprinting the introductions to two books he edited in 1854, *The Poetical Works of John Keats* and *The Poetical Works of William Wordsworth*. The first introduction, only thirty pages long, rehearses the facts of Keats's life and briefly analyzes his poetry for its "superabundance" of imagery, "over-languaged" style, youthful reliance on recent reading, and imaginative power. Keats, apparently, was the only great romantic Lowell truly liked. In the much longer second essay, Lowell clarifies his objections to Wordsworth and, by extension, to romanticism as a whole. The problem, in short, is egotism. Lowell had long diagnosed preoccupation with self as the chief cause of sentimentalism, vulgarity, and poor taste. He now claimed that it also blinded one to the ideal. As a result, Wordsworth "never quite learned the distinction between Fact, which suffocates the Muse, and Truth, which is the very breath of her nostrils. Study and self-culture did much for him, but they never quite satisfied him that he was capable of making a mistake." Such self-absorption produced very uneven poetry. Wordsworth's longer poems, such as "The Prelude" and "The Excursion," lack humor, drama, narrative pace, mental reach, and emotional power. But his best works, for instance the "Immortality Ode," achieve the "bare sincerity, the absolute abstraction from time and place, the immunity from decay, that belong to the grand simplicities of the Bible. They seem not more his own than ours and every man's, the word of the inalterable Mind." Only when poetry balances "Tendency" with a larger concern for "Form," a form that speaks to all humankind, does it truly succeed. Again borrowing a passage from his 1855 lectures, Lowell finally places Wordsworth in a lofty position, "fifth in the succession of the great English Poets" (presumably following Shakespeare, Milton, Chaucer, and Spenser). In that larger international pantheon of writers where Lowell customarily worshipped, however, Wordsworth ranks lower: "Compared with Goethe we feel that he lacks that serene impartiality of mind which results from breadth of culture; nay, he seems narrow, insular, almost provincial."

After this book, Lowell's energies increasingly turned to politics, always one of his chief interests. He served as a presidential elector in the disputed election of 1876, supporting the victorious Republican candidate Rutherford B. Hayes and thereby winning appointment as minister to Spain, followed in 1880 by appointment as minister to England. During this long stay in Europe (1877-1885) and after his return home he fulfilled his role as America's foremost man of letters by addressing varied audiences on both political and literary subjects, producing enough material to warrant the posthumous *Latest Literary Essays and Addresses* (1892), a miscellaneous collection of occasional speeches, lectures, and brief essays.

Three of these pieces were originally written to introduce editions of Milton, Walter Savage Landor, and Izaak Walton, and another to introduce a political work, *The History of the World's Progress* (1888). None is more or less than its genre promises. A lecture on Richard III delivered before the Edinburgh Philosophical Institution embarrassingly ascribes the play to another hand than Shakespeare's, and brief addresses on Coleridge, Browning, Fielding, and Wordsworth repeat his well-known opinions in a more flattering, generalized form. More valuable is a long essay on Thomas Gray, first published in the *New Princeton Review* in 1880 and written perhaps as early as 1876. Lowell makes his customary attack on the barrenness of eighteenth-century literature, and then goes on to praise Gray for overcoming the tendencies of his age by balancing a sturdy Johnsonian common sense with a pre-Wordsworthian imagination. Gray, unlike the egotistical Wordsworth, managed to blend form and tendency, aesthetics and morals, to become "the voice of emotions common to all mankind."

In his academic addresses, Lowell assumed ever more self-consciously the role of spokesman for liberal education and humane values. In 1887 he was named president of the Modern Language Association. The second person to serve in this position, he retained it for four years, longer than anyone ever has. He spoke before the association in 1889, staunchly defending the study of modern literature and praising the progress that had been made in the previous thirty years. Sounding some of the highest humanistic notes of his career, Lowell calls for a balance between the ancients and moderns, for a universal perspective that studies literature as "the unconscious autobiography of mankind." As Spenser's line "soul

Last photograph of Lowell

is form and doth the body make" implies, "we should judge a book rather by its total effect than by the adequacy of special parts, and is not this effect moral as well as aesthetic?" Literature offers both pleasure and instruction, and neither should be sacrificed to the other: "Perhaps the highest praise of a book is that it sets us thinking, but surely the next highest praise is that it ransoms us from thought."

On the surface, these views seem progressive. But for Lowell, "modern literature" meant writers from Dante to Goethe, and moral instruction meant humanistic idealism, not the grubby facts of social realism. In an address at the dedication of the Chelsea, Massachusetts, public library in 1885, he advised young readers to "confine themselves to the supreme books in whatever literature, or still better to choose some one great author, and make themselves thoroughly familiar with him." And Lowell's list was short. As he reiterated in an address before the Wordsworth Society in 1884, "Since Virgil there have been at most but four cosmopolitan authors,—Dante, Cervantes, Shakespeare, and Goethe. These have stood the supreme test of being translated into all tongues, because the large humanity of their theme, and of their handling of it, needed translation into none." In sharp contrast to the parochial "schoolmaster" Wordsworth, these writers avoided both "that provincialism which we call nationality" and the sentimentalism of overestimating the importance of their ego. Considering the occasion for these remarks, Lowell must be given credit for candor.

It was precisely such moralistic high-mindedness, of course, that blocked Lowell's appreciation of realism and dated him even in his own lifetime. In an important lecture on "Don Quixote" at the Working Men's College in London in 1885, he explicitly rejected realism in favor of a universal idealism, that "cosmopolitanism" he prized above all else. "I confess that in the production of what is called the realistic school I too often find myself in company that is little to my taste, dragged back into a commonplace world from which I was only too glad to escape, and set to grind in the prison-house of the Philistines. I walk about in a nightmare, the supreme horror of which is that my coat is all buttonholes for bores to thrust their fingers through and bait me to their hearts' content. Give me the writers who take me for a while out of myself and (with pardon be it spoken) away from my neighbors! I do not ask that characters should be real; I need but go into the street to find such in abundance. I ask only that they should be possible, that they should be typical, because these I find in myself, and with these can sympathize."

This opinion of realism is consistent with Lowell's lifelong principles and indicates his greatest weaknesses as a critic. Just as he detested minute analysis in fiction, so he detested it in criticism, and avoided systematic analysis all his life. As early as 1845 he praised another great American critic of the age, Edgar Allan Poe, for his "scientific precision and coherence of logic"; at the same time, however, he faulted him for failing to perceive "the profounder ethics of art." Poe's cold-blooded analyses illustrated "the great truth, too generally overlooked, that analytic power is a subordinate quality of the critic." The best criticism, thought Lowell, avoided such minutiae: "Facts in themselves are clumsy and cumbrous–the cowry-currency of isolated and uninventive men; generalizations, conveying great sums of knowledge in a little space, mark the epoch of free interchange of ideas, of higher culture, and of something better than provincial scholarship." He admitted that the best generalizations distill a lifetime of facts; but without such broad pronouncements, criticism lacks value and meaning for humanity at large.

Lowell spent his life trying to distill humane generalizations from five centuries of European literature and the masterpieces of classical antiquity. His insistence on high standards, humanitarian breadth, the fusion of form and substance, and a sympathetic historicism, bespeak a mind in advance of its age. Yet he failed to articulate these principles clearly, concisely, and consistently. Perhaps, as W. C. Brownell contended, he loved words more than ideas, and preferred to read rather than think, resulting in a criticism remarkable for sympathy, humanity, and scope, but equally remarkable for lack of system, disorderly presentation, and contradictoriness. To many readers today, Lowell must seem like the critic he derided in *A Fable for Critics:*

> No power of combining, arranging, discerning,
> Digested the masses he learned into learning. . . .
> He could gauge the old books by the old set of rules,
> And his very old nothings pleased very old fools;

> But give him a new book, fresh out of the heart,
> And you put him at sea without compass or chart.

If Lowell left no charts to steer by, it may be that such was his intention. He always recognized the limits of criticism and encouraged his readers, audiences, and students to think and feel for themselves. As he wrote in "Criticism and Culture," "I would not advocate a critical habit at the expense of an unquestioning and hearty enjoyment of literature in and for itself. Nay, as I think the great advantage to be gained by it is that it compels us to see two sides to every question, it should, when rightly understood and fairly applied, tend to liberality of mind and hospitality of thought." While some see this attitude as irresolute, others find in it a breadth and sympathy that make the critical act as natural and humane as the creative act. Always the humanitarian, Lowell realized that literature without life was pointless. Even though he devoted the better part of his life to criticism, he knew its subordinate place in the scheme of things and practiced his craft in humble awareness of the mighty literary presences that surrounded him in his Elmwood library. He never forgot his own early maxim, "All the critics on earth cannot crush with their ban/One word that's in tune with the nature of man."

Letters:

Letters of James Russell Lowell, 2 volumes, edited by Charles Eliot Norton (New York: Harper, 1894; London: Osgood, McIlvane, 1894);

New Letters of James Russell Lowell, edited by M. A. DeWolfe Howe (New York & London: Harper, 1932);

The Scholar-Friends: Letters of Francis James Child and James Russell Lowell, edited by Howe and G. W. Cottrell, Jr. (Cambridge: Harvard University Press, 1952).

Bibliography:

George Willis Cooke, *A Bibliography of James Russell Lowell* (Boston & New York: Houghton, Mifflin, 1906).

Biographies:

Horace Elisha Scudder, *James Russell Lowell: A Biography,* 2 volumes (Boston & New York: Houghton, Mifflin, 1901);

Ferris Greenslet, *James Russell Lowell: His Life and Work* (Boston: Houghton, Mifflin, 1905);

Richmond Croom Beatty, *James Russell Lowell* (Nashville: Vanderbilt University Press, 1942);

Martin Duberman, *James Russell Lowell* (Boston: Houghton Mifflin, 1966);

Edward Wagenknecht, *James Russell Lowell: Portrait of a Many-Sided Man* (New York: Oxford University Press, 1971);

C. David Heymann, *American Aristocracy: The Lives and Times of James Russell, Amy, and Robert Lowell* (New York: Dodd, Mead, 1980).

References:

William Crary Brownell, "Lowell," in *American Prose Masters* (New York: Scribners, 1909);

Harry Hayden Clark, "Lowell-Humanitarian, Nationalist, or Humanist?," *Studies in Philology*, 27 (July 1930): 411-441;

Norman Foerster, "Lowell," in his *American Criticism: A Study in Literary Theory From Poe to the Present* (Boston: Houghton Mifflin, 1928), pp. 111-156;

Richard H. Fogle, "Organic Form in American Criticism: 1840-1870," in *The Development of American Literary Criticism*, edited by Floyd Stovall (Chapel Hill: University of North Carolina Press, 1955), pp. 75-111;

Leon Howard, *Victorian Knight-Errant: A Study of the Early Literary Career of James Russell Lowell* (Berkeley & Los Angeles: University of California Press, 1952);

F. De Wolfe Miller, "Twenty-Eight Additions to the Canon of Lowell's Criticism," *Studies in Bibliography*, 4 (1951-1952);

Robert A. Rees, "James Russell Lowell," in *Fifteen American Authors Before 1900: Bibliographical Essays on Research and Criticism*, revised edition, edited by Rees and Earl N. Harbert (Madison: University of Wisconsin Press, 1984);

Joseph J. Reilly, *James Russell Lowell as a Critic* (New York & London: Putnam's, 1915).

Papers:

The largest collection of James Russell Lowell papers is at the Houghton Library, Harvard University. Major collections are also located in the Berg Collection at the New York Public Library, the Library of Congress, the Massachusetts Historical Society, the Morgan Library, and the University of Virginia Library.

George Perkins Marsh

(15 March 1801-23 July 1882)

Helen R. Deese
Tennessee Technological University

See also the Marsh entry in *DLB 1, The American Renaissance in New England.*

BOOKS: *The Goths in New-England; a Discourse Delivered at the Anniversary of the Philomathesian Society of Middlebury College, Aug. 15, 1843* (Middlebury: Cobb, 1843);

Address, Delivered before the New England Society of the City of New-York, December 24, 1844 (New York, 1845);

The American Historical School: A Discourse Delivered before the Literary Societies of Union College (Troy, N.Y.: Kneeland, 1847);

The Camel; His Organization, Habits, and Uses, Considered with Reference to His Introduction into the United States (Boston: Gould & Lincoln / New York: Sheldon, Blakeman, 1856);

Lectures on the English Language (New York: Scribners, 1860); revised and enlarged as *Lectures on the English Language: First Series* (New York: Scribners, 1861);

The Origin and History of the English Language, and of the Early Literature It Embodies (New York: Scribners / London: Low, 1862; revised edition, New York: Scribners, 1885);

Man and Nature; or, Physical Geography as Modified by Human Action (New York: Scribners, 1864; London: Low & Marston, 1864); revised and enlarged as *The Earth as Modified by Human Action* (New York: Scribners, 1874; London: Sampson, 1874; revised again, New York: Scribners, 1885);

Medieval and Modern Saints and Miracles, anonymous (New York: Harper, 1876).

OTHER: *A Compendious Grammar of the Old-Northern or Icelandic Language: Compiled and Translated from the Grammars of Rask* (Burlington, Vt.: Johnson, 1838);

Hensleigh Wedgewood, *A Dictionary of English Etymology,* volume 1, notes and additions by Marsh (New York: Sheldon, 1862);

George Perkins Marsh, 1861 (photograph by Mathew Brady)

Johnson's New Universal Cyclopedia, 4 volumes, 40 articles by Marsh on a wide variety of subjects (New York: Johnson, 1874-1878).

PERIODICAL PUBLICATIONS: "The Origin, Progress, and Decline of Icelandic Historical Literature, by Peter Erasmus Mueller ... Translated, with Notes by George P. Marsh," *American Eclectic,* 1 (May 1841): 131-146;

"Old Northern Literature," *The American Review: A Whig Journal,* 1 (March 1845): 250-257;

"Notes on the New Edition of Webster's Dictionary," *Nation,* 3 (16 August 1866): 125-127; (23 August 1866): 147-148; (6 September 1866): 186-187; (20 September 1866): 225-226; (4 October 1866): 268-269; (11 October 1866): 288-289; (8 November 1866): 369; (22 November 1866): 408-409; (27 December 1866): 515-517; 4 (3 January 1867): 7-9; (7 February 1867): 108-109; (14 February 1867): 127-128; (18 April 1867): 312-313; (9 May 1867): 373; (16 May 1867): 392-393; (27 June 1867): 516-517; 5 (4 July 1867): 7-8; (1 August 1867): 88-89; (12 September 1867): 208-209;

"The Origin of the Italian Language," *North American Review,* 105 (July 1867): 1-41.

The writings of George Perkins Marsh encompass one of the broadest ranges of those of any scholar and public figure in nineteenth-century America. A lawyer, legislator, philologist, linguist, diplomat, and geographer, he produced works on topics as varied as the Icelandic language and literature, the advisability of importing camels to North America, the dramatic effect which man was having on his natural environment, and the distinctiveness of American English. The student who meets Marsh for the first time almost invariably feels that there must be more than one George Perkins Marsh whom bibliographers have somehow confused.

Marsh was born in Woodstock, Vermont, into a prominent Vermont family. In 1820 he was graduated at the head of his class from Dartmouth, where he discovered a great gift for languages; he eventually mastered more than twenty. After teaching for a year, he studied law and in 1825 set up a law office in Burlington. In 1828 Marsh married Harriet Buell. They had two sons, the older of whom died in 1833, within a few days of Harriet Marsh's death. Marsh later married Caroline Crane. In 1843 he was elected to the first of two terms in Congress, where he distinguished himself as one of the guiding forces behind the establishment of the Smithsonian Institution.

During these years Marsh also built his reputation as a scholar. In 1838 he published *A Compendious Grammar of the Old-Northern or Icelandic Language,* a work based on the writings of R. K. Rask, which Marsh translated, compiled, and annotated. Along with his translation from Swedish for the *American Eclectic* magazine, it established him as the premier American student of Scandinavian languages and literature. Marsh drew further public attention, not all of it favorable, by some lectures delivered and published during this period. Most controversial were *The Goths in New-England* (1843) and *Address, Delivered before the New England Society of the City of New-York, December 24, 1844* (1845). Both of these lectures chauvinistically argued the point that the Goths were superior in intellect and character to the Romans, and that the Puritans of New England were the inheritors of Gothic virtues. In *The Goths in New-England* he wrote, "The Goths, the common ancestors of the inhabitants of North Western Europe, are the noblest branch of the Caucasian race. We are their children. It was the spirit of the Goth that guided the May-Flower across the trackless ocean; the blood of the Goth that flowed at Bunker's Hill." Marsh's position invited a parody from an anonymous critic: "About the only part of the human race worth mentioning is the Gothic race. About the only part of the Gothic race worth mentioning are the Puritans who emigrated to New England, and their present descendants. The circumstance of chief importance in the world's history is the emigration of the Puritans. The Reformation is important, for it led to this. The revelation of Christianity, at an earlier period, is also important, as a fact discovered at the time of the Reformation" (*Remarks on an "Address Delivered Before the New England Society of the City of New York"*). Perhaps well chastened, Marsh did not promote this theme in his later writings, except that the strain of anti-Catholicism here introduced was to survive to the end of his career. A theme more worthy of his abilities was sounded in *The American Historical School* (1847); in this address Marsh proved to be far ahead of his time in calling for a new kind of history, one "so totally different from existing models as to constitute a new field of literary effort. We require not so much a history of governments as the story of man; not a sketch of the outward relations of a people, but a picture of its social and domestic life, a revelation of its internal economy, and a philosophical investigation of the moral and political causes whose action and re-action have affected the personal liberties and the private interests and prosperity of its citizens." This idea of social history was not to be implemented for some three generations.

As United States Minister to Turkey (1849-1854), Marsh aided Lajos Kossuth and other political refugees, made the acquaintance of prominent European people of letters, includ-

Marsh, his sister-in-law Lucy Crane (standing), and his wife Caroline shortly after their marriage in September 1839
(Library of Congress)

ing Robert and Elizabeth Barrett Browning, and traveled. The main literary product of this period was the work preparatory to his odd book *The Camel; His Organization, Habits, and Uses, Considered with Reference to His Introduction into the United States* (1856), which had only a small sale and, it goes without saying, next to no effect in establishing the camel in America; but it illustrated Marsh's many-sidedness.

He returned home to find his financial affairs a shambles and himself facing bankruptcy. Reluctantly refusing, because of financial considerations, an offer of professorship of history at Harvard, Marsh turned to public service in Vermont and to lecturing. He delivered one course on the English language at Columbia College but finding that it did not pay enough, did not stay on. The publication of the lectures of that period, however, proved one of his most successful literary ventures; *Lectures on the English Language*

(1860) went through four editions in two years and was pirated in England, used as a text at Harvard, and widely acclaimed by American periodicals. His topics—among them the origin of speech and of the English language, the practical uses of etymology, the vocabulary of the English language, English as affected by the art of printing, principles of translation, corruptions of English, and the English language in America—were certain to prove instructive to an age in which American linguistic and philological studies were in their infancy. Recent literary and linguistic historians, including H. L. Mencken, have given attention almost exclusively to Marsh's last lecture, noting with interest his identification of an American English which is "necessarily much affected by the multitude of new objects, processes, and habits of life that qualify our material existence in this new world . . . , by the great influx of foreigners speaking different languages or dialects

Marsh as freshman congressman for Vermont, circa 1843
(Library of Congress)

. . . , by climatic and other merely material causes which affect the action of the organs of articulation . . . , [and] by the generally diffused habit of reading"–and to his defense of this language as being not inferior to the language of England.

A few years later he delivered a lecture series before the Lowell Institute of Boston, which he published as *The Origin and History of the English Language, and of the Early Literature It Embodies* (1862). In his introductory lecture he noted that "What is properly called philology . . . is much neglected by American scholars, and a professedly profound, but really most superficial research into linguistic analogies and ethnological relations is substituted instead." His ultimate object in this course, then, was philological rather than linguistic. His lectures cover the English language and literature from Anglo-Saxon times to the end of Queen Elizabeth's reign. They are replete with illustrative quotations from the major and the nearly obscure writers of the period and are sprinkled with occasional but generally sound critical evaluations. His major concern is the effect on the language of these writers; he admires Chaucer first and foremost for what he has meant to the English language: "From this

Babylonish confusion of speech [of the late middle ages in England] the influence and example of Chaucer did more to rescue his native tongue than any other single cause. . . . [H]e formed a vocabulary which, with few exceptions, the taste and opinion of succeeding generations has approved; and a literary diction was thus established, which, in all the qualities required for the poetic art, had at that time no superior in the languages of modern Europe." The modern student will miss from this generally thorough survey of early English literature any mention of *Sir Gawain and the Green Knight* or *Pearl,* a fact which illustrates the limitations under which Marsh labored in an age in which copies of many works of the Middle Ages commonly accepted today as masterpieces were extremely difficult to come by: although Marsh himself had one of the finest collections in the country of such materials, he had no copy of the one edition of *Sir Gawain and the Green Knight* which predates his lectures; *Pearl* had not yet been printed.

Marsh ranks Shakespeare with Chaucer as the great master of the English tongue. He makes the interesting observation that Shakespeare's vocabulary is relatively small, given the range of language available to him, and that "the affluence of his speech arises from variety of combination, not from numerical abundance." *The Origin and History of the English Language* was well received in scholarly circles, but was apparently too technical to attract an audience among the general public; it never went beyond one edition in his lifetime, but has been through several editions since his death. Today it is considered the best history of the language at the time of its publication.

In 1861 Marsh received a real political plum: an appointment by Abraham Lincoln as minister to the new Kingdom of Italy. He served in various Italian cities–Turin, Florence, and Rome–for twenty-one years, until his death in 1882. As a diplomat, able to make use of his broad knowledge of languages and to associate with the most cultured Europeans and Americans abroad, Marsh was in his element. He carried out his diplomatic duties with efficiency and still had leisure for literary pursuits. He published articles and reviews in periodicals and encyclopedias on a characteristically wide range of topics, from the latest English dictionaries to the pruning of forest trees. And he wrote the book for which he is remembered today as the father of the environmentalist movement, *Man and Na-*

Marsh in the library of Villa Forini, his home in Florence while he was Minister to Italy (Bailey-Howe Library, University of Vermont, Burlington)

ture (1864). Marsh's thesis that man was upsetting the balance of nature in his wanton abuse of natural resources was new to his age. The work was a popular success, and the modern ecology movement has revived interest in it today; it has been reprinted three times in the last quarter-century. Marsh's last book, *Medieval and Modern Saints and Miracles* (1876), was a warning to Americans of the machinations of the Catholic hierarchy. The work was written hastily and published anonymously; it had small sale or influence.

Marsh was a pioneer in Scandinavian studies in America. He left a significant mark on the study of language and literature and their interrelationships in his day. He was far ahead of his time in his thinking on man's relationship to his environment, as well as on the need for a new approach to history. He was a diplomat par excellence. Though his thinking on cultural and religious issues was sometimes bound, more than one would expect from a man of his intellect, by his place and time and background, surely his achievements place him among the handful of American "Renaissance men" in the nineteenth century.

Bibliography:

H. L. Koopman, *Bibliography of George Perkins Marsh* (Burlington, Vt.: Free Press, 1892).

Biographies:

Samuel Gilman Brown, *A Discourse Commemorative of the Hon. George Perkins Marsh, LL.D.* (Burlington, Vt.: Free Press, 1883);

Caroline Crane Marsh, *Life and Letters of George Perkins Marsh* (New York: Scribners, 1888);

David Lowenthal, *George Perkins Marsh: Versatile Vermonter* (New York: Columbia University, 1958);

Jane Curtis and others, *The World of George Perkins Marsh, America's First Conservationist and Environmentalist: An Illustrated Biography* (Woodstock, Vt.: Countryman, 1982).

Marsh's grave in the Protestant Cemetery, Rome

References:

Anonymous, *Remarks on an "Address Delivered Before the New England Society of the City of New York, December 24, 1844"* (Boston: Stimpson, 1845);

Richard Beck, "George P. Marsh and Old Icelandic Studies," *Scandinavian Studies,* 17 (May 1943): 195-203;

Catalogue of the Library of George Perkins Marsh (Burlington: University of Vermont, 1892);

Samuel Kliger, "George Perkins Marsh and the Gothic Tradition in America," *New England Quarterly,* 19 (December 1946): 524-531;

Mary Philip Trauth, *Italo-American Diplomatic Relations, 1861-1882: The Mission of George Perkins Marsh, First American Ambassador to the Kingdom of Italy* (Washington, D.C.: Catholic University of America, 1958).

Papers:

The bulk of George Perkins Marsh's papers is at the University of Vermont; this collection includes notebooks, diaries, letters to and from Marsh, unpublished manuscripts, and drafts of published ones. Also at the University of Vermont is the whole of Marsh's remarkable library of some 12,000 volumes. The Vermont Historical Society holds a significant collection of letters by Marsh; other letters are scattered in manuscript collections of many of the major libraries of the Northeast.

Cornelius Mathews

(28 October 1817?-25 March 1889)

Donald Yannella
Glassboro State College

See also the Mathews entry in *DLB 3, Antebellum Writers in New York and the South.*

BOOKS: *The Motley Book: A Series of Tales and Sketches,* as The Late Ben. Smith (New York: Turney, 1838);

Behemoth: A Legend of the Mound-Builders, anonymous (New York: J. & H. G. Langley, 1839);

The True Aims of Life: An Address Delivered before the Alumni of the New-York University (New York: Wiley & Putnam/J. & H. G. Langley, 1839);

The Politicians: A Comedy, in Five Acts (New York: Trevett, 1840);

Wakondah; The Master of Life. A Poem, anonymous (New York: Curry, 1841);

A Speech on International Copyright, Delivered at the Dinner to Charles Dickens (New York: Curry, 1842);

An Appeal to American Authors and the American Press, in Behalf of International Copyright (New York & London: Wiley & Putnam, 1842);

The Career of Puffer Hopkins (New York: Appleton, 1842);

The Better Interests of the Country, in Connexion with International Copy-Right (New York & London: Wiley & Putnam, 1843);

The Various Writings of Cornelius Mathews (New York: Sun Office / Harper, 1843);

Poems on Man, in His Various Aspects under the American Republic (New York: Wiley & Putnam, 1843);

An Address to the People of the United States in Behalf of the American Copyright Club, Adopted at New-York, October 18th, 1843 (New York: Published by the Club, 1843);

Big Abel, and the Little Manhattan (New York: Wiley & Putnam, 1845);

Americanism: An Address Delivered before the Eucleian Society of the New-York University, 30th June, 1845 (New York: Paine & Burgess, 1845);

Moneypenny, or, The Heart of the World. A Romance of the Present Day. Illustrated by Darley (New York: DeWitt & Davenport, 1849-1850);

Chanticleer: A Thanksgiving Story of the Peabody Family (Boston: Mussey / New York: Redfield, 1850);

Witchcraft: A Tragedy in Five Acts (London: Bogue / New York: French, 1852);

Calmstorm, the Reformer. A Dramatic Comment (New York: Tinson, 1853);

A Pen-and-Ink Panorama of New-York City (New York: Taylor, 1853).

PLAY PRODUCTIONS: *Witchcraft,* Philadelphia, Walnut Street Theater, 1846; New York City, Bowery Theatre, 1847;

Seeing the Elephant, New York City, Burton's Theatre, early 1848;

Jacob Leisler, the Patriot Hero, or, New York in 1690, New York City, Bowery Theatre, 8 May 1848;

False Pretences, or, Both Sides of Good Society, New York City, Burton's Theatre, 3 December 1855;

Broadway and the Bowery, or, the Young Mechanic and the Merchant's Daughter, New York City,

Brougham's Bowery Theatre, 10 November 1856.

OTHER: *Modern Standard Drama,* volumes 80-85 edited by Mathews (New York: Taylor, 1850);

The Minor Drama, volumes 37-39 edited anonymously by Mathews (New York: Taylor, 1850);

Henry R. Schoolcraft, *The Indian Fairy Book. From the Original Legends,* edited anonymously by Mathews (New York: Mason Brothers, 1856);

Hiawatha and Other Legends of the Wigwams of the Red American Indians, edited anonymously by Mathews (London: Sonnenschein, 1882).

Cornelius Mathews, a highly visible figure on the American literary scene from the 1830s to the 1850s, has been viewed mainly as a champion for international copyright and literary nationalism. But he was more: a creative writer, the author of nonfiction sketches and essays, fiction, plays, and poetry; an editor of book-length works as well as newspapers, magazines, and journals; a journalist who wrote numerous book reviews and notices for over forty years; and a humorist and satirist. He was not formally a literary theorist but a practical critic with a well-defined agenda.

Mathews's roles as a member of the Duyckinck Circle and the Young America group in the politically and ideologically charged literary frays of the American Renaissance period have provided the focus of virtually all contemporary and modern assessments of the man and his work, largely due to the vigorous, abrasive tone he frequently used when arguing his views. Widely held conceptions of the man derive little from serious analysis of his work or from considerations of a significant or even minimal number of documents, such as letters. Rather they are based largely on the impressions offered by his sometimes enemies, such as James Russell Lowell, Henry Wadsworth Longfellow, Oliver Wendell Holmes, and Edgar Allan Poe, among others. These circumscribed, even narrow, perceptions are due to the paucity of information available about his life and work as the antebellum New York literary scene, in which he played an important role, dissolved as the 1850s came to an end.

Mathews was born in Portchester, New York, a Westchester County suburb north of New York City, but his family apparently moved to the city shortly after his birth. A lifelong bachelor, he came from a hardworking, apparently middle-class family, supported by the cabinet-making skills and business acumen of his father. In 1834 he was graduated with the second class of the University of the City of New York (now New York University) and was admitted to the bar in 1837. Until 1848 *Trow's New York Directory* lists him as an attorney. It was not until 1850-1851 that the directory noted his occupation as author. From 1852 to 1856 he is identified only as an editor, with offices from 1852 to 1854 at the *Literary World,* published by the Duyckinck brothers.

Although Mathews lived until 1889, there has been virtually no accounting for his activities or fortunes from the middle 1850s through the late 1870s and early 1880s, some twenty-five years. His publication record testifies that he brought adaptations of certain Indian legends of Henry Schoolcraft through many editions in the 1850s, 1860s, and 1870s, and he asserted in a rare interview with George O. Seilhamer in 1881 that he had sustained his work in drama and theater over the years. According to Harrison Grey Fiske's obituary in the *New York Mirror,* he contributed articles to that journal and other periodicals during the 1880s. But many standard biographical sources have been silent about what work he did to support himself in his middle and old age.

The point is that the little hard information available on Mathews has not been added to substantially for more than a century. The outline of his life and career published in the *New York Times* and *New York Mirror* obituaries was derived essentially from information in the Duyckincks' *Cyclopædia of American Literature* (1855) which had been repeated in other standard period biographical dictionaries. This obscurity may also have been reflective of a withdrawal similar to that of his former friend and associate Herman Melville (there is no available evidence to connect the two after the early 1850s): a quietness, perhaps perverse, of the sort which caused Melville's Pierre (in *Pierre; or The Ambiguities,* 1852) to ignore those "Biographico solicito circulars" sent him by editors and publishers.

In fact Mathews was a journalist, editor, and publisher during this period of his life. *Trow's New York Directory,* in the annual appendix devoted to New York magazines and newspapers, lists him as the publisher and editor of the *New-Yorker* from 1858 through 1876, and of the *Comic World* from 1876 to 1878, near the end of his active professional career. At best his work in these journals is uninspired. This retreat into popular journalism, occasional book editing, and some play writing by a man who in his youth had been excited and engaged by the New York literary world may well explain his virtual silence in the world of higher literary authorship. The puzzle is complicated. On 7 and 8 February 1895 his collection of paintings and that of another, unnamed collector were auctioned by the Silo Art Galleries in New York. While it is impossible to identify which of the 161 pieces were Mathews's, it should be noted that there were numerous rural and urban landscapes, many of them European, as well as J. L. Eliot's portrait of Washington Irving, Winslow Homer's watercolor "Shoving Off," and Albert Bierstadt's "Old Faithful, Yellowstone Park." Who received the proceeds from this sale is unknown. But six years earlier Mathews had been buried in an unmarked pauper's grave, a charity case, in Brooklyn's Evergreen Cemetery—a rather unseemly circumstance.

The mysteries caused by partial and unretrieved or permanently lost biographical information are numerous, especially the issue of Mathews's birth date. Since the publication of the Duyckincks' *Cyclopædia of American Literature,* all but one of the sources located list it as 1817; the exception is Fiske's obituary. He records it as 1814, a date confirmed, for instance, by the 1850 census (in which the enumerator lists Mathews's age as thirty-five) and his death certificate which stipulates it at his decease as seventy-four-and-a-half years. No record of his birth appears to have survived.

Mathews's committed, occasionally strident, literary nationalism was a major professional concern and provided the fundamental raison d'être for his creative writing, reviewing, and editing. Among the many expressions of his insistence about a literature by Americans on American subjects was that made in the penultimate paragraph of a controversial speech he made at the muchpublicized dinner held in honor of Charles Dickens in 1842; he called for the cancellation of America's "great debt" to British writers on two counts, the second being the promotion of national "works of genius, the growth of our own soil, colored by our own skies, and showing something of the influences of a new community, where nature comes fresh and mighty to her task. A thousand voices now slumber in our vales, amid our cities, and along our hill-sides, that only await the genial hour to speak and be heard."

An abiding faith in democracy, in America's potential, was critical to the country's flourishing. In his speeches, many of which were subsequently published, he repeatedly insisted upon this—for example, in *An Appeal to American Authors and the American Press, in Behalf of International Copyright* (1842) and *The Better Interests of the Country, in Connexion with International Copy-Right* (1843). What he lamented in the latter speech was his countrymen's "dependency of Great Britain," their imitativeness. He exhorted readers to encourage their writers to address themselves to American subjects. This idealism, these aspirations, were to be discovered in the richness of the United States' growing cities as well as its pastoral grandeur; its varied people; its diversity and seemingly boundless possibilities for vibrant growth. The call was similar to those of Emerson in "The Poet" (1844), for example, and of Whitman in the preface to the first edition of *Leaves of Grass* (1855).

But Mathews's importance rests on more than such pronouncements. His creative writing itself is also a major factor, a working demonstration, to be considered in evaluating his contribution. The range of subjects on which he wrote and the variety of genres in which he experimented demonstrated a genuine hospitality to innovation. But he was by no means an author capable of discovering new rhythms, forms, and voices. Nevertheless, these are among his purposes in his first two books.

Initially published in seven individual parts, the first in early 1838, *The Motley Book: A Series of Tales and Sketches,* was reissued in two book editions prior to being reprinted in *The Various Writings of Cornelius Mathews* (1843). There are a few sentimental tales ("Potter's Field" and "The Druggist's Wife"), and one, "The Unburied Bones," which is sentimental with a gothic touch. But of the seventeen tales and sketches (Mathews discarded and added pieces in different editions), fourteen demonstrate his early ability with humor and satire. Almost half the works may be classified as light humor, employing some slapstick and irony, while others are partially satiric and offer some pointed criticism of professions and social institutions. "The Adventures of Sol Clarion," satiric in part only, is a serious exploration of the urban-pastoral motif, and "The Anniversary of the N. A. Society for the Encouragement of Imposture" presents a catalogue of some of Mathews's favorite subjects for satire: shady business practices, government maltreatment of

Indians, bureaucracy and spoils in government, and pseudoscientists, including a quack professor.

However, his most sustained efforts in satire focused on the American political scene as he observed it in New York. He was early active in the vibrant, fluid, and frequently ugly politics of the 1830s and 1840s. Mathews was one of the leading figures in Young America, the "Locofoco Politico-literary" group (as Stafford has described it) which had begun in the mid 1830s as the Tetrachtys Club. Young America championed the liberal, progressive social and political views and programs of the radical Democrats. But from the modern vantage, Mathews is perhaps more interesting for his dedication to exposing the chicanery and absurdity, among other flaws, rife in the political arena. He appears to have been less concerned with political parties than with a system that tolerated unscrupulous behavior by dishonest, self-serving functionaries within it who preyed upon an apathetic and gullible public, a subject he was to return to often.

The young writer had other interests, however, other subjects which aided his attempts to create an autochthonous literature. To be properly understood, *Behemoth: A Legend of the Mound-Builders* (1839) should be viewed within the context of Mathews's intense nationalism. The patriotism and democratic fervor expressed, for example, in *The True Aims of Life: An Address Delivered before the Alumni of the New-York University,* published the same year, offer useful frames in which the modern reader might consider the heroic role played by the "father of his country," Bokulla, in *Behemoth.* The sense of purpose he is able to inspire among the ancient mound builders in the face of the mastodon might well be read as a metaphor for the heroic leadership supplied by the founding fathers when confronting the English monarchy, and even as a message of encouragement for nationalists (including the literary) when faced with the oppressive weight of the continental and British traditions.

The heroic dimensions of the tale are established from the very beginning when Mathews introduces the massive beast in a setting remarkably similar to that constructed by James Fenimore Cooper in *The Prairie* (1827), when the Ishmael Bush family first spies the seemingly larger-than-life Natty Bumppo. Bokulla is of equally heroic stature, a culture hero in the fullest sense. His leadership, his sojourn in the wilderness in preparation for the conquest of Behemoth—even the armies, the battles, the

torment—and the landscape are conceived with the purpose of constructing a New World legend and mythology to rival those of European antiquity. Mathews is to be taken seriously when he asserts in his preface that "a green forest or a swelling mound is. . . . [A]s glorious as a Grecian temple," that we should be "as much affected by the sight of a proud old oak in decay near at home, as by the story of a baronial castle tottering to its fall three thousand miles off." Here he is of the party of Bryant and Emerson, not that of Irving twenty years earlier in his preface to *The Sketch Book of Geoffrey Crayon, Gent.* (1819-1820) or Hawthorne twenty-one years later in his preface to *The Marble Faun* (1860).

Before proceeding one should consider conditions in the publishing world during the formative years of Mathews's career. It was, after all, the milieu in which he was trying to make his way. The industry was undergoing a dramatic transition from the late 1830s through the early 1850s, and beyond. Technological advances made possible the production of printed material on a mass scale inconceivable earlier. Fresh markets, a new and much larger audience, were opening. Some of the desires implicit in the common man's assertions in Jacksonian America were to be satisfied in part by means of this revolution in printing technology. And these circumstances had profound effects on the identities, self-images, and the range of possibilities for members of the literary and publishing communities. Mathews worked in this fluid world. The early scene of which he was part had few fixed verities—certainly none universally accepted. The position the emerging mass culture (exemplified by P. T. Barnum and the influx of mammoth newspapers) was to have vis à vis the established high culture, which was itself changing and on the threshold of the American Renaissance, was an unanswerable question. An author was inevitably faced with the difficulty of determining for what audience to write and on what subjects.

These and similar problems were among those Mathews and his contemporaries considered. The questions are at the center of the frenetic activity, the petty and vicious rivalry, the excitement and drama of New York's literary, journalistic, and publishing worlds. The audience was young, democratic, large, and fluid—in search of itself and its taste. Such circumstances led Mathews to his concern about copyright legislation and his ongoing interest in editing periodicals—two pursuits that were to be critical in establishing the pattern of his career and, ultimately, his reputation.

Mathews thought that all four speeches he had made and published on the copyright issue between 1839 and early 1843 were of sufficient importance to warrant inclusion in the anthology of his works, *The Various Writings of Cornelius Mathews,* published by Harper in 1843. In these as well as in *An Address to the People of the United States in Behalf of the American Copyright Club* (1843) and *Americanism: An Address Delivered before the Eucleian Society* (1845), he made vigorous, sometimes eloquent assertions and pleas for enactment of an international law. He used a variety of emphases and rhetorical strategies to persuade his audiences that such legislation would improve the quality of reading matter available, protect authors on both sides of the Atlantic from exploitation, and nourish the growth of an indigenous American literature. Uneven as his arguments were, his sincerity and commitment were consistent. He was arguing not only for himself and his fellow authors (he was a founder and corresponding secretary of the Copyright Club) but for "the better interests of the country," as he phrased the cause in his 1843 lecture at the New York Society Library.

The just cause fought by authors for international copyright was not supported by some publishers and magazine and journal editors, especially in America. Printing and paying royalties for possibly unpopular books by Americans when one could pirate already popular, well-established European and British authors was deemed risky by most of the publishing industry. Mathews's militancy in opposing such an attitude was probably the main cause for his strained relations with the segment of the publishing community that also argued a conservative position contrary to Young America's stance on the related issue of literary nationalism. Such a copyright law was not to be passed until 1891, two years after Mathews's death.

Newspaper and journal editing were more practical ways for him to realize his agenda for a national, democratic literature, and as his career unfolded, he devoted himself increasingly to these labors. This work had infinitely greater impact than the relatively few pieces of extended criticism–basically undistinguished reviews rather than theoretical pieces–he published in his own and other periodicals. The vast majority of his criticism was published anonymously (in keeping with the conventions of time); in fact, most of the handful of reviews that can be attributed to Mathews can be done so mainly on external evidence, principally correspondence.

Mathews began his journal editing early in 1841 with *Arcturus: A Journal of Books and Opinion,* jointly edited with Evert A. Duyckinck. The tone of the monthly was serious, and it boasted such insightful criticism as that of William A. Jones, one of the best of the Young America group. In "An Appendix of Autographs" Poe noted that it had "attained much reputation," and in his sketch of Duyckinck in "The Literati of New York City," he judged it "decidedly the very best magazine in many respects ever published in the United States, . . . upon the whole, a little *too good* to enjoy extensive popularity." Poe was speaking from hindsight here in 1846, knowing that *Arcturus* had folded after a year-and-a-half run. This short-lived venture, however high its quality, may have pushed Mathews, and Duyckinck, to seek wider audiences by not applying such high standards in subsequent attempts. There is evidence that they proposed, most likely in the 1840s, to begin a "weekly folio newspaper," the *Millions*–the title probably suggesting the mass audience they sought, if not the profits they may have hoped for. But as far as is known, the paper was never published.

In 1846 Mathews and Duyckinck edited the *Saturday News.* Sometime after mid 1847, they bought a two-thirds interest in the London-based *Pictorial World,* but this connection, too, was brief. From 3 July to 2 October the same year, Mathews edited *Yankee Doodle* (he and Duyckinck had been involved in its founding in October 1846 and for a short period had written for it). A satiric weekly modeled on the English magazine *Punch,* it clearly sought popular appeal but not finding it, folded, another victim of financial failure. *Yankee Doodle* is best remembered for publishing, during Mathews's tenure, Melville's satires on Zachary Taylor and other pieces.

Next Mathews edited another satiric weekly, the *Elephant,* which met the same fate as *Yankee Doodle* after five issues early in 1848, and during 1849 he edited the weekly *People's Own, and Flag of the Free* (according to George L. Duyckinck's letter to Joann Miller, 11 April 1849). In 1850 Mathews founded two equally short-lived theater reviews, the *Prompter* and the *Prompter's Whistle,* perhaps realizations of his plans for such a paper as early as 1847. The same year, 1850, he began yet another brief effort, the *Weekly Review,* and in 1852 he possibly edited the *New York Reveille,* which ran from 1851 to 1854. During at least part of 1853 he edited the Duyckincks' *Literary World* with the younger of the brothers, George. This *Journal of American and Foreign Literature, Science, and Art,* as it was then subtitled, perhaps signaled a renewed commitment to higher quality journalism, more responsible criticism, but by the end of 1853 it too had failed. Scholars have long known of Mathews's contributions to the journal (for example, allowing him to write for it was the principal reason for Evert Duyckinck's being dismissed as editor in 1847); however, Mathews's long connection was not only editorial but financial, as indicated by his letter to George Duyckinck of 16 October 1852. He also had an interest in *Holden's Dollar Magazine,* as shown by the Duyckincks' 3 February 1851 memorandum to him. However, as already noted briefly, Mathews's longest tenure as an editor, from 1858 to 1876, was with the *New-Yorker,* and he concluded his editing career with two years at *Comic World,* beginning in 1876.

Turning again to Mathews's creative writing, we see that he continued to explore subjects such as politics and history treated in his first two books and even widened his thematic horizons. He continued to write long fiction and nonfictional prose and also tested other genres. These efforts were directed toward helping to establish firmly his country's literature.

Perry Miller's claim that *The Career of Puffer Hopkins* (1842) stands "at the head (crude though it be) of a long tradition in American writing"—the urban novel—may be an exaggeration, but there is no question that the majority of Mathews's efforts were directed toward capturing the urban scene which both enticed and appalled him. Urban subjects were the targets of his most sustained efforts in satire. Political life, the legal system, metropolitan journalism, reform, fashionable life, and the theater all came under his scrutiny. Urban satire was his jaundiced response to the claims of "civilization" as he saw it emerging. By capturing the sights, sounds, and colors of the metropolis, he was extending the Knickerbocker tradition of urban local color and making a major contribution to the cause of nationalistic literature.

He was explicit about the connection in the preface to *The Politicians: A Comedy, in Five Acts* (1840), in which, after echoing the claims of figures such as Bryant and Emerson about the appropriateness of American nature as a literary subject, he asserted that the city is as worthy a focus—especially, in Young American fashion, its political life. To comprehend the ideal against which he measured reality, one might best view his character Old Crumb in *The Politicians* as a projection of the sort of virtuous politician Mathews described in the *Arcturus* essay "Political Life" (reprinted in *The Various Writings of Cornelius Mathews* along with all the other important work he had so far published). The essay explores two faces: that of the noble, Adamic senator, the other of the common, urban ward hack preoccupied only with his own rise.

The Politicians, an unproduced play set in New York, reflected a jaundiced view of the dishonesty and hypocrisy of the professional, self-seeking politico, but it was also Mathews's most optimistic statement concerning the ultimate viability of the American democratic system. Although there was some small indictment of the naiveté of the common man as voter who allows himself to be hoodwinked, the responsibility for the wickedness of the election process and corruption in government was placed upon the cynical professional. A part of the play also served Mathews as the vehicle for introducing the relatively muted yet recurring and significant urban-pastoral motif. The theme, particularly as it is related to politics and other phenomena of urban life, was to become increasingly important in his writing, from *The Career of Puffer Hopkins* through *Big Abel, and the Little Manhattan* (1845) and *Moneypenny, or, The Heart of the World. A Romance of the Present Day* (1849-1850), and finally culminated in the dark vision of the play *Calmstorm, the Reformer. A Dramatic Comment* (1853).

In *The Career of Puffer Hopkins* Mathews again dramatized the dark side of politics he had outlined in "Political Life." While Miller's claim that the novel is "unreadable" is much too harsh, it is true that its plot or structure was weakened by the multiplicity of elements Mathews attempted to weave together. Some readers may take exception to the blurring of the satire by the intrusion of gothic and sentimental elements. But in light of the serialization of its first twenty-two chapters in *Arcturus,* perhaps it might help to recognize that Mathews's goal was to attract as wide an audience as possible and so, as was the case with the great bulk of contemporary popular fiction and remains so with modern soap opera, he was throwing in a little something for everyone. If such an approach does not improve our perception of the book's structure, it at least allows us to understand the principle by which it was probably constructed.

Although Mathews added no new dimensions to the criticism of the political scene he had treated in earlier works, there emerges, for example in chapter fourteen, a real sense of his judgment about the cynicism, hypocrisy, and stupidity which motivated the majority of the participants in the turbulent politics of the period. He also fired barbs at the literary and journalistic scenes. And about a quarter of the novel is woven of melodramatic, domestic-sentimental, and gothic threads.

In *Big Abel, and the Little Manhattan* Mathews was intent on asserting his faith in the emerging urban civilization over the primitive way of life. The book is in effect a ten-chapter tour of New York City during which the benefits and deficiencies of the urban scene are discussed and evaluated. Lankey Fogle, the Indian, the Little Manhattan, and Abel Henry Hudson, a great-grandson of the explorer, have been for some time attempting to divide the city between them, each claiming ownership by right of inheritance and possession. Tired of attempting to effect their purpose through the court system, they decide to wander about the metropolis and make their claims. In chapter nine the Little Manhattan has a vision of the ultimate decay and collapse of emblems of civilization such as houses and pierheads. But in this novel Mathews was asserting the virtue and predicting the triumph of this urban civilization over the primitive past which, however romantically attractive, was not viable.

Big Abel, and the Little Manhattan might be viewed as a celebration in one volume of the ordinary folk–the white settlers, that is–whose praises Mathews had sung in *Poems on Man, in His Various Aspects under the American Republic* (1843), and of their prevailing over the primitive; he had done the same in the poem *Wakondah; The Master of Life* (1841) in which he announced the native American's doom.

In 1846 and 1848 three of Mathews's known plays were produced. In two he promoted the national character and heritage by turning to colonial history rather than the primitive past to which he had addressed his imagination in *Behemoth*. *Witchcraft: A Tragedy in Five Acts*, which was at least among the most favorably received of his dramas, examined the assault upon individual liberty by the hysterical, authoritarian, and malign forces unleashed in Salem in the late-seventeenth

century (there may well have been some Yorker versus Yankee undercurrents in it). And *Jacob Leisler, the Patriot Hero, or, New York in 1690*, performed two years later, evidently successfully, reached back to the same period to celebrate the patriot who was its protagonist. Sandwiched between these two serious plays was *Seeing the Elephant* (George C. D. Odell dates its first performance as 15 September 1848, but Mathews in a letter to George L. Duyckinck of 20 March 1848 reported that it had already had twenty-seven performances). No doubt the comedy centered on some sort of confidence game or games, whether in the California gold fields or the New York streets, or elsewhere; it was a spin-off from Mathews's magazine, the *Elephant*, published from 22 January through 19 February 1848, which in turn was derived from one of the more popular series in *Yankee Doodle*. These three plays illustrate his commitment to national subjects, historical and contemporary, his ability to move from heavy drama to light comedy, and remind us once again of the wide range of genres he worked in.

They were followed in 1849-1850 by another novel, *Moneypenny, or, The Heart of the World*, a potboiler in many respects; Mathews reworked subjects and themes he had been handling for more than a decade. In this rambling and increasingly complex book, he in effect presented another tour of New York City, describing its unique scenes and personages, frequently with humor and satire, and assessing the quality of life it offered. His old concern with the civilized pastoral/primitive conflict is presented much the same as it had been in *Big Abel, and the Little Manhattan*. Introduced to the corrupting influences of the white urban civilization, the treachery of which is intensified by the whites' racially superior attitudes, the young Indian woman presented in the story gradually withers and, in utter disillusionment and despair about her city experience, commits suicide. But the melodramatic and sentimental plots and subplots are not the interesting or even important facets of the book. Considering Mathews's prior attempts to paint in prose what Theodore Dreiser would call "the color of a great city" and his later efforts in the virtual tour-guide book, *A Pen-and-Ink Panorama of New-York City* (1853), it appears that he used these stories in *Moneypenny* as a frame for urban local color. His ambivalence about the urban scene, essentially in New York, continued at least through the 1850s, probably for the rest of his life. In *Moneypenny* his satire is directed at a wide range of rascals endemic to city life—reformers and foppish English visitors who turn some Americans into toadying fools.

Mathews's work in the 1850s continued that which he had been doing for years and signaled the direction he was to follow for the rest for his career. In 1850 he published *Chanticleer: A Thanksgiving Story of the Peabody Family*, a domestic-sentimental evocation of the values of American culture implicit in its traditions. This was followed in 1853 by the apparently unproduced play *Calmstorm, the Reformer. A Dramatic Comment* which at once suggests the impending end of the socially conscious phase of Mathews's career and demonstrates the intensity of disillusionment, even despair, which he was experiencing after his years as a literary activist, an observer and recorder of life in the new nation.

The character Calmstorm grew out of the conception of the poet-journalist George Eaglestone, a young idealist and reformer in *Moneypenny*. The fiery activist apparently caught Mathews's imagination; in early 1850 the office of Mathews's *Weekly Review* issued a broadside which carried a note announcing the appearance of a volume titled "Eaglestone," but the book never appeared. Eaglestone's next appearance was in several sketches printed in *Holden's Dollar Magazine*, fragments cited as coming from "The Eaglestone Dramas." Sometime between 1851 and 1853 these became the dark verse play *Calmstorm*. Clearly, the disillusionment and bitterness that are at the heart of this Juvenalian statement had been festering in Mathews for several years.

Such a commentary was not dashed off hastily. Employing invective throughout, Mathews now assaulted the civilization and its institutions and conventions he had satirized, for the most part with good humor, earlier. As the action unfolds Calmstorm collides with those longtime targets of Mathews's criticism and exposure: corrupt judges, newsmen, and politicians. But it is not simply the inability of civilized institutions to assimilate the virtuous that spells the pessimism in the play. In it Mathews views the city—the symbol, the fruit, of civilized man—as inherently corrupt and incapable of reform. In essence he was addressing an old theme: the conflicts of the primitive and the civilized, the rural and the urban.

This is not to say that the issue of urban civilization's potential, particularly as it was represented in the Knickerbocker scene, was finally settled in his mind. In the same year he produced *Calmstorm* Mathews published *A Pen-and-Ink Panorama of New-York City*, the most unequivocally optimistic and readable of his "tours" of the metropolis. Unencumbered by efforts at plot and character, this book gracefully and enthusiastically captured once again the colors of a great city, gently poking at some of its deficiencies occasionally. Mathews used the book in adapted form in an 1880s series published in his friend Fiske's *New York Mirror*.

These works were punctuated, as already noted, by ventures in popular journalism and editorial work on the more serious *Literary World*. *False Pretences, or, Both Sides of Good Society* (produced in 1855), a five-act, sitting-room comedy of manners in the mode of Anna Cora Mowatt's popular play *Fashion* (1845), was apparently Mathews's last published attempt at belletristic writing. He exposed once again the materialism and essential vacuity of the fashionable life of the metropolitan wealthy. The play was balanced in a sense by the appearance the next year, 1856, of the first of at least seven editions, often reprinted, of Schoolcraft's Indian legends; in his sentimental rendering Mathews demonstrated his continuing interest in Native American culture.

The Schoolcraft editions might be viewed as a contrast to Mathews's writings on city life—illustrating, in effect, his lifelong concern with the urban-pastoral / primitive themes. In the same year his as yet unrecovered, perhaps lost, play, *Broadway and the Bowery*, was produced. And in 1858 he commenced his work as editor of the *New-Yorker*. Its eighteen-year life suggests that Mathews had at last found a substantial readership, but he was indeed writing or editing the "*other* way," as Melville would have described it. The paper's original subtitle was *A Complete Weekly Chronicle of the World: Literature, Romance, Business, and News;* the 24 April 1858 issue, for example, carried a strong statement that its editorial policy was to appeal to the commercial community and announced a "New Gallery" of verbal and pictorial portraits of businessmen.

It appears that Mathews's development was not all that unique for the times. His career spanned a period when the publishing industry was rapidly developing, moving from the relatively well-defined world of belles lettres for the few to entertainment for the masses. His following the trend contributes to his importance as much as do his earlier, book-length writings and his activity in the New York literary scene. In all instances he was attempting to promote nationalism by word, creative writing, and editing. Though he is a minor figure in America's cultural history, as his contemporaries and modern historians have judged, he is important, and the gaps in the record of his life and work make him an attractive subject for further scholarly inquiry, especially by students of journalism, magazine publishing, theater, and literature.

References:

James T. Callow, *Kindred Spirits: Knickerbocker Writers and American Artists, 1807-1855* (Chapel Hill: University of North Carolina Press, 1967);

Curtis Dahl, "Moby Dick's Cousin Behemoth," *American Literature*, 31 (1959): 21-29;

Dahl, "Mound Builders, Mormons and William Cullen Bryant," *New England Quarterly*, 34 (1961): 178-190;

Harrison Grey Fiske, "Obituary: Cornelius Mathews," *New York Mirror*, 6 April 1889, p. 6;

Robert W. Gladish, *Elizabeth Barrett Browning and the "Centurion": The Background to an Addition to the Elizabeth Barrett Browning Canon,* in *Baylor Browning Interests, No. 23* (Waco, Tex.: Baylor University, 1973);

Luther S. Mansfield, "Glimpses of Herman Melville's Life in Pittsfield: 1850-1851," *American Literature*, 9 (1938): 26-36;

Mansfield, "Melville's Comic Articles on Zachary Taylor," *American Literature*, 9 (1938): 411-418;

Perry Miller, *The Raven and the Whale: The War of Words and Wits in the Era of Poe and Melville* (New York: Harcourt, Brace, 1956);

Sidney P. Moss, "Poe, Hiram Fuller, and the Duyckinck Circle," *American Book Collector* (October 1967): 8-18;

Moss, *Poe's Literary Battles: The Critic in the Context of His Literary Milieu* (Durham, N.C.: Duke University Press, 1963);

Moss, *Poe's Major Crisis: His Libel Suit and New York's Literary World* (Durham, N.C.: Duke University Press, 1970);

Frank Luther Mott, *A History of American Magazines*, 5 volumes (Cambridge, Mass.: Belknap Press of Harvard University Press, 1938-1968);

George C. D. Odell, *Annals of the New York Stage*, 15 volumes (New York: Columbia University Press, 1927-1949);

John P. Pritchard, *Literary Wise Men of Gotham: Criticism in New York, 1815-1860* (Baton Rouge: Louisiana State University Press, 1963);

Arthur Hobson Quinn, *A History of the American Drama: From the Beginning to the Civil War* (New York: Harper, 1923);

Quinn, *A History of American Drama: From the Civil War to the Present Day* (New York: Crofts, 1937);

Claude Richard, "Poe and 'Young America,' " *Studies in Bibliography*, 21 (1969): 24-58;

George O. Seilhamer, *An Interviewer's Album: Comprising a Series of Chats with Eminent Players and Playwrights* (New York: Perry, 1881);

William Gilmore Simms, *Views and Reviews in American Literature, History and Fiction* (New York: Wiley & Putnam, 1845);

Benjamin T. Spencer, *The Quest for Nationality: An American Literary Campaign* (Syracuse: Syracuse University Press, 1957);

John Stafford, *The Literary Criticism of "Young America": A Study in the Relationship of Politics and Literature, 1837-1850* (Berkeley: University of California Press, 1952);

Allen F. Stein, *Cornelius Mathews* (New York: Twayne, 1974);

Daniel A. Wells, " 'Bartleby the Scrivener,' Poe, and the Duyckinck Circle," *ESQ*, 21 (1975): 35-39;

Donald Yannella, "Foreword," in separate-volume, photo-facsimile reprints of *Behemoth: A Legend of the Mound-Builders; Big Abel, and the Little Manhattan;* and *The Career of Puffer Hopkins* (New York: Garrett, 1970);

Yannella, "The Literary World," in *American Literary Magazines: The Eighteenth and Nineteenth Centuries,* edited by Edward E. Chielens (Westport, Conn.: Greenwood, 1986), pp. 224-230;

Yannella, " 'Seeing the Elephant' in *Mardi,*" in *Artful Thunder: Versions of the Romantic Tradition in American Literature in Honor of Howard P. Vincent,* edited by Robert J. DeMott and Sanford E. Marovitz (Kent, Ohio: Kent State University Press, 1975), pp. 105-117;

Yannella, "Writing the *'Other* Way': Melville, the Duyckinck Crowd, and Literature for the Masses," in *A Companion to Melville Studies,* edited by John Bryant (Westport, Conn.: Greenwood, 1986), pp. 63-81;

Yannella, *"Yankee Doodle,"* in *American Literary Magazines: The Eighteenth and Nineteenth Centuries,* edited by Chielens (Westport, Conn.: Greenwood, 1986), pp. 451-456.

Papers:
The major collection of Cornelius Mathews's letters, manuscripts, and other items is in the Duyckinck Family Papers and other collections at the New York Public Library. The Houghton Library at Harvard University also has significant holdings. Other archives holding substantial documents include the Historical Society of Pennsylvania, the Library of Congress (notably in the Schoolcraft and Minnie Maddern Fiske collections), and the Boston Public Library. Holdings of fewer than five items are scattered through major research libraries and even in some smaller facilities. For further guidance the reader should consult both editions of *American Literary Manuscripts*.

Charles Eliot Norton
(16 November 1827-21 October 1908)

Donez Xiques
Brooklyn College, City University of New York

See also the Norton entry in *DLB 1, The American Renaissance in New England.*

BOOKS: *Considerations on Some Recent Social Theories,* anonymous (Boston: Little, Brown, 1853);

Notes of Travel and Study in Italy (Boston: Houghton, Mifflin, 1859);

The Soldier of the Good Cause [pamphlet] (Boston: American Unitarian Association Army Series, number 2, 1861);

William Blake's Illustrations of the Book of Job with Descriptive Letterpress and Sketch of the Artist's Life and Work (Boston: Osgood, 1875);

Historical Studies of Church Building in the Middle Ages: Venice, Siena, Florence (New York: Harper, 1880; London: Low, Marston, Searle & Rivington, 1881);

The Poet Gray as A Naturalist with Selections from his Notes on the Systema nature of Linnæus and Facsimiles of his Drawings (Boston: Goodspeed, 1903);

Henry Wadsworth Longfellow: A Sketch of His Life by Charles Eliot Norton, Together with Longfellow's Chief Biographical Poems (New York & Boston: Houghton, Mifflin, 1907);

A Leaf of Grass from Shady Hill. With a Review of Walt Whitman's Leaves of Grass *Written by Charles Eliot Norton in 1855* (Cambridge: Harvard University Press, 1928).

Charles Eliot Norton.

OTHER: *Five Christmas Hymns,* edited by Norton (Cambridge, Mass.: Privately printed, 1852);

A Book of Hymns for Young Persons, edited by Norton (Cambridge, Mass.: Bartlett, 1854);

The Poetical Works of Coleridge and Keats with a memoir of Each, 4 volumes, edited by Norton (Boston: Houghton, Mifflin, 1855);

The New Life of Dante, An Essay with Translations (Cambridge, Mass.: Riverside Press, 1859);

The Poems of Arthur Hugh Clough with a memoir by Charles Eliot Norton (Boston: Houghton, Mifflin, 1862);

Philosophical Discussions by Chauncey Wright with a Biographical Sketch of the Author, by Charles Eliot Norton (New York: Holt, 1877);

The Correspondence of Thomas Carlyle and Ralph Waldo Emerson, 1834-72, edited by Norton (Boston: Osgood, 1883);

Early Letters of Thomas Carlyle, Edited by Charles Eliot Norton, 1814-1826, 2 volumes (London & New York: Macmillan, 1886);

Correspondence Between Goethe and Carlyle, edited by Norton (London & New York: Macmillan, 1887);

Reminiscences by Thomas Carlyle, 2 volumes, edited by Norton (London: Macmillan, 1887);

Letters of Thomas Carlyle, 1826-1836, 2 volumes, edited by Norton (London & New York: Macmillan, 1889);

Latest Literary Essays and Addresses of James Russell Lowell, edited by Norton (Cambridge, Mass.: Riverside Press, 1891);

The Divine Comedy of Dante Alighieri, 3 volumes, translated by Norton (Boston: Houghton, Mifflin, 1891-1892; revised and republished, 1902);

Letters of James Russell Lowell, 2 volumes, edited by Norton (New York: Harper, 1893);

The Heart of Oak Books, 5 volumes, edited by Norton and Kate Stevens (Boston: Heath, 1893-1894);

Orations and Addresses of George W. Curtis, 3 volumes, edited by Norton (New York: Harper, 1894);

"Harvard," in *Four American Universities: Harvard, Yale, Princeton, Columbia* (New York: Harper, 1895), pp. 1-43;

Last Poems of James Russell Lowell, edited by Norton (Boston & New York: Houghton, Mifflin, 1895);

The Poems of John Donne, from the Text of the Edition of 1633 revised by James Russell Lowell. With the various readings of the other editions of the sev-

Norton and Francis James Child, circa 1854

enteenth century, and with a preface, an introduction, and notes by Charles Eliot Norton, 2 volumes (New York: Grolier, 1895);

The Poems of Mrs. Anne Bradstreet (1612-1672); Together with Her Prose Remains, With an Introduction by Charles Eliot Norton (New York: Duodecimos, 1897);

Two Note-Books of Thomas Carlyle, from 23d March 1822 to 16th May 1832, edited by Norton (New York: Grolier, 1898);

Rudyard Kipling, *Plain Tales from the Hills,* revised, with a biographical sketch, by Norton (New York: Doubleday & McClure, 1899);

Letters from Ralph Waldo Emerson to a friend, 1838-1853, edited by Norton (Boston: Houghton, Mifflin, 1899);

Comments of John Ruskin on the Divina Commedia, compiled by George P. Huntington, with an introduction by Norton (Boston: Houghton, Mifflin, 1903);

The Love Poems of John Donne, selected and edited by Norton (Boston: Houghton, Mifflin, 1905).

PERIODICAL PUBLICATIONS: "Ancient Monuments in America," *North American Review*, 68 (April 1849): 466-496;

"Dwellings and Schools for the Poor," *North American Review*, 75 (April 1852): 464-480;

"Whitman's Leaves of Grass," *Putnam's*, 6 (September 1855): 321-323;

"The Laws of Race, as Connected with Slavery," *Atlantic Monthly*, 7 (February 1861): 252-254;

"Tambarini's Translation of the Commentary by Benvenuto da Imola on the *Divina Commedia*," *Atlantic Monthly*, 7 (May 1861): 629-637;

"The Advantages of Defeat," *Atlantic Monthly*, 8 (September 1861): 360-365;

"Abraham Lincoln," *North American Review*, 100 (January 1865): 1-21;

"America and England," *North American Review*, 100 (April 1865): 331-346;

"Dante and His Latest English Translators," *North American Review*, 102 (April 1866): 509-529;

"Arthur Hugh Clough," *North American Review*, 105 (October 1867): 434-477;

"The Cesnola Collection of Antiquities from Cyprus," *Nation*, 16 (23 January 1873): 62-63;

"Feminine Poetry," *Nation*, 22 (24 February 1876): 132-134;

"The Dimensions and Proportions of the Temple of Zeus at Olympia," *Proceedings of the American Academy of Arts and Sciences*, 13 (May-November 1877): 145-170;

"Painting and Sculpture in their Relation to Architecture," *American Art Review*, 1 (1880): 192-195, 249-253;

"Omissions by Mr. Froude in Carlyle's *Reminiscences*," *Nation*, 43 (22 July 1886): 74;

"The Intellectual Life of America," *New Princeton Review*, 6 (November 1888): 312-324;

"The Building of the Cathedral at Chartres," *Harper's Magazine*, 79 (November 1889): 944-955;

"The Educational Value of the History of the Fine Arts," *Educational Review*, 9 (April 1895): 343-348;

"The Work of the Archeological Institute of America . . . ," *American Journal of Archeology*, 4 (January-March 1900): 1-16;

"Tribute to William Wetmore Story," *Proceedings of the Massachusetts Historical Society*, 15 (1902): 368-371.

Charles Eliot Norton, scholar, editor, critic, teacher, and translator, was the distinguished son of a distinguished New England family. As an active and valued member of Boston's intellectual community from 1850 to 1900, Norton's influ-

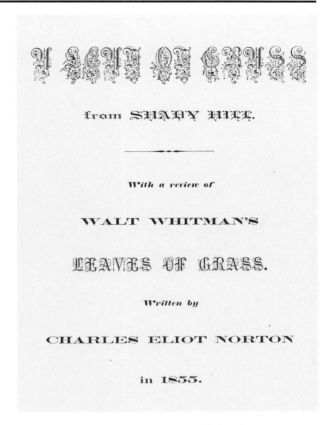

Title page for the 1928 book that includes the poem Norton wrote and pasted into his copy of Leaves of Grass *and his 1855 review of Whitman's book*

ence was considerable. His scholarly interest in the fine arts and literature enabled him to make lasting contributions to the life and letters of that period, and through his work as critic, translator, and Harvard professor to make an impact on succeeding generations as well.

After graduating Phi Beta Kappa from Harvard University in 1846, Norton engaged in business pursuits for about ten years. As part of his job with the East India Company, he was sent to Madras, Calcutta, and Bombay. Returning home by way of the Suez Canal, young Norton visited North Africa, Italy, and France. During that period he also made the acquaintance of a number of important literary figures, such as the English writer Elizabeth Gaskell, who was to become his lifelong friend. After his return to the United States in 1851, Norton, still a businessman, became actively involved in social issues such as popular education for the masses and better housing for Boston's poor. These concerns are reflected in his first book, *Considerations on Some Recent Social Theories* (1853), which was published anonymously.

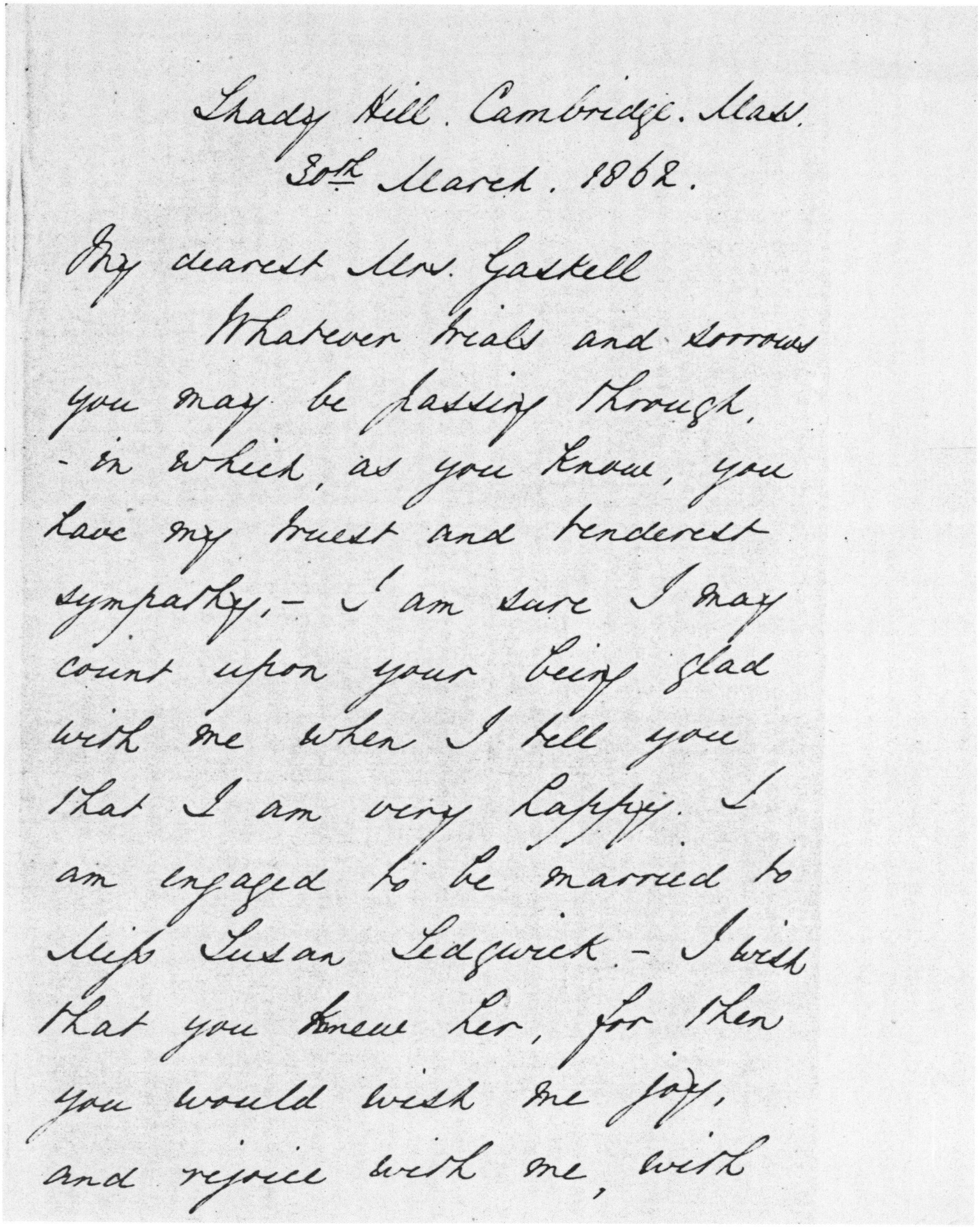

Shady Hill. Cambridge. Mass.
30th March. 1862.

My dearest Mrs. Gaskell

Whatever trials and sorrows
you may be passing through,
- in which, as you know, you
have my truest and tenderest
sympathy, - I am sure I may
count upon your being glad
with me when I tell you
that I am very happy. I
am engaged to be married to
Miss Susan Sedgwick. - I wish
that you knew her, for then
you would wish me joy,
and rejoice with me, with

Page from Norton's letter to his lifelong friend, the English novelist Elizabeth Gaskell, in which he announces his engagement to Susan Ridley Sedgwick (Charles Eliot Norton Papers, Houghton Library, Harvard University)

In addition, Norton contributed to various periodicals articles and reviews on a wide range of topics, including his experiences and observations in India. In 1855 he wrote a perceptive and favorable review (also published anonymously) of Walt Whitman's *Leaves of Grass,* which later was praised by the critic Kenneth Murdock who remarked, "[Norton] reviewed *Leaves of Grass* more enthusiastically and more justly than most of the baffled critics." In 1928 Norton's review was republished with Murdock's explanatory essay and Norton's poem "A Leaf of Grass from Shady Hill," the title indicating the impact of Whitman's verse on the young scholar.

In 1855, after the death of his father, Andrews Norton, Norton left the world of commerce and decided to go abroad with his mother, Catherine Eliot Norton, and two of his sisters, Jane and Grace. Remaining in Europe for about two years, Norton devoted most of his time and energy to the study of art and architecture, which he believed revealed the "social and moral development of a nation." By overlooking many political and religious aspects of life in medieval Italy, he was able to maintain that its art and architecture were evidence of that age's superior moral temper. He also was convinced that cathedrals in the medieval period represented "the decline of feudalism, and the prevalence of the democratic element in society." To Norton, the American abroad, the later "decline" of Italian art was the result of "immoral forces" in the Renaissance world. Many of these ideas appeared in *Notes of Travel and Study in Italy* (1859) and in a later work, *Historical Studies of Church Building in the Middle Ages: Venice, Siena, Florence* (1880). For the latter, Norton did a prodigious amount of research with original documents in the archives of those cities. Aside from Norton's bias toward relating the work of art to the moral caliber of the artist and the era, he was a very perceptive observer, with a keen eye for detail and an excellent grasp of history.

After his return to America in 1857, Norton continued writing and became seriously involved with several leading periodicals of the day, especially the *Atlantic Monthly,* the *North American Review,* and the *Nation.* His contribution over the years to the development and impact of American periodicals was but one of the significant influences he was to exert in American literature as a whole.

This aspect of his career was initiated in 1857 when James Russell Lowell informed Nor-

Susan Ridley Sedgwick in an 1861 crayon portrait by Samuel W. Rowse

ton of his plans to launch the *Atlantic Monthly* and solicited both advice and articles from him. Within a few years the magazine had over forty thousand subscribers. From *Atlantic Monthly*'s inception until about 1867, as Kermit Vanderbilt, Norton's able biographer, has pointed out, he principally wrote essays and reviews on art and scholarship and articles on the Civil War crisis.

In May 1862 Norton married Susan Ridley Sedgwick, ten years his junior. The following year, while the Civil War continued to rage, he became coeditor of the oldest quarterly magazine in the United States, the *North American Review,* where he subsequently exercised considerable influence over both the contributions and the format. In January of 1864 he wrote Frederick Law Olmstead a letter which reveals much about Norton's outlook toward the periodical: " 'I trust,' he said to Olmstead, 'that you will help us by writing for us,—in asking you to do so I do not feel that I am asking as for a contribution for the amusement of the readers of a magazine,—but rather for a patriotic work. . . . There is an opportunity now to make the "North American" one of the means of developing the nation, of stimulating its better sense, of setting before it and hold-

v. Assyrian Art.

Ἡ Νίνος μεν, ὦ πορθμεῦ, ἀπόλωλεν ἤδη
καὶ οὐδὲ ἴχνος ἔτι λοιπὸν αὐτῆς, οὐδ' ἂν εἴποις
ὅπου ποτὲ ἦν· ἡ Βαβυλὼν δέ σοι ἐκείνη ἐστὶν ἡ
εὔπυργος, ἡ τὸν μέγαν περίβολον, οὐ μετὰ πολὺ
καὶ αὐτὴ ζητηθησομένη ὥσπερ ἡ Νίνος·
Λουκ.Χάρων. 23.

Need of imagination to reconstruct the
lives of races now extinct. The function
of the historic imagination in its relation
to character, & the present time.

Babylonian Empire circa B.C. 2230 – 1270
Destruction of Nineveh B.C. 625
Conquest of Babylon 536.

Buildings of clay & wood; consequence in
use of this material.
Palace architecture, gorgeous barbaric splendour,
enormous extent, prodigality of labour.
No standard of excellence; no idea, principle.
Decorative & pictorial sculpture.

Page from Norton's lecture notebook for his "History of the Arts of Construction and Design, and their Relations to Literature" seminar (Charles Eliot Norton Papers, Houghton Library, Harvard University)

ing up to it its own ideal.' "

Norton's own ideals for good journalism had further opportunity for expression when in 1865 he was instrumental in founding the *Nation*, an important weekly, for which he also wrote essays and reviews until his death in 1908. Among the stated objectives of the *Nation* were the following: "to discuss legal and economic issues with less bias than the daily press; to champion the equal opportunity of the 'laboring class at the South,' and follow the social progress of the Negro; to spread true democratic principles in society and government; and to offer sound and impartial literary and art criticism."

In addition to Norton's involvement with these three leading periodicals, there was another rather singular contribution to journalism which began in 1863 during the Civil War. Norton himself described this as follows: "During the Civil War in America there was often need of enlightening and concentrating public opinion and of giving it unity throughout our vast territory. To this end a few of us in Boston agreed to form . . . the New England Loyal Publication Society." Its sole purpose was "to mould public opinion in favor of the Union."

Norton's responsibilities involved selecting articles (many of which had previously appeared in other publications), printing them as broadsides, and sending them to hundreds of editors of northern and border-state newspapers. It has been estimated that these broadsides reached over a million people each week.

For Norton, contemporary periodicals also provided an important avenue for reaching ordinary citizens. His own literary style frequently was hortatory, but that was consistent with his goals: to instruct and to correct. He felt that his country, especially at the time of the Civil War, was in moral danger because of a loss of idealism and unchecked pursuit of wealth. In his essays and letters he also frequently mourned the neglect of scholarship and the arts.

Over many years, Norton's contributions to American journalism, as writer, editor, and founder, extended from handling complex details of business to soliciting articles from some of America's finest essayists and scholars. His own essays, whether on current topics, the classics, or recent scholarship, reveal his keen powers of analysis, prodigious scholarship, and thoughtful cast of mind.

In 1868 Norton, exhausted from his literary and patriotic endeavors, sought respite in another European trip. This time the sojourn lasted almost five years. Norton, accompanied by his wife, Susan, their children, his mother, and two of his sisters, embarked in July 1868. His health improved, and the time abroad which he spent studying art and architecture and renewing acquaintances with many of the leading literary figures on the Continent was restorative. His wife and young family were interested and absorbed in the new surroundings, but while in Dresden during the winter of 1872, his wife became ill after giving birth to their third son and a few days later died. Norton, grief stricken, decided to take the family back to England. They remained there several months. While awaiting the opportunity to return to the States, Norton gave a series of lectures at Cambridge, wrote reviews, and met with important artists and writers such as William Morris, Sir Edward Coley Burne-Jones, John Ruskin, Leslie Stephen, and Thomas Carlyle. At last in 1873, the widower, who was forty-five, and his small children sailed for America and returned to Shady Hill, their home in Cambridge, Massachusetts.

Two years afterwards Norton was appointed professor of the history of the fine arts at Harvard University, a position which he held for almost twenty-five years. At that time collections of books, manuscripts, and artifacts in American libraries and museums were not particularly distinguished or comprehensive. Norton tried to remedy the situation by his own personal example, sharing his private collections with students, scholars, and museums. In addition, he was instrumental in founding the Archeological Institute of America in 1879 and the American School for Classical Study at Athens in 1882.

While Norton was professor of fine arts, he encouraged his students to develop a greater "sense of connection with the past and of gratitude for the efforts and labors of other races and former generations." He taught thousands of undergraduates, many of whom later held important positions in government, education, business, and commerce. "No profession," he once wrote, "is at once more depressing and more stimulating than that of the teacher of youth just entering manhood. The more keenly he sympathizes with them and desires to aid them, the more keenly he feels how far the best that he can do for them falls far short of their needs and of his own ideal of service." That ideal was manifest not only in Norton's published works but also in his lecture notes, manuscripts, and the notebooks

Shady Hill . Sunday
December 5. 1886.

My dear James, –

What a pleasant old-fashioned snow-storm we are having today! The hush of the earth is complete as this white blanket covers it, and it falls to sleep. We, like you, are having a quiet day. The pleasantest incident of the morning was the coming of your note, with the five dollars safe within it. No. the age of a bank-note has nothing venerable & attractive, like

that of a coin which had passed through many hands without being so defiled by them that it can never be made clean again. The dirty bank-note typifies the base used influences of money. Hawthorne somewhere, in one of his Note Books. if I remember rightly hints. at its suggestiveness.

I should have written to you yesterday, had I found your paper on Landor. I am glad you found it in the Massachusetts Review, which I did not think of looking in when I was at the

Letter from Norton to James Russell Lowell (Charles Eliot Norton Papers, Houghton Library, Harvard University)

College Library I fancy I should
have been better rewarded than
you, had I found it, and should
have discovered more than "one"
good sentence in it. As for
sentences that I can't understand there is one in your
'Democracy' volume, which I wait
for your coming to ask you to
explain to me. You will come,
we all hope, next Saturday, and
stay as long as you can be
content. If you do not want
to send off the manuscript before
then, pray bring what you write

on Landor to read to us. Do
you remember writing
"And Landor's self can Landor's
                         spell undo"?
A various reading, which I would
propose, runs
"And Lowell's voice" shall Landor's
                         spell renew?

Good bye, dear boy!
    We all send best love.
        Always your affectionate
            C. E. N.

Norton at work (Harvard University)

of some of his students which are now part of the Norton collection at Harvard University.

There is, of course, no satisfactory way to measure tangibly Norton's influence upon these young men, but letters from some of his former students offer evidence that it was not inconsiderable. "I speak only the bare truth," one of them wrote Norton, "when I say that in these thirty years I have not looked at a gorgeous sunset, or listened to exquisite music, or read a worthy book, without thinking of you, and by that thought expanding immeasurably within me the joy and delight which you taught us to derive from all beauty and nobility." Another former student wrote to Norton's daughter: "I have lived nearly fifty long years but not been fortunate enough to see another like him. . . . I have no doubt that, no less than his published works and the part of his life which was a more or less public property, his less known spoken works of instruction and deeds of kindness that touched men's mind and heart though difficult to trace are still working and will long work their part in this world of ours."

During more than two decades at Harvard, Norton taught men such as George Woodberry, James Loeb, William Vaughn Moody, and Irving Babbitt, who himself later became a distinguished professor, mentor of T. S. Eliot, and one of the leading figures in the New Humanist Movement. Norton's influence proved to be far-reaching indeed.

His primary concern has been described as "preaching the gospel of art to future generations," for he believed the fine arts revealed the moral fiber of a nation. The substance of his teaching "was ethical," wrote Edward Waldo Emerson. "He showed the sons of poor men mines of spiritual treasure; the sons of rich men the responsibility of having; that wealth demanded helpful use, and leisure unselfish work." In his classes, however, Norton not only considered the art of past ages but also took cognizance of contemporary events. One instance will serve to illustrate this. Norton, while a faculty member at Harvard, vigorously opposed America's declaration of war with Spain in 1898 and told the collegians that they "should not enlist in the 'criminal war' against

Spain, . . . their responsibilities lay in the civilizing work of peace rather than in fighting a weak country in an unnecessary war." Such remarks resulted in severe reprimands from some of his colleagues and neighbors.

In addition to his professional responsibilities at the university, Norton in 1878 invited a small group of young scholars to meet regularly with him at his home at Shady Hill for reading and discussion of the works of Dante. In 1881 that group inaugurated the Dante Society of America, and Norton became, after Henry Wadsworth Longfellow and James Russell Lowell, its third president.

Respect for Dante's achievement had been a constant in Norton's adult years. He was keenly interested in the *Vita Nuova*, for example, which he praised in these words: "[It has] the simplicity of youth, the charm of sincerity, the freedom of personal confidence; . . . so long as there are lovers in the world, and so long as lovers are poets, this first and tenderest love-story of modern literature will be read with appreciation and responsive sympathy." As early as 1859 Norton had published his own translation of this work, *The New Life of Dante, An Essay with Translations*, where, in characteristic fashion, he placed his own essay and notes at the back so that, as he said, Dante's work could first speak directly to the reader.

During the 1860s informal gatherings were held at Longfellow's home and Norton's home where friends and scholars met to discuss the translations of Dante which the two men were working on in poetry and prose respectively. Norton's prose version of the *Vita Nuova*, which was revised in 1867, went through a number of editions, receiving high praise from scholars and critics. William Dean Howells, for example, described it as "a work not less graceful than Longfellow's translation of the *Commedia*. . . . It joins the effect of a sympathy almost mounting to divination with a patient scholarship and delicate skill." In 1891-1892 Norton issued his translation of *The Divine Comedy*, carefully revised in 1902, which remains one of the best prose versions available in English.

Norton's high standards of scholarship and critical acumen were eagerly sought after until his death in 1908. He was esteemed as one of America's foremost critics of Dante scholarship. Some indication of his manner may be gleaned from his review of Tambarini's translation of Benvenuto Da Imola's commentary on the *Divina Commedia*. "The book," wrote Norton, "is worse than worthless to students; for it is not only full of mistakes of carelessness, stupidity, and ignorance, but also of wilful perversions of the meaning of the original by additions, alterations, and omissions." Norton then proceeded to demonstrate these points by quoting amply in Italian from the original and adding incisive comments about the period, the language, and the culture.

For more than forty years Norton found intellectual and aesthetic delight in Dante's work. As translator, critic, and teacher, he made a very substantial contribution to the development of Dante scholarship in America. When Norton retired from regular teaching duties in 1898 he continued for several years in the capacity of professor emeritus to hold a seminar on Dante and to write occasional articles for publication.

In his late seventies, his mood became more pessimistic and his letters reveal his hostility toward new immigrants and his concern that traditional American values somehow might be further eroded. He also believed that the newly rich who had wealth but lacked refined sensibility were a threat to the kind of moral and cultural development which he had hoped for and which he felt America sorely needed.

On his eightieth birthday, Norton was saluted by Harvard University, which published accolades from his colleagues, friends, and former students. In the months which followed, his health declined rapidly although he continued to be mentally alert, dictating letters to friends. Finally on 21 October 1908, with his grown children near him, Charles Eliot Norton died peacefully in the family home at Shady Hill.

In trying to assess Norton's significance as an American man of letters, one looks at his lengthy career as a scholar, critic, and teacher. Norton's critical theory and practical criticism do not exist in a single volume but rather are scattered among his reviews, essays, extant letters, lecture notes, introductions, and prefaces to volumes which range from studies of art and architecture (*Historical Studies of Church Building in the Middle Ages: Venice, Siena, Florence*, 1880), to the paintings of Blake (*William Blake's Illustrations of the Book of Job*, 1875), to a very thorough study of Thomas Gray as naturalist (*The Poet Gray as A Naturalist*, 1903).

Despite the fact that Norton wrote about an astonishing variety of subjects, he rarely lost sight of his conviction that his duty lay toward the aesthetic and ethical instruction of his countrymen.

Norton in his Ashfield garden

He was so convinced of his country's important place in history that, as one contemporary noted, he considered it a cheerful duty to correct its bumptiousness, prune its exuberance, and train its powers. Furthermore, his integrity enabled him to send an admonition such as the following to one who had sent him lavish verses on America. "We love our country, but with keen-eyed and disciplined passion, not blindly exalting her. . . . To do justice to the America that may be, we must not exalt the America that is, beyond her worth." His propensity for moralizing accompanied much of what he wrote. It is not surprising then that although his devotion to art and architecture filled a gap in American life and letters, his approach to modern literature and art was rather uneven. It was flawed by his determination to connect life and art, and his bias toward works from the Italian Gothic period.

Nevertheless, in his essays, letters, and numerous introductions to important literary works, he helped many Americans to appreciate and value the contributions of the past.

The fact that Norton was chosen to edit works by Carlyle, Ruskin, Emerson, and George Curtis, for example, shows the esteem in which he was held by his contemporaries. The results of Norton's efforts in these areas, however, have been subject to stern criticism. His work fails to meet the rigorous standard of twentieth-century literary scholarship because he deleted material and edited texts which he believed should not be made available to the general public.

His own writings and his life played a significant part in nineteenth-century intellectual life in America. As contributor to and editor of several leading periodicals, Charles Eliot Norton was in a unique position to influence public opinion. His efforts were not confined either to fine arts or literature. In 1879, for example, worried about the commercial and industrial exploitation of Niagara Falls, he and Frederick Law Olmstead launched a successful campaign to have both the Falls and the surrounding area designated as a state park. Several years later they again joined forces and led efforts to preserve the Adirondack Mountain area of New York State.

In addition to the many contributions which Norton made in the public domain, in his private life he also enriched the lives of those with whom he came in contact. His numerous trips abroad afforded him the opportunity of developing a lively correspondence and lasting friendships with leading intellectuals of the day. In fact, throughout his lifetime Norton was rich in friends whom he valued. He underscored this in a letter to James Russell Lowell saying, "If you see to the inscription over my grave, you need only say, 'He had good friends whom he loved.'"

As a member of Boston's famed Saturday Club from 1862 to his death in 1908, Norton's personality and scholarship contributed substantially to the intellectual climate of New England and his "gracious amity" was frequently noted. While current opinion about his lasting contributions as an editor are generally negative, nevertheless, his high esteem for the past and his idealism are noteworthy. He was, as his contemporary Edward Waldo Emerson remarked, "a scholar who had read the lesson of history and knew the wisdom, never outgrown, of the great spirits of the Past. He, in his day, worked for the right with tongue and pen—and showed its beauty."

Letters:

Letters of Charles Eliot Norton with Biographical Comment by his Daughter Sara Norton and M. A. De Wolfe Howe, 2 volumes (Boston & New York: Houghton Mifflin, 1913);

Letters of Mrs. Gaskell and Charles Eliot Norton, 1855-1865, Edited with an Introduction by Jane Whitehall (London: Oxford University Press, 1932).

Biographies:

Edward Waldo Emerson, *Charles Eliot Norton: Two Addresses* (Boston: Houghton Mifflin, 1912);

Kermit Vanderbilt, *Charles Eliot Norton: Apostle of Culture in a Democracy* (Cambridge: Belknap Press of Harvard University, 1959).

References:

Henry Adams, *Letters of Henry Adams,* 2 volumes, edited by Worthington C. Ford (Boston: Houghton Mifflin, 1930);

Van Wyck Brooks, *New England: Indian Summer 1865-1915* (New York: Dutton, 1940);

Rollo W. Brown, *Harvard Yard in the Golden Age* (New York: Current Books, 1948);

John Jay Chapman, *Memories and Milestones* (New York: Moffat, Yard, 1915);

Arthur Hugh Clough, *The Correspondence of Arthur Hugh Clough,* 2 volumes, edited by Frederick L. Mulhauser (Oxford: Clarendon Press, 1957);

T. S. Eliot, *Notes Towards the Definition of Culture* (New York: Harcourt, Brace, 1949);

Edward Waldo Emerson, *The Early Years of the Saturday Club, 1855-1870* (Boston: Houghton Mifflin, 1918);

Thomas W. Higginson, *Carlyle's Laugh and Other Surprises* (Boston: Houghton Mifflin, 1909);

Mark A. De Wolfe Howe, *The Atlantic Monthly and Its Makers* (Boston: Atlantic Monthly Press, 1919);

William Dean Howells, *Literary Friends and Acquaintances* (New York: Harper, 1900);

Henry James, *Notes on Novelists, with Some Other Notes* (New York: Scribners, 1914);

Howard Mumford Jones, *The Age of Energy: Varieties of American Experience 1865-1915* (New York: Viking, 1971);

Edward H. Madden, "Charles Eliot Norton on Art and Morals," *Journal of the History of Ideas,* 18 (June 1957): 430-438;

Frederic W. Maitland, *The Life and Letters of Leslie Stephen* (London: Duckworth, 1906);

F. O. Matthiessen, *American Renaissance: Art and Expression in the Age of Emerson and Whitman* (London: Oxford University Press, 1941);

Perry Miller, *The New England Mind* (New York: Macmillan, 1939);

Gordon Milne, *George William Curtis and the Genteel Tradition* (Bloomington: Indiana University Press, 1956);

Paul Elmer More, "Charles Eliot Norton," *Nation,* 97 (4 December 1913): 529-532;

Samuel Eliot Morison, *Three Centuries of Harvard* (Cambridge: Harvard University Press, 1936);

Frank L. Mott, *American Journalism* (New York: Macmillan, 1950);

Thomas R. Nevins, *Irving Babbitt: An Intellectual Study* (Chapel Hill: University of North Carolina Press, 1984);

Meyer Reinhold, *Classica Americana: The Greek and Roman Heritage in the United States* (Detroit: Wayne State University Press, 1984);

William Milligan Sloane, *Commemorative Tribute to McKim, Norton, Ward, Aldrich, and Jefferson* (New York: American Academy of Arts and Letters, 1910);

William R. Thayer, "Charles Eliot Norton," *Nation,* 87 (29 October 1908): 403-406;

John Tomsich, *A Genteel Endeavor: American Culture and Politics in the Gilded Age* (Stanford: Stanford University Press, 1971).

Papers:

Houghton Library, Harvard University, contains an extensive collection of Charles Eliot Norton materials. It includes his correspondence, journals, poems, scrapbooks, business account-books, manuscript copies of his public addresses, and miscellaneous other papers.

George Ripley

(3 October 1802-4 July 1880)

Henry Golemba
Wayne State University

See also the Ripley entry in *DLB 1, The American Renaissance in New England.*

BOOKS: *Discourses on the Philosophy of Religion Addressed to Doubters Who Wish to Believe* (Boston: Munroe, 1836);
Philosophical Miscellanies (Boston: Hilliard, Gray, 1838);
Letters on the Latest Form of Infidelity, Including a View of the Opinions of Spinoza, Schleiermacher and De Wette (Boston: Munroe, 1840).

OTHER: *Specimens of Foreign Standard Literature,* 15 volumes, edited by Ripley (volumes 1-11, Boston: Hilliard, Gray, 1838-1842; volumes 12-14, Boston: Munroe, 1842; volume 15, New York: Wiley, 1845);
A Handbook of Literature and the Fine Arts, compiled by Ripley and Bayard Taylor (New York: Putnam's, 1852);
New American Cyclopædia, 16 volumes, edited by Ripley and Charles A. Dana (New York & London: Appleton, 1863; revised 1883-1884).

PERIODICAL PUBLICATIONS: "De Gerando on Self-Education," *Christian Examiner,* 9 (September 1830): 70-107;
"Pestalozzi," *Christian Examiner,* 11 (January 1832): 347-373;
"Herder's Theological Opinions," *Christian Examiner,* 14 (November 1835): 172-204;
"Schleiermacher as a Theologian," *Christian Examiner,* 20 (March 1836): 1-46;
"Theological Aphorisms," *Christian Examiner,* 21 (January 1837): 385-398;
"Brownson's Writings," *Dial,* 1 (July 1840): 22-46;
"Letter to a Theological Student," *Dial,* 1 (October 1840): 183-187;
"Introductory Notice," *Harbinger,* 1 (14 June 1845): 8-10;
"Tendencies of Modern Civilization," *Harbinger,* 1 (28 June 1845): 33-35;

George Ripley

"Influence of Social Circumstances," *Harbinger,* 5 (26 June 1847): 46.

Known today primarily as the main force behind the communal experiment in transcendental socialism called Brook Farm, George Ripley's efforts as a literary critic and scholar are of real significance in that they mirror paramount intellectual concerns of nineteenth-century America. Ralph Waldo Emerson once commented that a biography of Ripley would provide a "fine historiette of the age."

Ripley's life can be divided into three phases. In the first phase he served as Unitarian minister from his ordination in November 1826 until his resignation from Boston's Purchase Street Church in May 1840. During this time he composed thirteen controversial essays for the *Christian Examiner*, wrote *Discourses on the Philosophy of Religion Addressed to Doubters Who Wish to Believe* (1836), edited *Specimens of Foreign Standard Literature* (1838-1845), debated theological principles with Andrews Norton in a series of published letters, participated in the Transcendental Club, and, in 1840, helped Emerson and Margaret Fuller edit the *Dial* in its first year.

In the second phase of his career, Ripley's increasingly radical transcendentalism manifested itself in Brook Farm. Founded in 1841 and located near West Roxbury, Massachusetts, in 1844, Brook Farm converted constitutionally to a socialist commune along the lines of Charles Fourier's plans as interpreted by the Americans Albert Brisbane and Horace Greeley. The most important literary aspect of this period was the transfer in 1845 of the Fourierist monthly the *Phalanx* from New York to Brook Farm where it was renamed the *Harbinger*, with Ripley replacing Brisbane as editor-in-chief. In the third phase of Ripley's career, from the demise of Brook Farm in 1847 until Ripley's death on 4 July 1880, he wrote thousands of articles, notes, and reviews which appeared in magazines from New York to San Francisco. However, his chief position during the period was as book reviewer for the *New York Tribune*, where, beginning in 1850, he served as one of the most prominent men of letters in America for thirty years. He reviewed all subjects from politics to philosophy, science to mysticism, history to theology, technology to poetry, as well as producing the first regular column of practical literary criticism in America.

The sheer bulk of Ripley's output makes it unwieldy, particularly since his topics are so diverse. One may, however, obtain a coherent sense of Ripley's life as a literary critic and scholar by concentrating on three aspects; first, his editorial projects, such as the fifteen-volume *Specimens of Foreign Standard Literature; A Handbook of Literature and the Fine Arts* (1852), which he compiled with the aid of Bayard Taylor; the sixteen-volume *New American Cyclopædia* (1863), which he edited with Charles A. Dana; and his editing of two of the most important mid-nineteenth-century periodicals, the *Dial* and the *Harbinger*. Second, one could study Ripley's literary and aesthetic theory as presented in his articles from the *Christian Examiner*, his *Discourses on the Philosophy of Religion*, and his unpublished notes. Finally,

Ripley's efforts at practical criticism can be assessed with respect to the articles and reviews he wrote for newspapers and magazines, primarily for the *New York Tribune*, in which he applied his aesthetic theory to the popular literature of his time. This method of structuring Ripley's critical career also has the advantage of reflecting crucial concerns which faced American intellectuals of his era.

The salient point of interest about Ripley's vast editorial projects is his definition of audience. The way an author defines his audience also defines the author's own image of himself; that is, the particular group to which he chooses to direct his message helps shape the content of that message. Ripley's encyclopedic endeavors represent a dramatic shift in his conception of audience. His first, *Specimens of Foreign Standard Literature* (1838-1845), attracted an elite cadre of American intellectuals who were interested in the newest Continental philosophical movements. The word "standard" in the title was a ruse, for the translations which Ripley presented of thinkers like Victor Cousin, Theodore Jouffroy, and Benjamin Constant de Rebecque would be considered radical, if not heretical, by mainstream America. By employing the term "standard," Ripley was also capitalizing on an innate American sense of inferiority, assuring even the most radical American intellectual that his or her notions would not seem at all odd or outré within the established European tradition. This rhetorical tactic is evident in his introduction to the first two volumes of the work which were called *Philosophical Miscellanies*: "The office of the true scholar in our republic is to connect himself in the most intimate and congenial relations with the energetic and busy population of which he is too often merely an insignificant unit. He is never to stand aloof from the concerns of the people; . . . he is never to set himself above them as their condescending instructor; . . . but he is called upon to honor the common mind, to commune with the instinctive experiences of the mighty heart of a free nation, and to bring the aid of learning and philosophy to the endeavor of the people to comprehend their destiny and to secure its accomplishment."

The emphasis in this passage upon the audience as the "common mind," an entity which Ripley would later emphasize and whose description is typically American, points to a narrative technique in which the writer pretends to be on a level no higher than the reader even though the writer is the one empowering the narrative, and is placed in the role of teacher with the reader as student.

In future editorial projects, Ripley placed himself in closer connection with what he targeted as "the common mind." In 1852 he and Bayard Taylor compiled *A Handbook of Literature and the Fine Arts,* which was aimed at an audience that was broader than the one for *Specimens of Foreign Standard Literature,* one that consisted of any readers interested in aesthetic principles or creative writing. In 1863, however, Ripley would come closest to "the common mind" and most fulfilled his self-concept of a "minister to the people" when he and Charles A. Dana edited the *New American Cyclopædia.* This project, which covered topics from archaeology to zoology, defined all literate and intellectually curious Americans as its audience, not just the aesthetes, theologians, and philosophers among them. Ripley's expanded sense of ministry was most rewarding financially with this endeavor which netted its editors between $40,000 and $45,000 and warranted a new edition in 1883. Ironically, some of those who had invested in Brook Farm, Ripley's deepest plunge into idealistic commitment, recalled their twenty-year-old debts and dunned Ripley for free copies to compensate for their losses in his transcendental socialist experiment.

These general editorial projects, with their increasingly broader definition of audience and Ripley's steadily widening self-characterization as an American intellectual, are functionally in marked contrast to his efforts in more specialized editorial projects such as the *Dial* and the *Harbinger,* which he undertook from 1841 to 1849. Just as both periodicals shared a similar concern with charting the historical progress toward a new and better era, Ripley's optimism in these two journals was at its sunniest. For example, he said he expected the *Dial* "will not only show how high the sun is up, but reflect a welcome, a healing light over our dark places." One way to achieve this was to keep the journal's pages open to all serious thinkers and writers while still emphasizing transcendentalism, an intellectual openness which seemed only right to the *Dial*'s editors since the policy of some journals to close their pages to transcendental writers had made the establishment of the *Dial* necessary in the first place.

For example, when James Freeman Clarke, upset by the radical nature of a piece on Schleiermacher, urged Ripley to omit it from the second number of the *Dial,* Ripley answered his close friend: "we must be governed by a sense of integrity towards the author, rather than of compassion towards the reader. Besides a few tough passages of the kind you allude to are of good use to aid the digestion of the rest, just as chickens thrive better with a little gravel to their corn." Ripley was pleased that the *Dial* succeeded in making the Philistines "wrathy as fighting cocks," but he was also disappointed that it did not have a more powerful impact on America. Perhaps the problem, Ripley surmised in one of his *Dial* articles, was that "What the age requires is not books but example, high, heroic example; not words but deeds. . . ."

In 1841 Ripley embarked on what he hoped would be such a "high, heroic example" when he founded Brook Farm, relinquishing his managing editorship of the *Dial* and eventually assuming the chief editorship of the *Harbinger,* a sixteen-page quarto which was published weekly from 14 June 1845 to 10 February 1849. Brook Farm had converted from a transcendental experiment in communal life to a socialistic phalanx in January 1844. Ripley believed that socialism needed two things to make it work in America–a model community and "a voice speaking daily to the people." As that voice, the *Harbinger,* like the *Dial,* gave access to many reform writers of various persuasions and sometimes published literature (offering a translation of George Sand's *Consuelo* in its first volume), but its thrust was Fourierist socialism.

The *Harbinger,* a Fourierite journal, opposed capitalism, slavery, and the Mexican-American War, while it supported prison reform, women's rights, labor unions, and other reforms. However, its insistence that America required what Ripley described as "an organic change in the structure of society" and that "society must be made to revolve on a new pivot" frustrated those attempting to achieve specific political reforms. Hence, while Ripley threw the weight of the *Harbinger* behind labor reforms, he idealistically maintained that the starting point would be to gain public control over capital and the tools of production since he saw industrial reform as a prerequisite to all other reforms. Feminists likewise had the *Harbinger*'s support, but the journal provided little practical advice by pointing out that women in Fourierist communes already had equal rights. Slavery too would be solved by the panacea of socialism, and so antislavery organizations were commended for their sentiments even as their efforts were branded ineffectual; only so-

Brook Farm, the utopian community founded by Ripley in 1842

cialism or war would resolve the problem of human bondage. Thus, association and socialism only could cure slavery, poverty, war, and other social ills: "The axe must be laid to the root of the tree," Ripley wrote, "or no universal good can be hoped for from the sincerest purposes of reform."

The major intellectual shift Ripley underwent while editor of the *Harbinger* was an increased awareness of the individual as a captive of history or as a product of social forces. Whereas the young Protestant minister might have boasted about the power of the individual's will to transform personal reality, in his socialist phase Ripley would write an essay for the *Harbinger* (26 June 1847) called "Influence of Social Circumstances" which stated: "Thus, the simple change of the position of an individual in the social mechanism in which he is born is sufficient to change entirely his ideas, his beliefs, his manners and habits, or in a word, his morality and his life. This no intelligent man will call into question."

Ripley's change in emphasis from the individual to society is one that took place individually with other American writers, such as Emerson, as well as on a cultural level. In literature, for example, the novel, with its social emphasis, came to replace poetry, with its personal voice, as the most flourishing genre, and the romanticism of early-nineteenth-century America was succeeded by realism in the last two decades of Ripley's life. This reorientation of the relationship of the individual to the matrix of society is the *primum mobile* of Ripley's thought; his conception of the way the human mind is shaped and works lay behind and informed whatever particular project he embarked upon. To describe this crucial topic, one had best look at Ripley's theories as presented in his essays and notes on theology and psychology.

Educated at Harvard (he graduated at the head of his class in 1823), with its emphasis on John Locke in philosophy and William Paley in theology, Ripley was firmly grounded in empiricist thought. However, matriculation at Harvard also enabled him to study under Levi Frisbee, one of the most radical proponents of liberal Christianity, and to become familiar with the writings of the German Romantics. In 1824 he entered the Harvard Divinity School. The standard theological line of Ripley's education was that the individual's mind at birth was a tabula rasa and all knowledge was derived from experience through the interplay of the senses with reality. Ideals therefore arose as the miracle of God's gift of grace; conceptions of Truth, Justice, Goodness, and Beauty were bestowed by the nonearthly power of Divinity. Ripley studied German scholars like Johann Gottfried Herder, Carl Ullman, and Friedrich Schleiermacher as well as Immanuel Kant because they emphasized the individual's inborn, innate intuitive faculties which were capable of perceiving divine truths without the intervention of an external, supernatural agency. For the same reasons he was also drawn to British philosophers like Dugald Stewart, Ralph Cudworth, Henry More, Samuel Clarke, Joseph Butler, Richard Price, John Smith, and Samuel Taylor Coleridge.

Ripley's philosophy as expressed in his *Christian Examiner* articles of the 1830s and his *Discourses on the Philosophy of Religion* as well as in his public debate with the conservative Unitarian Andrews Norton in 1839 was that one need not look beyond a study of the human mind in order to understand the reality that concerns humanity. As he said in his *Discourses on the Philosophy of Religion*, "It is from the cast and disposition of our souls that external nature derives its hues and conformations.... Forms are addressed to the eye, but the perception of beauty is in the soul." Hence, in his *Christian Examiner* articles he called for more psychological studies and less theology in the form of biblical exegesis: "We would see a more profound analysis of the soul, with its boundless capacities of suffering and enjoyment, its thirst for infinite good, its deep passions, its inexpressible wants, its lofty aspirations after the unseen and eternal. Man has been regarded too much as the creature of accidental circumstances, while the primary and indestructible laws of his being have been kept out of sight. We wish to see his whole nature clearly exhibited before us, with all the mysterious powers it involves." In addition to this analysis of the mind, Ripley also wanted these scientific descriptions presented in a distinguished literary style which would move the reader: "We would have these relations not only recognized, but felt.... We do not wish them to be treated as subjects of cold, logical discussion ... but to be held up in living colors, as everlasting realities, in which every human being has a deep and vital interest."

One can see why Ripley's psychological emphasis offended conservatives like Andrews Norton, for with Ripley God is relegated to the role of an artist whose human audience is of primary

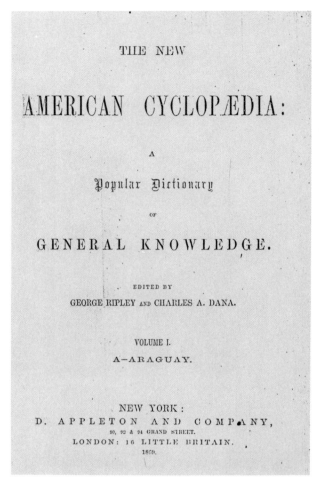

THE NEW

AMERICAN CYCLOPÆDIA:

A

Popular Dictionary

OF

GENERAL KNOWLEDGE.

EDITED BY

GEORGE RIPLEY AND CHARLES A. DANA.

VOLUME I.

A–ARAGUAY.

NEW YORK:
D. APPLETON AND COMPANY,
90, 92 & 94 GRAND STREET.
LONDON: 16 LITTLE BRITAIN.
1869.

Title page for volume one of a later edition of the highly successful compendium coedited by Ripley and Charles A. Dana

importance as interpreter, indeed as creator or recreator of His works. Without humanity as reader, the Divine Author's work consists of blank pages: "The sun might exist as the fountain of light ... and pour forth its streams over the earth, but [without] the inward nature of man ... the beauties of nature would be a lifeless blank, the variety of colors, of forms, of motions in the universe would be without significance, and the lavish bounty of Providence apparently bestowed in vain."

In awarding primary significance to human consciousness Ripley does not differ greatly from basic transcendentalism as propounded as early as 1819 by William Ellery Channing and as articulated by his more famous contemporaries like Emerson and Thoreau. But Ripley differed most markedly from other transcendentalists in that he placed less emphasis on individualism and more on the universality of human psychology. Hence, he was drawn to Schleiermacher in part because of his description of "primitive consciousness"; forty years later, in 1878, he would in like manner be "plunging deep in the current German philosophy, especially of [Arthur] Schopenhauer and [Eduard von] Hartmann" because of their emphasis on the universality of the will and the unconscious.

Ripley's concern with the universality of human psychology prevented him from being as thoroughgoing in his individualism as were some better-known transcendentalists. He could appreciate Emerson's insistence that one must "trust thyself " because the individual was the cynosure of the universe, but Ripley equally valued "common sense," which he described as the belief that individual perceptions were significant insofar as they reflected universal workings of the human mind, a belief that would be intensified during his *Harbinger* years as he gave more credence to the power of social forces. Thus, as editor he fought for an open editorial policy, and when he started Brook Farm he deliberately remained in the background instead of attempting to force his personal views on the community, an avuncular role that caused Margaret Fuller, for one, to complain of Ripley that he was a captain, not a conqueror.

In Ripley's literary criticism, his twin foci of individualism and common sense are often encoded as "genius" and "genuineness," the two essential components of his aesthetic. Genius involves diving into the author's personal wealth of inner experience, presenting that "deep inner experience" in language that is strikingly fresh and original. Yet the author's language must be accessible and not idiosyncratic, "genuine" in the sense that the language, as well as the events and experiences it describes, seems rooted in broad human context. Consequently, popular books like Ouida's *Under Two Flags* (1867) and Elizabeth Wetherell's *Wide, Wide World* (1850), which catered to sensationalism or proffered a mindless pleasantry, provoked Ripley's anger for they showed no signs of either genius or genuineness. However, William Makepeace Thackeray's novels, even though they offended Ripley's personal sense of morality because they showed "a slender faith in human virtue," were praised for their accuracy in description of the social context, their genuineness which was, because realistic, a kind of morality which was "not flattering to human pride but crushing out all conceit and nonsense."

Thackeray's authorial intrusions, however, spoiled Ripley's sense of genuineness, causing him to prefer George Sand and George Eliot on this score.

On the American scene, Edgar Allan Poe, among the romantics, showed unmistakable signs of genius, but Ripley could not detect much genuineness; instead of recognizing Poe's images as familiar psychological landscapes, he fretted that reading Poe was like "breathing the air of a charnel-house. The walls seem to sweat with blood, we stumble on skulls and dead men's hopes, and grinning spectres mock us in the dim sepulchral light." With respect to Henry David Thoreau, a romantic of a much different stripe, Ripley praised his style for being "true to life" and his language for being "alive with the deepest spirit of poetry." Even so, he complained of Thoreau's "ungracious isolation from the living interests of society," a complaint that seems curiously similar to the reservations Ripley had about Poe.

Herman Melville and Nathaniel Hawthorne were, according to Ripley, more successful. Ripley valued Melville's realistic scenes, which reminded him of the fidelity to detail in Dutch paintings, and admired the daring power of his originality, but Ripley warned of Melville's tendency to goad the natural play of his imagination on to "a monstrous activity." While he disdained the "mystic allegory" of *Mardi* (1849) "and this transcendental, glittering, soap-bubble speculation which he has done to death in that ambitious composition," he applauded *Moby-Dick* (1851) as an epic "whaliad" which penetrated like a harpoon "deep into the heart of things, showing that the genius of the author for moral analysis is scarcely surpassed by his wizard power of description." On the same grounds, Ripley praised Hawthorne for being a "sturdy realist" whose work offered a "singular lifelike reality." He appreciated the psychological penetration of *The Blithedale Romance* (1852) despite its oblique parody of Brook Farm, and he admired the way "the somber gloom" of *The Scarlet Letter* (1850) could be deftly counterpointed by Hawthorne's "refined comic humor."

The coarser humor of regionalist writers who inaugurated the realist movement in America was also welcome, and Ripley enjoyed the "sense of the manifold condition of life" and the "faithful pictures of actual human experience" in John Hay, Edward Eggleston, and Mark Twain, even though he did not live to see the appearance of Twain's mature work. He was well aware that these humorists were to be taken seriously, for they penetrated "beneath the crust of conventionalism to the depth of reality . . . while the shams and pretenses of artificial life fall to the ground." He also saw that William Dean Howells, as a purely realistic novelist, capitalized on the regionalists' efforts and excelled in expressive descriptions, a sense of humor, and an ear for dialect and the natural way people spoke. His novels provided a seemingly "unvarnished recital of events that but yesterday took place within the circle of our own experience." But while Howells could achieve a "refined and subtle analysis" of character and the psychological import of events, he was surpassed by Henry James whose style was rich, fluent, and copious, "so finely shaded yet capable of such varied service that it is in itself a form of genius." Bringing to bear his standards of genius and genuineness, Ripley defended James against his detractors, arguing that James "delights in the study and representation of personal traits which, though not eccentric, are original and illustrate natural but suggestive qualities of human character. He experiments with the passions as old alchemists did with the metals, not so much with the view of transmuting dross into gold, as of exhibiting accustomed forms in novel and original combinations."

Ripley's standards of genius and genuineness stood him in good stead in evaluating literature as a journeyman critic, but they also led him astray. He could, for example, believe that Frederick Goddard Tuckerman was a better poet than Walt Whitman, and he could wax wildly enthusiastic over an eight-volume poem by Edwin Arnold called *Light in Asia* (1879) which versified Arnold's experience with Buddhism. But more important than whatever critical judgments Ripley may have made is his function as a bridge between popular and intellectual thought in America, primarily in his position as book reviewer for the *New York Tribune* from 1850 to 1880. Ripley's essays may be interesting in themselves or biographically, but their greater significance is as a suprapersonal representation of generalized intellectual thought, as a mirror of the climate of intellectual opinion in America of the mid-to-late nineteenth century.

References:
Charles Crowe, *George Ripley: Transcendentalist and Utopian Socialist* (Athens: University of Georgia Press, 1967);

Octavius Brooks Frothingham, *George Ripley* (Boston & New York: Houghton, Mifflin, 1882);

Henry Golemba, *George Ripley* (Boston: Twayne, 1977).

Papers:
The Boston Public Library holds thirty-seven of George Ripley's letters in the Dwight collection; thirty-five in the Brook Farm collection; eighteen in the Antislavery collection; and seventeen in the Weston Papers; 1836-1847. The Fruitlands Museum, Harvard, Mass., holds ten letters written between 1841 and 1847. The Houghton Library at Harvard University has manuscripts, clippings, Brook Farm account books, and fifteen letters collected in four Ripley folders. The Massachusetts Historical Society holds Ripley's memorandum book, sermons, manuscripts, and thirty-four letters in the Frothingham collection, thirty-eight letters in the Bancroft collection, eighteen in the Parker papers, and seventeen in the Dana collection. The *New York Herald Tribune* files contain 106 letters, notes, and memoranda written from 1849 to 1880.

Henry Joseph Ruggles

(16 August 1813-6 March 1906)

Monica Maria Grecu
University of Nevada at Reno

BOOKS: *The Method of Shakespeare as an Artist, Deduced from an Analysis of His Leading Tragedies and Comedies* (New York: Hurd & Houghton, 1870);

The Plays of Shakespeare Founded on Literary Forms (Boston & New York: Houghton, Mifflin, 1895).

Henry Joseph Ruggles, a lawyer by profession, may be classed with a group of gentleman-scholars known as amateur critics. These non-academics, for whom literary criticism is an avocation, commonly display a tendency to push a thesis beyond its legitimate suitability, an earnest, almost driving need to be innovative and arresting, and a limited productivity in which depth is substituted for breadth. Ruggles does not wholly escape these perils, especially the tendency to push a thesis too far. As well, his choice of Shakespeare as the topic of his two books of criticism belie his desire to elicit attention and even controversy. Despite these failings, his work undeniably warrants attention. Schooled in the law, he emphasized the particulars of language to a degree uncommon for his period. He maintained that the vocabulary of a play—its metaphors and diction—is "the best key for unlocking . . . more hidden and secret meanings and beauties." This dedication to close reading saves him from making the kinds of extravagant propositions of which his contemporaries were often guilty and the support of which depends more on rhetorical ingenuity than analysis, even as it anticipates our current preoccupation with language as the coded integration and transmission of experience.

Only a few details of his life are known. He was born on 16 August 1813 in Milford, Connecticut, the second of three sons of Philo and Ellen Bulkley Ruggles. The father practiced law. Henry attended Columbia College, receiving his A.B. in 1832, and almost immediately took up the study and practice of law in the New York firm of his older and better-known brother, Samuel. All three brothers were active in New York

civic affairs, securing Union Square to the city, founding Grammercy Park, and laying out and naming Lexington Avenue. It is possible that Henry played a role in furthering the building of the Erie Canal and the Erie Railroad, since Samuel was central to these activities. There is no evidence that Henry ever married. In 1866 he retired from the law and either took up, or more likely continued, an avocational interest in Shakespeare. The results of his Shakespeare studies were two books published in 1870 and 1895. He died in 1906 at the age of ninety-two. Even these meager details suggest a man who, over-shadowed by an older brother, chose scholarship as a means of making his mark.

Ruggles's first publication was a study of *Twelfth Night, Hamlet,* and *Macbeth* entitled *The Method of Shakespeare as an Artist, Deduced from an Analysis of His Leading Tragedies and Comedies* (1870). Ruggles's intention is to dive below the seemingly "unsystematic and fortuitous" surfaces of the plays in order to explore how their language contributes "a wonderful harmony, coherence, and meaning." On this deeper level, language no longer appears adventitious; instead, study of Shakespeare's diction, metaphors, and similes reveals that throughout his work Shakespeare was "deliberate and philosophic" in his choice of words and images to convey meaning.

The shaping hypothesis of the book is the theory of organic form. Ruggles holds that readers intuitively recognize the "moral unity" of each of the plays, but neglect to follow this lead into an examination of characters, incidents, and language which would reveal how each of these expresses and reinforces the subject of a play. Shakespeare may have written for popularity and money, but the plays themselves are evidence that he sought to transcend these material concerns by creating art. Knowing that the complex of interrelationships "would be necessarily lost on the general audience and reader," Shakespeare's artistry can only be ascribed to the gratification of his own tastes or the exuberance of his imagination.

Ruggles's analyses are so detailed and extensive that they resist summation. Not many critics were, in 1870, interested in such attention to detail, or, indeed, thought it in any way worthy of their interest. There is a strong feel in the few reviews of minds being wrenched out of their familiar paths to confront a book both queer and inimical to them. Ruggles's failure to provide a chapter summarizing his conclusions implies that the book's many meanings could best be grasped by reading the work as a whole. It seems as if Ruggles was attempting to teach a new way of reading.

In any case he deals well with his three chosen plays. *Twelfth Night* is seen as a holiday piece written in a "spirit of license for a period of license." Viola observes taste and judgment, but for the other characters, self-ruling fancy, appetite, and desire make for a pleasant romp through life seen as a fiction. To Ruggles the elegance of the play lies in the way in which it doubles on itself: reason as the criterion for opinions and conduct is the backdrop, but in the foreground the play is all joyously fanciful about fancy, witty about wit, and buoyant about imagination.

On *Hamlet*, Ruggles is excellent as he probes the "seeming empire of chance" in the play in order to reveal how the "infinite complications" of the play finally coalesce into a "mighty scheme" so vastly predetermined that its understanding is beyond the scope of human intellect. Thus the play is not a tragic view of life, but a view of life as tragic. To reinforce this point, Ruggles engages in an exhaustive study of the play's diction as it complements theme, character, and action.

The same success is realized in the study of *Macbeth*, especially as he dissects the alternations in Macbeth's mind between reason and imagination, fear and hope. For example, in support of his contention that the play hinges upon the complicated relations of man and society in which personal will must necessarily manifest itself in overt acts, Ruggles points out how even innermost or subconscious thoughts are externalized: the three witches voicing the impulses of wicked ambition, Lady Macbeth's acting out her dreams, Macbeth seeing ghosts and phantom objects.

Twenty-five years later Ruggles again turned to the textual analysis of Shakespeare. *The Plays of Shakespeare Founded on Literary Forms*

(1895) is a much more ambitious effort, but like its predecessor, the work seems not to have caused any significant response from reviewers or critics. The twelve plays that Ruggles chooses to cover range in time between *Romeo and Juliet* and *The Tempest*. He eschews the history plays to focus on nine comedies and tragicomedies (*The Merchant of Venice, Much Ado About Nothing, The Merry Wives of Windsor, As You Like It, All's Well That Ends Well, Troilus and Cressida, Cymbeline, The Winter's Tale,* and *The Tempest*) and three tragedies (*Romeo and Juliet, Othello,* and *King Lear*). Obviously Ruggles's major interest was in the plays produced between 1596 and 1599 and again between 1608 and 1611, with *All's Well That Ends Well, Othello,* and *King Lear* occupying an intermediate position. Ruggles's approach, however, is not chronological.

His major intention in the book–actually something of a drawback–is to demonstrate a systematic reciprocal relationship, both structural and functional, between the plays and Francis Bacon's philosophy. Ruggles's contention is that the parallels that can be drawn between the two men are too numerous to be merely casual. They point to a correspondence that strongly suggests "some personal relation" between the two which remains shrouded in the silence of history and tradition. Each play is treated as a dramatic exemplification of some aspect of Bacon's philosophy, so that collectively the plays testify to "the system and technicalities of the Baconian philosophy." Ruggles's intention does not always serve him well. To see each play as centering on a single philosophical position introduces into the discussion an overly schematic approach which is ultimately unpersuasive. A second problem is structural: the many pages given over to exposition of key Baconian doctrines interrupt the flow of dramatic analysis. Finally, the parallels he educes, while sometimes startling in phrasing and point between the two men, often seem fortuitous and superficial. Ruggles professes to be aware of this possibility and claims that he strove to avoid it. If so, he was not altogether successful.

What saves his book, indeed what makes it interesting, is that Ruggles stayed close to the texts themselves and generally avoided flights of profundity that become neater and tidier the further they stray from what Shakespeare actually wrote. Furthermore, the *way* that Ruggles read a text made it easier to avoid digressing from his subject. His basic premise was that Shakespeare (as other great artists) explored the differences between "words and things." This view led him to concentrate on dramatic action and the resultant psychological conflict it causes for the characters. Rather than follow the nineteenth-century habit of viewing the characters as separate from the plays, Ruggles explored incidents and situations first and then sought to show how characters' responses diminished, intensified, qualified, or transformed them as human beings. In a word he began by analyzing plot and completed his study by determining the relationship between the exercise of correct or incorrect judgment and the way in which characters "read" their situations. He called plot "the constructive law of the piece," the frame within which we see the changing sentiments, purposes, and mental habits of the characters. This "law" established the particular "literary form" of a play, which meant to Ruggles that the "shortest road to the philosophy of the plays is through their art."

In his introduction Ruggles notes that *The Winter's Tale* most clearly illustrates how dramatic forms can serve as models of philosophical exposition through art, but he chooses to begin with *Cymbeline* as the clearest example of the application of Bacon's inductive system to a work of art. This critical viewpoint served him rather well, though it did not wholly deter him from engaging in the standard attention to character popular with his contemporaries. Its positive effect was to encourage Ruggles to concentrate on the action in terms of words, looks, and gestures which the various characters struggle to interpret. Such "signs" and "tokens" constitute "trials" insofar as they test the perceptual powers of the various individuals in the play. Ruggles points specifically to Posthumus's gestures at the time of his departure, the dumbshow scene, the misleading actions of Iachimo and the Queen, and Imogen's attempts to "read" what Pisanio is really "saying." Individual worth, then, is to be found in the relative success of the various characters in drawing correct inferences from signs and probabilities. Complicating this matter of assessing worth are traditional notions of blood, birth, and breeding as grounds of merit, as well as such occult methods as dreams and divinations, which the characters often employ to solve the riddles with which they are faced.

Having dealt with *Cymbeline* as a play which turns on the role of experience in determining correct inferences, Ruggles next turns to *The Winter's Tale* as a dramatic illustration of the conceptual role of honor as a standard by which to evaluate moral goodness. Experience is learned, but the sense of honor is rooted in opinion. Since opinion differs from belief in its relative dependence on reason, Ruggles analyzes in depth the various scenes of argumentation and disputation found in the play. This is a rewarding and nearly successful tactic, for it seems to have encouraged him to concentrate on the play's language to an unusual degree—not only metaphors and other stylistic features, but even interjections and individual words. Ruggles notes a kind of progression in the play. The notion of honor is central. Honor is defined in the polemics of language. Language thus *becomes* the play: as Ruggles says, "it is *ipsissima res* or the very thing itself." The play's unity, then, is located in its dependence on the instrumentality of language, which allows Ruggles to discount such "irregularities" as the apparently unmotivated jealousy of Leontes and the sixteen-year withdrawal of Hermione. The verbal controversy involved in defining honor constitutes the "action" of the play, which must necessarily follow its own pace. Its resolution can be the matter of a moment, and is, in fact, almost perfunctory.

This same sensitivity to language combined with an overemphasized thematic study of plot can be found in all of Ruggles's chapters. For example, he sees *Romeo and Juliet* as indebted to astrology, scarcely an original insight. The tenacity with which he pursues references to friendly or hostile "houses," however, underscores the uncertainties the characters feel in trying to anticipate the outcome of events which in the natural, uncontrollable order of things will turn out favorably or unfavorably. Similarly, he sees *Othello* as essentially a novel cast in dramatic form, certainly as valid a view as the tendency of some to see it as a "domestic tragedy."

In novelistic terms, *Othello* concentrates on a principal personage whose actions and characters propel him through a succession of conceivable events to a probable conclusion. Couched in public events and the accompanying intrigues and passions, the play nevertheless dwells on "the details of private and domestic life," as novels are supposed to. In support of this view, Ruggles closely analyzes the language of the play for its picture of civil society under the twin sway of law and religion, touching along the way matters of class and rank, civility as a guide to deportment, references to scriptural and Christian doctrines, and the elegant ceremonies designed to regulate social intercourse. Against this sway of law and religion is ranged the sensual, unbalanced side of man, so broadly malefic that human nature must finally be termed a puzzle.

Besides the usual murky statements commonly found in Ruggles's discussions of "organic form," there is in his criticism a nice blend of speculation and attention to particulars. This latter

bent was not characteristic of his period, of course, and may explain the ignoring of him then and thus our ignorance of him now. In many respects he was an original, but chiefly in the way he pored over literary expression, as lawyers pore over statutes. To that extent he seems almost an incongruity, out of place in his own time.

Arthur George Sedgwick

(6 October 1844-14 July 1915)

John Bird, Jr.
University of Rochester

BOOKS: *A Treatise on the Principles and Practice Governing the Trial of Title to Land,* by Sedgwick and Frederick S. Wait (New York: Baker, Voorhis, 1882); revised and enlarged as *A Treatise on the Trial to Land* (New York: Baker, Voorhis, 1886);

Elements of Damages, a Handbook for the Use of Students and Practitioners (Boston: Little, Brown, 1896); revised and enlarged as *Elements of the Law of Damages, a Handbook for the Use of Students and Practitioners* (Boston: Little, Brown, 1909);

English Political Development in the Century (New York, 1901);

The Democratic Mistake (New York: Scribners, 1912).

PERIODICAL PUBLICATIONS: "*Uncle Tom's Cabin,*" [play] *Nation,* 26 (11 April 1878): 241-243;

"Tolstoy's *The Cossacks,*" *Nation,* 27 (29 August 1878): 134-135;

"Wills' *Jane Shore,*" *Nation,* 27 (12 September 1878): 165;

"Bronson Howard's *Hurricanes,*" *Nation,* 27 (12 September 1878): 165;

"Charles Reade's *Double Marriage,*" *Nation,* 28 (9 January 1879): 33-34;

"Howells' *Counterfeit Presentment,*" *Nation,* 28 (9 January 1879): 34;

"Trollope's *An Eye For an Eye,*" *Nation,* 28 (24 April 1879): 290;

"Trollope's *Thackeray,*" *Nation,* 29 (21 August 1879): 127-128;

"Boucicault's *Octoroon,*" *Nation,* 29 (27 November 1879): 367;

"Recent Novels" [Zola's *The Markets of Paris*], *Nation,* 29 (25 December 1879): 443;

"T. W. Higginson's *Short Studies of American Authors,*" *Nation,* 30 (8 April 1880): 273-274;

"Mr. Trollope's Last Novel" [*The Duke's Children*], *Nation,* 31 (19 August 1880): 138-139;

"Oscar Wilde," *Nation,* 34 (12 January 1882): 28-29;

"James Fenimore Cooper," *Nation,* 36 (1 February 1883): 107;

"Crane's *Red Badge of Courage, Maggie,* and *George's Mother,*" *Nation,* 63 (2 July 1896): 15;

"Bellamy's *Utopia,*" *Nation,* 65 (26 August 1897): 170-171;

"*Twelve Types* by G. K. Chesterton," *Nation,* 76 (5 February 1903): 119-120;

"*A Reader's History of American Literature,*" *Nation,* 78 (18 February 1904): 136;

"*The Wampum Library of American Literature,*" *Nation,* 79 (1 December 1904): 443;

"The *Nation's* Critics," *Nation,* 101 (8 July 1915): 54-57.

In an era of rapidly changing literary tastes and movements, the last half of the nineteenth century and the first decade of the twentieth, Arthur George Sedgwick wrote criticism which resembled the judicial criticism of the eighteenth century. Sedgwick seemed continually involved in a rearguard action against what he perceived to be a loosening of prescribed rules of taste and decorum. Despite his high moral and formal tone, his reviews sparkle with Johnsonian wit, making them, despite his strict and sometimes eccentric viewpoints, eminently readable and consistently interesting.

Sedgwick was born in New York City on 6 October 1844. He attended Harvard and earned an A.B. in 1864. Upon graduation, he enlisted in the Union army. As a first lieutenant of the 20th Massachusetts Infantry, he was captured by Confederate troops at Deep Bottom, Virginia, in July 1864, and held in Libby Prison, where he suffered a serious illness. In September of that year, he was paroled, then discharged from the army in February 1865 because of physical disability. He entered Harvard Law School a month later, and in 1866 received his LL.B. In November 1868 he was admitted to the bar and secured a position with a Boston law firm.

His brother-in-law, Charles Eliot Norton, advised him to spend time writing, and Sedgwick began what was to be a lifelong association with the newly founded *Nation*. In 1868 or 1869, he claimed to have written an article a week for the publication. He became an assistant editor of the *Nation* in 1872 and remained on the staff until 1905. In all, he contributed well over 800 articles and reviews on law, politics, history, current events, and literature. Aside from his work for the *Nation*, he certainly took very seriously Norton's advice to write: he edited (with Oliver Wendell Holmes, Jr.) the *American Law Review* from 1870 to 1873; he was briefly managing editor of the *New York Evening Post* in 1872, resigning because of editorial interference from the business office, then served as assistant editor of that paper from 1881 to 1885; and he wrote and edited a number of law books. In 1912 he published *The Democratic Mistake*, taken from lectures he gave at Harvard in 1909, in which he argued that the United States had erred in expecting responsible government solely through the ballot box, reinforcing the kind of aristocratic argument one finds in his literary reviews. Among his friends were many of the important literary people of the day, most notably Henry James.

Sedgwick's literary reviews for the *Nation* can be roughly divided into three categories: reviews of plays, reviews of novels, and reviews of biography and criticism. In an age when the actors often overshadowed the play, Sedgwick paid as much attention to the form of a drama as to its execution. For example, in his review of the play version of *Uncle Tom's Cabin*, he attempts to explain

its continued popularity, noting that "the thrilling story of Uncle Tom's suffering has now acquired a sort of historical character," and that the fact that the world of slavery was now past "ought to make the play, as a play, just as attractive as it once was morally and politically." He reviews the acting as well, calling the performance of the villains "awful enough to blanch the cheek of the most hardened spectator," but objects that the actress who plays Topsy, instead of dancing the "real Negro break-down," dances ballet instead, complete with pointed toes. The best feature of the play, he claims, is the use of authentic Negro songs and dances–performed by black actors and actresses–which constitutes for Sedgwick an uncharacteristic appreciation of realism.

Returning to formal matters, in a review of William Gorman Wills's *Jane Shore*, he objects to the ending, since "tradition ought, it seems to us, to have counted for something and have secured us against a happy melodramatic termination of a career which popular belief brought to its end in a London ditch." He finds the main actress too studied, but admits that "this is a fault to which, in the present condition of the American stage, we are disposed to be very lenient." His moral tone is preeminent in his review of *Hurricanes*, "a lively comedy of the farce order," which he says "is full of life and spirit," but adds that "it must be said that it is vulgar, as all plays of this school seem doomed to be." Even more stringently, he says of *Joshua Whitcomb*, a depiction of the stage Yankee, that "it would go against our conscience to recommend any one to go to see 'Joshua Whitcomb,' for a more hopelessly vulgar entertainment we have never seen."

Aside from such moral judgments, his reviews nearly always exhibit great wit, as in his review of Charles Reade's *Double Marriage*, where he finds the lead actress's performance so fine and so full of "genuine tragic feeling" that it made him wish that the play could "have ended at its real climax, where she attempts suicide. Never have we been more sorry to see a life saved." Similarly, in a short notice that Howells's *A Counterfeit Presentment* was rumored to be coming into production, Sedgwick applauds the play's American qualities and decries the common practice of turning French plays into American ones by changing character names and place references; "after the process is completed," Sedgwick writes in a mixture of formal judiciousness and witty sarcasm, "these plays usually present a picture of life about as like that which usually goes on in America as it is like life in Hindustan." In a review of Dion Boucicault's *Octoroon,* he reverses what he said about *Uncle Tom's Cabin,* and more characteristically, he calls the use of black performers "a mistaken sacrifice to realism; that the corked Caucasian is, for theatrical purposes, a far better negro than the African, seems to us hardly to admit of a doubt." Despite his iconoclasm, Sedgwick's general critical judgment of the quality of the nineteenth-century American stage coincides with the modern view.

His reviews of novels read like a succession of reactions against whatever new movement was at hand. He finds Tolstoy's *The Cossacks* "more a collection of national types than a novel," claiming that Tolstoy does not rank with Turgenev, that he lacks "dramatic power." In his continual Aristotelian demand that plot, action, and characters be inextricably wed, Sedgwick accuses Tolstoy of controlling his characters too strictly and concludes that, "consequently, although as a description of a certain sort of Russian life the story is valuable, it does not, as fiction, seem to us to be of great interest." In a similar vein, of Trollope's *An Eye For an Eye* (1879) he observes that "we feel at once that we are in the presence of a novelist's puppet rather than a real human being." Trollope is not alone in this, Sedgwick asserts, but merely normal, since only one or two novelists a century transcend this flaw. Thackeray seems to have been Sedgwick's ideal model, but in later reviews he showed a much deeper appreciation of Trollope's work.

The movement which most raised Sedgwick's critical hackles was naturalism. Even so, he could praise Zola's *The Markets of Paris* (1879), since " it shows his ability, when he is at his best, to sink his theorizing in an acute and dispassionate study of life and character." That is as far as he will go; he later uses a review of "Mr. Trollope's Last Novel" (*The Duke's Children,* 1880) to point out the flaws of naturalistic fiction. Since "there is no beginning or ending to anything" in real life, and since "the function of the novelwriter is to bring out this great fact," the theory is bound to fail in practice. Sedgwick posits that "the difficulty with the naturalistic theory, as a theory, is that fiction based on the idea of photographically representing life itself would be a bald series of statements of facts, like those in the columns of a newspaper."

Thus, Sedgwick heaves a nearly audible sigh of relief that naturalism is a product of France and doesn't seem to have yet corrupted British or American fiction. When that lamentable event finally occurs, Sedgwick vents his critical spleen on Crane's *Maggie: A Girl of the Streets* (1893), *Red Badge of Courage* (1895), and *George's Mother* (1896). Although he finds *Red Badge* "undeniably clever," he classifies Crane as a "rather promising writer of the animalistic school." Crane's characters, he contends, are "types . . . mainly human beings of the order which makes us regret the power of literature to portray them. . . . We resent the sense that we must at certain points resemble them." He bewails the fact that naturalism deals only with man as a low animal, and thus rejects all the higher attainments of men: "Real life is full of the contrasts between these conflicting tendencies, but the object of the animalistic school seems always to make a study of the *genus homo* which shall recall the menagerie at feedingtime rather than human society."

Sedgwick's wit does not mask his growing indignation at the reversal of old orders, both in literature and in real life. When he reviews Bellamy's *Utopia* (1897), he complains that formerly, when a writer reached fifty thousand readers, he was "almost certainly a man of real literary distinction," since the educated were previously almost totally of the upper class, but "now, for every one of these there are a hundred readers who have had all the avenues to speculation opened to them, without ever having been taught to think." Such elitism pervades his criticism and parallels the mistrust of democracy Sedgwick revealed in *The Democratic Mistake.*

In his review of biography and criticism, Sedgwick strikes many of the same notes that he does in his reviews of plays and novels. Trollope's *Thackeray* (1879) allows him to set forth his critical dicta for biographers—"It may be difficult to lay down abstract rules for the guidance of biographers, but one thing is absolutely essential: that they should sympathize with and appreciate their subject." In a later review, of Thomas Raynesford Lounsbury's biography of James Fenimore Cooper, Sedgwick praises the biographer for avoiding "most of the faults of current biography," primarily that "he has not made any attempt to enhance the interest of his subject by tearing away the veil from the privacy of family life, nor to stimulate the appetite of the reader with newly-discovered gossip and scandal, or those petty personal details which make biography so often read like tittle-tattle prepared for the delectation of cooks and chambermaids."

Of contemporary critical movements, Sedgwick had much to say. In his review of Thomas Wentworth Higginson's *Short Studies of American Authors* (1880), Sedgwick discusses impressionistic criticism, calling it "unsystematic." "It professes," he says, "to have no fixed rules or canons. The critic performs his office not by comparing the subject with a standard imposed by the laws of taste, but by 'seeing the thing as it is.'" The value of such criticism "will depend upon his [the impressionistic critic's] capacity for observation, comparison, and reproduction of impressions," a value which Sedgwick seems to find dubious at best. He takes a dim view of aestheticism, which he attacks in his review of Oscar Wilde's lecture on the subject. Wilde, he claims, is not really saying anything new, and besides, since aestheticism is regrettably already here, Wilde is merely preaching to the converted. In reviewing *Twelve Types* (1902), Sedgwick calls Chesterton "a liberal of the latest type–and this, we take it, means a kind of opportunism in matters literary and social, analogous to the opportunism which everybody recognizes as the 'note' of liberalism in the political world."

In two final reviews of critical trends, Sedgwick seems to look back longingly at the old standards of the past. "What the future has in store for us we cannot say," he says in his review of Higginson's *A Reader's History of American Literature* (1903), "but of one thing we may be sure, that all good literature, here as elsewhere, will be produced by those who keep the traditions of good literature alive, and aim, not at Americanism, but excellence." His review of *The Wampum Library of American Literature* sounds the lament of the critic who feels that the old, proper standards have been cast aside, only to be replaced by new-fangled methods of dubious quality: "No doubt we have passed, within a century, quite beyond the old theory of hard and fast canons of taste and judgment, and we all know, or may know if we wish, how to apply the Taine method or the Sainte-Beuve method to the 'Transcendental School,' or to Hawthorne, or to Cooper's novels; but are we really any more at one as to the function of art or criticism than we were when Poe became an editor, or when Lowell wrote the 'Fable for Critics'?" Indeed, Sedgwick sounds like many traditional critics today in an era of rapidly changing methods when he casts his glance to the future. "If we were to hazard a guess," he writes, "we should be inclined to think that the progress of democracy had made criticism everywhere a highly eclectic species of literature, in which what was wanted was not so much balance, measure, and judgment, as some new and catching theory." He goes on: "Reading one after another of these specimens, we are inclined to exclaim, 'What is truth?' when we are recalled to ourselves by recollecting that, according to more than one master, criticism has nothing whatever to do with Truth."

Sedgwick's last contribution to the *Nation* was "The *Nation's* Critics," for the fiftieth anniversary issue, in which he recounts his long association with the magazine, as well as answers charges leveled at the magazine over those fifty years. The summer before, Sedgwick had been injured in an automobile accident and had not fully recovered; in the spring of 1915, he suffered a severe case of pneumonia. A week after his last article appeared, despondent over his ill health, he committed suicide in a Pittsfield, Massachusetts, hotel. In a letter written not long before his own death, Henry James called Sedgwick's suicide a "fine conclusive act, . . . in fact I regard it as an act of high reason, of the finest deliberation in face of all the facts, and of the greatest wisdom and beauty." W. C. Brownell's tribute in the *Nation*, "The Late A. G. Sedgwick," sums up the taste and style of a critic who wrote well, but perhaps outside the main currents of his time: "His taste was sure, and based on the standards, but it was catholic and uninterested in heated and superfine discriminations. . . . His own style–and it was very much his own–was the exact envelope of his way of thinking. It sought no external graces and eschewed the figures of speech, though it had great personal savor and a truly idiosyncratic energy, combined with economy."

References:

W. C. Brownell, "The Late A. G. Sedgwick," *Nation*, 101 (29 July 1915): 146;

Leon Edel, *Henry James: A Life* (New York: Harper & Row, 1985);

Edel, ed., *Henry James Letters: Eighteen Ninety-five to Nineteen Sixteen* (Cambridge: Belknap Press of Harvard University Press, 1984), IV: 774-775;

Allan Nevins, *The Evening Post: A Century of Journalism* (New York: Boni & Liveright, 1922);

Gustave Pollak, *Fifty Years of American Idealism: The New York Nation, 1865-1915* (Boston: Houghton Mifflin, 1915), pp. 15-17.

William G. T. Shedd

(21 June 1820-17 November 1894)

Monica Maria Grecu
University of Nevada at Reno

BOOKS: *Lectures Upon the Philosophy of History* (Andover, Mass.: Draper, 1856);

Discourses and Essays (Andover, Mass.: Draper, 1856; enlarged edition, Andover, Mass.: Draper, 1862);

A History of Christian Doctrine, 2 volumes (New York: Scribners, 1863; Edinburgh: Clark, 1888);

Homiletics and Pastoral Theology (New York: Scribners, 1867; London: Banner of Truth Trust, 1965);

Sermons to the Natural Man (New York: Scribners, 1871);

Orthodoxy and Heterodoxy, a Miscellany (New York: Scribners, 1873);

Theological Essays (New York: Scribner, Armstrong, 1877);

Literary Essays (New York: Scribners, 1878);

Sermons to the Spiritual Man (New York: Scribners, 1884);

The Doctrine of Endless Punishment (New York: Scribners, 1886);

Dogmatic Theology, 3 volumes (New York: Scribners, 1888-1894);

Calvinism: Pure and Mixed; a Defence of the Westminster Standards (New York: Scribners, 1893).

OTHER: *The Complete Works of Samuel Taylor Coleridge,* 7 volumes, edited by Shedd (New York: Harper, 1852).

The Confessions of Augustine, edited, with an introduction, by Shedd (Andover, Mass.: Draper, 1864);

TRANSLATIONS: Franz Theremin, *Eloquence a Virtue; or, Outlines of a Systematic Rhetoric,* translated by Shedd (New York: Wiley, 1850);

Heinrich Ernst Ferdinand Guericke, *A Manual of Church History,* translated by Shedd (Andover, Mass.: Draper/New York: Wiley & Halstead, 1857-1870).

A brilliant exponent of Old Light theology in particular and of Reformation theology in gen-

William Greenough Thayer Shedd

eral, William G. T. Shedd was a biblical scholar who adapted the principles of biblical criticism to the study of literature. In this he was early influenced by James Marsh, under whom he studied at the University of Vermont, who introduced him to the work of Kant and Coleridge. As professor of English literature at the University of Vermont from 1845 to 1852, Shedd was among the first generation of American scholars to teach formally that discipline in American colleges. He did not engage in practical literary criticism as such, but devoted himself to exploring the role that the historical sense could play in critical theory.

By temperament and training Shedd was disposed to systematic and philosophical thought, and these two characteristics provide the basis for his reflections upon literature. He accepted and applied Kant's distinction between the understanding and the reason. According to Kant, understanding operates on the scientific and mathematical level of abstraction, whereas reason imposes mental constructions upon our "objective" world by virtue of knowledge already existing in the human mind. From Coleridge he adopted the distinction between fancy and imagination. Fancy is a faculty which summons up light inventions and fantasies. Imagination, on the other hand, reinterprets reality in order to reach fundamental truths embedded in human experience. To these concepts Shedd grafted theological and historical considerations. He felt that Christian eschatological views had profoundly affected and altered the human view of history by establishing a universal history of substitutionary atonement and subsequent redemption. Hence, history could be seen as a continuum progressing toward morality in which the major way-stations were paganism, Romanism, and finally the Reformation. It stood, then, that post-Reformation literature would also be morally superior. Shedd's exemplar was Milton.

Within this broad historical range Shedd focused on literature as an institutional expression of a nation's character which could be used to analyze a national psychology. His mentors here were undoubtedly Edwards A. Park, the elder Leonard Woods, Moses Stuart, and Edward Robinson, all of whom he knew at Andover Theological Seminary. While humanity constituted one "race," a narrower environmental and genetic inheritance differentiated national groups from one another. The scholar had to familiarize himself with the peculiarities of language that result from that inheritance. Literary study, as a result, required mastery of a number of disciplines: among them, anthropology, philology, general psychology, religious and political history.

Shedd was born the son of Marshall and Eliza Thayer Shedd, both parents representing distinguished New England lines of descent. Following college preparatory work at Westport, New York, he entered the University of Vermont at age fifteen and graduated in 1839. Shortly afterwards he entered Andover Theological Seminary and graduated in 1843. The following year he was ordained a minister. He followed this voca-

THE

COMPLETE WORKS

OF

SAMUEL TAYLOR COLERIDGE.

WITH AN INTRODUCTORY ESSAY

UPON HIS

PHILOSOPHICAL AND THEOLOGICAL OPINIONS.

EDITED BY

PROFESSOR SHEDD.

IN SEVEN VOLUMES.

VOL. I.

NEW YORK:
HARPER & BROTHERS, PUBLISHERS,
Nos. 329 AND 331 PEARL STREET,
FRANKLIN SQUARE.
1871.

Title page for a later edition of Shedd's edition of Coleridge's works

tion only for a short time, from 1843 to 1845 in Brandon, Vermont, and from 1862 to 1863 as co-pastor of the Brick Presbyterian Church in New York City; teaching and scholarship were his true interests. In 1845, the year he accepted the teaching position at the University of Vermont, he married Lucy Ann Myers of Whitehall, New York, by whom he had two daughters and two sons.

All of his literary criticism was written within his seven-year tenure as professor of English at Vermont, although a clear literary interest can be detected throughout his publications. His first published book was a translation of Franz Theremin's *Eloquence a Virtue* (1850), a work highly indebted to current German theories of rhetoric. Shedd's interest in style predisposed him to Theremin, for both men viewed eloquence from an ethical rather than an artistic perspective. It was not a "mere collection of rules" that made rhetoric valuable, but the organic blend of idea and expression a new kind of rhetoric might encourage. Furthermore, Theremin's book addressed the area of moral freedom which Kant had made the prerequisite of pure reason. The book was rich in theory but unfortunately did not lend itself to practical application.

Two years later, during his last year at Vermont, Shedd published a seven-volume edition of Coleridge's work. Shedd's editorial contribution is small, consisting of a long "Introductory Essay" and the excisions of essays by English editors that were deemed unnecessary to an American edition. The remaining volumes are those of the English edition edited by Henry Nelson Coleridge. The "Preliminary Essay" of James Marsh to his 1829 edition of *Aids to Reflection,* so important to Coleridge's reputation in America, was retained, and Shedd extended an affecting tribute to Marsh in his own introduction. It is the philosophical and theological side of Coleridge to which Shedd addresses himself in his introduction, but literary references are not entirely absent. He pays tribute to the "remarkable universality" and "wonderful variety" of Coleridge's genius and argues that, with the exception of Wordsworth, Coleridge had done most to elevate the literature of his time, to promote a sense of style and tone in emerging writers, and to "revolutionize" the period's literary criticism. And he points to *Literary Remains* as "unquestionably the best philosophy of Art and of Criticism, and the very best actual criticism upon the great creative minds in Literature" which one might find. The question of Coleridge's plagiarism is directly confronted and resolved in Coleridge's favor, though Shedd apparently finds disturbing the "striking" parallels in conception, statement, and trains of discussion with the work of Schelling and Jacobi.

In 1852 Shedd resigned from the University of Vermont to accept a position as professor of sacred rhetoric and pastoral theology at Auburn Theological Seminary. In the winter of 1853-1854 he gave a series of prelections in the Department of Ecclesiastical History, published in 1856 as *Lectures Upon the Philosophy of History.* By then he had already been a professor of church history at Andover Theological Seminary for two years. The book contains his most extended statement on the historical spirit. After observing that historical theory depends upon an "antecedent idea" which exists a priori in the mind, Shedd

quickly turns to its explication. History is defined as development: continuous, organic, and dynamic. In short, the investigator "never comes to a point where there are no connected antecedents until he reaches the beginning of human history, where the basis for the whole process was laid by a fiat, supernatural, and creative." Shedd's observation ascribes an origin to historical process which allows him to take issue with those materialists who posit motion in matter. He denies that there can be "evolution of heterogeneous germs out of homogeneous ones," a shading of one species into another, or development in terms of upward improvement.

This view of history is a central theme in the essays published as *Discourses and Essays* (1856), the majority of which were written during his Vermont years and three of which bear directly on literature. The essay on rhetoric adds little to what he had said in his translation of Theremin, though it is better phrased and the analyses run deeper. In a consideration of language and style, Shedd has some interesting things to say. He sees language as man's supreme accomplishment: pliant, precise, and vital, infinitely superior in range to the particularized expression of poetry and oratory. Sincerity becomes the gauge of style. Some styles correspond to the spirit of the age, while other, personal styles undergo great changes corresponding to particular stages in the author's development. Throughout, however, good writers are faithful to those variations of thought. As riveting as style might be, Shedd nevertheless upholds the side of man as opposed to language or style. Language and style are manifestations of human discourse, but the mind as the originating power should remain "the chief object of culture."

Much the same thing is said in his forceful essay on "The True Nature of the Beautiful, and Its Relation to Culture." As a good Platonist he sees Beauty, Truth, and Good as archetypal ideas which form a basis for the elements of culture so that art falls under the aegis of Beauty. But Shedd links beauty to a preoccupation with form without substance. Art may contain Truth and Good, but only as the means to its primary purpose of formally addressing the imagination. Shedd turns to history to demonstrate that too particular a focus on Beauty leads to cultural enervation and decline. History empirically reveals that only when Truth and Good constitute the substance of art, with Beauty but a "property and shadow," does a culture grow in strength and

Shedd in a portrait by Mathew Brady (Library of Congress, Brady-Handy Collection)

grandeur. The golden ages of Greece and Rome occurred when their art was "intellectual and moral, rather than aesthetic." Similarly, the superiority of Teutonic art to Italian can be attributed to the primacy it gives to intellect and morality: Teutonic art has "given origin to all the literatures, philosophies, and systems of government and religion, that constitute the crowning glory of the modern world." In English literature the Elizabethan age and the example of Milton confirm the feasibility of preferring substance to form, whereas the age of Queen Anne and younger romantics such as Keats reveal what can happen when the imagination is not seen in its proper perspective, that is, when it is too subservient to traditional literary forms or is left unbridled.

The last collection of essays on humanistic studies that Shedd published is *Literary Essays* (1878), mainly an anthology of articles written in the 1850s. A reprint of "The True Nature of the Beautiful, and Its Relation to Culture" begins the

book, and in his preface Shedd justifies this position by claiming that the essay is "the key-note to the whole" insofar as it reveals the "unity and system" of his approach. This unity rests on his conviction that the study and welfare of human beings is the proper subject of the scholar, to which all other considerations must be subordinate. The goal is intellectual virtue, though he does not discount moral virtue. The venality and profligacy of the Reconstruction period made clear that America had somehow lost intellectual discipline and had to regain it. A "national malady" was abroad, marked by frivolity, sensuality, and a "modern softening of the brain." The only feasible counter, Shedd thinks, is to accept these facts and seek to regain a sense of historical purpose.

Of the various essays on rhetoric, education, national and racial character, as well as theological considerations, "The Influence and Method of English Studies," first published in *Bibliotheca Sacra* in 1856, most typifies Shedd's point of view. His Teutonism disinclined him from giving serious consideration to the literatures of the "southern races," and between the literatures of Germany and England he preferred the latter on grounds of scope and "masculine vigor." His main contention is that philological familiarity with the English vernacular is necessary to an understanding and appreciation of the literature. In comprehending the beauty of the Middle English of Chaucer we equip ourselves to best comprehend the flowering of the Elizabethan period—to Shedd representative of England's highest cultural achievement. Milton's centrality to what is excellent in English literature is reaffirmed, and following Wordsworth and Coleridge he sees in the younger romantics and in Tennyson a sad falling off into syrupy "feminism."

In 1874 Union Theological Seminary appointed Shedd Professor of Systematic Theology. He remained in that position until 1890, when he retired. Four years later Shedd died, survived by his wife and four children. *Dogmatic Theology* (1888-1894) was his last major published work. As a vigorous exposition of Reformation theology, it is second only to the work of Jonathan Edwards. It is obvious, in reviewing his work, that theology was Shedd's metadiscipline. Basically he was a religious humanist, his work all of a piece, in which literature was enlisted on the side of intellect and cultural scholarship. The spirit of quest is less apparent than a sincere, earnest presentation of a point of view grounded in a fixed and unwavering theology. Like Edwards before him he set himself in opposition to a prevailing liberalism, and like Edwards he lost. What one appreciates is his dignified level of discourse and his commitment to the life of the mind.

Reference:

John DeWitt, "William Greenough Thayer Shedd," *Presbyterian and Reformed Review*, 5 (April 1895): 295-322.

Edmund Clarence Stedman
(8 October 1833-18 January 1908)

Robert J. Scholnick
College of William and Mary

SELECTED BOOKS: *Poems, Lyrical and Idyllic* (New York: Scribners, 1860);

Alice of Monmouth: An Idyl of the Great War, with Other Poems (New York: Carelton/London: Low, 1863);

The Blameless Prince and Other Poems (Boston: Fields, Osgood, 1869);

The Poetical Works of Edmund Clarence Stedman (Boston: Osgood, 1873; enlarged edition, Boston: Houghton, Mifflin, 1884);

Victorian Poets (Boston: Houghton, Osgood, 1875); revised and enlarged edition, Boston & New York: Houghton, Mifflin/London: Chatto & Windus, 1887);

Favorite Poems (Boston: Osgood, 1877);

Hawthorne and Other Poems (Boston: Osgood, 1877);

Lyrics and Idylls, with Other Poems (London: Kegan Paul, 1879);

Edgar Allan Poe (Boston: Houghton, Mifflin/London: Low, Marston, Searle & Rivington, 1881);

Poets of America (Boston & New York: Houghton, Mifflin/London: Chatto & Windus, 1885);

The Nature and Elements of Poetry (Boston & New York: Houghton, Mifflin/London: Cassell, 1892);

Poems Now First Collected (Boston & New York: Houghton, Mifflin, 1897);

The Poems of Edmund Clarence Stedman (Boston & New York: Houghton Mifflin, 1908);

Genius and Other Essays (New York: Moffat, Yard, 1911).

OTHER: *A Library of American Literature from the Earliest Settlement to the Present Time*, 11 volumes, edited by Stedman and Ellen M. Hutchinson (New York: Webster, 1888-1890);

The Works of Edgar Allan Poe, 10 volumes, edited by Stedman and George E. Woodbury (Chicago: Stone & Kimball, 1894-1895);

A Victorian Anthology, 1837-1895, edited by Stedman (Boston & New York: Houghton, Mifflin, 1895);

An American Anthology, 1787-1900, edited by Stedman (Boston: Houghton, Mifflin, 1901; London: Gay & Bird, 1901);

The New York Stock Exchange; Its History, Its Contribution to National Prosperity, and Its Relation to American Finance, 2 volumes, edited by Stedman (New York: Stock Exchange Historical Company, 1905).

On 26 April 1888 Walt Whitman told his young friend Horace Traubel that "I advise everybody to read Stedman. Stedman is an education. I do not deny him power." Whitman's recommendation of the New York-based poet, critic, anthologist, and literary scholar was not, however, unqualified. Speaking particularly of Stedman's criticism, Whitman commented, "But I do not think him conclusive—beyond him is another Stedman whom he never seems able to reach." The problem, Whitman observed, is that "Stedman always feels that he must be judicial—the dominance of that principle has held him down from many a noble flight. Stedman seems often just about to get off for a long voyage and stops himself on the shore." Nevertheless, Whitman considered Stedman "our most generous

Photograph made in 1903 by Frederick Stuart Stedman

man of letters" and "our best man in his speciality—criticism." At the time of Whitman's conversation with Traubel, Stedman had published two critical studies that had become standards: *Victorian Poets* (1875) and *Poets of America* (1885). He was then completing work on the eleven-volume *Library of American Literature* (1888-1890), an anthology of works in a variety of forms drawn, as the subtitle indicates, "from the earliest settlement to the present day." A champion of the widely scorned Poe and Whitman, an outspoken opponent of didacticism and moralism, Stedman, through his wide-ranging criticism and scholarship, did more than anyone else in the late nineteenth century to define the American tradition in literature and lay the groundwork for American literary scholarship as it is known today.

Still, what Whitman termed the "dominance" of the "judicial principle" severely limited Stedman's ability to respond to the new. He perceived realistic prose fiction as a threat to the traditional supremacy of poetry, and so slighted the most vital literary expression of the time—clearly

a serious limitation of his criticism. Stedman's formal aesthetic statement, *The Nature and Elements of Poetry* (1892), stresses only those elements which differentiate poetry from prose and thus propounds an unsupportably grand view of the poet and his function.

Stedman was born in Hartford, Connecticut, on 8 October 1833. Tragically, his father, Edmund Burke Stedman, died of consumption in December 1835, leaving his young wife Elizabeth Clementine Dodge Stedman to care for Stedman and a second son, Charles Frederick, born only five months before his father's death. Her husband, a lumber merchant, did not leave Elizabeth enough money to support her family, and so she was forced to take up residence in the Plainfield, New Jersey, home of her parents. Her father, David Low Dodge, a staunch Calvinist and prosperous New York merchant, refused to be the sole support of the boys. The boys' paternal grandfather agreed to contribute to his grandsons' education but only if they were sent to Norwich, Connecticut, to live with his brother James, a lawyer and classicist who "raised" boys as a means of supplementing his income. Their mother, who as Elizabeth Kinney would achieve a modest reputation as a poet in the 1860s, attempted to earn enough money to support her family by publishing prose and poetry in *Godey's, Knickerbocker,* and other magazines. But the monetary returns were insufficient, and the young widow was forced to send each son to Norwich when he reached the age of six.

For the preternaturally sensitive and precocious Ned Stedman, as the boy was called, the separation from his mother was particularly painful. Mother and first-born son shared a love for poetry. As his mother recalled, "as soon as he could speak, he lisped in rhyme, and as soon as he could write, he gave shape and measure to his dreams. Often on being put to bed, when he was between five and six, he would get on his knees, bury his head in the pillow, and if told to lie down and go to sleep, would answer, 'Let me alone, please, the *poetry* is coming.' " It is understandable, then, why the separation from his mother was a traumatic experience. As Stedman wrote in 1875 to the Boston writer Thomas Wentworth Higginson, a distant relative, he was raised in the "Calvinistic back-country, where I was injured for *life,* and almost perished of repression and atrophy."

Young Stedman's loss was compounded by a deep sense of rejection when his mother married William B. Kinney in 1841 and she acceded to her husband's decision not to allow the two Stedman boys to come live with them. The birth of two daughters to his mother and her new husband exacerbated Stedman's sense of abandonment and deprivation. A Newark editor, Kinney became American chargé d'affaires in Turin in 1850, and Stedman, then a Yale freshman, had to watch from the dock as his mother sailed away with her husband and their two daughters to Italy. When he returned to New Haven for his sophomore year, he suffered from a sense of abandonment, and so, he later recalled, "from utter loneliness, trouble, and inexperience, I fell into the dissipation that drew me from my proper studies." For his rather harmless mischief making about the streets of New Haven, Stedman was rusticated to Northampton, Massachusetts, where he got into yet more trouble and was permanently separated from Yale.

The chastened, repentant Stedman returned to Norwich determined to atone for his transgression and "to accomplish something that

Stedman in 1851 (daguerreotype by Case)

would gain me an honorable name." After reading law for a short period, in 1852 he purchased a weekly paper with an associate. The next year, on 23 November 1853, he eloped with Laura Hyde Woodworth, a seamstress. Then, after dissolving his newspaper partnership in Norwich, Stedman moved to Winstead, Connecticut, where he became a partner, with Stephen A. Hubbard, in the *Mountain County Herald.* Despite his growing success as an editor, Stedman still dreamed of a literary career. His Tennysonian "Amavi" appeared in *Putnam's Monthly* in October 1854, but he found that his responsibilities as editor left little time for composition. In 1855 he moved to New York, working first for a clock company and then as a real estate and general commission broker. His plan was to earn his living as a businessman during the day and devote his evenings and vacations to art.

His early friends in New York were the poets Richard Henry Stoddard, his wife Elizabeth Barstow Stoddard, Bayard Taylor, and Thomas Bailey Aldrich, all devoted to poetry as an expression of beauty—in contrast to the didacticism associated with the New England tradition. As he recalled in a 1906 essay, "Stoddard's Last Poem," the poems of Stoddard, Taylor, Aldrich, as well as those of his own, "were fresh with the ardor of a new clan, devoted to poetry for its own sake, to art and beauty and feeling; and this in no spirit of preciosity, but as a departure from—though not a revolt against—the moralizing and reformatory propaganda, howsoever great in purpose and achievement, of the venerated 'elder bards'" of New England. Yet, as a poet, Stedman could never free himself from the inhibiting influence of his New England predecessors. He did not see the necessity of "revolt." His liberation would come only through criticism.

For most of the next fifty-five years—until he sold his seat on the New York Stock Exchange in 1900—Stedman attempted to reconcile the demands of two very different lives: financial speculation and art. Unfortunately, he suffered from the vicissitudes of an erratic, barely regulated stock market; periods of prosperity would be followed by serious reverses, and at the end of his life he was barely solvent. The extraordinary demands of his divided life left him little concentrated time for composition, and the separation of his literary life from his daily business endeavors undermined his attempts to create a unified, lasting body of work. However, he continued to write poetry throughout his life, producing his first volume, *Poems, Lyrical and Idyllic*, in 1860.

Although over the course of his career he would regularly publish volumes of poetry and his work was welcome at such magazines as the *Atlantic Monthly* and *Scribner's Magazine*, he never fulfilled his ambitions as a creative artist. As he wrote in an 1879 essay on Bayard Taylor, "Men do not escape from tasks they once assume, and he had undertaken to earn a large income, and survey the world, on the one hand, and to hold the Muse by her pinions on the other. His poetry had to be composed 'between spells,' and on the wing." Stedman undertook to succeed in the stock market, earn a large income, and be a leading figure in the New York literary and artistic circle that centered around the Century Club; his poetry, itself "composed . . . on the wing," was not his central purpose, and so his own creative work would continue to disappoint him.

Stedman spent the early years of the Civil War as a reporter for the *New York World*. Based in Washington, he also traveled in the field with the troops. But when his paper wavered in its support of the war effort he left journalism, accepting a clerkship in the office of the Attorney General, Edward Bates. He joined a commercial banking firm in 1863 and in 1864 opened his own brokerage firm. But Stedman allowed his commission business to expand beyond his ability to handle it, and he began to lose money in his own trading account through inattention.

To escape the intense pressures of this life, he temporarily withdrew from business early in 1865, devoting his mornings to translating the Greek poets Theocritus, Bion, and Moscus into English hexameters. When he visited his old haunts in Wall Street in the afternoons, he felt himself to be the "Pan in Wall Street" of his characteristic poem of this time. Pan sounded "a strange, wild strain" which was heard "high above the modern clamor,/Above the cries of greed and gain,/The curbstone war, the auction's hammer." For the first time Stedman devoted himself seriously to criticism, publishing a theoretical essay, "Elements of the Art of Poetry," in the New York magazine *Galaxy* in July 1866 and "English Poetry of the Period" in Boston's *North American Review* issue of the same month. These early essays would set the direction of Stedman's career as critic.

"English Poetry of the Period" is an essay-review of Richard Henry Stoddard's anthology *The Late English Poets* (1865). Drawing a comparison with the Alexandrian period, Stedman characterizes the contemporary age as intellectual, introspective, and critical. But the poets, Stedman charges, are unable to distance themselves from their times and produce lasting work. With the exception of Alfred Tennyson, Robert Browning, and Matthew Arnold, contemporary English poetry is "lacking in freshness, synthetical art, and sustained imaginative power." In "Elements of the Art of Poetry," Stedman, defining poetry as "rhythmical, imaginative language interpreting nature," calls upon the poet to display the high imaginative power so notably absent in contemporary poetry and somehow transcend the restrictions of an unpoetical era.

Yet, Stedman was unable to produce the elevated, spontaneous poetry which his theory demanded. His mistake was in thinking that poetry could supply the high imaginative satisfaction of the Renaissance and Romantic eras, even in the prosaic 1860s and 1870s. As a poet, then, he cut himself off from a vital relationship with his own time. He refused to exploit his genuine talent for light, comic verse of the sort that was in great demand and which paid well, and he would become dissatisfied with the "magazine poems," which he could turn out easily, but which seemed to mean little. He nevertheless recognized, as he

Stedman's 1861 letter to Richard and Elizabeth Stoddard expressing his condolence for the death of their son Wilson (Laura Stedman and George M. Gould, Life and Letters of Edmund Clarence Stedman, *1910)*

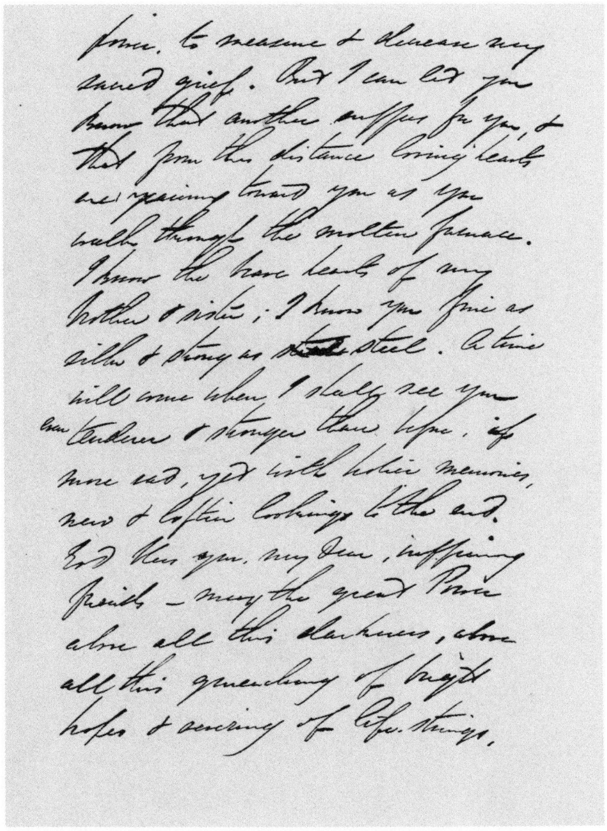

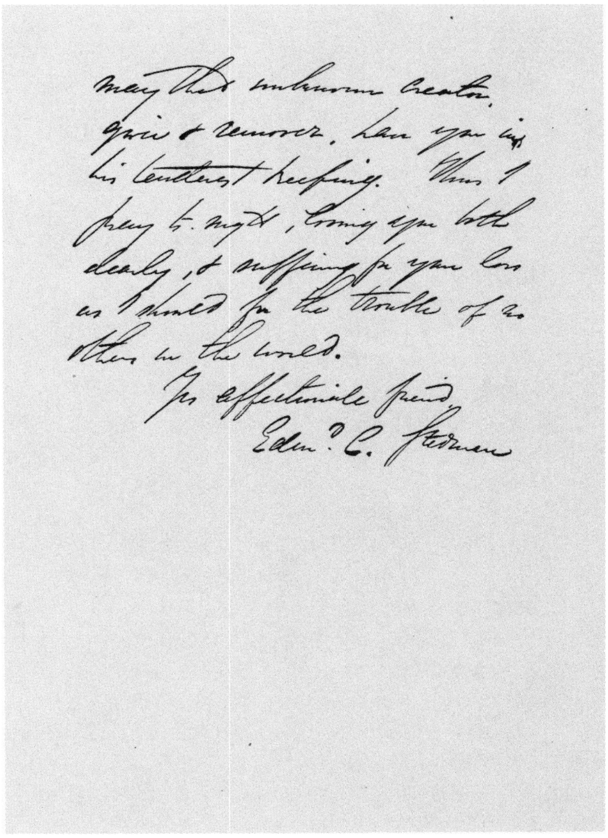

wrote to a friend, a "kind of dogged, critical faculty within me" and so returned to criticism. In November 1871 the *Atlantic Monthly* published "Tennyson and Theocritus," an essay extending the comparison between the Alexandrian and Victorian periods of "English Poetry of the Period" by brilliantly demonstrating the extraordinary parallels in the work of Theocritus and Tennyson, both dominant voices of their respective ages. The critical success of this essay prompted Stedman to write an extended study of contemporary British poetry.

Stedman arranged to publish in *Scribner's Monthly* a series of essays (collected as *Victorian Poets*) on "the lives and productions of such British poets as have gained reputation within the last forty years." Affirming Hippolyte Taine's critical principle that the literary scholar must examine "the insensible molding of an author's life, genius, manner of expression, by the conditions of race, circumstances, and period in which he is seen to be involved," Stedman placed the work of both major and minor poets in the context of the period. Still, he allowed for the ability of the literary genius "to overcome all restrictions, create their own styles, and even . . . determine the lyrical character of a period." Hence, after a general essay exploring the intellectual characteristics of the period, he devoted essays to the major poets Walter Savage Landor, Elizabeth Barrett Browning, Alfred Tennyson, Robert Browning, Matthew Arnold (treated with Thomas Hood and Bryan Waller Proctor) and Algernon Charles Swinburne. He concluded with an essay on Dante Gabriel Rossetti, William Morris, and Robert Buchanan and another on the minor poets. Reflecting the influence of Taine and aware that the temper of the age was scientific, Stedman attempted to proceed systematically, producing a more disciplined and systematic criticism than was being practiced in America.

Writing in *The Victorian Poets: A Guide to Research* (1968) Jerome H. Buckley has provided a summary of Stedman's achievement in *Victorian Poets,* praising him for being "the earliest to prepare a substantial critique" of the entire period "without special bias" and for being "less reluctant than some later critics to reach general conclusions." Assuming that the "Victorian era is virtually at an end," Stedman, as Buckley writes, "argued that poetry must now move in new directions. The Victorian poets, as Stedman sees them, have been highly self-conscious and distrustful of emotion, modern men living in an 'age of

Laura Hyde Woodworth Stedman in 1864 (photograph by Mathew Brady)

prose.' . . . They 'have flourished in an equatorial region of common-sense and demonstrable knowledge,' and some of them have been beguiled by 'Science, the modern Circe, from their voyage to Hesperides' and transformed 'into voiceless devotees.' But the best, finding in art relief from an unaesthetic time, have achieved a formal excellence much to be admired. . . . But by 1875 the virtuosity of Swinburne seems to have carried expression to its ultimate extreme. . . . The hope for poetry lies only in a return to dramatic themes." Buckley concludes by observing that Stedman's "criticism, Arnoldian as it is in tone, relates Victorian poetry to the context of an analytic age and emphasizes a problem still too often neglected by the scholar: the problem of style." *Victorian Poets,* Stedman's first book of criticism, became a popular as well as a critical success. Stedman revised the book and added a "Supplementary Review" of later poets for the thirteenth edition, published in 1887. Such was the demand that Houghton, Mifflin, successor to Osgood, published new editions regularly, the last in 1917.

The strain of writing *Victorian Poets* while simultaneously running his brokerage business and trying to function as a poet was so great that as 1874 came to an end, the harried Stedman felt himself on the verge of a nervous breakdown. He escaped from the pressures of his dual career by taking a long Caribbean vacation, explaining to Whitelaw Reid, editor of the *New York Tribune,* "I don't know whether it's the stock-side of my head that's given way, or the book-side–but they don't trot together any longer. I make a living in Wall Street, but it is an incessant strain, and if I go back there next Fall, I shall run down again. Neither can I stand daily writing."

When Stedman returned to New York following his Caribbean vacation, he faced a difficult stock market and was forced to devote long hours to his business simply to remain solvent. He had little time for criticism, but did occasionally accept an invitation to write a poem for some special event. Most notably, he delivered the popular "Hawthorne" as the Phi Beta Kappa poem at Harvard in 1877. The sudden death of his close friend and literary ally Bayard Taylor in December 1878 provided the necessary impetus for him to begin his long-delayed history of American poetry. His essay on Taylor, which appeared in *Scribner's Monthly* in November 1879, unsparingly revealed the limitations of Taylor's art, treating him as an example of a talented writer whose life was "consecrated to poetry but not dedicated to it." A penetrating analysis of Taylor's failed career, the essay is also a tacit admission on Stedman's part of his own limitations as a creative artist. The writing of this essay was the necessary first step in his major revaluation of his American contemporaries and immediate predecessors in *Poets of America.*

Stedman clearly signaled his intention to challenge the accepted shape of the tradition by publishing in *Scribner's Monthly* appreciative essays on two poets who were widely thought to be disreputable, Poe (May 1880) and Whitman (November 1880). In "Our Garnered Names," published in the October 1878 issue of *Scribner's Monthly,* the journal's moralistic and powerful editor, Josiah Gilbert Holland, had attacked Whitman for his immorality as well as his "abominable dissonances" and also excoriated Poe, whose works he termed "the crazy products of a crazy mind." Holland heaped praise on the established luminaries of American literature, and included Stedman on the list of significant poets. But now Stedman

used the pages of Holland's influential middle-class monthly to deflate the reputations of the "garnered names" of American poetry: Bryant, Whittier, Longfellow, Holmes, and Lowell. He had the ability to write appreciatively of these figures, identifying their genuine achievements while reducing their overinflated statures. He continued Poe's attack on the didacticism and moralism of the New England worthies.

In *Poets of America,* the first critical history of the subject, Stedman successfully balances Poe's emphasis on beauty of expression with Emerson's orphic vision. Emerson he treats as the "forerunner and inspirer, and when the true poet shall come to America, it will be because such an one as Emerson has gone before him and prepared the way for his song, his vision, and his recognition." Stedman's most important book, *Poets of America* remains a penetrating analysis of American poetry.

In the concluding chapter Stedman conceded the artistic insignificance of his own generation. "There is, if not a decadence, at least a poetic interregnum," he wrote. Prose fiction had become the important form; significant poetry was not being published. But Stedman, of course, could not admit defeat. As a way out, he sensibly urged poets to learn from novelists, who "depict *Life* as it is, though rarely as yet in its intenser phases." If the poets learn to write more dramatically, depicting "individuals, men and women, various and real," then, Stedman predicted, there would be a new "dawn," a new era of poetic greatness. Here he did help point the way; in the 1890s the work of such young poets as Edwin Arlington Robinson and Stephen Crane was notable for its strongly dramatic qualities.

While working on *Poets of America* Stedman agreed to produce a full-scale anthology of American literature. His extensive research into the earliest periods of American literary history left its mark on the introductory chapters of *Poets of America.* Speaking of Moses Coit Tyler's *History of American Literature* (1878), he observes, "How hard for our amiable historian to make poetical finds that can lighten the pages of his record!" The colonial American poets, Stedman asserts, "were simply third-rate British rhymsters, who copied the pedantry of the tamest period known. The only marks of distinction between their prose and verse were that, while the former might be dull, the latter must be, and must pay a stilted regard to measure and rhyme."

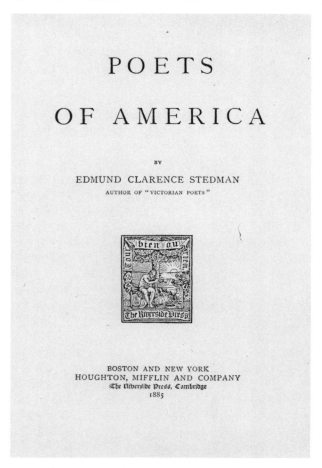

POETS

OF AMERICA

BY

EDMUND CLARENCE STEDMAN

AUTHOR OF "VICTORIAN POETS"

BOSTON AND NEW YORK
HOUGHTON, MIFFLIN AND COMPANY
The Riverside Press, Cambridge
1885

*Title page for Stedman's landmark critical history of
American poetry*

Clearly Stedman underestimates the work of Anne Bradstreet and others. His major thesis, however, is that the literary historian must look "elsewhere" for "the manifest, the sincere genius of the colonies . . . than in their laborious verse." And Stedman knew where to look: "Noble English and a simple, heroic wonder give zest to the writings of the early chroniclers, the annals of discovery and adventure. Such traits distinguish the narratives of the gallant and poetic Captain John Smith, and of Strachey, whose picture of a storm and wreck in the Bermudas so roused the spirit that conceived 'The Tempest.' They pervade the memorials of Bradford and Winthrop, of Johnson and Gooken, of Francis Higginson and Winslow and William Wood. There are power and imagination in the discourses of the great preachers—Hooker, Cotton, Roger Williams, Oakes. . . . Law, religious fervor, superstition, were then the strength of life; and the time that produced Increase and Cotton Mather fostered a

progeny quite as striking and characteristic as the melodists of our late Arcadian morn."

This statement expresses the critical rationale for his *A Library of American Literature,* which would be published in eleven volumes in the years 1888-1890 by Samuel Clemens's publishing firm, Charles L. Webster and Co. If American literature is to be found, Stedman is saying, the writing produced on this continent must be approached on its terms. It makes little sense to measure the American literary genius entirely by its achievement in the established forms of British literature. Instead, it is necessary to widen the conception of the nature of literature itself, and accept as literature such forms as sermons, travel accounts, spirituals, and folk songs. At a time of pervasive Anglophilia, when, as Howard Mumford Jones has written, "the inference that American topics, American genius, and American culture were inevitably barren was extensively discussed," Stedman demonstrated the existence of an American literary tradition by presenting lively examples in a variety of forms that spoke for themselves.

In this endeavor Stedman was moved by the broad literary nationalism of Walt Whitman, whose poetry was well represented in *A Library of American Literature.* As Stedman wrote Whitman in sending him the first seven volumes as a gift, "*You* will justly estimate its significance, and this quite irrespectively of its literary or artistic qualities. There are masterpieces in it. But it is *not* a collection of masterpieces: it is something of more moment to you and me. It is *America.* It is the symbolic, the essential, America from her infancy to the second Century of her grand Republic. It is the diary, the year-book, the Century-book, of her progress from Colonialism to Nationality. All her health and disease are here: her teething, measles, mumps, joy, delirium, nuptials, conflicts, dreams, delusions, her meanness and her nobility. We purposely make the work *inclusive*—trying to show every facet of this our huge, as yet half-cut rose-diamond."

A Library of American Literature deserves credit for giving strong support to at least five ideas which have come to undergird the study of American literature today. First and most important, through the extent and quality of its selections, many of which were simply not otherwise available, it presented American literature as a distinct and unified body of work. Secondly, drawing this literature from the "earliest settlement," it showed the importance of approaching our liter-

Stedman in 1879 (photograph by Mora)

ature with a historical sense. It also demonstrated the value of interpreting major writers in the context of lesser authors from the same period. And by the force of the vitality of its works in a variety of forms, it expanded the canon, at the same time serving to broaden the definition of literature beyond the belletristic. Clearly, the field of American literature, especially in the earlier periods, would not exist had it been confined to drama, poetry, and fiction. Finally, it presented the national literature organically, that is, as reflecting a natural and evolving relationship between the development of the national life and changing literary forms. Although Stedman was not a professional literary scholar, his work on *A Library of American Literature* helped prepare the way for academic scholarship and study in American literature as it exists today. For instance, in 1917 the editors of the *Cambridge Literary History* wrote that it had proven "indispensable" to their work.

The costly project was a critical and popular success, but a commercial disaster. The expensive books were sold by subscription, but because of mismanagement of this aspect of the business by

Clemens's firm, Stedman's monumental work proved to be a tremendous drain on the resources of the company and contributed to its bankruptcy in 1894.

A significant impetus for Stedman's next important work, *The Nature and Elements of Poetry* (1892), was his friend William Dean Howells's review of *Poets of America* in his "Editor's Study" column in *Harper's Monthly* in March 1886. There he took issue with Stedman's confident prediction of a revival of poetry. Noting that no one took poetry seriously anymore, Howells wrote that "If . . . we are now at the end of our great poets for the present, we do not know that we shall altogether despair." The champion of Critical Realism and prose fiction, Howells warned against the excesses of the poet, the bard, the self-involved and self-styled "genius," whose work did not contribute to the social consciousness that was vitally important to him at this time. In fact, the egalitarian Howells doubted the very existence of genius as a factor in achievement in literature or elsewhere.

Stedman responded with his essay "Genius," published in the *New Princeton Review* in September 1886. Drawing from the statements of philosophers from Plato to Schopenhauer and von Hartmann, as well as the examples of great artists such as Mozart, Stedman defined genius as a quality "*inborn*, not alone with respect to bodily dexterity and the fabric of the brain, but as appertaining to the power and bent of the soul itself." Stedman framed his conception of the genius as inspired truth-teller in order to insure that the great poet would remain a conspicuous example of the literary genius. It remained for him to develop his thesis and justify the ways of poetry in an age of prose realism.

In the spring of 1891 he accepted an invitation to inaugurate the Turnbull lectureship in poetry at Johns Hopkins University, delivering a series of lectures that would become *The Nature and Elements of Poetry*. Feeling himself to be on the defensive, he adopted the self-defeating strategy of attempting to prove the superiority of poetry by stressing its high, spiritual elements–just those qualities which differentiate poetry from prose. For him poetry was, to use the title of his concluding chapter, "The Faculty Divine: Passion, Insight, Genius, Faith." He emphasizes the truth-telling powers of poetry, not its aesthetic or formal qualities. According to Stedman, Emerson, "our seer of seers," takes precedence over Poe, the foe of didacticism and exponent of beauty. Stedman is moved to give the true poet virtually God-like powers: "As far as the poet, the artist, is creative, he becomes a sharer of the divine imagination and power, and even of the divine responsibility." For the poet has the function of portraying the elements of our world not "as they are, but as they are or may be at their best. This lifts them out of the common, or, rather, it is thus we get at the 'power and mystery of common things.' His most audacious imaginings are within the felt possibilities of nature. But the use of poetry is to make us believe also in the impossible." As was not the case in his practical criticism, Stedman holds his ideal poet to an impossible standard as truth-giver, and no real-life poet could live up to it.

In the decade of the 1890s Stedman, while continuing his brokerage business, produced several impressive scholarly and editorial projects. With George E. Woodbury he edited *The Works of Edgar Allan Poe*, a ten-volume edition published by the young Chicago firm of Stone and Kimball in 1894-1895. In 1895 he also produced *A Victorian Anthology*, conceived as a companion to *Victorian Poets*, published twenty years before. And in 1901 he compiled another massive anthology of poetry, *An American Anthology, 1787-1900*. In their day these two volumes were praised as masterpieces of the anthologist's art, and the American work, which included virtually all American poets—major, minor, and justly forgotten—was hailed as an authoritative demonstration of the range and extent of the American poetic achievement. But as anthologist Stedman lacked that which Whitman had charged dominated his criticism: the "judicial principle."

Stedman took particular pleasure in including such younger poets as Edwin Arlington Robinson, William Vaughn Moody, and Stephen Crane. Here he represented the generation of American poets who would find a way to escape the "twilight interval" whose features he had analyzed acutely. And as Harriet Monroe, the founder of *Poetry* magazine, had observed, Stedman was a generous "friend and helper" to many of these younger artists, assisting them in placing their work, entertaining them in his suburban Bronxville home, and—perhaps most importantly—lending a sympathetic ear to their work. In his role as elder statesman, Stedman, who had "almost perished from repression and atrophy" as a child cruelly separated from his mother, was able to serve as a father figure, ex-

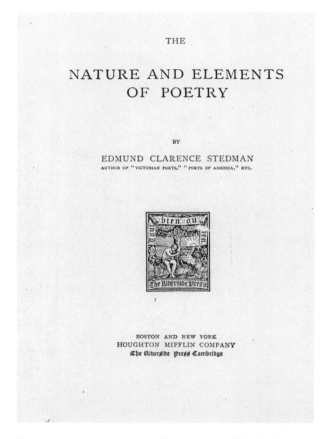

THE

NATURE AND ELEMENTS
OF POETRY

BY

EDMUND CLARENCE STEDMAN
AUTHOR OF "VICTORIAN POETS," "POETS OF AMERICA," ETC.

BOSTON AND NEW YORK
HOUGHTON MIFFLIN COMPANY
The Riverside Press Cambridge

Title page for the collection of lectures in which Stedman attempts to prove the superiority of poetry over prose

tending a generous concern for the works and lives of his young friends.

But at last the strain of Stedman's fractured existence caught up with him. In 1899 he suffered a serious heart attack and the next year he sold his seat on the stock exchange and retired from business. Although he had spent a lifetime on Wall Street, he was far from being a wealthy man. In fact, he had spent the previous seventeen years paying off debts incurred when his elder son, Frederick Stuart, who had joined him in business, embezzled large sums from the firm. His younger son, Arthur, assisted him on such literary projects as *A Library of American Literature* and was also a free-lance editor, bringing out editions of Melville and Whitman, but he remained financially and emotionally dependent upon his parents until he died in 1906. The year before, Stedman's wife, Laura, had died. Such was Stedman's financial condition that, despite his weak health and personal losses, he still had to depend on his journalism to make ends meet. Financial necessity, not a genuine interest in the subject, led him to edit *The New York Stock Exchange* which was published in two volumes in 1905. He was loyally and skillfully assisted in his various literary projects in the last years of his life by his granddaughter Laura Stedman, the daughter of his elder son, Frederick.

On 18 January 1908 Stedman succumbed to a massive heart attack. Characteristically, the night before he died he outlined to the young poet and playwright Percy McKaye his plans to write a critical history of American poetry of the first decade of the new century. But as critic, scholar, anthologist, and man of letters Stedman had already made a singularly original and valuable contribution to the comprehension and enjoyment of American literature.

Letters:

Laura Stedman and George M. Gould, *The Life and Letters of Edmund Clarence Stedman,* 2 volumes (New York: Moffat, Yard, 1910);

Edmund W. Gosse, *Transatlantic Dialogue: Selected American Correspondence,* edited by Paul F. Matthiesen and Michael Millgate (Austin: University of Texas Press, 1965).

References:

Jerome H. Buckley, "General Materials," in *The Victorian Poets: A Guide to Research,* second edition, edited by Frederic E. Faverty (Cambridge: Harvard University Press, 1968), pp. 1-32;

Richard Cary, *The Genteel Circle* (Ithaca: Cornell University Press, 1952);

George DeMille, *Literary Criticism in America* (New York: Dial, 1931);

Margaret Fuller, *A New England Childhood* (Boston: Little, Brown, 1916);

Thomas W. Higginson, *Carlyle's Laugh* (Boston: Houghton Mifflin, 1909);

William Dean Howells, "Editor's Easy Chair," *Harper's Monthly,* 81 (February 1911): 471-474;

Howard Mumford Jones, "Introduction," in *American Prose Masters,* by William Cary Brownell (Cambridge: Harvard University Press, 1967);

Ralph N. Miller, "Associationist Psychology and Stedman's Theory of Poetry," *Markham Review,* 5 (Summer 1976): 65-71;

John Paul Pritchard, *Criticism in America* (Norman: University of Oklahoma Press, 1956);

Robert J. Scholnick, *Edmund Clarence Stedman* (Boston: Twayne, 1977);

Scholnick, "The Shadowed Years: Mrs. Richards, Mr. Stedman and Robinson," *Colby Library Quarterly,* 9 (June 1972): 510-531;

Willard Thorp, "Defenders of Ideality," in *Literary History of the United States,* third revised edition, edited by Robert E. Spiller and others (New York: Macmillan, 1963), pp. 809-826.

Papers:

The major collection of Edmund Clarence Stedman's correspondence, manuscripts, photographs, and other literary material is at Columbia University. Major collections of Stedman's letters may be found at the Houghton Library at Harvard University, the Huntington Library, and the libraries of Princeton, Duke, and the University of Virginia.

Richard Henry Stoddard

(2 July 1825-12 May 1903)

Robert D. Harvey
University of Nevada at Reno

See also the Stoddard entry in *DLB 3, Antebellum Writers in New York and the South.*

BOOKS: *Foot-prints* (New York: Spalding & Shepard, 1849);

Poems (Boston: Ticknor, Reed & Fields, 1852);

Adventures in Fairy-land (Boston: Ticknor, Reed & Fields, 1853);

Songs of Summer (Boston: Ticknor & Fields, 1857);

Town and Country, and the Voices in the Shells (New York: Dix, Edwards, 1857);

The King's Bell (New York: Carleton, 1863; London: B. M. Pickering, 1864);

The Story of Little Red Riding Hood (New York: Gregory, 1864);

Abraham Lincoln: An Horatian Ode (New York: Bunce & Huntington, 1865);

The Children in the Wood, Told in Verse (New York: Hurd & Houghton, 1866);

The Book of the East, and other poems (Boston: Osgood, 1871);

A Century After: Picturesque Glimpses of Philadelphia and Pennsylvania (Philadelphia: Allen, Lane & Scott/Lauderbauch, 1876);

Poets' Homes (Boston: Lothrop, 1877);

In Memory of William Cullen Bryant, 1794-1878 (New York: Evening Post Steam Presses, 1878);

Nathaniel Hawthorne (New York: Scribners, 1879);

The Poems of Richard Henry Stoddard, Complete Edition (New York: Scribners, 1880);

The Homes and Haunts of our Elder Poets (New York: Appleton, 1881);

Henry W. Longfellow. A Memoir (London: Warne, 1882);

The Life of Washington Irving (New York: Alden, 1883);

Putnam the Brave (Cincinnati: Thomson, 1884);

The Lion's Cub; With Other Verse (New York: Scribners, 1890; London: Elkin Matthews, 1891);

Under the Evening Lamp (New York: Scribners, 1892);

Photograph taken by Rockwood for the Authors Club, 1902

Recollections, Personal and Literary, edited by Ripley Hitchcock (New York: Barnes, 1903).

OTHER: *The Life, Travels and Books of Alexander von Humboldt,* edited by Stoddard (London:

230

Low & Son/New York: Rudd & Carleton,
1859);

The Last Political Writings of Gen. Nathaniel Lyon, edited by Stoddard (New York: Rudd & Carleton, 1861);

The Loves and Heroines of the Poets, edited by Stoddard (New York: Derby & Jackson, 1861);

The Late English Poets, edited by Stoddard (New York: Bunce & Huntington, 1865);

Melodies and Madrigals; Mostly from the Old English Poets, edited by Stoddard (New York: Bunce & Huntington, 1866);

Remember: A Keepsake, edited by Stoddard and Elizabeth Stoddard (New York: Leavitt & Allen, 1869);

Rufus W. Griswold, ed., *The Female Poets of America,* revised edition by Stoddard (New York: Miller, 1873);

Griswold, ed., *Poets and Poetry of America,* revised, with additions, by Stoddard (New York: Miller, 1874);

Prosper Merimee's Letters to an Incognita, with Recollections by Lamartine and George Sand, edited by Stoddard (New York: Scribner, Armstrong, 1874);

Anecdote Biographies of Thackeray and Dickens, edited by Stoddard (New York: Scribner, Armstrong, 1874);

Personal Reminiscences by Barham, Homes, and Hodder, edited by Stoddard (New York: Scribner, Armstrong, 1874);

Personal Reminiscences by Chorley, Planché, and Young, edited by Stoddard (New York: Scribner, Armstrong, 1874);

Personal Reminiscences by Cornelia Knight and Thomas Raikes, edited by Stoddard (New York: Scribner, Armstrong, 1875);

Personal Reminiscences by O'Keefe, Kelly and Taylor, edited by Stoddard (New York: Scribner, Armstrong, 1875);

Edgar Allan Poe, *Poems,* selected, with an original memoir, by Stoddard (New York: Widdleton, 1875);

Personal Reminiscences by Moore and Jerdom, edited by Stoddard (New York: Scribner, Armstrong, 1875);

Charles Cavendish Fulke Greville, *Memoirs: A Journal of the Reigns of George IV and William IV,* edited by Stoddard (New York: Scribner, Armstrong, 1875);

Personal Recollections of Lamb, Hazlitt and Others, edited by Stoddard (New York: Scribner, Armstrong, 1875);

Portrait of Stoddard as a young man

Life, Letters and Table Talk of Benjamin Robert Haydon, edited by Stoddard (New York: Scribner, Armstrong, 1876);

Personal Reminiscences by Constable and Gillies, edited by Stoddard (New York: Scribner, Armstrong, 1876);

Elizabeth Barret Browning, *Letters, Addressed to R. H. Howe,* preface and memoir by Stoddard (New York: Miller, 1877);

Elizabeth Barret Browning, *Mrs. E. B. Browning's Letters and Essays,* with a memoir by Stoddard (New York: J. Miller, 1877);

Anecdote Biography of Percy Bysshe Shelley, edited by Stoddard (New York: Scribner, Armstrong, 1877);

Poetical Works of William Cullen Bryant, edited by Stoddard (New York: Appleton, 1878);

John Doran, *Lives of Queens of England of the House of Hanover,* preface by Stoddard (New York: Armstrong, 1880);

Wit and Wisdom of Rev. Sidney Smith, edited by Evert A. Duyckinck, with a prefatory mem-

Elizabeth Drew Barstow, whom Stoddard married in December 1852

oir of Duyckinck by Stoddard (New York: Armstrong, 1880);

Poems of William Wordsworth, edited, with an introduction, by Stoddard (New York: Johston, 1881);

Henry Wadsworth Longfellow, *A Medley in Prose and Verse,* edited by Stoddard (New York: Harlan, 1882);

English Verse, 5 volumes, edited by Stoddard and William J. Linton (New York: Scribners, 1883);

Reading and Recitations from Modern Authors, Being Pearls Gathered from the Fields of Poetry and Romance: Choicest Gems of Miss Muloch, Tom Hood and Many Others, edited by Stoddard and Elizabeth Stoddard (Chicago & New York: Belford, Clark, 1884);

Selections from Poetical Works of A. C. Swinburne, edited by Stoddard (New York: Crowell, 1884);

Mayne Reid, *The Bush-boys; or, The History and Adventures of a Cape Farmer and the Family in the Wild Karoos of Southern Africa,* edited, with a

memoir, by Stoddard (New York: Knox, 1885);

Hippolyte Taine, *History of English Literature,* edited by H. Van Lann, with a preface by Stoddard (New York: Worthington, 1889);

The Complete Poems of William Cullen Bryant, edited by Stoddard (New York: Stokes, 1894);

Works of Lord Byron with his Letters and Journals, and His Life by Thomas Moore, edited, with an introduction, by Stoddard (Boston: Nicolls, 1900);

Henry Cady Sturges, *Chronologies of the Life and Writings of William Cullen Bryant,* with a memoir by Stoddard (New York: Appleton, 1903).

Though none of his prose or verse has genuine value today, there are three interesting things about the life of Richard Henry Stoddard, which comprised a half-century of poetic effusion, literary journalism, and editorial hackwork. First, he found genteel culture a means of escaping from a boyhood of proletarian penury, finally achieving a sincere testimonial dinner at his beloved Authors Club in 1897. Second, in 1851 he married Elizabeth Barstow and lived for fifty years with a spirited woman of superior mind and personality, whose realistic novels, especially *The Morgesons* (1861), and tales of New England domestic life tear away genteel masks and reveal psychological depths in eccentric and mordant dialogue. (It is questionable whether Stoddard, who once said his wife had genius, but he more talent, ever read her work with real understanding. Even so, he realized that she "was not cursed by mediocrity," but had "the misfortune to be original.") Finally, Stoddard's failure to develop in historical or literary awareness (unlike his genteel contemporaries George William Curtis and Edmund Clarence Stedman—to say nothing of the younger and more penetrating William Dean Howells and Henry James) corresponds to a similar lag in the vast American popular audience during the Gilded Age. Stoddard *was* his audience. Like them, he clung to his youthful reverence for William Cullen Bryant, Henry Wadsworth Longfellow, James Russell Lowell, John Greenleaf Whittier, and his close friend Bayard Taylor, while the writings of Walt Whitman, Mark Twain, Henry James, and Henry Adams passed him by.

Stoddard's father, Reuben Stoddard, the last of a line of Hingham, Massachusetts, sailors, was lost at sea in 1828. The boy's pious paternal grandparents took in Stoddard and his mother, Sophia Gurney Stoddard, though soon the unedu-

Stoddard in his East Fifteenth Street house, New York

cated widow and her son moved in with her parents. Stoddard's mother later sewed sailors' outfits in Boston, married another sailor, and took the then ten-year-old boy to New York. Brief schooling there started his interest in poetry, but there was not enough money to support a quality education. At fifteen Stoddard was on the streets bringing home a pittance as an errand boy, a shop boy, a legal copyist, and a bookkeeper. He remembered his ineffectual stepfather as kindly, never letting his mother "lay the weight of her hand on me. 'Boys will be boys' he said; and he always remained one." At eighteen he began a three-year apprenticeship in a foundry as an iron molder. His boyhood was almost Dickensian, perhaps, but without bitterness. He looked to literature as a way out–and up.

In the late 1840s he met Edgar Allan Poe and the surviving Knickerbockers, sought out acquaintance with editors and publishers, and began to place poems in periodicals. At this time he met his wife, and also a close friend in Bayard Taylor, as well as Nathaniel Hawthorne, who got him a position in the New York Custom House where he later met Herman Melville. Modestly secure, he went in for a literary career.

Stoddard thought he was a poet, and the

nineteenth-century American audience, mesmerized by Longfellow, edified by Lowell, put off by Whitman, Thoreau, and Melville, forgetting Emerson, only amused by Twain, and of course unaware of unpublished Dickinson, pleasantly agreed. His poetry, a thin, melodious lyricism faintly echoing Tennyson and introducing clichés from the exotic East, may be found in *Poems* (1852), *Songs of Summer* (1857), *The Poems of Richard Henry Stoddard, Complete Edition* (1880), and *The Lion's Cub; with Other Verse* (1890).

As a literary critic his views follow his poetic practice. It is mostly literary journalism done as publishers' hackwork in the 1860s, 1870s, and 1880s. He was a reviewer for the *New York World* (1860-1870), editor of the *Aldine* (1869-1874) and literary editor of the *New York Mail and Express* (1880-1903). He produced anthologies: *The Late English Poets* (1865), revised editions of Rufus W. Griswold's *Female Poets of America* (1873) and *Poets and Poetry of America* (1874), and *English Verse*, edited with William J. Linton (1883). He edited parlor table compendia: *The Loves and Heroines of the Poets* (1861), *Melodies and Madrigals; Mostly from the Old English Poets* (1866), and *Readings and Recitations from Modern Authors, Being Pearls Gathered*

Richard Henry and Elizabeth Barstow Stoddard, 1902 (photograph by Rockwood for the Authors Club)

from the Fields of Poetry and Romance (1884), with Elizabeth Stoddard.

Stoddard wrote prefaces galore, to various works of von Humboldt (1859), Mérimée (1874), Poe (1875), Benjamin Haydon (1876), Elizabeth Barrett Browning (1877), Bryant (1878 and 1894), Sidney Smith (1880), Wordsworth (1881), Longfellow (1882), Swinburne (1884), and Byron (1900) and Van Lann's translation of Taine's *History of English Literature* (1889). He also edited popular biographies of artists and writers sold in vast editions in the 1800s–the "Bric-a-Brac" and "Sans Souci" series–and wrote sketches of Revolutionary War heroes (originally published in *National Magazine*), a collection of essays *Under the Evening Lamp* (1892), and the posthumous *Recollections, Personal and Literary* (1903). There are also periodical short pieces in *Lippincott's Magazine, Appleton's Booklovers' Magazine, Harper's Monthly,* and *Scribner's Monthly,* some bits of which were collected in *Recollections, Personal and Literary.* Stoddard was a fair-sized cog in the East's publishing machine trying to "sivilize" the "territory" (as Huck Finn would put it)–at a profit.

One asks Ezekiel's question, Can these bones live? Let the answer depend on his *Appleton's Booklovers' Magazine* article on Whittier (April 1871), his preface to Taine's *History of English Literature* and the posthumously published *Recollections, Personal and Literary.* The article on Whittier provides a clear definition of Stoddard's notion of poetry's relation to life; he objects to Whittier's antislavery element: "It may be said, indeed, to have dominated over him during the greater part of his life. We may like it or we may not; but there it is, and there it was, and there it will be to the end . . . . We do not believe in the poetry which is inspired by morals or politics. It is not poetry; it is politics and morals in verse."

In the preface to Taine's history he cannot see the mind at work in the poetry of Dryden or Pope; intellect, genuine moral concern with history, is "unpoetical." Stoddard goes on to expand this view; he states that the reader should be interested in Chaucer's narrative skill (reincarnated as Stoddard sees it in the poems of William Morris), and in Shakespeare's use of the dramatic (alive again, he feels, in Browning), but not in attempting to organize an intellectual thesis to comprehend a whole people's literature and historical development. But Stoddard had no gift for analysis and took no pains to define the genres he mentions here; it's an oddly desultory preface which quickly rejects Taine's method (all too French) but replaces it with nothing but the kind of random personal delight which Stoddard feels Taine's method cannot account for.

In *Recollections, Personal and Literary* there might have appeared source materials for understanding the changing personalities and issues of literary experience in New York from 1845 to 1900, but what does appear is only superficial anecdote. Stoddard fails to see those personalities otherwise than as part of the tale of his own rise—acquaintances who used him well, such as Hawthorne, or ill, such as Poe. There is no grasp of the movement of ideas or of minds here. He seems mainly fascinated to have actually chatted with Thackeray, found Griswold and Nathaniel Parker Willis kindly disposed to him, received letters from Whittier or Lowell (Stoddard kept a large collection of autographs). His experiences must have been extraordinary, but his sensibility makes very little that is interesting of them.

He does, however, move the reader by his account of reading and writing his way out of boyhood poverty, of the joy of being young, unknown but confident, in New York, and of finding a smart wife and congenial friends in Grub Street, including George Boker, Bayard Taylor, E. C. Stedman, George Henry Curtis, Thomas Bailey Aldrich, and the somewhat younger Howells—all of whom testify to Stoddard's geniality and love of literature and to Elizabeth Stoddard's vital and dangerous wit. For a while in the 1860s and 1870s, indeed, their lower eastside Manhattan house was a kind of literary salon. However, New York's only genuises, Melville and Whitman, were notably not present. The Bayard Taylors roomed with the Stoddards for a while in that house—later encroached upon by immigrant slums and crowded with books and souvenirs (a lock of Milton's hair)—and Taylor has provided in *Diversions of the Echo Club* (1871) a sense of their vitality and their ambitious high jinks.

Taylor of course lost himself in travel, lecturing, and diplomatic work. Stoddard found shelter in the kind of verse which Melville satirized in book eighteen of *Pierre; or, The Ambiguities* (1852), with such titles as "The Tropical Summer: A Sonnet"; "The Weather: A Thought";

"Life: an Impromptu"; "The Late Mark Gracemen: an Obituary"; "Honor: a Stanza"; "Beauty: an Acrostic"; "Edgar: an Anagram"; and "The Pippin: a Paragraph." Stoddard found a living in the New York world of publishers, editors, and journalists. His "criticism" raised no real questions; his "scholarship" found no answers. His life with his brilliant, perceptive, no-nonsense wife is an enigma. Even with genius, Poe and Melville found literary life hard in nineteenth-century New York. For Stoddard's mediocrity it was somehow easier.

References:

Mrs. Thomas Bailey Aldrich, *Crowding Memories* (Boston & New York: Houghton, 1920);

Edward Sculley Bradley, *George Henry Boker: Poet and Patriot* (Philadelphia: University of Pennsylvania Press, 1927);

L. Buell and S. A. Zagarell, eds., "Biographical and Critical Introduction," in Elizabeth Barstow Stoddard's *The Morgesons* (Philadelphia: University of Pennsylvania Press, 1984): xi-xxv;

Richard Cary, *The Genteel Circle: Bayard Taylor and His New York Friends* (Ithaca: Cornell University Press, 1952);

William Dean Howells, *Literary Friends and Acquaintance* (New York & London: Harper, 1900);

A. R. Macdonough, "Stoddard's *Poems*," *Scribner's Monthly*, 20 (September 1880): 686-94;

Albert H. Smyth, *Bayard Taylor* (Boston & New York: Houghton, Mifflin, 1899);

Edmund Clarence Stedman, *Genius and Other Essays* (New York: Moffat, Yard, 1911);

Laura Stedman and George M. Gould, *Life and Letters of Edmund Clarence Stedman*, 2 volumes (New York: Moffat, Yard, 1910);

Marie Hansen-Taylor and Horace E. Scudder, eds., *Life and Letters of Bayard Taylor*, 2 volumes (Boston: Houghton, Mifflin, 1884);

Marie Hansen-Taylor, *On Two Continents* (Garden City: Doubleday, Page, 1905).

Papers:
Two large collections of Richard Henry Stoddard's manuscripts are in Cornell University Library and the Library of American Antiquarian Society. E. C. Stedman's papers, useful for his relations to both R. H. and Elizabeth Stoddard, are at Columbia University.

Henry Theodore Tuckerman

(20 April 1813-17 December 1871)

Janice L. Edens
Macon Junior College

BOOKS: *The Italian Sketch Book,* anonymous (Philadelphia: Key & Biddle, 1835); enlarged and republished under Tuckerman's name (Boston: Light & Stearns, 1837; revised and enlarged again, New York: Riker, 1848);

Isabel; or, Sicily: A Pilgrimage (Philadelphia: Lea & Blanchard, 1839); republished as *Sicily: a Pilgrimage* (New York: Putnam's, 1852);

Rambles and Reveries (New York: Giffing, 1841);

The Sad Bird of the Adriatic: An American Tale (London: Clements, 1841);

Thoughts on the Poets (New York: Francis/Boston: Francis, 1846; London: Slater, 1850);

Artist Life, or Sketches of American Painters (New York & Philadelphia: Appleton, 1847); republished as *Sketches of Eminent American Painters* (New York & Philadelphia: Appleton and Appleton, 1849);

Characteristics of Literature, Illustrated by the Genius of Distinguished Men (Philadelphia: Lindsay & Blakiston, 1849);

The Life of Silas Talbot, a Commodore in the Navy of the United States (New York: Riker, 1850);

The Optimist (New York: Putnam's, 1850); republished as *The Optimist: A Series of Essays* (New York: Putnam's, 1852);

Poems (Boston: Ticknor, Reed & Fields, 1851);

Characteristics of Literature, Illustrated by the Genius of Distinguished Men. Second Series (Philadelphia: Lindsay & Blakiston, 1851);

Leaves from the Diary of a Dreamer: Found Among his Papers (London: Pickering, 1853);

A Memorial of Horatio Greenough (New York: Putnam's, 1853);

Mental Portraits; or, Studies of Character (London: Bentley, 1853); revised and enlarged as *Biographical Essays: Essays, Biographical and Critical; or, Studies of Character* (Boston: Phillips, Sampson, 1857);

A Month in England (New York: Redfield, 1853);

A Memorial of the Life and Character of John W. Francis, Jr. (New York: Printed by J. F. Trow, 1855);

Henry T. Tuckerman

The Criterion, or, The Test of Talk about Familiar Things (New York: Hurd & Houghton, 1856); republished as *The Collector: Essays on Books, Newspapers, Pictures, Inns, Authors, Doctors, Holidays, Actors, Preachers* (London: Holten, 1868);

The Character and Portraits of Washington (New York: Putnam's, 1859);

The Rebellion: Its Latent Causes and True Significance, in Letters to a Friend Abroad (New York: Gregory, 1861);

America and Her Commentators (New York: Scribners, 1864);

A Sheaf of Verse Bound for the Fair (New York: Alvord, 1864);

Book of the Artists (New York: Putnam's, 1867);

Maga Papers about Paris (New York: Putnam's, 1867);

The Life of John Pendleton Kennedy (New York: Putnam's, 1871);

Little Journeys to the Homes of American Authors (New York & London: Putnam's, 1896); extracted and republished as *Irving* (New York & London: Putnam's, 1896).

OTHER: *The Boston Book, Being Specimens of Metropolitan Literature, Occasional and Periodical,* edited by Tuckerman (Boston: Light & Horton, 1836);

"Genius," in Felicia Hemans, *Poems,* edited by Rufus W. Griswold (Philadelphia: Sorin & Ball, 1845);

The Poems of Samuel Taylor Coleridge, with an introductory essay by Tuckerman (New York: C. S. Francis/Boston: J. H. Francis, 1848);

The Poems of Elizabeth Barrett Browning, with an introduction by Tuckerman (New York: C. S. Francis/Boston: J. H. Francis, 1850);

"Over the Mountains; or, The Western Pioneer," in *Home Book of the Picturesque: or, American Scenery, Art, and Literature,* (New York: Putnam's, 1852);

Poems, Plays and Essays by Oliver Goldsmith, M.B., with an introductory essay by Tuckerman (Boston: Phillips, Sampson, 1854);

The Poetical Works of Robert Southey, with a memoir by Tuckerman (Boston: Little, Brown, 1864);

John W. Francis, *Old New York, or, Reminiscences of the Past Sixty Years,* with a memoir by Tuckerman (New York: Widdleton, 1866);

Thomas Budd Shaw, *Outlines of English Literature,* with a sketch of American literature by Tuckerman (New York: Sheldon, 1867);

Shaw, *A Complete Manual of English Literature,* edited, with notes, by William Smith with a sketch of American literature by Tuckerman (New York: Sheldon, 1868).

Henry Theodore Tuckerman, Washington Irving's contemporary and fellow Knickerbocker, was a highly regarded romantic, idealistic critic during the mid-nineteenth century. Considered a genius in the United States, he also had a small but appreciative following in England. Additionally, he was included in Vapereau's *Dictionnaire Universel* of 1857 as one of America's better essayists. Evert A. Duyckinck, whose easygoing critical style was similar to Tuckerman's, pointed out in a laudatory essay in his *Cyclopædia of American Literature* (1855) that Tuckerman contributed "to all the best magazine literature of the day," including *Walsh's Review,* the *North American Review,* the *Democratic, Graham's Magazine,* the *Literary World,* the *Southern Literary Messenger,* and the *Christian Examiner.* As editor for the *Boston Miscellany of Literature and Fashion* in 1842-1843, Tuckerman exerted tremendous influence over what was considered publishable. For example, when Tuckerman refused to publish Edgar Allan Poe's "The Tell-Tale Heart" in the *Miscellany,* James Russell Lowell published it in the *Pioneer* (January 1843), though he said he was perhaps being presumptuous "to dissent from" Tuckerman's "verdict."

Tuckerman was born in Boston on 20 April 1813 to Henry Harris and Ruth Keating Tuckerman. He began preparing for Harvard at the Latin School, but was forced to withdraw after two years because of illness. On a trip abroad to strengthen his health he acquired his love for art, letters, and Italy, which was to remain with him and influence his career for the rest of his life. After returning to the United States, he wrote *The Italian Sketch Book* (1835), a work which set the tone for his later writing. After a second journey abroad, he returned home once more and wrote *Isabel; or Sicily, A Pilgrimage* (1839). He edited the *Boston Miscellany of Literature and Fashion* in the early 1840s, then moved to New York City in 1845. There he joined Anna Lynch's salon, with which he was involved for over twenty years and where he met and formed a sympathetic association with the Young America group. In 1850 Tuckerman received an honorary M.A. from Harvard, and because of his effort in behalf of Italian exiles in the United States, the Italian king presented him with a special order.

Tuckerman was one of the vague, sentimental, romantic critics of the nineteenth century whom Poe so detested. In fact, Tuckerman and Poe were at completely opposite ends of the critical spectrum. In contrast to Poe's frequently scathing attacks, Tuckerman said, "Let us recognize the beauty and power of true enthusiasm; and whatever we may do to enlighten ourselves and others, guard against checking or chiding a single earnest sentiment." Like Rufus Griswold and Duyckinck, Tuckerman believed that both literature and criticism should be sweet and uplifting. As Nelson Adkins said in the *Dictionary of American Biography,* "Tuckerman is best understood in the light of his essay on Hazlitt, where he finds the function of the critic that of feeler and sympathizer, as well as of analyst." In addition, as Charles Lombard has pointed out, Tuckerman's criticism was greatly influenced by French Romanticism. From Madame de Staël he learned to use biographic and personal details about writers in evaluating their work, and from Rousseau, Lamartine, and Chateaubriand he perceived the value of using religious sentiment as a literary theme.

Tuckerman began his writing career with *The Italian Sketch Book,* which was published anonymously in 1835. It is a collection of impressionistic travel essays mixed with reflections on art, literature, and politics as well as a few narratives. Two years later the book appeared in a second edition, enlarged and signed by the author. His next book, *Isabel; or Sicily: A Pilgrimage,* is a fictionalized account of a journey through Sicily by a young woman named Isabel Otley and her uncle, Clifford Frazier. According to Charles Lombard, the scene in which the heroine is drawn to prayer when she hears vesper bells shows the influence of Chateaubriand's *Génie du Christianisme* (1802).

Tuckerman's first book of criticism, *Rambles and Reveries* (1841), a collection of travel sketches, miscellaneous essays, and evaluations of various English poets, attempts to use the personal lives of writers as a tool for understanding their works. *Thoughts on the Poets* (1846) continued in this vein. For example, Tuckerman considered Byron's writing in light of his exploits, and, despite his disapproval of Byron's personal life, he found value in the poet's work and felt readers could savor the man's wilder side vicariously without being unduly influenced by it.

With *Artist Life, or Sketches of American Painters* (1847), a discussion of twenty-three American artists, Tuckerman ventured into the world of art criticism, evincing a preference for the romantic over the neoclassical, the sublime emotion over the well-rendered detail. Twenty years later he published *Book of the Artists* (1867), which discussed over one hundred American painters and sculptors, some of whom he grouped into categories such as "early portrait painters" and "landscape painters." Also included were individual chapters on twenty-seven artists, as well as an introductory essay tracing the rise and progress of art in America. In this essay he noted some of the drawbacks encountered by American artists, such as the absence of accepted standards and, with the exception of those fortunate enough to live in major cities, a lack of exposure to fine art. He

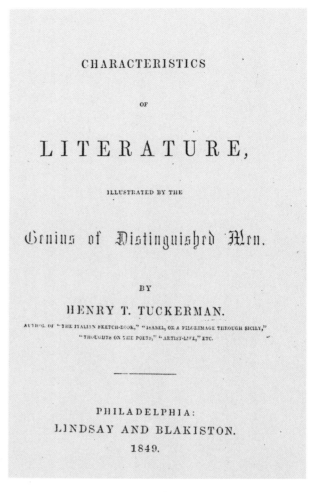

CHARACTERISTICS

OF

LITERATURE,

ILLUSTRATED BY THE

Genius of Distinguished Men.

BY

HENRY T. TUCKERMAN.

AUTHOR OF "THE ITALIAN SKETCH-BOOK," "ISABEL, OR A PILGRIMAGE THROUGH SICILY," "THOUGHTS ON THE POETS," "ARTIST-LIFE," ETC.

PHILADELPHIA:
LINDSAY AND BLAKISTON.
1849.

Title page for Tuckerman's 1849 work in which he discusses writers as examples of certain types, such as "the novelist," "the magazine writer," and "the reformer"

also cited a need for more specific standards of judgment in art criticism.

His next work of literary criticism, *Characteristics of Literature, Illustrated by the Genius of Distinguished Men* (first series, 1849; second series, 1851) discussed various writers as examples of certain types, such as "the novelist," "the magazine writer," and "the reformer." It also continued to reflect his preference for the gentle over the biting, as he criticized Swift for his harsh and vulgar satire.

The Optimist (1850) was a curious collection of miscellaneous essays on topics ranging from "The Weather" and "Hair" to "Lyric Poetry" and "The Profession of Literature." *Southern Quarterly Review* praised *The Optimist* for its "nice analysis, delicate discrimination, . . . gentle taste, harmonious style, and . . . pleasant discursive vein of thought" and said Tuckerman deserved "highest distinction" among American essayists. Tuckerman was also a minor poet, publishing the collection *Poems* in 1851 and *A Sheaf of Verse Bound for the Fair* in 1864. His *Leaves from the Diary of a Dreamer* (1853) was a series of impressionistic sketches after the fashion of Irving.

Another book about his travels, *A Month in England* (1853), charted his visit to Westminster, with reflections on other writers who had preceded him, such as Johnson and Chateaubriand. In the same year he published in England another collection of miniature biographies entitled *Mental Portraits; or, Studies of Character*, which, like *Characteristics of Literature, Illustrated by the Genius of Distinguished Men*, discussed various people as representative types. Daniel Boone, for instance, represented the pioneer, and Jenny Lind represented the vocalist. In his discussion of Charles Brockden Brown, whom he classified as "The Supernaturalist," he called the writer America's first "literary genius," though he wasn't blind to Brown's lack of polish. Later Tuckerman published a somewhat revised and enlarged edition in America under the title *Biographical Essays: Essays, Biographical and Critical; or, Studies of Character* (1857).

In the 1850s Tuckerman began working on longer biographies, a task which was to culminate in his famous biography of John Pendleton Kennedy. His first such venture was *The Life of Silas Talbot, a Commodore in the Navy of the United States* (1850). Next came *A Memorial of Horatio Greenough* (1853), *A Memorial of the Life and Character of John W. Francis, Jr.* (1855), and *The Character and Portraits of Washington* (1859). *The Life of John Pendleton Kennedy* (1871), a eulogy which praised Kennedy for his abilities in politics, society, and literature, is still considered the authorized biography, though it is not impressive by modern critical standards. In 1896 *Irving*, a small book about Washington Irving drawn from material Tuckerman had written earlier for inclusion in Putnam's Homes of American Authors series, was published as a separate volume.

In addition to articles and books Tuckerman also wrote numerous introductory essays about famous writers. In these he continued to insist that literature's mission was to inspire and elevate. His discussion of Elizabeth Barrett Browning, for example, though predominantly favorable, criticized her poetry for an "absence of spontaneous, artless and exuberant feeling" and "a certain hardness and formality, a want of *abandon* of manner, a lack of gushing melody, such as

takes the sympathies captive at once." Calling her a poetess, Tuckerman found her too intellectual for a woman: "She labors to reconcile herself to life through wisdom and her religious creed, and justifies tenderness by reason. This is a rather masculine process." A few years later in an introduction to Oliver Goldsmith's works, he praised the versatile writer for his honesty and his lack of "malignant satire." In the same essay he criticized modern writers for abandoning simplicity and gravitating toward the "startling and peculiar."

At the close of the Civil War, Tuckerman published *America and Her Commentators* (1864), which traced writings about America from its beginnings, culminating in a discussion of various Americans' reflections about their native land. The book seems to be at least partially an attempt to create a new sense of unity and patriotism after the devastation of the war.

Tuckerman's tenure as editor of *The Boston Miscellany* led to his famous dispute with Edgar Allan Poe, perhaps due to Tuckerman's refusal to print "The Tell-Tale Heart," though according to a letter from James Russell Lowell dated 17 December 1842, the refusal could well have been precipitated by Poe's essay entitled "A Chapter on Autography," in which Poe called Tuckerman "an insufferably tedious and dull" writer. Finally, in July 1845 they ended their quarrel when Poe, Tuckerman, and W. D. Snodgrass served on a committee to award a prize for the best poem from the graduating class at Rutgers Institute commencement.

Tuckerman, who never married, died on 17 December 1871 in New York City and was buried in Mount Auburn Cemetery in Cambridge, Massachusetts. His sister Ruth set up a memorial to him consisting of a complete set of his writings in an ebony case at Newport in the "Redwood Library." During his day Henry Tuckerman was well regarded by the public as well as fellow writers and critics. Griswold highly praised Tuckerman, whom he placed right between Edgar Allan Poe and Margaret Fuller in *The Prose Writers of America* (1849). Irving complemented him for his "liberal, generous, catholic spirit." Evert Duyckinck appreciated the kindness and generosity of his criticism. Although *Appleton's Cyclopædia of American Biography* (1889) admitted his style lacked "vigor," it praised his writing as "graceful, melodious, and refined" and claimed that his "prose writings are a valuable contribution to polite literature."

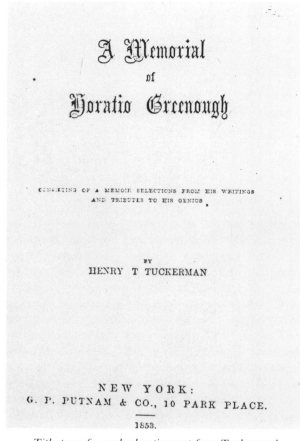

Title page for and advertisement from Tuckerman's second biographical work, a tribute to the noted American sculptor

Yet not all of his contemporaries were so approving, most notably Edgar Allan Poe, whose long-standing disagreement with Tuckerman has already been mentioned. Later generations have agreed with Poe. Twentieth-century critics find Tuckerman's writing shallow. In *The Times of Melville and Whitman* (1947), Van Wyck Brooks says Tuckerman "expressed the intelligent commonplace on a high level." Though he is mildly appreciated for his biographical essays, most scholars now feel he was highly overrated in his own day.

The final verdict is perhaps best summed up by the *Cambridge History of American Literature*, which declared in 1917: "His pleasantly pedantic essays are no longer either novel or informing."

References:

S. A. Allibone, *A Critical Dictionary of English Literature* (1871), III: 2466-2467;

Van Wyck Brooks, *The Times of Melville and Whitman* (New York: Dutton, 1947; London: Dent, 1948);

Evert A. Duyckinck and George L. Duyckinck, eds., *Cyclæpedia of American Literature* (New York: Scribners, 1855), pp. 582-586;

Rufus Wilmot Griswold, *The Prose Writers of America*, third revised edition (Philadelphia: Carey & Hart, 1849), pp. 531-536;

Stanley J. Kunitz and Howard Haycraft, eds., *American Authors 1600-1900: A Biographical Dictionary of American Literature* (New York: Wilson, 1938);

Charles M. Lombard, "Gallic Perspective in the Works of Henry T. Tuckerman," *Bulletin of Bibliography*, 27 (1970): 106-107;

Lombard, "A Neglected Critic–Henry T. Tuckerman, *Etudes Anglaises*, 22 (1969): 362-369;

Edmund C. Stedman and Ellen Mackey Hutchinson, eds., *A Library of American Literature from the Earliest Settlement to the Present Time* (New York: Charles L. Webster, 1889), pp. 224-228;

James Grant Wilson and John Fiske, eds., *Appleton's Cyclopædia of American Biography* (New York: Appleton, 1889).

Papers:

The Historical Society of Pennsylvania in Philadelphia houses a significant collection of Henry Theodore Tuckerman's letters, manuscripts, and other documents. Other letters are scattered around the country, though some of the larger holdings may be found at Duke University, the Boston Public Library, the Henry E. Huntington Library and Museum in San Marino, California, and Yale University. Tuckerman's manuscripts can be found at the New Hampshire Historical Society in Concord, the University of Virginia, the University of Texas, Johns Hopkins University, and the Redwood Library and Athenaeum in Newport, Rhode Island.

Moses Coit Tyler

(2 August 1835-28 December 1900)

Doreen Alvarez Saar
Drexel University

See also the Tyler entry in *DLB 47, American Historians, 1866-1912.*

BOOKS: *The Brawnville Papers: Being Memorials of the Brawnville Athletic Club* (Boston: Fields, Osgood, 1869);

A History of American Literature, 1607-1765, 2 volumes (New York: Putnam's, 1878; London: Low, Marston, Searle & Rivington, 1879); revised as *A History of American Literature During the Colonial Time,* 2 volumes (New York: Putnam's, 1897);

Patrick Henry (Boston & New York: Houghton, Mifflin, 1887; revised, 1899);

Three Men of Letters (New York & London: Putnam's, 1895);

The Literary History of the American Revolution, 1763-1783, 2 volumes (New York & London: Putnam's, 1897);

Glimpses of England, Social, Political, Literary (New York & London: Putnam's, 1898).

OTHER: "The New Gymnastics as an Instrument in Education," in *The New Gymnastics for Men, Women, and Children,* by Dio Lewis (Boston: Ticknor & Fields, 1868);

Henry Morley, *A Manual of English Literature,* revised by Tyler (New York: Sheldon, 1879);

"The Educational Value of the Study of History," in *Library of Universal History,* 8 volumes (New York: Peale & Hill, 1897), I: iii-x.

PERIODICAL PUBLICATIONS: "Mr. Emerson as a Teacher of Eloquence," *Independent,* 22 (5 May 1870);

"The Literary Labors of Charles Sumner," *Independent,* 22 (12 May 1870);

"Gentlemen and Scholars in Politics," *Independent,* 22 (22 December 1870);

"Mr. Bancroft's Last Volume," *Independent,* 26 (3 December 1874);

"Neglect and Destruction of Historical Materials in this Country," *Papers of the American Historical Association,* 2 (1887): 20-22;

Moses Coit Tyler in 1875 (University of Michigan Library)

"Doyle's Puritan Colonies," *Literary World,* 19 (3 March 1888): 69-70;

"A Half Century of Conflict, by Francis Parkman," *Political Science Quarterly,* 7 (December 1892): 726-729;

"The Party of the Loyalists in the American Revolution," *American Historical Review,* 1 (October 1895): 24-45;

"The Life of Thomas Hutchinson," *Nation,* 62 (26 March 1896): 258-259;

"The Declaration of Independence in the Light of Modern Criticism," *North American Review,* 163 (July 1896): 1-16.

Moses Coit Tyler has been called the father of American studies for his pioneering work in the scholarly study of colonial and revolutionary literature. Considered a member of the Critical School of American history, Tyler combined an interest in literature and history in two great and enduring studies of the formative years of American literature: *A History of American Literature, 1607-1765,* published in 1878, and *The Literary History of the American Revolution: 1763-1783,* published in 1897. Praised by such scholars as Perry Miller, Howard Mumford Jones, W. E. H. Lecky, and George Otto Trevelyan, Tyler's works remain a part of the standard scholarship on the period. Like many of the great American historians of the late nineteenth century, Tyler had no formal training in history and was an educational innovator. In an era when universities had just begun to move away from a curriculum based on classics and religion, Tyler actively promoted American history and literature as objects worthy of study. In 1881 he became the first scholar to hold the position of professor of American history. In 1884 he helped found the American Historical Society.

Throughout his life Tyler searched for consistency and moral meaning. Although he was able to see both in American literature, he was less successful in finding the qualities in his personal life. In his diaries, Tyler recognized much of his life was spent in "flounderings." Despite his eventual success with his scholarly work and the fact that he always felt he would make his mark in the field of history and literature–"As a literary and philosophical servant of American society, I might be first rate"–Tyler was still plagued by doubt. Identifying a "tripartite concern for history, health, and religion" in Tyler's many careers, Michael Kammen ascribes Tyler's concern to his "persistent perplexity about his vocation and identity."

In his memorial address for Tyler in the 1901 *Annual Report of the American Historical Association,* George L. Burr suggested Tyler's varied experiences may have been the necessary ingredients of a great historian: "His Eastern birth and Western rearing, the Puritan traditions and convictions which shaped his earlier life, and the humanizing studies, the wider acquaintance, the freer air of the lecture field and of travel which gave breadth and color to . . . his experiences as a Congregational pastor and the widely differing environment whose influence long after ripened

in his entrance as a deacon and as priest into the Episcopal clergy, all these, aye, even the accident of name which cousined him to the Virginia Tylers had their share in the making of that historian."

Moses Coit Tyler was born in Griswold, Connecticut, on 2 August 1835 to Elisha and Mary Greene Tyler. Tyler came from old colonial stock: he was a direct descendent of Job Tyler who landed with his brother, Henry, at Plymouth around 1653. While Job remained in Massachusetts, Henry moved to Virginia. The Virginia branch of Tylers would produce the tenth president of the United States, John Tyler. A turning point in the Massachusetts Tylers' lives was the trial of Job's daughter-in-law. In 1692, Mary Tyler was called before Judge John Hathorne, Nathaniel Hawthorne's ancestor, to answer charges of witchcraft. She was acquitted by the grand jury, but four years later, her husband, Hopestill Tyler, moved his family to Connecticut where the Tylers remained until 1835.

In 1835 Tyler's father, a restless and ambitious failure, moved the family to Constantia, New York, and then to a series of small towns in Michigan. In 1842 the Tylers moved to Detroit. After graduating from the first graded school in Detroit at age fifteen, Tyler taught school in Romeo, Michigan. After short stints as a teacher and book agent, he enrolled in the University of Michigan in 1852. Through the intervention of his Connecticut relatives, Samuel and George Coit, Tyler was able to leave Michigan for Yale University in 1853. *A History of American Literature, 1607-1765* is dedicated "in token of unceasing gratitude" to Samuel and George Coit.

Tyler's years at Yale were unremarkable. During his senior year, Tyler became friends with Andrew Dickinson White. Tyler and White were to remain friends, and, later, White–historian, president of Cornell, and diplomat–was to be a profound influence on Tyler and on the direction of American education.

After graduating from Yale in 1857, Tyler prepared for the ministry. He studied at the Yale Theological Seminary for one year. In 1858 he moved to Andover, Massachusetts, where he enrolled in Andover Theological Seminary. Although Tyler did not receive a degree from either institution, in 1859 he was offered the pastorship of a Congregational church in Owego, New York, and was ordained there as a Congregational minister. In 1859 he married Jeannette Hull Gilbert. They had two children: Jessica,

Tyler's parents, Mary and Elisha Tyler, in 1851

born in 1860, and Edward, born in 1863. Tyler remained in Owego until 1860 when he accepted a pastorship in Poughkeepsie, New York. In October 1862, Tyler's ill-health caused him to give up his congregation in Poughkeepsie. Although his resignation would mean the end of his career in the church, Tyler's quest for spiritual meaning was to continue. As F. O. Matthiessen noted in his 1934 review of the Jones-Casady biography of Tyler, Tyler "shared to the end of his days in the spiritual restlessness of his era, harassed by doubt and yet driven on by the necessity of faith." In 1877 Tyler became an Episcopalian. He was invested as a Episcopal deacon in 1878. Five years later, he was ordained an Episcopal priest. Tyler often lamented his failure to remain in the ministry. In an 1890 letter he remarked: "Once more rolls upon me the longing to be a preacher. What human employment compares with it! Oh, that I had persisted in it even unto death!"

Following his physical breakdown in 1862, Tyler embarked on a quest for good health. His search led him to Doctor Dio Lewis of Boston. Lewis had invented a system of calisthenics which

he called musical gymnastics. He believed these exercises had health-giving properties. Converted to Lewis's ideas by the return of his health, Tyler went to England in April 1863 to spread the gospel of fitness through musical gymnastics.

Tyler was heartened by his experience in England. Aided perhaps by the Victorian enthusiasm for "muscular Christianity," his lectures on Lewis's gymnastics were well received. He was able to expand his lectures and include such subjects as "The Pilgrim Fathers," and "American Humor." Tyler's report that upon reaching Wales in 1866 he found placards announcing him as "The Great American Orator" gives an indication of his success. Tyler supplemented the income from his lectures by writing for American publications. His work appeared in the *Independent*, the *Herald of Health*, and the *Nation*, among others. He also published anonymously a long, satirical poem, *The Omnibus*, in 1865.

Tyler's first book, *The Brawnville Papers: Being Memorials of the Brawnville Athletic Club*, draws on Tyler's experiences with musical gymnastics. Published in 1869, *The Brawnville Papers* is de-

Jeannette Hull Gilbert in 1857. She and Tyler were married on 26 October 1859.

scribed by Jones and Casady as the fictional account of the "struggles of an intelligent minority in a small New England town to found a gymnasium." *The Brawnville Papers* was not great art and Tyler later found it an embarrassment. However, its existence is a sign of Tyler's inner turmoil. Tyler wanted to be a great writer. In his diaries, he records his vacillations between what he believed were his three career choices: the ministry, academia, and literary life. In 1869 he wrote: "The question which for many years I have continually put to myself is this: Am I to be a literary artist, or am I to be a literary man applying his art to affairs?" Even in 1889, after his greatest academic success, he would still feel the lure of literary life: "Shall I go on with my *History of American Literature,* or write a history of *The birth of the revolution,* or write a series of historical novels beginning with one in Governor Berkeley's time; and perhaps also take time for more miscellaneous literary work—essays, American ballads, dialogues *a La Imaginary conversations,* and other projects more purely literary."

After having been separated from his family for three-and-a-half years, Tyler returned to

the United States in 1866. By the fall of 1867 he had accepted a position as professor of rhetoric and English literature at the University of Michigan. At the same time, Andrew D. White persuaded Ezra Cornell to establish a new university in Ithaca, New York. Confident Tyler would add to the academic luster of Cornell University, White, newly appointed to the presidency, urged Tyler to join the faculty. Although Tyler returned to Michigan, he would still feel White's presence in the changes Michigan had undergone since Tyler's undergraduate days. White had joined in the movement for educational change, particularly in the study of history, that swept through American universities during the late nineteenth century. From 1857 to 1867, as a member of the faculty at the University of Michigan, White had introduced a program in scientific history along German models, and aided in the revision of Michigan's curriculum and of the elective system.

During his early years at Michigan, Tyler was known as a memorable teacher who had revolutionized the teaching of literature. Before Tyler's innovations, students read only summaries of great works, or when they were allowed to read an original text, they were limited to an examination of the text's linguistic structure. Tyler insisted students read the texts they studied. To further this project, he assembled a library of literary texts. In his teaching he emphasized the importance of independent thought and research. In Herbert Baxter Adams's *Special Methods of Historical Study,* Tyler is quoted as saying that only through research can students "get into an attitude that is inquisitive, eager, critical, originating." Not only did he try to change teaching methods but he also tried to change curriculum: he was one of the first in this country to suggest that American literature belonged in the college curriculum.

Although Tyler confidently wrote in 1871 that he had found his life work in the study of the history of American literature, he still must have been assailed by doubts. In 1873 he had resigned from Michigan to become literary editor of Henry Ward Beecher's *Christian Union.* Among the reasons for his move may have been that Beecher had been one of the idols of Tyler's youth: in 1863 Tyler had written that Beecher's prayers possessed an "exquisite, wonderful, emyrean spirituality and tenderness of filial reverence which makes one of Beecher's prayers worth going around the globe to hear."

Tyler's writings for *Christian Union* show that he was already considering some of the ideas which would become important for his scholarly writing. For example, in a review of John S. Hart's *A Manual Of American Literature,* Tyler was heartened to find evidence that Americans had begun to recognize the worth of their native culture, noting with amusement, "Who shall explain the odd contradiction in our national habits of furiously boasting about American history, and steadily refusing to know anything about it?" In the same review he suggested the establishment of an Early American Text Society, a concern which would become even more important to him when he did the preliminary research for his book on colonial and revolutionary American literature.

Tyler's career as an editor was brief. A scandal surrounding Beecher's relationship with a married woman destroyed Tyler's faith in Beecher and his taste for journalism: "I hate the newspaper and its work but I must work on faithfully until I have paid the penalty for my blunders and sins." In 1874 a chastened Tyler returned to Michigan. During that same year, George Putnam suggested that Tyler do a review of American literature. Putnam's request was to launch Tyler on a far more ambitious enterprise, Tyler's monumental *A History of American Literature, 1607-1765.*

Although Putnam had hoped to publish Tyler's review during the excitement of the Centennial celebration, *A History of American Literature, 1607-1765* was not published until 1878. Tyler's intention was to write a history of American literature that was not an "indiscriminate dictionary" but "the intellectual history of a nation." Some years before, while pondering the work of Henry T. Buckle, Tyler had discovered the principles that would govern his interpretation of history: "As a historical writer, he indicates nobly . . . the path to be taken by every other historical writer–the exhaustive preparation; the recognition of a spirit of the age as ruling the evolution of the events of the age, and using kings, presidents, statesmen, warriors, as the tide uses the chips that are carried upon its top; the necessity, therefore, of finding for each period and for each people the hidden law of progress."

A History of American Literature, 1607-1765 fulfills Tyler's definition of good history. It is an encyclopedic narrative history of the progress of American literature from the landing at Jamestown to the eve of the Revolution. For Tyler, en-

Tyler in England, circa 1865 (William L. Clements Library, University of Michigan)

during values of democracy were already evident in the literature of the colonies. His biographies of colonial writers showed their unconscious recognition of the historical tide that was moving them ever closer to the fulfillment of the yet unborn American nation.

Although Tyler chose works which had "some noteworthy value as literature," analyzing literature *as* literature is secondary to Tyler's vision of a consistent developing national morality in colonial writing. Like many Victorian historians, Tyler used biography to write about history, using "authors, not books merely, as texts for literary discourse." Often, Tyler's characterization of an author seems to determine how he looked at the work; Tyler was unable to judge the work without judging the writer's morality. For example, the reader is invited to share Tyler's belief that Captain John Smith's chronicles must be treated as an expression of the man, seen as a highly dramatized historical personality: "As students of literature we shall be drawn to Captain John Smith as belonging to that noble type of manhood of which the Elizabethan period produced so many examples."

Spanning over one hundred and fifty years, and describing the works of almost one hundred and fifty writers, *A History of American Literature* is remarkable in its thoroughness. Tyler had little scholarship to guide him, and he searched for colonial books and manuscripts in dusty libraries and archives all over the country: "I have studied, as I believe, every American writer of the colonial time, in his extant writings." The comprehensiveness and accuracy of Tyler's research enabled scholars to survey, for the first time, the whole of early American literature. Considering the enormous scope of the task, the work is balanced and fair. The work restored the reputation of Daniel Gookin and discovered the work of John Wise. Tyler's decision to omit Thomas Morton and others antagonistic to the Puritans is one of the rare instances where Tyler's scholarly judgment was swayed by personal bias. Finally, the most striking quality of the work is its value as entertainment: Tyler tried to make history accessible by engaging readers in the drama of personality.

The book affected attitudes toward the preservation of the American heritage. Tyler's toil with colonial manuscripts increased his concern about the potential loss of irreplaceable documents. (See "Neglect and Destruction of Historical Materials in this Country" in the American Historical Association's Papers for 1887.) The enthusiasm generated by his work eventually resulted in the reprinting of important colonial texts.

A History of American Literature reflects the influence of the Critical School of American historians, as well as the prejudices of American Victorian culture. The Critical School believed that the study of history should be the study of morality, that biography helped the reader to understand the ethical content of history, and that history is a science; that is, historians must be factually accurate. Tyler shared in these convictions and added a further innovation by putting them to use to study American history. Many of Tyler's ideas in his landmark history were also influenced by the perceptions of American Victorian culture. Like his generation, Tyler asserted the Englishness of America, finding the descendants of the English colonies to be the "most numerous and . . . dominant portion" of the American people. Because he shared the Victorians' contempt for the Indians, Tyler was surprised by European

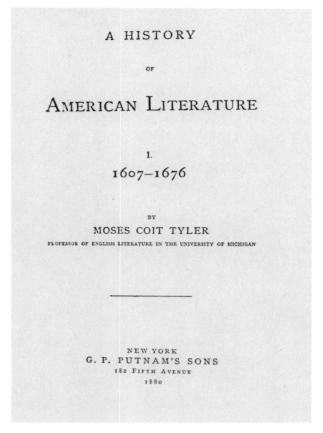

A HISTORY

OF

AMERICAN LITERATURE

I.

1607–1676

BY

MOSES COIT TYLER
PROFESSOR OF ENGLISH LITERATURE IN THE UNIVERSITY OF MICHIGAN

NEW YORK
G. P. PUTNAM'S SONS
182 FIFTH AVENUE
1880

Title page for volume one of a later edition of Tyler's encyclopedic narrative history of American literature

interest in colonial literature about the Indians, those "uncouth dusky creatures, the savage proprietors of the continent." Like many of his contemporaries, he viewed the Indian as "simply a fierce dull biped standing in our way." Finally, for Tyler, and for the Victorians, the literature of New England exemplified the literature of the nascent nation. Of the eighteen chapters in *A History of American Literature*, eleven are devoted to New England. Tyler praised the inhabitants of colonial New England for being a "thinking community," devoted to religion where men were "self-consistent in theory and practice." Tyler's appreciation of the Puritans differentiates his work from that of another important American historian of the late nineteenth century, Edward Eggleston, who deprecated Puritan culture.

Tyler's unified vision of the American character overwhelms aesthetic considerations. Tyler considers literature as a source of social information: he opens the canon to include journals, diaries, and travel literature as proper objects of literary study while reducing belles lettres to a category of American self-expression. In the opening chapter, Tyler justifies this approach by asserting that the colonists did not regard aesthetics as important but treated literature "as an instrument of humane and immediate utility." For many years, his view of the character of literary endeavor held sway over critical evaluations of this period: for example, Tyler's notion that Puritans eschewed aesthetic concerns has only recently been challenged.

Tyler's history was a great success and he was acknowledged as a leading scholar in the field of American literary history. In 1881 Cornell became the first American university to create a professorship of American history. In recognition of Tyler's eminence and at the urging of Andrew D. White, Henry Sage, president of Cornell, invited Tyler to fill this new position. Encouraged by White, Tyler accepted Sage's offer and became the first professor of American history in the country. Tyler remained at Cornell for the rest of his life.

Although, as Michael Kammen records, in 1880 there were only eleven professors of history in the United States, the time was ripe for a recognition of the profession. In 1884 Tyler joined with Charles Kendall Adams, professor of history at the University of Michigan and former student of Andrew White, Herbert Baxter Adams of Johns Hopkins, and Frank B. Sanborn, secretary of the American Social Science Foundation, to found the American Historical Association. This group of historians rejected the romantic/patriotic school and its uncritical mythology of America and sought historical accuracy, thus anticipating the scientific school of history. Tyler wrote that the Critical School was "characterized preeminently by simplicity both in material and form; and that means it seeks for the whole absolute truth of history sincerely, skeptically, untiringly, and then tries to tell it plainly."

Although Tyler and the Critical School rejected unthinking patriotism, Tyler nonetheless believed that history must teach civic duty: "While history should be thoroughly scientific in its method, its object should be practical. To this extent I believe in history with a tendency. My own interest in our own past is chiefly derived from my own interest in our own present and future: and I teach American history, not so much to make historians as to make citizens and good leaders for the State and Nation."

In 1887, while Tyler was still hard at work on the sequel to A History of American Literature, John Tory Morse's American Statesmen series published Tyler's Patrick Henry. Many famous historians including Henry Adams and Albert Bushnell Hart wrote for the series. In an introduction to Patrick Henry, Lance Banning says Tyler's biography corrected many of the errors of Henry Wirt's Sketches of the Life and Character of Patrick Henry (1817), a work that had been considered the standard biography of Henry for over seventy years. Wirt had characterized Henry as uncouth and unlettered: after examining many of the original records of the period, Tyler was able to show that Wirt's description was inaccurate. Tyler's work was "immediately acclaimed as one of the best of a distinguished series" and remained "definitive for sixty years."

In 1895 Three Men of Letters was published. In his introduction, Tyler explained that the three chapters of this book represent "an incidental product" of his researches on colonial and Revolutionary American literature and these chapters, to his mind, could not properly have been included in his earlier and larger work. The first chapter details the "true secret" of the circumstances surrounding the Very Reverend George Berkeley, Dean of Derry's sojourn in Newport, Rhode Island, during the years 1729 to 1731. The remaining two chapters are literary biographies of Timothy Dwight and Joel Barlow.

Tyler's second major work, The Literary History of the American Revolution, 1763-1783, was published in 1897. William Dean Howells, George W. Cable, W. E. H. Lecky, and William E. Gladstone were among those who praised this encyclopedic work. Fredrick Lewis Pattee wrote to Tyler's publisher to say, "One has the impression constantly that every pains [sic] that patience and scholarship can give have been exhausted to make the work a complete and final authority.... I cannot conceive how a more thorough and accurate history could be made." The book, covering only twenty years and less than fifty writers, is more limited in scope than Tyler's history of the colonial period.

While in his earlier work Tyler conceives of literature as a reflection of national character, in The Literary History of the American Revolution Tyler sees art as the embodiment of the forces of political development. In the writings of the Revolutionary period, Tyler finds not "art for art's sake" but art "swept into universal conscription, and enrolled for the service of the one party or of the other in the imperilled young Republic." As early as 1880 Tyler had begun to see the forces of political revolution as the operative and formative prin-

Tyler as a professor at Cornell University (William L. Clements Library, University of Michigan)

ciple of the literature of this period: "First grasp the idea that it is a period in which political and military struggles are the great trait; that these struggles converge on the effort for complete detachment of America from Europe; and that the literature of the time is chiefly an expression of these energies." Because Tyler's narrative was tightly organized around a chronological study of the "origin and growth and culmination" of the spirit of Revolution, Tyler moved with greater control in *The Literary History of the American Revolution* and the relation of history and literature seems more seamless than in his work on the colonies.

Despite these surface differences between the two books, Tyler's method remains the same. Once again, he defines the contours of the whole of the Revolutionary era through historical biography. He includes the work of many figures who had not received much critical attention, such as Michel-Guillaume Jean de Crèvecœur and Loyalist writers, and he includes unusual forms of litera-

ture, such as diaries and prison literature. Like his history of the colonies, Tyler's history of the Revolution reflected the literary and historical tastes of his age as Howard Mumford Jones notes in his preface to a later edition of the volume: "His is an Anglo-Saxon history; it is a New England history; it is a true-blue Protestant history; it is a history which records the moral triumph of a pure and virtuous patriotism over a 'brain sick' king, a corrupt Parliament, and an invading army. He makes small reference to . . . any system of ideas outside the British empire. . . . For him American writing is born out of an 'Elizabethan world,' which is, as it were, a piece of Victorian mythology. . . ."

At the time, one of the important contributions of *The Literary History of the American Revolution* was its balanced treatment of the Loyalists. Albert T. Klyberg records that Tyler was one of the first historians to tell both sides of the Revolutionary controversy. Tyler's stance was a controversial one, breaking with the American "Whig" historians' portrayal of the Loyalists. Before he had published this history, Tyler had argued for fair treatment of the Loyalists. In an article in the inaugural issue of the *American Historical Review* (October 1895) he denied the common perception that the Loyalists were simply agents of the British, and in Klyberg's words, described the Loyalists as "conservatives wanting to maintain the *status quo*, as much in love with liberty and America as any patriot."

Tyler's analysis of the Loyalist cause has not stood the test of time. In *The Ordeal of Thomas Hutchinson*, Bernard Bailyn claims Tyler did not understand "the peculiar mental and psychological dispositions of the late eighteenth century which alone make sense" of the Loyalist experience. According to Bailyn, Tyler's interest in restoring the history of the Loyalists is, in part, an attempt to reconcile what Tyler and his generation considered a "deplorable race-feud" between members of the "English-speaking race."

In his last years Tyler received ample recognition for his scholarly achievements. In 1898 Putnam's published *Glimpses of England, Social, Political, Literary*, a representative sampling of the essays Tyler had written in England. Tyler added an honorary doctor of laws from the University of New Brunswick to degrees he had received from Columbia in 1888, and Wooster in 1875. He was elected to the American Philosophical Society, and in 1900 was elected first vice president of the American Historical Association. Leaving behind many projects in manuscript form, Tyler died in Ithaca on 28 December 1900.

Despite the great changes in the study of literature, Moses Coit Tyler's scholarship remains an important contribution to the study of early American literature. His encyclopedic works on the literature of America from 1620 to 1783 were remarkable feats of research and diligence, representing the first time that any critical survey of the literature of this period had been undertaken. Tyler believed literature should be read for its intellectual, social, and political implications, and he studied American literature as a reflection of the mind of the nation. For many years his literary/historical approach dominated American scholarship in this field, and the thoroughness and comprehensiveness of his research made critical reevaluation of early American literature slow in coming. As Howard Mumford Jones says in his preface to *The Literary History of the American Revolution*: "As in the more magnificent case of Gibbon, later investigators have found new materials, unearthed new authors, corrected emphases, but Tyler remains the supreme master in his field."

Letters:
Moses Coit Tyler: Selections from his Letters and Diaries, edited by Jessica Tyler Austen (Garden City: Doubleday, Page, 1911).

Biography:
Howard Mumford Jones, *The Life of Moses Coit Tyler, Based upon an Unpublished Dissertation*

from Original Sources by Thomas Edgar Casady (Ann Arbor: University of Michigan Press, 1933).

References:
Bernard Bailyn, *The Ordeal of Thomas Hutchinson* (Cambridge: Harvard University Press, 1974);

Deborah L. Haines, "Scientific History as a Teaching Method: The Formative Years," *Journal of American History,* 63 (March 1977): 892-912;

Michael Kammen, "Moses Coit Tyler: The First Professor of American History in the United States," *History Teacher,* 17 (November 1983): 61-87;

Albert T. Klyberg, "The Armed Loyalists as Seen by American Historians," *Proceedings of the New Jersey Historical Society,* 82 (1964): 101-108;

Robert Skotheim, "The Writing of American History of Ideas: Two Traditions in the Twentieth Century," *Journal of the History of Ideas,* 25 (1964): 257-278.

Papers:
Moses Coit Tyler's papers, including drafts of articles, materials gathered for his publications, and research notes, as well as his commonplace books and private correspondence, are located at Olin Library, Cornell University, Ithaca, New York. A small collection of his letters is at the Bentley Historical Library, University of Michigan, Ann Arbor.

Charles Dudley Warner

(12 September 1829-20 October 1900)

Peter Van Egmond
University of Maryland

BOOKS: *My Summer in a Garden* (Boston: Osgood, 1870; London: Low, Marston, Low & Searle, 1871);

Saunterings (Boston: Osgood, 1872);

Backlog Studies (Boston & New York: Houghton, Mifflin, 1873);

The Gilded Age: A Tale of To-Day, by Warner and Samuel L. Clemens (Hartford: American Publishing Company, 1873; 3 volumes, London: Routledge, 1874);

Baddeck, and That Sort of Thing (Boston: Osgood, 1874);

My Winter on the Nile, Among the Mummies and Moslems (Hartford: American Publishing Company, 1876; revised edition, Boston: Houghton, Mifflin, 1881);

In the Levant (Boston: Houghton, Mifflin, 1876; London: Low, Marston, Searle & Rivington, 1877);

Being a Boy (Boston: Houghton, Mifflin, 1877);

In the Wilderness (Boston: Houghton, Osgood, 1878);

Captain John Smith, Sometime Governor of Virginia, and Admiral of New England: A Study of His Life and Writings (New York: Holt, 1881);

Washington Irving (New York: Houghton, Mifflin, 1881);

A Roundabout Journey (London: Chatto, 1883; Boston & New York: Houghton, Mifflin, 1884);

Papers on Penology, by Warner and others (Elmira, N.Y.: Reformatory Press, 1886);

Their Pilgrimage (New York: Harper, 1886);

A-hunting of the Deer and Other Essays (Boston: Houghton, Mifflin, 1888);

On Horseback: A Tour in Virginia, North Carolina, and Tennessee, with Notes on Travel in Mexico and California (Boston & New York: Houghton, Mifflin, 1888);

A Little Journey in the World: A Novel (New York: Harper, 1889; revised, New York & London: Harper, 1899);

Studies in the South and West, with Comments on Canada (New York: Harper, 1889; London: Unwin, 1890);

Charles Dudley Warner (Mark Twain Memorial)

As We Were Saying (New York: Harper, 1891);

Our Italy, Southern California (New York: Harper, 1891; London: Osgood, 1892);

The Work of Washington Irving (Boston & New York: Houghton, Mifflin, 1893);

As We Go (New York: Harper, 1894);

The Golden House: A Novel (New York: Harper, 1894; London: Harper, 1899);

The Relation of Literature to Life (New York: Harper, 1897);

The People for Whom Shakespeare Wrote (New York: Harper, 1897);

That Fortune: A Novel (New York & London: Harper, 1899);

Fashions in Literature: And Other Literary and Social Essays and Addresses, edited by Hamilton W. Mabie (New York: Dodd, Mead, 1902).

Collection: *The Complete Writings of Charles Dudley Warner,* 15 volumes, edited by Thomas R. Lounsbury (Hartford: American Publishing Company, 1904).

OTHER: *The Book of Eloquence,* compiled by Warner (New York: Chappell, 1866);

A Library of the World's Best Literature, 30 volumes, edited by Warner (New York: Hill, 1896-1897);

Biographical Dictionary and Synopsis of Books Ancient and Modern, 2 volumes, edited by Warner (Akron, Ohio: Werner, 1902).

In the *Biographical Dictionary and Synopsis of Books Ancient and Modern* (1902), Charles Dudley Warner is described as "an American man of letters and novelist." Something of his personality and literary judgment may also be revealed in the descriptions of other prominent American writers, for Warner was the overseeing editor. Ralph Waldo Emerson is described as "an eminent American philosopher, poet, essayist, and lecturer"; Walt Whitman "a celebrated American poet"; and Samuel L. Clemens "a distinguished American humorist."

Warner's minimalist description of Clemens may have its source in a series of misunderstandings and disagreements between Warner and Clemens after the appearance of their collaborative effort, *The Gilded Age: A Tale of To-Day* (1873), which is Warner's chief claim to fame. For example, a letter dated 1 June 1911 (reprinted in the *Twainian,* May-June 1965) from Warner's close friend and traveling companion Joseph H. Twichell to A. B. Paine tells that Clemens paid Warner nothing for relinquishing his right to share in the profits of *The Gilded Age* as a play, and adds, "There was some unpleasantness between them about it." It is understandable that Warner's description of Clemens would not be entirely objective, and perhaps this helps to explain the essential tone of his literary and social criticism—it is purely personal.

Warner was born in Plainfield, Massachusetts, to farming parents, Sylvia Hitchcock and Justus Warner. His father died when Warner was five. When he was eight Warner was taken in by a relative who would be his guardian until 1848,

THE

GILDED AGE

A TALE OF TO-DAY

BY

MARK TWAIN
(SAMUEL L. CLEMENS)
AUTHOR OF "INNOCENTS ABROAD," "ROUGHING IT," ETC.
AND
CHARLES DUDLEY WARNER
AUTHOR OF "MY SUMMER IN A GARDEN," "BACK LOG STUDIES," ETC.

FULLY ILLUSTRATED FROM NEW DESIGNS
BY HOPPIN, STEPHENS, WILLIAMS, WHITE, ETC., ETC.

SOLD BY SUBSCRIPTION ONLY.

HARTFORD:
AMERICAN PUBLISHING COMPANY.
W. E. BLISS & CO., TOLEDO, OHIO.
1874.

Title page for the second edition of Warner's collaboration with Samuel Clemens. A satire of political greed and corruption, the book's title became the descriptive phrase for the era.

when he enrolled at Hamilton College as a sophomore. In *Being a Boy* (1877) he describes his formative years as idyllic when not interrupted by the chores of a farm. The Puritan ideals of his home and community, forbidding such worldly recreations as card-playing and dancing, created his lifelong value system and outlook. As a collegian Warner began a life of steady and discriminating reading, and he wrote articles for the *Knickerbocker Magazine* before graduating in 1851. After college he worked at a variety of menial jobs vaguely associated with books and printing, and in 1853 he produced a limited printing of *The Book of Eloquence,* a collection of quotations and fragments from British and American literature which was published commercially in 1866.

As a child and young man, Warner was in poor health, but the outdoor life seemed to be the best tonic for him. "Roughing it" was beneficial not only physically but morally as well. The turning point in his physical condition seems to have occurred in 1853 and 1854 when he was part of a survey party for a railway in Missouri. After that he returned east to Binghamton, New York, in 1855 to live with an uncle and to study law, working part of the time as a conveyancer in real estate. In 1856 he married Susan Lee of New York City; they were to have no children. He received a bachelor of law degree from the University of Pennsylvania in 1858 and moved to Chicago to begin a practice, although his interests were still primarily scholarly and literary. He preferred studying law to practicing it. Moreover, the Panic of 1857 caused economic uneasiness throughout the country generally and in Warner's law office particularly.

In 1860 an acquaintance and fellow college alumnus, Joseph Roswell Hawley (1826-1905), urged Warner to come to Hartford to be associate editor of the *Hartford Press* (in 1867 to be consolidated with the *Hartford Courant*), which was already influential and had a solid readership. Hawley entered the Union Army in 1861, leaving Warner as chief editor, writing articles and editorials and determining editorial policy. In 1868, with the newspaper functioning smoothly, Warner and his wife left for a yearlong trip to England and Europe, the first of five lengthy overseas trips. He continued to file articles from various places back to the *Courant*. These were later collected under the title *Saunterings* (1872).

After his return to Hartford, Warner bought a house with three acres on what was then the outskirts of the city. This was to be the setting for frequent social and literary gatherings, including such people as Twichell, Samuel Clemens, Harriet Beecher Stowe, Henry Ward Beecher, and most of the Hartford luminaries of the day. Warner eventually named his estate Nook Farm, and indeed he was something of a gentleman farmer, cultivating a large vegetable garden, a grape arbor, and a small orchard. A series of philosophical-agricultural essays for the *Courant* dealt with the garden's lessons in "patience and philosophy, and the higher virtues. . . ." The essays were so popular with Hartford readers that they were collected and published as *My Summer in a Garden* in 1870, with an introduction by Beecher, who had interceded with his own publisher in their behalf. The book went through several editions, with later editions including an essay on the Warners' family cat, Calvin.

Warner's essay-writing career was now established, and his views were as diverse as his subjects. Besides his signed essays for the *Courant* and other popular journals of the day, many others appeared unsigned and thus have not been collected. His next collection, *Backlog Studies* (1873), consists of essays published in *Scribner's Magazine*. This represents his first important social and literary criticism. Interestingly, Warner laments in 1871 the disintegration of the family unit, the loss of respect for the elderly, imitation gas logs, and confusion of the personality and attire of the two sexes. In praise of the family fireside, he describes the importance of the backlog, a large log which burns slowly, radiating the heat of the fire, and continuing throughout the day. This log, he notes, may be compared to the life of a good man, and the hearth itself, he considers "an emblem of the best things." In this work Warner makes his first attempt at defining the work of the critic: "Criticism is not necessarily uncharitableness, but a wholesome exercise of our powers of analysis and discrimination. It is, however, a very idle exercise, leading to no results when we set the qualities of one over against the qualities of another, and disparage by contrast and not by independent judgment. And this method of procedure creates jealousies and heartburnings innumerable." This is evidently a foreshadowing of the modern New Criticism. "Criticism by comparison is the refuge of incapables," he declares.

His book *Saunterings* (1872), is the first of nine travel books and describes his year in Europe. The others deal with trips in North America, the Iberian peninsula, North Africa, France, and on the Nile. His travel observations can be described as those of a wealthy American who laments the decline of older cultures and yet stays thoroughly American wherever he goes. His descriptions of various locales and their historic sites are described in almost minute detail, perhaps bearing in mind his Hartford reader who likely could not afford similar trips nor expend so much time as Warner could. (He spent just over five months on or around the Nile.)

The publication of *The Gilded Age* brought increased fame, although both Warner and Clemens were uneasy about their mixed product. Clemens's colorful descriptions and biting satire are evident in the novel, and Warner's romantic plot twists and attempts at gothic mystery are clearly at odds with Clemens's own aims. The sat-

ire upon political greed and corruption domi-
nates, however, and the book had some success,
as did a dramatization the following year (1874).
The title became the descriptive phrase for the
last quarter century in the United States.

Most of Warner's notions as a critic have as
their purpose social improvement through Christian values of morality and classical ideals of culture. Two critical books, *As We Were Saying* (1891)
and *As We Go* (1894), are collections of articles written for the general reader. They offer observations on many subjects, not only literary but on
fashions, family values, American tourists, personal hygiene, eating habits, and anything else
that Warner felt his reader ought to know in
order to "be correct." Perhaps his greatest contribution to American literary criticism is the American Men of Letters series of critical biographies
of American authors (1881). His *Washington Irving* was the first volume published, inaugurating
a distinguished series which helped establish a
scholarly frame of study lasting for many years.

In response to the increasing demand for
his books, Warner again turned to criticism in
The Relation of Literature to Life (1897), essays primarily about literature. The title essay suggests
that the contemplative man who writes, especially
the poet, has a more lasting influence than does
the active man. Literature uplifts and sustains the
spirit of a people. "Simplicity" is opposed to
superfluity—in dress, in thought, and in artistic expression. Warner's point is itself simplistic. He violates his own rule of simplicity many times in his
own books, especially in his arcane, remote literary and historical references. In the essay "Equality," Warner argues that this term does not mean
uniformity but does mean equal rights in education, gender, and race.

Another book published in 1897, *The People
for Whom Shakespeare Wrote,* is a grand disappointment to anyone but the general reader with only
a vague interest in literature, because most of the
information is taken, only slightly paraphrased,
from William Harrison's *The Description of England* (1877-1881), edited by Frederick J. Furnivall and published by the New Shakespeare
Society. Warner acknowledges the debt but does
little to provide the humor and grace characteristic of his other books.

His *Fashions in Literature: And Other Literary
and Social Essays and Addresses* (1902) illustrates
Warner's critical approach to social and literary issues and provides a synoptic view of his main critical opinions. These are essays and addresses

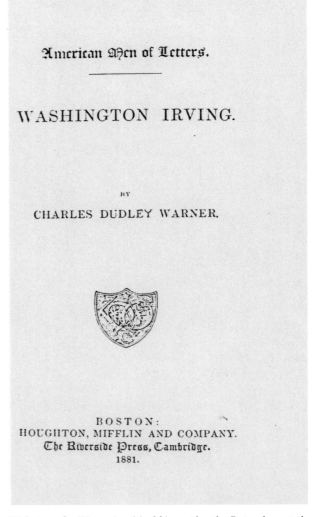

American Men of Letters.

WASHINGTON IRVING.

BY

CHARLES DUDLEY WARNER.

BOSTON:
HOUGHTON, MIFFLIN AND COMPANY.
The Riverside Press, Cambridge.
1881.

*Title page for Warner's critical biography, the first volume pub-
lished in the American Men of Letters series*

spanning more than twenty years, published after
his death by his longtime friend and editorial associate Hamilton W. Mabie. The title essay declares
that, like changing fashions in attire, literary judgment is often subjective to the individual critic.
There are, however, three characteristics common to all literary masterpieces: simplicity, knowledge of human nature, and charm, which is
defined as "the agreeable personality of the
writer." In "The American Newspaper," Warner
presents an overview that includes reporting, advertising, editorials, and readers; he concludes
that, despite many ills, "the moral tone . . . is
higher than that in the community in which it is
published." In "Certain Diversities of American
Life" Warner describes the American's eagerness
to attain wealth and urges a turn from material

Warner, circa 1895 (Mark Twain Papers, Bancroft Library, University of California, Berkeley)

to moral values. Speaking at the University of the South in Tennessee, Warner praises the geographical diversity which makes up the United States in scholarship and the arts. He also urges Negro suffrage and improvements in education.

In "Some of the Causes of the Prevailing Discontent," Warner describes one such cause as the misunderstanding of "equality" in the American democratic philosophy. Another cause he notes is the meager condition of the American laborer, and another the poor quality of public education. The remedy, he says, is to develop the intellectual person; then "discontent will be of a nobler kind." In "The Education of the Negro," Warner prescribes a focus on mechanical and agricultural skills in order to serve the overall economy, especially in the South; and liberal studies, he contends, would improve morality.

Warner's most forward-looking proposal as social critic is described in "The Indeterminate Sentence." He writes that there is a "well-defined criminal class" for whom open-ended prison sentences should be given. The criminal can decide whether to lead an honest life or remain in prison. "The Life-Saving and Life-Prolonging

Art" is a brief talk before the Hartford County Medical Association in praise of the physician. Warner's "Literary Copyright" states a common plea of American authors in the nineteenth century—a time extension of copyright for Americans and development of a similar international copyright.

"The Pursuit of Happiness" is yet another attempt to urge an optimistic outlook for the general reader. Happiness, Warner writes, is an inner condition which may be found in the present rather than by waiting for it to appear in the future. Defining "Truthfulness" in literature Warner writes that it means faithfulness to life or the author's remaining true to his conception. In the very brief essay "Literature and the Stage," he laments that contemporary American drama is commercialistic and lacking in literary merit. Finally " 'H. H.' in California" is a reminiscence of Helen Hunt Jackson and her novel *Ramona* (1884).

While *Fashions in Literature* illustrates the variety of Warner's interests, it also reveals the shallowness of his audience—though not necessarily of Warner himself. His formal education, his wide reading and extensive travel, and his selected circle of friends and correspondents made him well-suited for more incisive and penetrating commentary. But the requirements of a daily newspaper and the demanding details of popular authorship no doubt prevented him from becoming more than a romantic novelist and a witty and charming writer of travel books.

Papers:

The Louis Robert Trilling papers (over 3,000 items) for a proposed biography of Warner, collected from 1936 to 1965, are in the Columbia University Libraries. The Houghton Library at Harvard has over 100 letters by Warner in the Houghton Publishing Company collection. The Watkinson Library, at Trinity College, Hartford, has a sizable collection of Warner manuscripts, journals, and letters, along with nearly 3,000 letters to Warner. There are more than ninety other repositories in the United States with some holdings of Warner material, largely in connection with his association with Samuel Clemens.

Edwin Percy Whipple

(8 March 1819-16 June 1886)

Gerald E. Gerber
Duke University

See also the Whipple entry in *DLB 1, The American Renaissance in New England.*

BOOKS: *Essays and Reviews,* 2 volumes (New York: Appleton/Philadelphia: Appleton, 1848-1849);

Lectures on Subjects Connected with Literature and Life (Boston: Ticknor, Reed & Fields, 1849; London: John Chapman, 1851); enlarged as *Literature and Life* (Boston: Osgood, 1871);

Character and Characteristic Men (Boston: Ticknor & Fields, 1866);

The Literature of the Age of Elizabeth (Boston: Fields, Osgood, 1869);

Success and Its Conditions (Boston: Osgood, 1871);

Some Recollections of Rufus Choate (New York: Harper, 1879);

Works, 6 volumes (Boston: Houghton, Mifflin, 1885-1887)—includes *Literature and Life, Essays and Reviews, Character and Characteristic Men, Success and Its Conditions,* and *The Literature of the Age of Elizabeth;*

Recollections of Eminent Men, with Other Papers (Boston: Ticknor, 1886);

American Literature, and Other Papers (Boston: Ticknor, 1887);

Outlooks on Society, Literature and Politics (Boston: Ticknor, 1888);

Charles Dickens, The Man and His Works, 2 volumes (Boston & New York: Houghton Mifflin, 1912).

OTHER: Thomas Babington Macaulay, *Critical, Historical and Miscellaneous Essays,* 6 volumes, with an introduction by Whipple (New York: Sheldon/Boston: Gould & Lincoln, 1860);

Men of Mark: Bryant, Longfellow, Poe, Turner, Macaulay, Freeman, Curtius, Ticknor, Sumner, Mill, by Whipple and Edward A. Freeman (New York: Barnes, 1877);

Thomas Starr King, *Christianity and Humanity: a Series of Sermons,* edited, with an introduction, by Whipple (Boston: Osgood, 1877);

Edwin Percy Whipple

King, *Substance and Show and Other Lectures,* edited, with an introduction, by Whipple (Boston: Osgood, 1877);

The Family Library of British Poetry from Chaucer to the Present Time, edited by Whipple and James T. Fields (Boston: Houghton, Osgood, 1878);

Daniel Webster, *The Great Speeches and Orations of Daniel Webster, with an Essay on Daniel Webster as a Master of English Style,* essay by Whipple (Boston: Little, Brown, 1879);

Charles Dickens, *The Writings of Charles Dickens, with Critical and Bibliographical Introductions and Notes by Whipple and Others,* 32 volumes

(Boston & New York: Houghton, Mifflin, 1894).

PERIODICAL PUBLICATIONS: Review of *The Scarlet Letter, Graham's Magazine,* 36 (May 1850): 345-346;
"The Vital and the Mechanical," *Graham's Magazine,* 37 (July 1850): 1-6;
"Doctrine of Form," *Graham's Magazine,* 37 (September 1850): 170-174;
Review of *The House of Seven Gables, Graham's Magazine,* 38 (June 1851): 467-468;
Review of *The Blithedale Romance, Graham's Magazine,* 41 (September 1852): 333-334;
"Nathaniel Hawthorne," *Atlantic Monthly,* 5 (May 1860): 614-622.

Edwin Percy Whipple's literary criticism received wide acclaim before he was thirty-five. During the 1840s and early 1850s he contributed articles to many periodicals, including the *North American Review, Graham's Magazine,* the *American Review,* the *Literary World,* and the *Methodist Quarterly Review.* In 1847, when Whipple was twenty-eight, Rufus Griswold, introducing the selections from Whipple's work which appeared in *The Prose Writers of America* (1847), judged that he gave "promise of occupying a higher rank than has been attained by any other American" among critical essayists. After Whipple published a collection of articles as the two-volume *Essays and Reviews* in 1848, the *Literary World* (23 December 1848) asserted that he now was "generally reputed to stand at the head of American critics," and the *Christian Review* (April 1850) announced that he was "considered on all hands the most accomplished" of contemporary critical essayists and lecturers. Emerson considered Whipple "a superior critic"; Hawthorne regarded him very highly; and Poe called him "perhaps," America's "best critic."

Although Whipple's early reputation has not been sustained, he remains significant in part because he was an important disseminator of romantic organic critical theory in an ethical New England environment. Whipple's central purpose, his friend Thomas Starr King wrote in 1850, was "to know the essence, laws, and philosophy of genius" from which literature grew, "and therefore he reads a book not only to discover what the characteristics of the book are . . . but also to determine what *the man is,*" what the "quality" and reach of his power are. In addition to seeing literature as an organic expression of the author (and,

to some extent, the author's roots), the critic's job was to expose (in the light of Whipple's own Boston Whig and Unitarian attitudes) health or sickness in the author's spirit. Literature was to be a moral force, although not an overly didactic one. Moral idealism functioned as a restraint on the historical relativism which was inherent in his organic theory.

With characteristic modesty, Whipple wrote to Rufus Griswold, who was seeking biographical information to be used in *The Prose Writers of America,* "My biography is very short, not much taller than my person." Indeed surprisingly little is known about his personal and family life. Even his letters are rather silent about such matters. He was born in Gloucester, Massachusetts, on 8 March 1819 to Matthew W. and Lydia Gardiner Whipple. In 1820 when Edwin was only eighteen months old, his father died of cholera; Edwin's mother was left with four small boys. The family soon moved to Salem, where Whipple went to school until he was fifteen, graduating from Salem High School in a business preparatory curriculum. He then served as a clerk at the Bank of General Interest, where a brother had worked for three years since its founding in 1831. These early years were filled with reading, so extensive (by his own account to Griswold) that by twenty-seven there was "hardly a prose-writer in English literature" that he had missed. He frequented bookstores and at times worked in the Salem Athenaeum Library, where he could remember Hawthorne's messengers depositing and picking up books.

In 1837 he made "a triumphal entrance," he joked, into Boston and became employed until 1845, first as a clerk and later as the chief clerk with the banking and brokerage firm of Dana, Fenno and Henshaw. In Boston his experiences in the Mercantile Library Association, which Whipple later said offered "an education such as can be given by no school or counting-house," and in the Attic Nights Club afforded the future reviewer and lecturer an opportunity to develop his abilities as critic, writer, and speaker. The Association provided lectures, a library, and an opportunity for practice in debate and for reading one's own poetry and prose. Members also took turns serving as critics of the virtues and deficiences of their creative offerings. The Attic Nights Club, formed by Whipple and five other members of the association, met Saturday nights in an antique-looking building, perhaps in an attic room, where, according to the

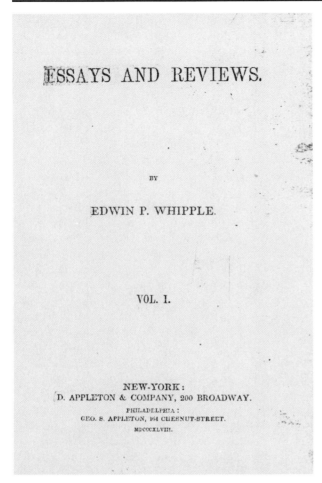

ESSAYS AND REVIEWS.

BY

EDWIN P. WHIPPLE.

VOL. I.

NEW-YORK:
D. APPLETON & COMPANY, 200 BROADWAY.
PHILADELPHIA:
GEO. S. APPLETON, 164 CHESNUT-STREET.
MDCCCXLVIII.

Title page for the first volume of Whipple's collection which established him as a leading literary critic

Duyckincks, Whipple displayed "his quick intellectual fence and repartee, extensive stories of reading, and subtle and copious critical faculty." Here he also had his first opportunity to discuss German, British, and American authors.

No comprehensive list of Whipple's very early publications exists. He told Griswold that he first wrote for "various newspapers," such as the *Boston Times* and *Boston Notion*. In the 18 December 1841 *Notion*, for example, he provided anonymously his earliest known treatment of Poe; a "rather savage" review, Whipple later noted, of one of Poe's chapters on autography. This foreshadowed Whipple's later, more widely known call for a critic with eclectic taste. His final assessment of Poe's criticism would be less harsh, but here he charged that Poe was not qualified "for a general critic." Poe confused his own "likes and dislikes" with "enlarged principles of taste" and hence was guilty of "a collossal [*sic*]

piece of impertinence . . . to exalt himself into a literary dictator." Whipple recalled four decades later that he also had contributed to "a penny paper" a review of the first volume of Emerson's essays. Whipple had been struck by "the quaint, keen, homely good-sense" in the volume: "A transcendentalist of the type of Emerson was as good judge of investments on earth as he was of investments in the heavens above the earth." Thus Emerson was not inappropriately called a "Greek-Yankee—a cross between Plato and Jonathan Slick," a frequently borrowed appellation which Whipple took credit for coining, "a dubious honor or dishonor" of his "youthful presumption."

His reputation as a critic grew because of magazine contributions, which often reflected his interest in an organic critical theory, traceable in part to August Wilhelm von Schlegel's *Lectures on Dramatic Art and Literature* (1809-1811) and to Samuel Taylor Coleridge's *Biographia Literaria* (1817). In the first magazine piece, on Macaulay (whose style Whipple's own did not imitate, he contended, but resembled enough to have warranted a letter from Griswold addressed "For Hon. T. Babington Macaulay Whipple") in the February 1843 *Boston Miscellany*, Whipple focused on the authorial seeds and roots of Macaulay's essays, which included "depth of feeling," "a fine sense of the beautiful," "a quick sensibility," "a comprehensive and penetrating judgment," "intellectual and moral sympathy," impartiality, and a love of liberty and hatred for despotism. Striving for the balanced view of the subject that marks some of Whipple's criticism, he also found deficiencies, for example, judgments sometimes dogmatic and haughty, wit sharpened by contempt rather than restrained by kindliness, and a style marked by "incessant brilliancy" that at times fatigues the reader. All of these merits and defects could be seen organically as outgrowths from the original seed of "vigor," the most prominent trait of his writing and personality.

Whipple later quipped that the short-lived *Boston Miscellany* died with the number in which his Macaulay essay appeared. In the same year he began a long, beneficial association with the *North American Review*, although at first he feared that the well-established, eminently respectable, well-printed journal was somewhat of a cemetery, "the Mount Auburn of literature, affording a most beautiful mausoleum wherein an article could be buried" in the cerements of an insufficiently circulated quarterly. In essays on *The Critical and Miscellaneous Writings of T. Noon Talfourd*

(October 1843) and on Griswold's *The Poets and Poetry of America* (January 1844) Whipple again focused on the mind and personality which flourished in the literature. "Love, beauty, goodness, sincerity, pure thoughts, and fine sympathies," sprang "as from a celestial seed" in Talfourd's essays.

But the dominance of Whipple's "kindliness of temper and tenderness of sentiment," his "sweet disposition," often made him too much an advocate and too infrequently a judge. In the essay on American poetry (which, if it was to be a part of a true national literature, should emerge organically from the history, scenery, society, and politics—the life and inner spirit—of this country) Whipple asserted that Charles Sprague's poem "Curiosity" grew out of the author's "most exact sense of moral distinction" and "fine perception of the ridiculous." Richard Henry Dana's works were marked by "an acute observation of nature, a deep feeling of beauty, a suggestive and shaping imagination, a strong . . . sensibility," and "a dark vein of despondency." Whittier had all the requisites for writing great poetry: soul, vigor, truthfulness, manliness of character, and independence of nature. The deficiencies of his poetry were explained as "faults of the mind," coming in part from "excessive fluency and a too excitable sensibility." Although extended analysis of the verbal and structural properties of poetry typically did not interest Whipple, occasionally he used organic analogies to comment on specific stylistic traits which, even though faulty on other grounds, were justified as emanations of the artist's personality or valued for their contributions to the organic unity of the work.

Thoughts on the moral function of poetry were especially prominent in his lengthy consideration of Griswold's *The Poets and Poetry of England in the Nineteenth Century* (1842) in the *American Review* (July 1845). The common view of poetry as "unreal"—that is, the judgment that the ideal or the imaginary is only a beautiful illusion—he believed had its origin in the excessive reliance on the senses and the understanding characteristic of the age. The world around us, he argued, was actually "an imperfect embodiment of real life"; and poetry, which "convicts convention of being false to the nature of things . . . by perceiving what is real and permanent in man and the universe," is the "protest of genius" and a catalyst for reform.

Whipple—who once inspired a listener to laud him for his mastery of the science of literary

THE

LITERATURE

OF

THE AGE OF ELIZABETH.

BY

EDWIN P. WHIPPLE.

BOSTON:
JAMES R. OSGOOD AND COMPANY,
LATE TICKNOR & FIELDS, AND FIELDS, OSGOOD, & CO.
1871.

Title page for a later edition of Whipple's collected lectures on Elizabethan dramatists and poets originally delivered in 1859 at the Lowell Institute

appraisal and classification and compare him with the natural historian Agassiz—divided the reformers into two classes: the intense and comprehensive. The intense poet is more subjective; his individuality "overmasters his mind." He has keen insights into realities, but his "poetry is often marked by an eloquent intolerance, a beautiful fanaticism, a most sublime wilfulness of vision" which "is lightning, not sunlight." The comprehensive poet has no desire to reshape nature and man into his own personality. His aim is to reach the general truth which includes all varieties; in doing so, he can be praised for his universality.

Whipple observed that no poet falls in only one of these classes, but English poets in the nineteenth century tended to be more intense; they were less interested in "correct" representations

Frontispiece and title page for Whipple's collected essays on Charles Dickens, many of which had appeared as introductory material in a thirty-two-volume edition of Dickens's work published by Houghton, Mifflin in 1894

and judgments than in impassioned statements. Of these, Scott alone deserved to be called comprehensive. Unfortunately his range of vision and his freedom from egotism also meant that Scott's individual soul was not observable in his poetry which, therefore, provided "no very subtile [*sic*] perception of the spiritual mysteries of the universe" that one often found in the more intense Wordsworth or Shelley.

Whipple focused on the principles of literary criticism in "British Critics" (*North American Review*, October 1845) and "Coleridge as a Philosophical Critic" (*American Review*, June 1846). The critics of the period exhibited an egotistical tendency like that which had urged the distinction between intense and comprehensive poets. Francis Jeffrey, for example, tested "the value of all things by their agreement or discordance" with an individual mode of thinking and, therefore, understood "little but himself" and was not able to do justice to many authors. The self-effacement Whipple called for was evident in the

exposition of the ideas of Coleridge, for him a primary shaper of the proper approach to criticism. Nature was Coleridge's (and Whipple's) guide: just as one would not disparage a willow tree because it is not an oak, one should not judge a poem with criteria foreign to it. Consequently, after determining first that the literary composition had life, the critic should concentrate on the organic nature of the product—how it grew from the thoughts and feelings of its author.

This orientation, Whipple argued, requires a comprehensive taste and brings the critic to the "peculiar individuality of the man" and his work, rather than the critic's own peculiarities and biases. Criticism thus becomes "interpretive both of the spirit and form of works of genius" instead of merely censorship, a change Whipple thought had been brought about by Coleridge. By seeking laws appropriate to each work of art, criticism also took its place among the sciences, Whipple wrote later in "Shakespeare's Critics" (*North American Review*, July 1848). A scientific examination of a plant, insect, or a fish entailed an investigation of the "inward mechanism," its purpose, and the physiognomy of its own "peculiar life." Whipple argued that *Hamlet* and *King Lear* were equally worthy of this treatment.

In *Essays and Reviews,* published in 1848 and 1849 in two volumes, Whipple collected these magazine essays along with others on topics such as Daniel Webster, Daniel Neal's *The History of the Puritans* (4 volumes, 1732-1748), Sydney Smith, Wordsworth, Byron, and English dramatists. A second edition appeared in 1851, a third in 1853, and nine more by 1888. The early critical response to the volumes clearly marked Whipple's rise in American literary criticism, a stature also reflected in awards of honorary degrees from Harvard University in 1848 and from the University of Vermont in 1851. Charles C. Smith in the *Christian Examiner* (March 1849) observed that he had "a widespread reputation" and "an honorable position" among critics and showed "promise of future eminence." Henry Norman Hudson, first in the *Literary World* (16 December 1848) and then in the *American Review* (February 1849), labeled Whipple "unquestionably one of the . . . brightest, and shrewdest living writers." The *Southern Literary Messenger* (February 1849) praised him as "one of the raciest and most brilliant essayists of the day." Responding to the second edition, *Harper's New Monthly Magazine* (April 1851) noted that "Whipple has attained a deserved eminence as a critical authority, which is certainly not surpassed in the field of American letters, and with but few exceptions, by a writer in the English language."

The acclaim for the work, of course, was not universal. At times the inevitable charges of "puffing" were voiced. Others, including a few supporters, found him too genial to be properly judicial–a trait Poe observed in a "eulogy" on Tennyson and lampooned as "critical Boswellism." Still others found that Whipple's talent and learning could not eclipse his lack of original thought. A reviewer in *Holden's Dollar Magazine* (April 1849), for example, underscoring Whipple's commercial training, called him a retailer of literature who manufactured nothing but kept on hand "an immense stock of ready made goods imported from all nations."

In 1850 Whipple published "The Vital and the Mechanical" (*Graham's Magazine,* July 1850) and "Doctrine of Form" (*Graham's Magazine,* September 1850), two disappointingly slight commentaries on organicism. In the first piece he was content to observe in religion, politics, science,

and literature the operation of the principle that "every thing . . . either grows or is put together, is a living organism or a contrived machine." In the second he argued that form does not occur accidentally, that there is an inevitable connection between the form and the nature of each thing in the mineral, vegetable, and animal worlds.

Much more significant in the 1850s were his growing friendship with Nathaniel Hawthorne and an important role in creating the novelist's contemporaneous reputation. Whipple recalled that Hawthorne, who had no literary vanity, needed to be cheered about the prospects of *The Scarlet Letter* (1850) when it was still in the press, a result perhaps achieved by some aspects of his review in *Graham's Magazine* (May 1850). If *The Scarlet Letter,* a "beautiful and touching romance" from "the fine and deep genius which lies within" the author, had any fault, Whipple wrote, it was an excessive gloom traceable to Hawthorne's intense interest in the "working of dark passions." Yet the fault seemed to enhance the underlying moral tone Whipple often looked for, since Hawthorne had so mastered the portrayal of guilt that even "the most abandoned libertine" reader would have to be thrilled "into something like virtuous resolution."

In his review of *The House of the Seven Gables* (*Graham's Magazine,* June 1851) Whipple found the gloom and humor better balanced (due in part, perhaps, to Hawthorne's sensitivity to Whipple's remark) and, while insistent that fiction should instruct subtly and not moralize, he took pains to emphasize the moral lessons which Hawthorne had introduced so quietly: few realize the "pernicious consequences" of expediency and that the influential classes are just as liable to error as are members of the mob. Hawthorne's growing respect for Whipple's judgment was reflected in his request that Whipple keep his promise to look over the manuscript that became *The Blithedale Romance* (1852). Hawthorne wanted "a keen, yet not unfriendly eye" to look for defects and wanted some help in choosing a title. It is probable not only that Whipple's advice influenced his choice of a title but the treatment of Hollingsworth in the conclusion as well.

In his subsequent review (*Graham's Magazine,* September 1852) Whipple provided a studied reflection on Hawthorne's genius and praised the work as "a real organism of the mind with the strict unity of one of Nature's own creations. It seems to have grown up in the author's nature, as a tree or plant grows from the earth, in

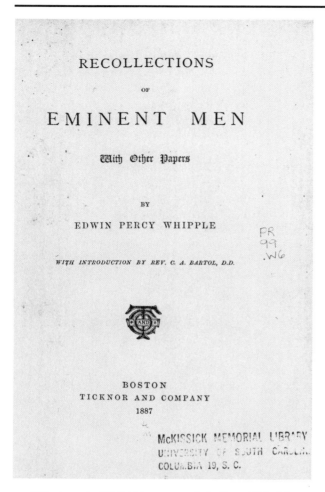

RECOLLECTIONS

OF

EMINENT MEN

With Other Papers

BY

EDWIN PERCY WHIPPLE

WITH INTRODUCTION BY REV. C. A. BARTOL, D.D.

BOSTON
TICKNOR AND COMPANY
1887

Title page for Whipple's essays, originally published in
Harper's Monthly, *on famous men he had known*

obedience to the law of its germ." Unfortunately, Whipple's ability to deal with the stylistic properties of the romance was not equal to his perceptions, for he added weakly that the unity was felt and could not be made clear by analysis. When *The Marble Faun* was published, Whipple surveyed Hawthorne's career in the *Atlantic Monthly* (May 1860) in a review which Hawthorne called "really keen and profound." Here Whipple observed that Hawthorne's misanthropy, not sufficiently relieved, and his use of characters less as feeling, thinking beings than as illustrations of thought were evident in his short stories. The romances, however, marked a distinct advance in his career; they provided the treatment of individuality (and the intrusion of Hawthorne's own passion) which created an intensity before lacking.

During the 1850s Whipple's celebrity as a public speaker also spread. Often restricted by the miscellaneous character of his audiences,

"Wit and Humor" and "The Ludicrous Side of Life" were the most popular of the six lectures he gave regularly from 1843 to 1849; he published the six in 1849 as *Lectures on Subjects Connected with Literature and Life* which had three printings during that year. Six new lectures on topics (such as "Character," "The American Mind," and "The English Mind") with broad appeal were given between 1849 and 1856 from Maine to Ohio. Five were published in *Harper's Monthly* in 1857; all were included in *Character and Characteristic Men* in 1866.

The most significant of his literary lectures were those in 1859 for the Lowell Institute which provided an opportunity for a semiweekly series of twelve lectures on Elizabethan dramatists and poets. They were subsequently printed in the *Atlantic Monthly* (February 1867-December 1868) and then in *The Literature of the Age of Elizabeth* (1869), Whipple's most developed commentary on the Renaissance. He was captivated especially by Shakespeare, in part because he was able to follow nature and feel human life from many points of view. Shakespeare could look through the eyes of Caliban as well as Othello, Dogberry as well as Mark Antony, Whipple noted; he could "seize the essence of all the excitements of human nature–terrible, painful, criminal, rapturous, or humorous"–because he was "thousand-souled." He was not merely an aristocrat of intellect and conscience like Milton, who could "do justice to the Devil" but not to "poor devils." In a word, Shakespeare demonstrated "toleration" (which Whipple emphasized belonged "to the highest class of virtues") beyond that demonstrated by other authors. Moreover, Shakespeare's work exhibited a living "unity in variety." Whipple compared Shakespeare's literary product to that of an oak tree; a Ben Jonson drama, by contrast, was "a cunningly fashioned box, made of oak-wood, with some living plants growing in it."

Most of Whipple's literary criticism written after 1860 deserves less attention. He had left the brokerage house of Dana, Fenno and Henshaw in late 1844 or early 1845 to become superintendent of the newsroom in the Merchants' Exchange Building in Boston, a position he held until 1860. Thereafter for some years he was a contributor and later an editor for the *Boston Transcript* and briefly, in the early 1870s, the literary editor of the *Boston Daily Globe*. In 1871 he published *Success and Its Conditions*, twelve essays (published separately over the previous twenty-five years), which dealt only occasionally with literature and focused, Whipple noted optimistically in the preface, on the proposition that in all departments of life "truth is mighty and *has* prevailed."

In 1876 he contributed an often superficial survey of American literature, an exercise which he felt required him to "condense paragraphs into epithets," to the *Harper's Monthly* series entitled "The First Century of the Republic." It was included in 1887 in *American Literature, and Other Papers.* A leader in providing a perceptive appreciation of Dickens's fiction beginning with an 1844 lecture, he also published individually some of the valuable essays which in 1894 would become introductory material in a thirty-two volume edition of Dickens's works. In 1912 Arlo Bates collected the essays in *Charles Dickens, The Man and His Works.* Whipple also contributed to *Harper's Monthly* sketches of famous men he had known. After his death in 1886, the sketches were included in *Recollections of Eminent Men* (1886). A miscellany of other previously published essays appeared in a posthumous volume, *Outlooks on Society, Literature and Politics* (1888).

After 1870 his reputation faded noticeably. In 1886 he was remembered as an important critic largely in obituaries and eulogies. John Greenleaf Whittier, a longtime friend, called him "the ablest critical essayist of his time," except, perhaps, for James Russell Lowell and Matthew Arnold. Thomas Wentworth Higginson ranked him as a critic with Margaret Fuller and "far above" Poe. But in general, as the *New York Tribune* (26 June 1886) reported, Whipple "may have suspected that he had survived the generation that comprehended him most fully." Twentieth-century assessments have been very infrequent. In 1946 Denham Sutcliffe published the only extensive modern scholarly article on Whipple; it is remarkable for its singularity as well as for it sensitive survey of Whipple's work. Whipple also has been the sole subject of three dissertations. Usually he has been relegated to the brief surveys provided in histories of literature and literary criticism, where he is remembered for his contributions to nineteenth-century criticism.

In isolating the deficiencies which contributed to the decline of Whipple's reputation, it is easy to be less than "interpretive"–in the genial sense Whipple himself preferred. William Dean Howells gave him too little credit when he voiced his doubt that Whipple "had any theory of criticism except to find out what was good in an au-

Engraved portrait used as the frontispiece for Whipple's Recollections of Eminent Men *(1886)*

thor and praise it," but clearly he was less a theorist than a reviewer and lecturer. Consequently, due to his lack of wide reading in the history of philosophy and his primary attention to matters other than the solution of philosophical problems, he was not likely to produce a lengthy treatise of organic theory. Unfortunately, his scattered comments on theory often sounded as if they were parts of successful lyceum lectures, devoid of discussion of some of the troublesome ramifications of his critical stance only in part because of the "perpetual scepticism," he once observed, "as to the patience of audiences which torments the lecturer during the brief hour in which he attempts to hold their attention."

Whipple did not seem aware, for example, that his organic theory and the catholic taste it required also encouraged an anarchy of tastes. In judging literature he was confident that one could rely on "the instinctive processes of every tolerant reader," an ideal democratic taste–which he assumed was not different from his own when he spoke of beauty or the essence and purpose of moral and spiritual laws. He also seemed unaware of the extent to which organic interpretation and literary judgment might be incompatible. He found no inconsistency in seeking Hawthorne's individuality in his work and then judging the work as excessively gloomy because of the absence of "spiritual joy." Organic theory was at times easily and comfortably set aside in favor of his own moral and aesthetic biases.

Moreover, his criticism seems less worthy and interesting because Whipple too often yielded to his own geniality, a common complaint not frequently enough tempered with a recognition of Whipple's comments on writers' deficiencies. Bayard Taylor admired this spirit of tolerance, but many others judged that it encumbered his discussions. At times Whipple was simply myopic, as is evident in his high praise of Charles Sprague and Richard Henry Dana, Sr. and his neglect of Poe and Whitman. Whipple also provides little analytical discussion of the stylistic properties of literary works, understandable considering his primary interest in the author's mind and personality but nevertheless disappointing to modern formalists. Some also denigrate aspects of his prose style, for example, his distracting fondness for antitheses, which Thoreau saw as evidence of Whipple's inability to deal with weighty subjects. Others have insisted that his style is too elaborately epigrammatic, although one cannot read (and reread) Whipple's essays without relishing his wit.

These deficiencies tarnish his reputation but do not obscure Whipple's considerable accomplishments. Because of his essays and lectures he became a highly respected voice in Boston culture and American literary criticism for several decades. He has been referred to as the best critic writing for the *North American Review* before the Civil War. He has been mentioned often as one of the first American critics to recognize and discuss the historical significance of Wordsworth's poetry. He was influential in urging American critics to look more closely at Shelley's poetry in order to find its essential morality. He contributed significantly to Tennyson's poetic reputation in the United States. He also helped to enhance respect for the novel as a literary form with challenging artistic and moral dimensions. In this regard, he provided perceptive early attempts to explain

Hawthorne's special genius and was one of the most important American interpreters of Dickens's fiction in the nineteenth century.

In the movement of literary nationalism, he argued strongly the need for an American literature less dependent on foreign influences. He also helped to elevate the profession of criticism by emphasizing an interpretive spirit rather than the censorious "grating of one individual mind against another." Interpretation, he urged, should be a science (but not "a kind of intellectual anatomy" that eclipses the life of a literary work) and should therefore follow laws appropriate to the work, not arbitrary rules or individual impressions. In this spirit Whipple was a notable speaker for romantic organic theory.

References:
Cyrus A. Bartol, "Whipple's Lectures on Literature and Life," *Christian Examiner,* 47 (November 1849): 370-384;

Francis Bowen, "Whipple's Lectures on Literature and Life," *North American Review,* 70 (January 1850): 153-165;

"E. P. Whipple," *Graham's Magazine,* 42 (April 1853): 448-455;

R. H. Fogle, "Organic Form in American Criticism: 1840-1870," in *The Development of American Literary Criticism,* edited by Floyd Stovall (Chapel Hill: University of North Carolina Press, 1955), pp. 75-111;

Thomas W. Higginson, "Edwin P. Whipple," *Atlantic Monthly,* 58 (September 1886): 344-348;

Julia W. Howe, "Edwin P. Whipple as a Critic," *New Princeton Review,* fifth series 3 (January 1887): 98-105;

Henry Norman Hudson, "Whipple's *Essays and Reviews,*" *American Review,* 9 (February 1849): 148-172;

T. W. Hunt, "E. P. Whipple as an English Essayist," *Bibliotheca Sacra,* 50 (January 1893): 30-51;

Thomas S. King, "Whipple's *Lectures,*" *Universalist Quarterly,* 7 (January 1850): 77-90;

Leishman A. Peacock, "Edwin Percy Whipple, A Biography," Ph.D. dissertation, Pennsylvania State University, 1942;

Bliss Perry, "Edwin Percy Whipple," in *The Early Years of the Saturday Club, 1855-1870,* by Edward Waldo Emerson (Boston & New York: Houghton Mifflin, 1918), pp. 117-123;

Edgar Allan Poe, "About Critics and Criticism," *Graham's Magazine,* 36 (January 1850): 49-51;

"Popular Lecturing," *Christian Review,* 15 (April 1850): 237-254;

John Paul Pritchard, "Edwin Percy Whipple," in his *Criticism in America* (Norman: University of Oklahoma Press, 1956), pp. 140-145;

John W. Rathbun, *American Literary Criticism, 1800-1860* (Boston: Twayne, 1979);

Robert E. Streeter, "Critical Thought in the *North American Review, 1815-1865,*" Ph.D. dissertation, Northwestern University, 1943;

Frederick Alvin Smith, "E. P. Whipple, Nineteenth Century American Literary Critic," Ph.D. dissertation, University of Illinois, 1969;

Denham Sutcliffe, "Our Young American Macaulay," *New England Quarterly,* 19 (March 1946): 3-18;

Luetta Wolf, "The Literary Criticism of Edwin P. Whipple," Ph.D. dissertation, University of Michigan, 1972.

Papers:
Edwin Percy Whipple materials, usually letters from and to Whipple, are widely scattered in libraries in the United States. The larger collections are in the Beinecke Library, Yale University; Houghton Library, Harvard University; Boston Public Library; Historical Society of Pennsylvania; University of Illinois Archives, Urbana; and the Alderman Library, University of Virginia.

Richard Grant White
(23 May 1821-8 April 1885)

Glen M. Johnson
Catholic University of America

BOOKS: *Companion to the Bryan Gallery of Christian Art: Containing Critical Descriptions of the Pictures, and Biographical Sketches of the Painters* (New York: Baker, Godwin, 1853);

Shakespeare's Scholar: Being Historical and Critical Studies of His Text, Characters, and Commentators, with an Examination of Mr. Collier's Folio of 1632 (New York: Appleton/London: Trubner, 1854);

National Hymns: How They Are Written and How They Are Not Written: A Lyric and National Study for the Times (New York: Rudd & Carleton Elliott, 1861; London: Low, 1862);

The New Gospel of Peace, According to St. Benjamin (volumes 1 and 2, New York: Tussey, 1863; volume 3, New York: American News Agency, 1864; republished in one volume, New York: American News Company, 1866);

Memoirs of the Life of William Shakespeare, With an Essay Toward the Expression of His Genius, and an Account of the Rise and Progress of the English Drama (Boston: Little, Brown, 1865);

The Adventures of Sir Lyon Bouse, Bart., in America During the Civil War: Being Extracts from His Diary (New York: American News Company, 1867);

Words and Their Uses, Past and Present: A Study of the English Language (New York: Sheldon, 1870; revised, 1872);

The Chronicles of Gotham, 2 volumes (New York: Carleton/London: Low, 1871-1872);

The Fall of Man; or, The Loves of the Gorillas, A Popular Scientific Lecture upon the Darwinian Theory of Development by Sexual Selection, by a Learned Gorilla (New York: Carleton/London: Low, 1871);

Every-Day English: A Sequel to "Words and Their Uses" (Boston: Houghton, Mifflin, 1880);

The American View of the Copyright Question . . . With a Postscript (London & New York: Routledge, 1880);

England Without and Within (Boston: Houghton, Mifflin, 1881);

Richard Grant White

Mr. Washington Adams in England (Edinburgh: Douglas, 1883); republished in *The Fate of Mansfield Humphreys, With the Episode of Mr. Washington Adams in England, and an Apology* (Boston: Houghton, Mifflin, 1884);

Studies in Shakespeare (Boston & New York: Houghton, Mifflin/London: Low, Marston, Searle & Rivington, 1886);

Opera in New York (New York, 1887).

OTHER: *The Works of William Shakespeare: The Plays Edited from the Folio of MDCXXIII, With Various Readings from All the Editions and All the Commentators, Notes, Introductory Remarks, A Historical Sketch of the Text, An Account of the Rise and Progress of the English Drama, A Memoir of the Poet, and an Essay upon the Genius,* 12 volumes, edited by White (Boston: Little, Brown, 1857-1866);

Poetry, Lyrical, Narrative, and Satirical, of the Civil War, edited by White (New York: American News Company, 1866);

The Confessions of William Henry Ireland, Containing the Particulars of His Fabrication of the Shakespeare Manuscripts, introduction by White (New York: Bouton, 1874);

The Dramatic Works of Richard Brinsley Sheridan, introduction by White (New York: Dodd, Mead, 1883);

Selections From the Poetry of Robert Browning, introduction by White (New York: Dodd, Mead, 1883).

PERIODICAL PUBLICATIONS: "Holbein and the Dance of Death," *Atlantic Monthly,* 3 (March 1859): 265-282;

"A Norse Love Story: Frithoif's Saga," *Galaxy Magazine* (June 1867);

"The Public-School Failure," *North American Review,* 131 (1880): 537-550;

"The Business of Office-Seeking," *North American Review,* 135 (1882): 27-49.

Richard Grant White was a visible figure in New York during the time when that city was emerging as a world center for the arts, for publishing, and for the cultural institutions supported by a wealthy and ambitious society. As a leisured gentleman of excellent pedigree, inherited money, aesthetic sensibility, and wide reading, White affected to hate New York and its brashness. But the city's cultural institutions and its many periodicals provided a forum for his strong opinions and his aristocratic persona. White's critical writings covered music, the visual arts, drama, and poetry. He wrote on such political issues as international copyright, public schools, and office seeking. He published satires on the peace movement during the Civil War, on postwar New York politics, and on Darwinism. His most important work, however, was as a scholar of Shakespeare. His edition of the plays, and his essays on Shakespeare's texts and the performing tradition, are of enduring value.

White belonged to no school, acknowledged no mentor, and left no disciples. He found his voice in opposition, on the one hand, to pedantic commentators and fussy scholarship and, on the other, to the "vulgar" consumption of art without the support of personal cultivation and restraint. His advice to new readers of Shakespeare is typical: "The way to read Shakespeare is–to read him. . . . Throw the commentators and the editors to the dogs" (*Studies in Shakespeare,* 1886). On the other hand, as White wrote of music, "It is not safe to measure the power" of an art "by the effects that it produces." Art is "a relief and a stimulus," but "it originates no sentiment, it develops none." Rather, in the properly educated consumer, it "subtilizes"–"not food for the soul but wine" (*National Hymns,* 1861). Such wine, to be sure, is no intoxicant but a subtle bouquet to be sipped and savored.

White molded his career on the English gentleman-amateur of letters. As William Charvat describes the type in *The Profession of Authorship in America* (1968), a gentleman author wrote for his own amusement, never for money, and as the by-product of learning and personal culture; he addressed what he wrote to a small group of presumed equals. White insisted on his heritage and assiduously cultivated a genteel persona. Born in New York in 1821, he was a direct descendant of one of the early English settlers of Massachusetts. Anyone who knew him knew, as he wrote in 1861, "how I prize my English birthright" (*National Hymns*). He prefaced his *Words and Their Uses, Past and Present: A Study of the English Language* (1870) with a letter to James Russell Lowell in which he imagined their ancestors meeting in a "newly laid out street of Cambridge" and taking satisfaction in a vision of their families' status–in the persons of Richard Grant and James Russell–"some two hundred and thirty or forty years" later.

The eldest child of a prosperous South Street merchant and Episcopal layman, "Grant" White attended the grammar school of Columbia College and then the University of the City of New York, from which he graduated at eighteen. His father wanted him to enter the ministry and opposed his youthful desire to be a musician. The son studied both medicine and law and was admitted to the bar in 1845, but never practiced. He drifted into writing, collaborating in two periodicals, the *Alleghanian* and the humorous *Yankee Doodle,* both of which failed. Financial troubles in the family gave new impetus to his writing career, and White associated with the *Morning Courier and New-York Enquirer* as music critic. In 1850 he married Alexina Black Mease. One of their two sons, Stanford White, became a central figure in the history of architecture in America.

White's first book, *Companion to the Bryan Gallery of Christian Art* (1853), catalogues the holdings of a New York museum. A modest work, the book briefly describes the paintings collected by T. J. Bryan and classifies them, in a general way, within each painter's work or a national tradition. The opinions are standard nineteenth-century wisdom—for example, that Raphael "stands unquestioned at the head of his art." White's short introduction is unremarkable, derived from authorities whom he cites—principally John Ruskin, William Hazlitt, and Jonathan Richardson. It remained characteristic of White to base his writings on extensive reading (and properly to credit his sources). The handbook, however, is his last publication in the field of visual arts, where he labored under the obstacle of never having seen most of the works that an art critic must draw upon for his generalizations.

Music was more available than painting to an American of the mid-nineteenth century. Although it was White's first subject and his most lasting interest, he never collected his writings on music, which are now for the most part buried in periodical files. A review of 1852, quoted in White's *Opera in New York* (1887), gives the flavor of White's early music criticism. Madame Alboni's voice, White wrote, had a "sumptuous quality," a "cool lusciousness," "bubbling" from "generously parted lips." Alboni "seems to give no thought to what she does, but merely to let the flood of song pour itself forth . . . large, simple, and grand." The emphasis here, on the person of the singer and on how this dramatic presence serves a work which will "pour" forth, is consistent with White's later focus, in discussing various arts, on the autonomy of the work and on performance as the realization (unself-conscious) of what a work contains. Throughout his career, White continued to draw on his knowledge of music and to use that knowledge to oppose studied "interpretations" in all genres. Arguing in *Studies in Shakespeare* against philosophical commentators on Shakespeare's plays, for example, White supported his position by reference to Mozart's symphonies: "Now, I venture to say that there is no . . . consecutive train of thought, and no . . . ethical import in the Jupiter and in the 'Zauberflote' or correspondence between them! Mozart did not evolve musical camels out of his moral consciousness."

MEMOIRS

OF THE LIFE OF

WILLIAM SHAKESPEARE,

WITH

AN ESSAY TOWARD THE EXPRESSION OF

HIS GENIUS,

AND

AN ACCOUNT OF THE RISE AND PROGRESS OF

THE ENGLISH DRAMA.

BY RICHARD GRANT WHITE.

BOSTON:
LITTLE, BROWN, AND COMPANY.
1865.

Title page for the three essays that first appeared in volume one of The Works of William Shakespeare, *which White began to edit in 1857*

White's book *National Hymns* derived from his music criticism. It grew out of a competition, inspired by the outbreak of the Civil War and judged by White and twelve associates, to produce an appropriate anthem. ("The Star Spangled Banner" was judged by White to be too difficult for "ordinary voices" to sing; "Hail Columbia" was "common-place, vulgar, and pretentious.") The judges decided that none of 1,200 entries was worthy of the $500 prize; but White salvaged the occasion by writing an account of the event. His book opens with a statement about "the power of music." The position he takes here is consistent with his later writings on literature. Music, he says, "addresses itself to man's entire nature." To the extent that it can be analyzed, this statement means that an art's value is not to be made too specific. Music "does not refine; it does not elevate; it does not strengthen. . . . It has no moral, nay, no intellectual influence whatever."

What is left after these exclusions is a kind of exquisite refinement, which "quickens and subtilizes" sentiments already present. That critical position seems, from a twentieth-century perspective, merely vague. But its significance, for White, comes inescapably from the assumption that aesthetic appreciation is a complement of being born well. As Edwin Cady has shown in *The Gentleman in America* (1949), heredity was an essential component of the idea of the gentleman, an attitude that America's upper classes took over from England and maintained well beyond White's time. In that sense, what White called "birthright" remained fundamental to his sense of himself and to his valuations as a critic. The snobbishness of this position became glaring later in White's writings on English usage. In the meantime, White cultivated his English heritage in producing the works that are his most lasting claim to critical recognition—his Shakespearean scholarship.

White had read Shakespeare since his earliest days. He was thankful, he said, that his father's library contained only unannotated editions of the plays; this had kept him "free from the contamination and perversion" of pedants and commentators. The immediate impetus for White's writings on Shakespeare was the faked corrected folio put forward by John Payne Collier. White produced an analysis of Collier's text, published in *Putnam's Magazine* in 1853 and then revised for *Shakespeare's Scholar* in 1854. Although others joined White in discrediting Collier's claims, no one did a more meticulous analysis of the spurious edited folio. (Like a gentleman White refrained from accusing Collier of intentional fraud—even though the evidence clearly indicated that.) White's examination highlighted textual anomalies—such as erasures in the annotations—drew upon knowledge of Elizabethan usage and dramatic contexts, and considered how the annotations affected, mostly for the worse, Shakespeare's "poetry," "humor," and "manifest dramatic purpose." White's case was solid: no one could deny conclusions based on such meticulous research and close readings.

Shakespeare's Scholar contained the criticisms of Collier's work, as well as notes, mainly textual, on each of the plays. These discussions pointed toward what White already had in process, his edition of *The Works of William Shakespeare*, which appeared in twelve volumes between 1857 and 1866. In 1883 a later printing of this edition became known as the first "Riverside" Shakespeare.

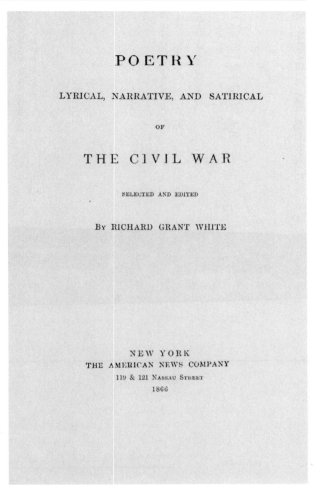

POETRY

LYRICAL, NARRATIVE, AND SATIRICAL

OF

THE CIVIL WAR

SELECTED AND EDITED

BY RICHARD GRANT WHITE

NEW YORK
THE AMERICAN NEWS COMPANY
119 & 121 NASSAU STREET
1866

Title page for the collection of poems White gleaned from wartime periodicals. White included poems written by Southerners in an appendix, stating "they will write better . . . in a better cause."

Volume 1 of the completed *Works* included White's biography of Shakespeare, along with "An Essay Toward the Expression of his Genius" and "An Account of the Rise and Progress of the English Drama." These three essays were also separately published, as *Memoirs of the Life of William Shakespeare* (1865). A number of periodical pieces on various topics, produced over the years, were revised by White shortly before his death and published posthumously as *Studies in Shakespeare* (1886).

White introduces the *Works* with a modesty unusual among editors of Shakespeare, claiming not an epoch-making text but "a better presentation of that which has been presented tolerably well before." An editor, White adds, is a "necessary evil" and should be tolerated only so far as is necessary to achieve an authoritative version of

Shakespeare's words. White's work will be "confined . . . to the text": interpretive notes will not be "thrust between a poet and his reader." In compiling his text White followed the accepted principle of granting "the authority which goes with authenticity" preeminently to the First Folio. White's text is "founded exclusively" on the Folio, though he will not scruple to alter "boldly" when that authority is found to be "manifestly corrupt or imperfect." Of course, lacking the scientific approach that was to be developed by the "new bibliography" in the twentieth century, White and his contemporaries had few methodological restraints on deciding what was imperfect or where to claim authority for bold "corrections." White, however, is consistently conservative, avoiding wild guesses and drawing emendations from the best quarto evidence. (White had at his disposal two copies of the folio and James Lenox's excellent collection of quartos.)

In explaining his principles of emendation, White places primary emphasis on "syllabic faithfulness." Decisions about contractions and endings "-ed" were based on White's (fortunately excellent) ear for rhythm. Elizabethan orthography interested him little except when it affects rhythm. On the other hand, he retains distinctions among possessive "it," "it's," and "its," as "evidence of a change in the language which took place during Shakespeare's career." His decisions were generally sound and his scholarship meticulous for the time. Even some things that contemporaries found quirky–such as White's insistence that *Nothing* in the title of *Much Ado* was pronounced "Noting," thus creating a pun–are today taken seriously. Early reviewers, notably James Russell Lowell, caught White making some claims for discoveries that others had made before and identified inevitable inconsistencies in the twelve volumes; but there was general agreement that White's edition was the most accurate to date. Unfortunately perhaps for White, it was almost immediately superseded, as the authoritative text, by Clark and Wright's Cambridge *Shakespeare* of 1863-1866.

White's *Memoirs of the Life of William Shakespeare* is less authoritative than his edition. Although he did his research and claimed to be counteracting pretentious claims by earlier writers, he put forward an interpretation of Shakespeare's life and motives that is extreme in what it refuses to grant the playwright. Rejecting the view that Shakespeare wrote out of large philosophical perspectives and for aesthetic purposes,

White claims that his motive was purely financial– "solely that he might obtain the means of going back to Stratford to live the life of an independent gentleman." The playwright chose his subjects to serve "the taste of the day," so as to fill the theaters. Moreover, "we may be sure that he wrote with no moral purpose." On the positive side, White does grant Shakespeare "his peculiar power as a dramatist . . . in his treatment of character." "So real" are his characters "in their individuality, so sharply outlined and completely constructed, that the men and women that we meet seem but shadows compared with them; and yet each one of them is so purged of the accidental and nonessential as to become typical, ideal." As for style, Shakespeare's is distinctive and preeminent, but "it is not to be defined at all; it is a mystery," a "nameless something." Perhaps that is because "his style corresponded entirely to the character of his mind" as "essentially a Goth." Shakespeare's "genius," as White sees it, is preeminently that of the Anglo-Saxon race: "universal as he was," Shakespeare "marked himself peculiarly ours by raising his dizzy pile of fancy and imagination upon the broad and solid foundation of English common-sense. The eminence of the rugged and solid English mind in all departments of poetry is a noteworthy intellectual phenomenon." As often with White, the "nameless something" that produces distinction is Anglo-Saxon "birthright."

White's collection of periodical essays, *Studies in Shakespeare*, opens with a long, avuncular piece titled "On Reading Shakespeare." Addressed to the "young" reader, it shows White in a less formal, sometimes quirky, frame. He says, for example, that women generally do not like Shakespeare, "with the exception of a few who are not always the most lovable or the happiest of the sex," because his writings are not "fanciful," "external," and "sentimental" enough for females. Beyond the quirks, White's advice is simple and good: begin by reading the plays, read for plot first, then "begin to study Shakespeare as a poet." As before, White maintains that the plays are accessible to any careful reader: "the help of critics" is needed–if at all–only at an advanced stage of appreciation. In that regard, "On Reading Shakespeare" contains White's strongest statements against "criticism of what has been called the higher kind"–the abstract, philosophical approach pioneered by Germans and imported into English by Coleridge. "Not a little of the Shakespearean criticism of this kind . . . is the

WORDS AND THEIR USES,

PAST AND PRESENT.

A STUDY OF THE ENGLISH LANGUAGE.

BY

RICHARD GRANT WHITE.

THIRD EDITION, REVISED AND CORRECTED.

BOSTON:
HOUGHTON, MIFFLIN AND COMPANY.
The Riverside Press, Cambridge.
1881.

EVERY-DAY ENGLISH.

A SEQUEL TO

"WORDS AND THEIR USES."

BY

RICHARD GRANT WHITE.

Ratio imperatrix supra grammaticam

BOSTON:
HOUGHTON, MIFFLIN AND COMPANY.
The Riverside Press, Cambridge.
1880.

Title pages for White's two most-popular books, compilations of articles on the correct usage of the English language which first appeared in the Galaxy *and the* New York Times

mere result of an effort to say something fine about what needs no such gilding. . . . Avoid them."

Included in *Studies in Shakespeare* is "The Bacon-Shakespeare Craze," an essay in which White reveals that, in 1856, he refused an invitation to write an introduction to Delia Bacon's book upholding Francis Bacon and others as authors of the plays. (An introduction was eventually written by Hawthorne.) Although White is acerbic about the "hapless" or "insane" upholders of the Baconian theory ("pene-literary people"), he maintains himself "wholly indifferent" at last: the authorship of the plays "affects in no way their literary importance or interest, their ethnological or their social significance, their value as objects of literary art, or their power as a civilizing, elevating influence upon the world." Several other essays, notably "The Case of Hamlet" and

"On the Acting of Iago," deal with contemporary performance practices, which White knew well, and argue for changes on the basis of close readings of the plays. In the Iagos of Edwin Booth and others, for example, White finds "a very exaggerated form of a very commonplace scoundrel" and argues for a more complex type "whom we all have often seen"—socially ambitious and successful, with no "spontaneous malice" but "utterly selfish, stony-hearted, and grasping." Simultaneously, although White doesn't mention Coleridge, the essay is arguing against his interpretations of Iago's "motiveless malignity."

During the Civil War years, White worked as chief of the revenue bureau of the New York Custom House and was occupied with his Shakespeare edition. But he found time to produce a satire on the Copperheads, or Northerners who sympathized with the South, published anonymously in three parts as *The New Gospel of Peace, According to St. Benjamin* (1863-1864). The pamphlets mimicked Elizabethan English and were divided into "verses" in imitation of the King James Bible. They were successful enough to encourage White to continue, and after the war he produced *The Chronicles of Gotham* (1871-1872), a satire on New York money and society, and *The Fall of Man* (1871), a burlesque of Darwinism "by a Learned Gorilla." Another postwar publication was an edition of *Poetry, Lyrical, Narrative, and Satirical, of the Civil War* (1866). White gleaned his selections from wartime periodicals offering little perspective which perhaps explains why there is included little that has lasted. White, indeed, seemed to be aware that the collection could be justified mainly for "historical value": it is "generally true," he wrote, that "great events do not inspire great poems." As a last reflection of his wartime radicalism, White banished Southern war poems to an appendix: "they will write better . . . in a better cause."

Once his Shakespeare was completed, White found a new career as arbiter of "the right use and the abuse" of English. Beginning in 1867 in the *Galaxy*, and later in the *New York Times*, he published regular articles on usage. There were two compilations, *Words and Their Uses* (1870) and *Every-Day English* (1880). These books were White's most popular—the former had reached its thirty-third "edition" by 1899. White's books on usage are very much of a piece with similar writings of a century later. Like Edwin Newman, John Simon, and William Safire in the 1970s, White sets himself up as an arbiter of "correctness and fitness of verbal expression," in the face of a perceived decline in "taste and reason." The stakes are thought to be high: "The mental tone of a community may be vitiated by a yielding to the use of loose, coarse, low, and frivolous phraseology. Into this people fall by mere thoughtless imitation of slovenly exemplars." His twentieth-century successors blame television; White blamed newspapers— "big words for small thoughts." Although White's basic advice about usage makes sense—"the higher the culture, the simpler the style and the plainer the speech"—the origins of his criticism in class-consciousness are obvious. The desire to hold off "vulgar" usage does not disguise the need to put down "vulgar" people.

As before, White did his research and thought out his positions. Although he lacked the vocabulary to follow them up, some of his perceptions anticipate later scholarship. For example, when he claims that "English is, to all intents and purposes, without formal grammar," he looks toward the discounting of Latin-based rules in the description of English. White always comes back, however, to his emphasis on class: "to protect against the contamination of debasing influences," he says, we must choose "usage of the most cultivated society" as the "only guide." Like John Simon after him, White admits that the language has changed over time, but maintains that change should now be stopped: further drift is likely to be "degradation" caused by "the very superficial instruction of a large body of people." A look at White's examples of degradation–he considers the verb "donate" to be "utterly abominable," for example–shows how futile are efforts such as his to hold an imagined line in usage.

In 1876 the lifelong Anglophile visited England for the first and only time. The resulting book, *England Without and Within* (1881), was compared at the time with Emerson's *English Traits* (1856); in retrospect, it seems at best comparable to the least inspired of Washington Irving's celebrations of old Britain. Like Irving in *The Sketch Book of Geoffrey Crayon, Gent.* (1819-1820), White begins by celebrating the skies visible during his Atlantic voyage; and the celebratory tone is maintained. As Allison Lockwood says in *Passionate Pilgrims* (1981), White's book "fairly glows with approval and enthusiasm for everything British." That glow is earned, and the enthusiasm maintained, partly through willful exclusions. White notes, for example, that he "kept away from mills and mines and everything connected with them." Perhaps more revealing, White declined to seek out Carlyle, Tennyson, "nor others of their order." His reason was that a man's prominence as a thinker or writer is no guarantee that he will not be "ill-natured or ill-bred, or at least uncompanionable." White spent his time with the well-bred and companionable; his 600-page account suffers as a result.

In his last years, White published a second satirical novel, *Mr. Washington Adams in England* (1883); like *The Adventures of Sir Lyon Bouse* (1867), it attracted little attention. Two critical publications of the 1880s are worth noting, however. "Opera in New York," which appeared in *Century* magazine in 1882 and was privately printed as a book in 1887, is a narrative history with mildly gossipy anecdotes about singers, entrepreneurs, and socially ambitious patrons of the arts. White, who had been involved in the musical scene, as critic and as patron, almost since the first appearance of Italian opera in New York in the 1820s, drew upon his own memories, and a collection of programs and playbills, to produce a valuable history of the institutions that supported art in Manhattan during his time. The next year (1883) brought an influential introduction, by White, of *Selections From the Poetry of Robert Browning*. White also was final arbiter of the selections based on Browning's own recommendations. White's enthusiastic support of "the intellectual phenomenon of the last half century" was long-standing and culminated in this edition. His reasons for a high evaluation of Browning are not surprising: "To say that Browning is the greatest dramatic poet since Shakespeare is to say that he is the greatest poet, most excellent in what is the highest form of imaginative composition, because it is the most creative."

After White's death in 1885, he was remembered primarily (in the words of the *Dictionary of American Biography*) as "a disagreeable, humorless snob, coxcomb, and Anglomaniac." The high-handed tone of his writing left him open to that characterization. But from the perspective of a century we can appreciate the breadth of his interests, the quality of his scholarship, and the value of his accomplishment in several areas. White was one of the last gentleman-amateurs of letters, a nonspecialist of wide reading and cultivated tastes, more than a little snobbish but an upholder of aesthetic standards in the middle of a rapidly expansive materialistic society. White lived in a city exploding with money and ambitious for everything, including "culture." No doubt the culture that New York and America developed was better for White's influence and example, if only slightly so.

Walt Whitman

(31 May 1819-26 March 1892)

Hisako Yamauchi
Kurume Institute of Technology

See also the Whitman entry in *DLB 3, Antebellum Writers in New York and the South.*

BOOKS: *Franklin Evans; or the Inebriate* (New York: New World, 1842);

Leaves of Grass (Brooklyn, N.Y.: Rome Brothers, 1855; London: Horsell, 1855; revised and enlarged, Brooklyn, N.Y.: Fowler & Wells, 1856; revised and enlarged again, Boston: Thayer & Eldridge, 1860-1861; London: Trubner, 1860-1861; revised and enlarged again, New York: Chapin, 1867; revised and enlarged again, Washington, D.C.: [New York: Redfield], 1871; revised and enlarged again, Boston: Osgood, 1881-1882; London: Bogue, 1881-1882; revised and enlarged again, Philadelphia: McKay, 1891-1892;

Drum-Taps (New York: Eckler, 1865); republished with *Sequel to Drum-Taps* (New York: Eckler, 1866; London: Chatto & Windus, 1915);

After All, Not to Create Only (Boston: Roberts, 1871);

Democratic Vistas (Washington, D.C.: [New York: Redfield], 1871); republished as *Democratic Vistas, and Other Papers* (London: Scott/ Toronto: Gage, 1888);

Passage to India (Washington, D.C.: [New York: Redfield], 1871);

As a Strong Bird on Pinions Free and Other Poems (Washington, D.C.: Green, 1872);

Memoranda During the War (Camden, N.J.: New Republic Print Shop, 1875-1876);

Two Rivulets—including *Democratic Vistas, Centennial Songs As a Strong Bird on Pinions Free, Memoranda During the War,* and *Passage to India* (Camden, N.J.: New Republic Print Shop, 1876);

Specimen Days & Collect (Philadelphia: Rees Welsh, 1882-1883; Glasgow: Wilson & McCormack, 1883); republished as *Specimen Days in America* (London: Scott, 1887);

November Boughs (Philadelphia: McKay, 1888; Paisley & London: Gardner, 1889);

Walt Whitman

Good-Bye My Fancy (Philadelphia: McKay, 1891);

In Re Walt Whitman, edited by Horace L. Traubel (Philadelphia: McKay, 1893);

Calamus, edited by Richard Maurice Bucke (Boston: Maynard, 1897);

The Wound Dresser, edited by Bucke (Boston: Small, Maynard, 1898);

Notes and Fragments, edited by Bucke (London, Ontario: Privately printed, 1899);

An American Primer, edited by Traubel (Boston: Small, Maynard, 1904);

Walt Whitman's Diary in Canada, edited by William Sloane Kennedy (Boston: Small, Maynard, 1904);

The Gathering of the Forces, edited by Cleveland Rodgers and John Black, 2 volumes (New York & London: Putnam's, 1920);

The Uncollected Poetry and Prose of Walt Whitman, edited by Emory Holloway, 2 volumes (Garden City & Toronto: Doubleday, Page, 1921);

Pictures, edited by Holloway (New York: June House, 1927);

The Half-Breed and Other Stories, edited by Thomas Ollive Mabbott (New York: Columbia University Press, 1927);

The Eighteenth Presidency! (Montpellier, France: Gausse, Graille & Castelnay, 1928); edited by Edward F. Grier (Lawrence: University of Kansas Press);

Walt Whitman's Workshop, edited by Clifton Joseph Furness (Cambridge: Harvard University Press, 1928);

A Child's Reminiscence, edited by Mabbott and Rollo G. Silver (Seattle: University of Washington Book Store, 1930);

I Sit and Look Out, edited by Holloway and Vernolian Schwartz (New York: Columbia University Press, 1932);

Walt Whitman and the Civil War, edited by Charles I. Glicksberg (Philadelphia: University of Pennsylvania Press, 1933);

Walt Whitman's Backward Glances, edited by Scully Bradley and John A. Stevenson (Philadelphia: University of Pennsylvania Press, 1933);

New York Dissected, edited by Holloway and Ralph Adimari (New York: Wilson, 1936);

Walt Whitman of the New York Aurora, edited by Joseph Jay Rubin and Charles H. Brown (State College, Pennsylvania: Bald Eagle Press, 1950);

Walt Whitman Looks at the Schools, edited by Florence Bernstein Freedman (New York: King's Crown Press, 1950);

Whitman's Manuscripts: Leaves of Grass (1860), edited by Fredson Bowers (Chicago: University of Chicago Press, 1955);

An 1855-56 Notebook Toward the Second Edition of Leaves of Grass, edited by Harold W. Blodgett with additional notes by William White (Carbondale: Southern Illinois University Press, 1959);

Portrait of Whitman used as the frontispiece in the first edition of Leaves of Grass *(1855)*

The Early Poems and the Fiction, edited by Thomas L. Brasher (New York: New York University Press, 1963);

Prose Works 1892, edited by Floyd Stovall, 2 volumes (New York: New York University Press, 1963);

Walt Whitman's Blue Book, edited by Arthur Golden, 2 volumes (New York: New York Public Library, 1968);

Walt Whitman's Autograph Revision of the Analysis of Leaves of Grass, edited by Quentin Anderson and Stephen Railton (New York: New York University Press, 1974);

Daybooks and Notebooks, edited by William White, 6 volumes (New York: New York University Press, 1977).

Collections: *Complete Poems and Prose of Walt Whitman, 1855-1888* (Philadelphia: Ferguson, 1888);

Complete Prose Works (Philadelphia: McKay, 1892);

The Complete Writings of Walt Whitman, edited by Richard Maurice Bucke, Thomas B. Harned, and Horace L. Traubel, 10 volumes (New York: Putnam's, 1902);

First page of Whitman's 1873 will (Anderson Galleries, sale number 2198, 25 November 1927)

The Collected Writings of Walt Whitman, general editors, Gay Wilson Allen and Sculley Bradley, 22 volumes (New York: New York University Press, 1961-1984);

Walt Whitman's Memoranda During the War and Death of Abraham Lincoln, edited by Roy P. Basler (Bloomington: Indiana University Press, 1962);

Leaves of Grass: Comprehensive Reader's Edition, edited by Harold Blodgett and Bradley (New York: New York University Press, 1965).

Walt Whitman did not aspire to be a literary critic, yet in the course of his career he did review the works of a large number of writers ranging from the ancient classicists to his contemporaries. In form and length Whitman's criticism is journalistic, reflecting his long training and experience on various newspapers. Although his attitudes toward writers and literature matured with experience, his critical principles stayed remarkably consistent. Most notably he sought to disassociate American literature from its English origins in order that America might have a "democratic" literature. To this end he viewed all literature of the past as material from which might be winnowed a literary canon that could be the bedrock of a literature for the commonalty. Hence literature was to be valued less for its "professional quality" than for its reflection of and sympathy with humanity. Certain corollaries followed. Overpreoccupation with revision and polish encouraged too much method and formalism at the expense of vitality. "The best writing," he was later to say, "has no lace on its sleeves." Modern ideas, practices, and standards, especially as associated with emerging democratic humanity, should prevail against those of the past. Indirection informed by imaginative vision was better than slavish imitation–a view that led him to be impatient with post-Civil War realism. The true visionary was the poet, who in Whitman's view would eventually replace Christ as the true son of God. The poet that Whitman consistently prized was intuitive, imaginative, vital, robust, perspicuous, sympathetic, and above all prophetic of the new democratic order of things to come.

Whitman, the second of nine children, was born 31 May 1819 in West Hills, Long Island, to parents of Quaker background, Walter and Louisa Van Velson Whitman. In 1823 the family moved to Brooklyn, where for six years Whitman attended public schools. It was the only formal

educaton he ever received. At age eleven he worked as an office boy for lawyers and a doctor, then in the summer of 1831 became a printer's devil for the *Long Island Patriot.* Unsuccessful in trying to land a job as a compositor he rejoined his family, who in the meantime had returned to Long Island.

On Long Island he taught at several schools and in 1838-1839 edited *Long Islanders.* The next few years he alternated between teaching school and contributing or editing newspapers in Long Island, Brooklyn, and New York. This journalistic activity expanded to the point that between 1841 and 1850 he either edited or contributed to over thirteen newspapers and magazines in the greater New York area. A novel, *Franklin Evans; or the Inebriate,* was published in 1842. In 1848 he journeyed to New Orleans and worked a short stint with the *New Orleans Crescent,* the first of a number of journeys he would make to familiarize himself with the breadth of America.

Among the newspapers and magazines with which Whitman was associated, the *New York Aurora* and the *Democratic Review* especially provided him important opportunities to acquaint himself with the world of literature. The *Aurora* assigned him to report on a series of lectures by Ralph Waldo Emerson, the most famous New England transcendentalist of the day, and at the time at the peak of his powers; Whitman would later say that it was Emerson who "brought me to boil." The *Democratic Review,* the organ of liberal Young America, provided him the opportunity to read works by such major American writers as Hawthorne, Poe, Bryant, Longfellow, and Thoreau; he read, too, the Bible, Shakespeare, and the "Gaelic" poet Ossian, Greek and Hindu poets, Dante, Dickens, Scott, and Carlyle. The published criticism that emerged from this reading, together with Kenneth M. Price's study of Whitman's marginalia, reveal certain capricious characteristics that Whitman never abandoned. Most notable is verdict by fiat. Whitman was quick to judge, slow to reason why. On occasion this was due to the fact that he had not read the work under review: ironic in view of his later statement that book reviewers were "like so many monkeys on the limb of a tree chattering in concert." When the works under review *had* been read, his judgments are often so arbitrarily personal as to defeat the cause of criticism.

Thus some of his early views can be startling. Samuel Johnson is dismissed as a "sour, malicious, egotistical man." The prudery behind his

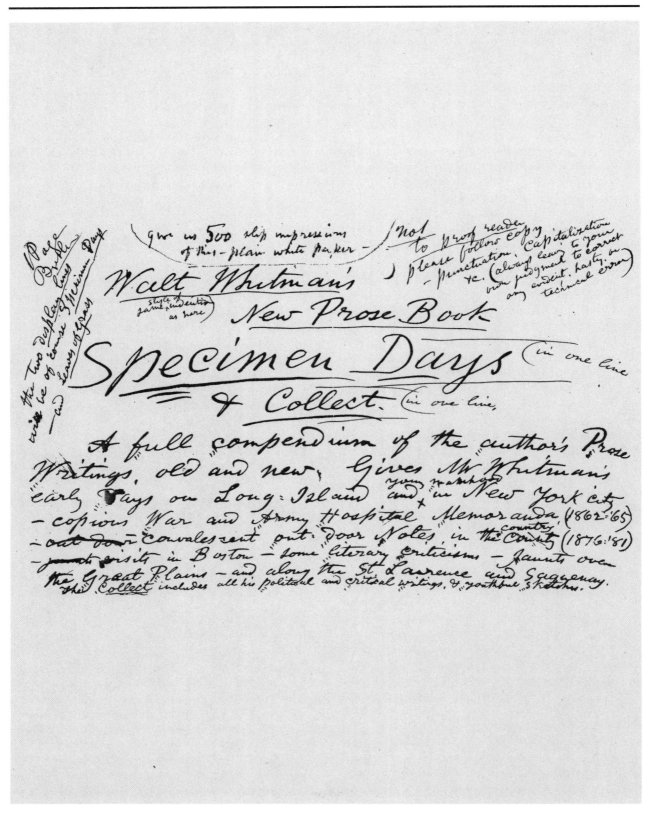

Title page with notes to the printer from the manuscript for Whitman's Specimen Days & Collect *(1882-1883) (Charles E. Feinberg Collection, Library of Congress)*

attack on William Gillmore Simms's *The Wigwam and the Cabin* (1845) as "lewd" and "coarse and indelicate in its details" is simply bewildering. His positive responses were less myopic. He always respected William Cullen Bryant as a poet of nature and even felt personal fondness for the man. Henry Wadsworth Longfellow, whose poems Whitman sometimes published in the *Brooklyn Eagle* (which he edited from 1846-1848), was another for whom Whitman had warm admiration. The writings of Margaret Fuller and George Sand provided him with evidence for his lifelong assertion that women are the intellectual equals of men, so that consideration of gender differences has no place in either literature or criticism. He had as one would expect an almost extravagant admiration for Emerson. In fact, his continued emphasis on self-reliant originality, democratic nationalism, modernity, and obstinate independence, while certainly native to his temperment, owed much to Emerson's influence.

Between 1848 and 1855 Whitman lived mostly in Brooklyn with his family, where he operated a printing office and stationery store and occasionally contributed to newspapers. In July of 1855 the first edition of *Leaves of Grass* was published by Rome Brothers in Brooklyn. About 1,000 copies were printed, though not all of them were bound at once. The book contained a long prefatory essay and twelve untitled poems. For the most part, public reaction was unfavorable. Many readers were utterly startled by Whitman's irregular verse form; most could not fully understand his poems; more perceptive readers were distressed and sometimes outraged (as was Oliver Wendell Holmes) by the explicitness of Whitman's sensuality. Emerson, however, upon reading a complimentary copy, wrote to Whitman saying that it was "the most extraordinary piece of wit and wisdom that America has yet contributed." Whitman continually added more poems to the volume, tinkered with others already included, and revised the book's structure. The number of editions totaled seven by the time of his death on 26 March 1892.

The preface to the 1855 editon of *Leaves of Grass* has since become one of the most famous manifestos in literature. It is a lyrical statement of belief in the possibility of a democratic poetry for America and in the inevitable emergence of a poet who will be a bard to the people. Whitman exalts the poet to divine rank and makes him a redeemer of the people even as he reflects their native wisdom, spiritual yearnings, and earthly appetites. The poet's power derives from his intuitive knowledge of divinely ordained universal history and of the fundamental laws and precepts which unify all creation. He incarnates this knowledge and through his poetry enlightens the people to their own divine destinies. The poetry is thus revelatory in the sense that it takes up what appears to be incomplete and discrete and shows how it fits into the cosmic whole. The result is a response marked by a whole lexicon of emotional terms: ardor, enthusiasm, gusto, passion, receptivity, ecstasy among them. Needless to say, this lofty vision of the poet demanded poetry that corresponded in scale and form. Traditional forms and conventions were cast off because Whitman felt that they narrowed poetry into a given course of expression utterly familiar and ineffectual. "Of ornaments to a work nothing outré can be allowed." To Whitman, honest expression would spontaneously dictate form and rhythm: "The rhyme and uniformity of perfect poems show the free growth of metrical laws and bud from them as unerringly and loosely as lilacs or roses on a bush, and take shapes as compact as the shapes of chestnuts and oranges and melons and pears, and shed the perfume impalpable to form."

In several reviews that Whitman anonymously wrote to puff the book, he gave a further critical cast to his creative aspirations. "Walt Whitman and his Poems," which appeared in *The United States Review* (1855) mocks those literary ideas which reveal their origins in London and Paris. Mainly Whitman rejects caste and class while enthusiastically embracing amelioration and progress. Dismissing the "rules of polite circles" and all such categories as classic or romantic, materialism or spiritualism, Whitman centers on his book's "fierce affection for persons." "Persons" constitute the common people, promote the great democratic undertaking, dwell in and react to the American landscape. In Whitman, he proclaims, the people have found "An American bard at last!" The style is described as "transcendent and new," so organically complex that its rhythms and consistency are concealed in the "roots of his verses, not to be seen by themselves." Despite the questionable ethics involved in the review's authorship, the points that Whitman makes are ones that posterity has since confirmed.

Democratic Vistas (1871) is Whitman's first published book of prose. Written during the Reconstruction, it reflects the feeling that the great

Whitman, with his nurse Warren Fitzenger, in 1890 (Charles E. Feinberg Collection, Library of Congress)

American experiment in democracy had failed and would continue to fail without a greater commitment to individual conscience and personal integrity. Here Whitman emphasizes the concept of brotherhood, especially in his argument that individuals should give up some liberties in order to promote the welfare of the group. The reconciliation of individualism and brotherhood, Whitman thinks, can be best fulfilled by new American writers who will crystallize his own ideals. He seldom specifies poets or novelists, but he does criticize literary practices in general and claims that literature "has never recognized the People."

In January 1873 he suffered a partial paralytic stroke which compelled a move to Camden, New Jersey, where his brother George lived with his mother. The mother died shortly after. *Two Rivulets* (1876) and *Specimen Days and Collect* (1882-1883) were collections of early journalism,

including literary criticism and reviews; their republication at a time when Whitman was becoming accepted earned them a second and more extensive readership. Steadily failing health prompted him to move to a house on Mickle Street in Camden, where he lived with a housekeeper until his death. Among his visitors was the young Horace Traubel, who in 1888 began to take notes for what would become his series of memoirs, *With Walt Whitman in Camden* (1906-1964).

November Boughs (1888) and *Good-Bye My Fancy* (1891) contain a significant amount of literary criticism. Whitman's attitudes and values are essentially the same as found in the work of his apprenticeship years, but his positions are explained in more detail and there is a certain depth present which is lacking in his earlier work. A late article, "Have We an American Literature?" provides a convenient vantage point for putting the later criticism in context. Written in response to an invitation from the editor of the *North American Review* and published in the March 1891 issue, his answer to the question in his title is a "no." He predicts a "yet to be" body of American literature, but even that is undercut by a conditional phrase—"if it ever comes"—which establishes a basic uncertainty. Given the late date of the article Whitman's hesitation is simply astonishing. By 1891 there existed a substantial body of native literature. However, not a single writer is mentioned: not Emerson or Thoreau, Hawthorne or Melville; realists of the stature of Howells, Clemens, and James (elsewhere dismissed as producing dainty "fragile literary vessels"); or any of the emerging naturalist writers.

Whitman's shortsightedness can be explained in terms of his personal views. He was not looking at American literature as it *was* but as it *should* or *could be*. Implicit in his argument is the idea that no "great literatus" had emerged other than himself, and he saw none on the horizon. Characterizing the American people as possessed of decorum, intelligence, and a sense of noblesse oblige, they yet lacked voices who would translate these attributes into literary forms. Patriotism, nationality, and ensemble—Whitman's trinity of American ideas—were scarcely visible in American books, and without them no national literature was possible. In support of this position he quoted the "high-pitch'd taunt" of Margaret Fuller: "It does not follow, because the United States print and read more books, magazines, and newspapers than all the rest of the world, that they really have therefore a literature."

Whitman's nationalism appears to have a political cast, but it is its expression amounting to religious ecstasy that is important. Since democratic nationalism was a late development, it logically stood that the ecstatic voice would be missing in earlier writers. Yet a nationalist spirit that could serve as the basis of further growth and development could be detected in earlier writers, and Whitman was responsive. Robert Burns was celebrated for his close empathy with his people, and on somewhat similar grounds Whitman was prepared to accept Tennyson. Even Shakespeare, always suspect as the voice of feudalism, not to speak of the "sickly sulking and sniffling" of *Hamlet*, could be appreciated for the nationalist fervor of his history plays. In 1884 Whitman was prepared to go further. Following the lead of his friend and benefactor William Douglas O'Connor, he speculated that the "real meaning and purposes" of the history plays were to "record the first full exposé" of the futilities of feudalism and to proclaim "the scientific (Baconian?) inauguration of modern Democracy."

On the evening of 26 March 1892 Whitman died, and four days later was buried at Harleigh Cemetery in Camden. Primarily the poet of transcendentalism and democracy and the prophet of self, the considerable bulk of his prose writings is situated within the programmatic intentions of his literary theory and objectives. He was therefore unable to approximate the dispassionate stance of the committed literary critic. To Traubel he said on occasion that the reviewer and the critic should focus on what the writer intended rather than indict the writer for failing to accomplish what he never meant to do. This admirable precaution, however, was seldom observed in his own critical practice. He was fairer with writers that he personally liked or was attracted to: Emerson, Bryant, Longfellow, Carlyle, Burns, Dickens, Tennyson. His literary criticism of others is chiefly of interest for his evaluations of writers relative to his own purposes.

Letters:

Letters Written by Walt Whitman to His Mother from 1866 to 1872, edited by Thomas B. Harned (New York: Putnam's, 1902);

The Letters to Anne Gilchrist and Walt Whitman, edited by Harned (Garden City: Doubleday, Doran, 1918);

Whitman and Rolleston: A Correspondence, edited by Horst Frenz (Bloomington: Indiana University Press, 1951);

The Correspondence of Walt Whitman, edited by Edwin Haviland Miller, 6 volumes (New York: New York University Press, 1961-1977).

Bibliographies:

Frank Shay, *The Bibliography of Walt Whitman* (New York: Friedmans', 1920);

Carolyn Wells and Alfred F. Goldsmith, *A Concise Bibliography of the Works of Walt Whitman* (Boston: Houghton Mifflin, 1922);

Gay Wilson Allen, *Twenty-Five Years of Walt Whitman Bibliography: 1918-1942* (Boston: Faxon, 1943);

Allen, *Walt Whitman Handbook* (Chicago: Packard, 1946);

14

¶ The word I should put primarily as indicating the character of my own poems would be the word "Suggestive- ness." I round and finish little or nothing; I could not, consistently with my scheme. If "Leaves of Grass" satisfies those who, to use a phrase of Margaret Fuller's, "expect suggestions only and not ful- filments," I shall be quite content.

Pages from the manuscript of "A Backward Glance on My Own Road" (Critic, 5 January 1884), Whitman's assessment of the signifi-cance of his poetry following publication of the 1881-1882 edition of Leaves of Grass *(Walt Whitman's Backward Glances, University of Pennsylvania Press, 1947)*

15

¶ That I have not been accepted during my own time — that the largely prevailing range of criticism on my book has been either mockery or denunciation — that my relation with publishers has been that of victim — and that I have been the marked object of two or three (to me pretty serious) official buffetings — is all (not more than I ought to have expected. I had my choice when I commenced. I bid neither for soft eulogies, nor big money returns, nor the approbation of existing schools and conventions. As now fulfilled after thirty years, the best of the achievement is, that I have had my say entirely my own way, and put it unerringly on record — the value thereof to be decided by time.

Photograph of Whitman in 1891 made by painter Thomas Eakins, who had painted a portrait of Whitman in 1888 (courtesy of Yale University Library)

Walt Whitman: A Catalog Based upon the Collections of the Library of Congress (Washington, D.C.: Government Printing Office, 1955);

James T. Tanner, *Walt Whitman: A Supplementary Bibliography 1961-1967* (Kent, Ohio: Kent State University Press, 1968);

William White, *Walt Whitman's Journalism: A Bibliography* (Detroit: Wayne State University Press, 1969);

Roger Asselineau, "Walt Whitman," in *Eight American Authors,* edited by James Woodress, revised edition (New York: Norton, 1971), pp. 225-272;

Allen, *The New Walt Whitman Handbook* (New York: New York University Press, 1975);

Gloria A. Francis and Artem Lozynsky, *Whitman at Auction, 1899-1972* (Detroit: Gale, 1978);

Jeanetta Boswell, *Walt Whitman & the Critics: A Checklist of Criticism, 1900-1978* (Metuchen, N.J.: Scarecrow Press, 1980);

Scott Giantvalley, *Walt Whitman, Eighteen Thirty-Eight to Nineteen Thirty-Nine: A Reference Guide* (Boston: G. K. Hall, 1981);

Donald Kummings, *Walt Whitman, 1940-1975: A Reference Guide* (Boston: G. K. Hall, 1982).

Biographies:

William Douglas O'Connor, *The Good Gray Poet: A Vindication* (New York: Bunce & Huntington, 1866);

John Burroughs, *Notes on Walt Whitman as Poet and Person* (New York: American News, 1867);

Richard M. Bucke, *Walt Whitman* (Philadelphia: McKay, 1883);

Thomas Donaldson, *Walt Whitman, the Man* (New York: Harper, 1896);

William Sloane Kennedy, *Reminiscences of Walt Whitman* (London: Gardner, 1896);

John Townsend Trowbridge, *My Own Story* (Boston: Houghton, Mifflin, 1903);

Whitman's tomb, built from his own design, in Harleigh Cemetery, Camden, New Jersey

Henry Bryan Binns, *A Life of Walt Whitman* (London: Methuen, 1905);

Edward Carpenter, *Days with Walt Whitman* (London: Allen/New York: Macmillan, 1906);

Bliss Perry, *Walt Whitman: His Life and Work* (London: Constable/New York: Houghton, Mifflin, 1906);

Horace Traubel, *With Walt Whitman in Camden, March 28-July 14, 1888* (Boston: Small, Maynard, 1906);

Traubel, *With Walt Whitman in Camden, July 16-October 31, 1888* (New York: Appleton, 1908);

James Thompson, *Walt Whitman, the Man and the Poet* (London: Dobell, 1910);

Traubel, *With Walt Whitman in Camden, November 1, 1888-January 20, 1889* (New York: Kennerley, 1914);

Charles N. Elliot, *Walt Whitman as Man, Poet and Friend* (Boston: Badger, 1915);

Leon Bazalgette, *Walt Whitman, the Man and His Work*, translated by Ellen Fitzgerald (Garden City: Doubleday, 1920);

Elizabeth Leavitt Keller, *Walt Whitman in Mickle Street* (New York: Kennerley, 1921);

John Bailey, *Walt Whitman* (New York: Macmillan, 1926);

Emory Holloway, *Whitman: An Interpretation in Narrative* (New York: Knopf, 1926);

Clara Barrus, *Whitman and Burroughs: Comrades* (Boston: Houghton Mifflin, 1931);

Edgar Lee Masters, *Whitman* (New York: Scribners, 1937);

Newton Arvin, *Whitman* (New York: Macmillan, 1938);

Katherine Molinoff, *Some Notes on Whitman's Family: Mary Elizabeth Whitman, Edward Whitman, Andrew and Jesse Whitman, Hannah Louisa Whitman* (Brooklyn, N.Y.: Privately printed, 1941);

Hugh I'Anson Faussett, *Walt Whitman: Poet of Democracy* (New Haven: Yale University Press, 1942);

Henry Seidel Canby, *Walt Whitman: An American* (Boston: Houghton Mifflin, 1943);

Gay Wilson Allen, *The Solitary Singer: A Critical Biography of Walt Whitman* (New York: Macmillan, 1955; revised edition, New York: New York University Press, 1967);

Horace Traubel, *With Walt Whitman in Camden, January 21-April 7, 1889*, edited by Sculley Bradley (Carbondale: Southern Illinois University Press, 1959);

Emory Holloway, *Free and Lonesome Heart: The Secret of Walt Whitman* (New York: Vantage, 1960);

Allen, *Walt Whitman* (New York: Grove, 1961);

Horace Traubel, *With Walt Whitman in Camden, April 8-September 14, 1889*, edited by Gertrude Traubel (Carbondale: Southern Illinois University Press, 1964);

Joseph Jay Rubin, *The Historic Whitman* (University Park: Pennsylvania State University Press, 1973);

Justin Kaplan, *Walt Whitman: A Life* (New York: Simon & Schuster, 1980).

References:

Gay Wilson Allen, *Aspects of Walt Whitman* (Philadelphia: Folcroft Library Editions, 1961);

Allen, *A Reader's Guide to Walt Whitman* (New York: Farrar, Straus & Giroux, 1970);

Allen, *Walt Whitman as Man, Poet, and Legend* (Carbondale: Southern Illinois University Press, 1961);

Allen, ed., *Walt Whitman Abroad* (Syracuse: Syracuse University Press, 1955);

Roger Asselineau, *The Evolution of Walt Whitman*, 2 volumes (Cambridge: Harvard University Press, 1960-1962);

Stephen A. Black, *Whitman's Journey into Chaos* (New Brunswick: Rutgers University Press, 1975);

Harold Blodgett, *Walt Whitman in England* (Ithaca: Cornell University Press, 1934);

Harold Bloom, ed., *Walt Whitman* (New York: Chelsea House, 1985);

Helena Born, *Whitman's Ideal Democracy* (Boston: Everett Press, 1902);

Arthur E. Briggs, *Walt Whitman: Thinker and Artist* (New York: Philosophical Library, 1952);

Richard M. Bucke, *Cosmic Consciousness* (New York: Dutton, 1923);

John Burroughs, *Whitman: A Study* (Boston: Houghton, Mifflin, 1896);

E. Fred Carlisle, *The Uncertain Self: Whitman's Drama of Identity* (East Lansing: Michigan State University Press, 1973);

Richard Chase, *Walt Whitman Reconsidered* (New York: Sloane, 1955);

Leadie M. Clark, *Walt Whitman's Conception of the American Common Man* (New York: Philosophical Library, 1955);

Sarah Blacher Cohen, "Walt Whitman's Literary Criticism," *Walt Whitman Review*, 18 (June 1972): 39-50;

Walter H. Eitner, *Walt Whitman's Western Jaunt* (Lawrence: University Press of Kansas, 1981);

Norman Foerster, *American Criticism* (Boston: Houghton Mifflin, 1928);

William Gay, *Walt Whitman: His Relation to Science and Philosophy* (Melbourne, Australia: Firth M'Cutcheon, 1895);

Clarance Gohdes and Rollo G. Silver, eds., *Faint Clews and Indirections: Manuscripts of Walt Whitman and His Family* (Durham: Duke University Press, 1949);

Douglas Grant, *Walt Whitman and His English Admirers* (Leeds: Leeds University Press, 1962);

Conrad L. Hartley, *The Spirit of Walt Whitman* (Philadelphia: Folcroft Library Editions, 1973);

Will Hayes, *Walt Whitman: The Prophet of the New Era* (London: Daniel, 1921; Philadelphia: Folcroft Library Editions, 1973);

Milton Hindus, ed., *Walt Whitman: The Critical Heritage* (London: Routledge & Kegan Paul, 1971);

Maurice O. Johnson, *Walt Whitman as Critic of Literature* (Lincoln: University of Nebraska Press, 1938);

D. H. Lawrence, *Studies in Classic American Literature* (New York: Boni, 1923);

Henry E. Legler, *Walt Whitman: Yesterday & Today* (Philadelphia: Folcroft Library Editions, 1973);

R. W. B. Lewis, ed., *The Presence of Walt Whitman* (New York: Columbia University Press, 1962);

Jerome Loving, *Emerson, Whitman & the American Muse* (Chapel Hill: University of North Carolina Press, 1982);

Andrew Macphail, *Essays in Puritanism: Jonathan Edwards, John Winthrop, Margaret Fuller, Walt Whitman, John Wesley* (Port Washington, N.Y.: Kennikat Press, 1905);

F. O. Matthiessen, *American Renaissance* (New York: Oxford University Press, 1941);

Charles R. Metzger, *Thoreau and Whitman: A Study of Their Aesthetics* (Seattle: University of Washington Press, 1961);

James E. Miller, Jr., *Walt Whitman* (New York: Twayne, 1962);

Carleton Eldredge Noyes, *An Approach to Walt Whitman* (New York: Houghton Mifflin, 1910);

Roy Harvey Pearce, ed., *Walt Whitman: A Collection of Critical Essays* (Englewood Cliffs, N.J.: Prentice-Hall, 1962);

Kenneth M. Price, "The Margin of Confidence: Young Walt Whitman on English Poets and Poetry," *Texas Studies in Language and Literature* (Winter 1983): 541-557;

Esther Shephard, *Walt Whitman's Pose* (New York: Harcourt, Brace, 1938);

Jan Christian Smuts, *Walt Whitman: A Study of the Evolution of a Personality*, edited by Alan L. McLeod (Detroit: Wayne State University Press, 1973);

John Addington Symonds, *Walt Whitman: A Study* (London: Routledge, 1893);

Oscar L. Triggs, *Browning and Whitman: A Study in Democracy* (Chicago: University of Chicago Press, 1893);

James Woodress, *Critical Essays on Walt Whitman* (Boston: G. K. Hall, 1983).

Papers:
The bulk of Walt Whitman's manuscripts, proofs, and printed works, including the collection assembled by Charles E. Feinberg, is at the Library of Congress.

Checklist of Further Readings

Aderman, Ralph M. "Contributors to the *American Quarterly Review, 1827-1833*," *Studies in Bibliography*, 14 (1961): 163-176.

Andrews, Donald Frank. *"The American Whig Review*, 1845-1852: Its History and Literary Contents," Ph.D. dissertation, University of Tennessee, 1977.

Asquino, Mark Louis. "Criticism in the Balance: The Literary Anthologist as Literary Critic and Promoter in Nineteenth-Century America," Ph.D. dissertation, Brown University, 1978.

Brown, Clarence, ed. *The Achievement of American Criticism: Representative Selections from Three Hundred Years of American Criticism.* New York: Ronald Press, 1954.

Buell, Lawrence. "Identification of Contributors to the *Monthly Anthology and Boston Review, 1804-1811*," *Emerson Society Quarterly*, 23 (Second Quarter 1977): 99-105.

Buratti, David. *"The Spirit of the Times:* Its Theatrical Criticism and Theories as a Reflection of Cultural Attitudes," Ph.D. dissertation, Indiana University, 1977.

Calhoun, Richard J. "The Ante-Bellum Literary Twilight: *Russell's Magazine*," *Southern Literary Journal*, 3 (Fall 1970): 89-110.

Calhoun. "Literary Criticism in Southern Periodicals During the American Renaissance," *Emerson Society Quarterly*, no. 55 (Second Quarter 1969): 76-82.

Calhoun. "Literary Criticism in Southern Periodicals, 1828-1860," Ph.D. dissertation, University of North Carolina, 1959.

Chambers, Stephen, and G. P. Mohrmann. "Rhetoric in Some American Periodicals, 1815-1850," *Speech Monographs*, 27 (June 1970): 111-120.

Charvat, William. *The Origins of American Critical Thought, 1810-1835.* Philadelphia: University of Pennsylvania Press, 1936.

Christophersen, Merrill G. "Early American Dramatic Criticism," *Southern Speech Journal*, 21 (Spring 1956): 195-203.

Clark, Harry Hayden. "Literary Criticism in the *North American Review*, 1815-1835," *Transactions of the Wisconsin Academy of Sciences, Arts and Letters*, 32 (1940): 299-350.

Clark, ed. *Transitions in American Literary History.* Durham: Duke University Press, 1953.

Cutting, Rose M. "America Discovers Its Literary Past: The Anthology as Literary History in the Nineteenth Century," Ph.D. dissertation, University of Minnesota, 1972.

Delano, Sterling F. *"The Harbinger:* A Portrait of Associationism in America," Ph.D. dissertation, Southern Illinois University, 1974.

DeMille, George E. *Literary Criticism in America: A Preliminary Survey.* New York: L. Mac Veagh, Dial Press/ Toronto: Longmans, Green, 1931.

Dorn, Minda Ruth Pearson. "Literary Criticism in the *Boston Quarterly Review,* the *Present,* and the *Massachusetts Quarterly Review,*" Ph.D. dissertation, Southern Illinois University, 1975.

Feuer, Lewis S. "James Marsh and the Conservative Transcendentalist Philosophy: A Political Interpretation," *New England Quarterly,* 31 (March 1958): 3-31.

Firda, Richard Arthur. "German Philosophy of History and Literature in the *North American Review,* 1815-1860," *Journal of the History of Ideas,* 32 (January-March 1971): 133-142.

Flood, Verle Dennis. "A Study in the Aesthetics of Taste in America: The Role of Common Sense Philosophy in the Literary Criticism of the Boston Anthologists," Ph.D. dissertation, University of Iowa, 1959.

Foerster, Donald M. "Homer, Milton, and the American Revolt against Epic Poetry: 1812-1860," *Studies in Philology,* 53 (January 1956): 75-100.

Foerster, Norman. *American Criticism; A Study in Literary Theory from Poe to the Present.* Boston & New York: Houghton Mifflin, 1928.

Frederick, John T. "American Literary Nationalism: The Process of Definition, 1825-1850," *Review of Politics,* 21 (January 1959): 224-238.

Habich, Robert D. "'An Annotated List of Contributions to the *Western Messenger,*" *Studies in the American Renaissance* (1984): 93-179.

Habich. *Transcendentalism and the Western Messenger: A History of the Magazine and its Contributors, 1835-1841.* Rutherford, Madison & Teaneck, N.J.: Fairleigh Dickinson University Press/London & Toronto: Associated University Presses, 1985.

Jacobs, Robert D. "Campaign for a Southern Literature: The *Southern Literary Messenger,*" *Southern Literary Journal,* 2 (Fall 1969): 66-98.

Jones, Howard Mumford. *America and French Culture 1750-1848.* Chapel Hill: University of North Carolina Press, 1927; London: Oxford University Press, 1927.

Lewis, Benjamin Morgan. "A History and Bibliography of American Magazines, 1800-1810," Ph.D. dissertation, University of Michigan, 1956.

Lombard, Charles M. "Mme. de Staël's Image in American Romanticism," *College Language Association Journal,* 19 (1975): 57-64.

Long, Orie William. *Literary Pioneers: Early American Explorers of European Culture.* Cambridge, Mass.: Harvard University Press, 1935.

Miller, Perry. *The Raven and the Whale; The War of Words and Wits in the Era of Poe and Melville.* New York: Harcourt, Brace, 1956.

Mott, Frank. *A History of American Magazines,* 5 volumes. Cambridge: Harvard University Press, 1938-1968.

Mulqueen, James E. "Conservatism and Criticism: The Literary Standards of American Whigs, 1845-1852," *American Literature*, 41 (November 1969): 355-372.

Parks, Edd Winfield. *Ante-Bellum Southern Literary Critics*. Athens: University of Georgia Press, 1962.

Pochmann, Henry. *German Culture in America: Philosophical and Literary Influences, 1600-1900*. Madison: University of Wisconsin Press, 1957.

Pritchard, John Paul. *Criticism in America; An Account of the Development of Critical Techniques from the Early Period of the Republic to the Middle Years of the Twentieth Century*. Norman: University of Oklahoma Press, 1956.

Pritchard. *Literary Wise Men of Gotham: Criticism in New York, 1815-1860*. Baton Rouge: Louisiana State University Press, 1963.

Pritchard. *Return to the Fountains: Some Classical Sources of American Criticism*. Durham: Duke University Press, 1942.

Queenan, John T. "The *Port Folio*: A Study of the History and Significance of an Early American Magazine," Ph.D. dissertation, University of Pennsylvania, 1955.

Rathbun, John W. *American Literary Criticism, 1800-1860*. Boston: G. K. Hall, 1979.

Rathbun. "The Historical Sense in American Associationist Literary Criticism," *Philological Quarterly*, 40 (October 1961): 553-568.

Rusk, Ralph. *The Literature of the Middle Western Frontier*, 2 volumes. New York: Columbia University Press, 1925.

Schilling, Hanna-Beate. "The Role of the Brothers Schlegel in American Literary Criticism as Found in Selected Periodicals, 1812-1833: A Critical Bibliography," *American Literature*, 43 (January 1972): 563-579.

Sherzer, Jane. "American Editions of Shakespeare: 1753-1866," *Publications of the Modern Language Association*, 22, no. 4 (1907): 633-696.

Shrell, Darwin. "Nationalism and Aesthetics in the *North American Review*, 1815-1850," in *Studies in American Literature*, edited by Waldo McNeir and Leo B. Levy. Baton Rouge: Louisiana State University Press, 1960, pp. 11-21.

Sibley, Agnes. *Alexander Pope's Prestige in America 1725-1835*. New York: King's Crown Press, 1949.

Simpson, Lewis P. *The Federalist Literary Mind*. Baton Rouge: Louisiana State University Press, 1962.

Spencer, Benjamin. *The Quest for Nationality; An American Literary Campaign*. Syracuse: Syracuse University Press, 1957.

Spiller, Robert. "Critical Standards in the American Romantic Movement," *College English*, 8 (April 1947): 344-352.

Spiller, et al., eds. *Literary History of the United States*, 3 volumes. New York: Macmillan, 1948.

Stafford, John. *The Literary Criticism of "Young America." A Study in the Relationship of Politics and Literature, 1837-1850.* Berkeley: University of California Press, 1952.

Stovall, Floyd, ed. *The Development of American Literary Criticism.* Chapel Hill: University of North Carolina Press, 1955.

Streeter, Robert. "Association Psychology and Literary Nationalism in the *North American Review,* 1815-1825," *American Literature,* 17 (November 1945): 243-254.

Vogel, Stanley. *German Literary Influences on the American Transcendentalists.* New Haven: Yale University Press, 1955.

Williams, Stanley Thomas. *The Spanish Background of American Literature.* New Haven: Yale University Press, 1955.

Woodall, Guy R. "Nationalism in the Philadelphia *National Gazette and Literary Register,* 1820-1836," *Costerus,* 2 (1972): 225-236.

Contributors

Howard G. Baetzhold..*Butler University*
Dennis Berthold... *Texas A&M University*
John Bird, Jr...*University of Rochester*
Stephen A. Black...*Simon Fraser University*
Richard J. Calhoun...*Clemson University*
Peter Crawford ....*Statement Magazine*
Jack De Bellis... *Lehigh University*
Helen R. Deese .... *Tennessee Technological University*
Sterling F. Delano.. *Villanova University*
Janice L. Edens..*Macon Junior College*
Heyward Ehrlich ....*Rutgers University, Newark*
Gerald E. Gerber ....*Duke University*
Henry Golemba .... *Wayne State University*
Monica Maria Grecu ....*University of Nevada at Reno*
Robert D. Harvey ....*University of Nevada at Reno*
Glen M. Johnson ....*Catholic University of America*
Steven Swann Jones............................. *California State University, Los Angeles*
David Laird .... *California State University, Los Angeles*
Gloria Martin ....*Pacific Lutheran University*
Rayburn S. Moore.. *University of Georgia*
Dennis R. Perry .... *University of Missouri-Rolla*
John W. Rathbun............................... *California State University, Los Angeles*
Doreen Alvarez Saar ....*Drexel University*
Robert J. Scholnick... *College of William and Mary*
David E. E. Sloane .... *University of New Haven*
Herbert F. Smith .... *University of Victoria*
James W. Tuttleton .... *New York University*
Peter Van Egmond.. *University of Maryland*
Bette S. Weidman .... *Queens College, City University of New York*
George P. Winston ....*Nichols College*
Donez Xiques................................*Brooklyn College, City University of New York*
Hisako Yamauchi......................................*Kurume Institute of Technology*
Donald Yannella...*Glassboro State College*
Christina Zwarg .... *Harvard University*

Cumulative Index

Dictionary of Literary Biography, Volumes 1-64
Dictionary of Literary Biography Yearbook, 1980-1986
Dictionary of Literary Biography Documentary Series, Volumes 1-4

Cumulative Index

DLB before number: *Dictionary of Literary Biography,* Volumes 1-64
Y before number: *Dictionary of Literary Biography Yearbook,* 1980-1986
DS before number: *Dictionary of Literary Biography Documentary Series,* Volumes 1-4

B

C

Cumulative Index

D

G

I

M

N

S

T

U

V

Y

Z